Crude

SALLY O'REILLY

EROS PRESS

PROLOGUE

Ida O'Dewey's first memory was of shocking pain, of white heat bursting behind her eyes, then flashing through her whole body. At the time this was a purely visceral experience, although she would soon be able to recount it as 'spilling boiling soup into my lap', finessing this some years later with 'my mons came up like a football'.

First memories are formed when the senses are subjected to some new intensity: the clamour and brilliance of a fairground, the faintly troubling smell of Tupperware, the surge of adrenaline at being abandoned at the nursery, the crack of a piggy bank giving way under a hammer, an uncle's too-tight grip around the wrist... These vignettes are the only access we have to our enigmatic prehistories, before we learned to preserve our thoughts and actions in language and lay them down for posterity. They tell us not so much about our personal stories, as our collective origin in the sensuous, meaningless slime.

But whereas most of us retrieve these memories from the third or fourth relatively inarticulate year of existence, Ida was already nineteen and fully verbal. The Spill happened one nondescript evening in the shared kitchen of her halls of residence. She assumed it was her halls, but could recall nothing of the circumstances that led up to the accident. And not just the immediate circumstances. There was a silent, colourless, odourless blank where there should have been memories of parental warmth, the rush of school days, the purple mist of teenage angst, the pinker, more pungent crushes, the intangible dreams, the all-too concrete disappointments and the stretch and shimmer of learning, growing experiences. She was clearly possessed of a personage that had been formed socially, for she knew what was funny and how to be angered, could use her manners and usually observed consensual morality. And although later in life she would occasionally be haunted by childhood sensations – the reassuring pressure of the bar brought down on to her socked big toe to measure her for new school shoes, or the itch of melted ice cream drying on her chin in briney sunshine – there was no existing narrative to explain any of this, no circumstantial evidence to place her anywhere particular. And no one had ever turned up to claim her. There were no birthday cards or Sunday evening phone calls, no one came to her graduation or expected her to visit during the holidays. According to the records she bore the surname O'Dewey, but all other descendants of the infamous librarian had changed their name to Browse during the Great Methodologies War. She was conspicuously without clan.

In the days following her sudden emergence into consciousness, Ida had taken to her room and wandered through the empty regions of her mind, like a family returning from holiday to find themselves burgled, her distress not mounting so much as dilating, as room upon room proved empty. With no inventory of what was missing, she was unable to express grief at nameable losses. Her anguish was paralysingly general. Within a week, needing something specific to cling to, she had spun herself an autobiography: a dreadful accident had wiped out all her immediate family in one go, the traumatic news of their loss causing her to knock over her soup, which in turn triggered a profound, self-protecting amnesia.

But there was no letter or telephone hanging off the hook to corroborate this, and before long she would come to accept that she simply had not existed until she was nineteen. She had been born a fully formed adult, which, she decided, had its advantages. She was not burdened with the memory of tottering and falling during early attempts to walk, or forming wet sounds that no one else could understand in a mouth lacking the finer control required of articulation. And, as far as she was concerned, she hadn't packed her own kit bag of common sense through a painful process of lesson learning, but had always instinctively known that flames were hot, strangers posed dangers and the morning-after pill was not an honourable form of contraception. On her darkest days, not having had any experience of failing, trying harder and failing less completely, she felt she could never again learn anything new. Generally though, she was given to brightness and, with the attitude of one unaccustomed to embarrassment, tended to throw herself into situations where most would be wary.

A clarification is necessary at this point. When Ida said she had no memories, she was referring to the autobiographic sort that explain how one has come to be where and what one is. She did, however, discover a substantial deposit of memories of the impersonal kind, which described the wider world in general, if not her position within it.

A few weeks after The Spill, once her alienation had come to feel familiar enough to be called her sense of self, she tentatively began quizzing that self for clues to its past. She had started with trivial questions, for safety's sake: What was the name of your first pet? What is your mother's maiden name? Who did you have a crush on as a teenager? Do you prefer cake or trifle? Surrealism or Existentialism? She had drawn a blank each time, until this last question. Why, that was easy: 'Existentialism of course. Surrealists were completely misguided in their assertions that their subconscious acted freely of their egos. Their egos became their ultimate product: they canned and sold their own breath. And don't get me going on misogyny! When they weren't sawing up their mistresses' bodies or filling up their vaginas with teeth and concrete, they were elevating women to symbolic stereotypes and then butchering and stuffing them. At least with Existentialism, in an amoral, Dogless universe, everyone and everything is equally meaningless. This is a profound eradication of capitalist hegemony, which Surrealism never even came close to. Surrealism simply condoned the indulgence and visibility of deeper desires, making them acceptable and visible enough for marketing departments to get their claws into. No, the only thing that Surrealism revolutionised was the advertising industry, by negligently building a motorway right up to the front door of the subconscious.'

She was breathless. Where had this opinion come from? Her excitement swelled. She asked more questions: What is Surrealism? Who were its main proponents? Why do teenagers think it's cool? Does the recent return to the moustache as a motif of eccentricity operate along Surrealist lines, or is it merely a cynical and empty signifier adopted by a media-conscious generation? She was stunned to note that not only did she know how to ask these questions, but that the answers radiated from her, lecture-sharp.

Blocking out the sounds of other students sparring, bickering and loving around her, she paced what little of the room wasn't filled by bed or desk and began to excavate her find with care and amazement. She muttered and muttered, paced and paced, moving from Surrealism to French Lettrism to the Canadian Group of Seven to the New Objectivity of Weimar… She barely knew which link to follow, which periods, styles, concepts or aesthetics to choose from. Art-historical facts were jostling to be voiced, like rabbits at the chicken wire when lettuce is offered.

Hours later she fell to the bed exhausted. This knowledge that possessed her was bewildering. She was not studying art history. She was enrolled on a vocational arts administration course. Where could it have come from? You hear of people being raised by wolves or nuns. Maybe she had been raised by art historians. She spent another week assessing her grasp of the subject and the nature of its content. It was beyond her current ability to test its depth and detail, but its historical scope seemed to reach right up until about twenty years ago, when she would have been born, if she was the age she supposed. This curious coincidence lodged in her mind like a splinter, provoking a throb that displaced all other thoughts. Art history became her creation myth, and contemporary art a cipher for her personal story. If she could understand art of the last twenty years, she would become whole.

She applied for a departmental transfer, underwent rigorous oral examination and within weeks was attending classes on temporality and spaciality, sociality, radicality and many other adjectives-turned-nouns. Her new curriculum became her intrinsic structure, her lecturers her parental figures and artspeak her genetic argot. By the time she graduated, with distinction, she had learned so much about herself from the reflective qualities of contemporary art that she came to realise, even if she were to track down her biological parents, they could not provide a truer image of herself.

She would consult artworks for emotional guidance – a strategy that could be confusing, since art relates human concerns more complex and grave than the average post-graduate's. But this, she found, put things in proper perspective. When her college sweetheart proposed to her on the day of their MA graduation, for instance, dozens of paintings of drab eighteenth-century Dutch women trapped in the barren psychology of their domesticity flashed before her eyes, and she turned him down flat. For progressive advice on handling her first overbearing editor she consulted the Futurist Manifesto, but reviling her editor's decaying spirit (he was over forty) and throwing him aside like an old manuscript was not a course of action available to someone with ambition but no private income. And so she turned to the eighteenth-century Romantics instead, who taught her to feed off the horror and awe of his edits.

And now, twenty years on, with first-hand experience up to her elbows, art was no longer a subject external to her, to be learned; it grew within her like kettle fur. She was now a producer of knowledge who drew fragile respect from a capricious public. The momentum she had built up through the enthusiasm of her twenties and the mild arrogance of her thirties had propelled her to a supposedly powerful position. But since visibility and vulnerability had always been entangled in her mind, she undertook her more prominent roles – as a regular reviewer in a quality newspaper and an advisor on a primetime television soap opera – with wary ambivalence. She was never so intoxicated by the heights of success that she did not notice the upturned faces willing her to fall.

CHAPTER 1

'So,' said Preston the insomniac lead scriptwriter, 'we've got a murder scene: the life-drawing room, tastefully cluttered with easels and drapes. And I think there should be an art-historical reference in the positioning of the body. Firstly, because it's classy...'

'Yes, definitely,' said Chip. 'There's always a heavy mailbag after an art-historical reference. Excellent.' The producer liked to coincide a dramatic new subplot with the start of each term, but the start of the academic year should be extra-special.

'And secondly, in case we need a serial killer. He could commit a whole series of murders and arrange the bodies in poses from paintings. People love a killer with a "thing".'

'Or she could,' said Ida. 'Why not a female serial killer?'

Chip exhaled smoke with a long hiss.

'Would the feminists like that? I never can tell. It seems that equality is desirable to them only when what is being shared out is something they particularly want.'

'Speaking as a feminist,' said Ida, tossing her copper curls, 'I'd like to see a woman break free of the murderer's sidekick mould. I for one would be interested to hear she had a psychotic personality disorder. Men always grab the best excuses for themselves.'

'From a dramatic perspective, I think it's a great idea,' said Preston, removing his glasses to rub his bruised eyelids. 'She could be a vengeful, menopausal life model, returning the male gaze in the form of a dagger. And she only kills the men who have painted her.'

'Oh yes,' said Chip. 'The network'll love it – it has tragedy, gender politics and—'

'Stereotyping?' Lack of sleep, thought Ida, can darken an imagination, but it can also make it lazy. 'And basing the body's pose on a painting is going to be a problem. Male nudes aren't exactly prominent in art history. You could open it up to sculpture, because there's your Classical Greek statues, of course. But when is a murder victim ever upright and about to throw a discus?'

‘She could hang her victims then,’ said Preston.

‘Great, that’s it. Daisy,’ said Chip, addressing the art director, who stood to one side, drawing frantically as everyone spoke, and crossing out furiously as they changed their minds. ‘You’ll need to research ropes and knots for that. And Ida …’

‘Not so many famous paintings of hangings, I’m afraid. And the pose tends to be a bit samey. Doesn’t naturally lend itself to variations on a theme.’

‘Ok, so maybe she could crucify her victims then,’ said Chip. The others grimaced. Even Preston found it a touch too gothic. ‘Hmm, yes, you’re right – still too samey. This isn’t really working out, is it? Sorry Preston, can we revert to male murderer, female victim?’ Preston nodded matter-of-factly, not quite hiding his disappointment. ‘So Ida, you’re back on reclining female nude duties, if you don’t mind.’

‘Just close your eyes, pick any art history book off the shelf, open it and point,’ said Ida with a sigh.

‘And Preston,’ said Chip, ‘to keep the feminists happy, let’s have the victim be a lady professor. I’ll check the cast list for any pending maternity leave.’

‘Ok. So then we have Sam and Pamantha’s first kiss,’ said Preston.

‘And a bloody long time coming too. I was starting to think they were frigid. So, go on.’

‘It would be great to have it happen in the lecture theatre with a nice big slide projected in the background. There could be a close-up with a lovely pan upwards to an image of something sexy, beautiful, spiritual even—’

‘Nothing too blue now,’ warned Chip. ‘No ecstatic St Theresa with a cum-face or cherubs pointing their willies about. Ida? Any thoughts?’

She closed her eyes, hummed and twiddled her ear like a radio dial.

‘I’m getting a … a … a foot, yes a drawing of a foot.’

‘Stop pissing about,’ said Chip.

‘No, actually, I think that’s quite good,’ said Ida. ‘An anatomical drawing of a foot. They’re kissing, with their mouths.’

‘Naturally.’

‘And they’re thinking about working their way down to one another’s vaginas. It always starts at the mouth …’

‘Speak for yourself,’ said Preston.

‘On television it always starts and ends at the mouth,’ said Ida. ‘The rest is usually left to the imagination. But here we go too far, so to speak.

We've already overshot.'

'Hey, that's great actually,' said Preston. 'You know, in the black-and-white days you could only show a kiss onscreen if both actors had one foot on the floor.'

'I think you mean at least one foot,' said Ida.

'Ok, ok. But anyway, a foot image would make for a nice riff on that. I like it.'

'Oh yes,' said Chip, 'the viewers like that subtle cultural studies stuff, don't they, where they have to invent the associations.'

'Not invent – excavate. Sorry, I forgot, they don't teach you these thinky things on those vocational courses,' said Ida, 'but trust me – it's a classy bit of media critique that will generate a good few column inches.'

'Listen. Communications is a three-year academic course that's just as long and difficult as art appreciation, or whatever it is you pretended to study,' said Chip, pocketing his cigarettes, which was always a sign that things were drawing to a close. 'And anyway, who's top of this little hierarchy here? Now, as I was saying, I don't suppose anyone could be rubbed up the wrong way by a large foot – present company excepted, on account of you being filthy sensualists – so, if you think it's a goer, I'll run with it. Pardon the pun.'

A herd of gutter-press smudgers lived in the production office forecourt and pumped off a few rounds of flash-photos whenever anyone exited or arrived, whether they recognised them or not. Ida accommodated them with a brief pose, deflecting with smiles their standard questions regarding her next project, her personal life and career ambitions, before heading for the stationer's to stock up on skinny, hard-balled biros and slippery fibre-nibs. She also needed a new notebook for her big new project. She loved stationery. Half the job was done already if you had fresh tools lined up for it. They represented an exciting state of potential, in which there were as yet no compromises made, no sub-standards accepted with bad grace. A project was at its best in these first throes.

Central Academia was in a similar state of potential. September was the most verdant month of the academic year, when any leaves so inclined in the deciduous and evergreen mix forest had a way to go yet before they turned. Even greener freshers were arriving by train and tram in the outer districts, where halls of residence showed off their new coats of paint, beaming in the sunshine. In the centre, standing at their allotted clearings hacked out of the forest, the Greco-Roman

Etymology Department, the neo-baroque Philology Block and the art nouveau Critical Faculty Building bore newly planted blooms in their many borders, balconies and baskets with the grace of well-brought-up women who know how to wear jewellery appropriate to age and occasion. But while the stone and marble façades served up a potent cocktail of awe, anxiety and ambition, the sprawling television centre inspired a very different sentiment. Its hodgepodge of architecture told of goals achieved through incremental increases in budget, know-how and populist appeal, upgrading over decades from a shanty of single-floor portacabins to glass towers that forged upwards with the launch of each new channel – six at present, with a seventh under construction.

In the stationer's, a busy three-floor emporium that peddled every hue and tone ever manufactured, Ida picked out a fine-nibbed green ink pen with a transparent barrel that seemed more technical than it was. It was of no relevance to her big new project though. She was distracted by more immediate appointments and deadlines, and in particular her appearance on a radio panel game show that evening. Having been on the programme numerous times before, she knew there was no possibility of preparing for it, other than generally clearing the mind and limbering up the geniality muscles. And so, on quitting the shop, she decided to walk about for a bit to see who else might be on the prowl.

Among the first trickle of students in their best outfits, she ran into a shambling man she could never remember the name of, although she knew plenty about him: he was a point-two in the Etymology Department and had a penetrative sibilance that barred him from the career in broadcasting he had so dearly wished for. He had emerged, carrier bag in hand, from among the television executives in suits and lecturers in gowns, like a camouflaged predator leaping from a sand trap to engage Ida in small talk.

'Ida, hello! It'ß been an age. ßo, tell me, what are you working on at the moment?' This was a conversational gambit she particularly hated.

'Oh, you know – the usual. Bits and pieces.'

'C'mon, there'ß always ßomething ßpecial bubbling on the O'Dewey ßtove. I hear you've got ßomething big cooking up, no?' He was always interested to hear what the a- and b-list were up to, and felt no trace of resentment. He was relieved to be mediocre. It was infinitely less stressful than leading the sort of life he enjoyed spectating.

'Well, I am revving up to start a new book.' She waggled her new pen at him.

‘Great. What iß it? More on affectß of functiveß?’

‘Dog, no, I think I’ve done my bit on that ßubject – er, topic. No, I’m researching a new area I’m in the process of making up. It’s always hard to say at the beginning, but, loosely speaking, I think it’s about measuring.’

‘Wow – amazeballß!’ He seemed genuinely impressed, which was sweet of him, Ida thought. He always spoke positively. Very rare, she thought. Very undignified.

‘There goes someone important,’ said Ida as a professorial limousine pulled out of the professorial car park and nudged along the elevated road that only professors could use. All other traffic was consigned to zigzagging about the pitted streets engulfed by the forest below, which served every last outhouse and offered no direct route between any two places that a normal person might need to use. This was why, besides service and goods vehicles, train and tram were the primary modes of transport in Academia.

‘ßo, yes, anyway…’ said the man. ‘I’m ßtill campaigning for “doing” to be pronounced “doing”,’ which he made rhyme with ‘boing’ instead of ‘wooing’.

‘Of course, yes, it’s important work, taking on those dictionary cartels. You must explain your etymological revisionism to me some time.’ She always said this to him, although they both knew that she didn’t really want him to and that she would never lend her name to the campaign, despite the list of quite reputable endorsements he had already garnered. His uncle, a Reader in the Linguistics Department, had backed him, not through nepotism, but because the nephew was a usefully inert body to have on the staff. His academic mediocrity ensured he was a team player by nature, averse to intellectual liberty, risk and innovation. This ‘doing’ campaign gave the impression of intellectual progressiveness required of even entry-level academics, but would never actually upset any theoretical or institutional apple carts.

‘Well, I must prepare myself for the radio this evening.’ She looked him, whatever-he-was-called, in the eye for perhaps the first time during their exchange and smiled warmly. The final impression is the one that lasts, she always thought.

‘Oh Ida, you do live the life…’

‘Shit, have you seen the time?’ she interrupted, in case another avenue of chat had occurred to him, and tilted towards a busy tram stop round the corner, out of sight, while he, floored by this metaphysical parting shot, shook his head and rubbed the back of his neck in bewilderment.

'Have I ßeen the time?' he muttered. 'Have I ßeen it? How do they do it, theße high-flyerß? They have a mind, just like I have a mind, but how do theirß come up with theße abßtract and brilliant thingß?'

CHAPTER 2

A turquoise and grey jumpsuit-clad woman with an earpiece and a clip-board sprang on to the stage and, with outstretched arms, lowered the audience babble to an expectant silence. She held the crowd in suspension just long enough to demonstrate her power over it, then made a swift, sharp signal, triggering a disembodied voice, deep and intense, like Dog speaking from beyond reality.

'Welcome, ladies and gentlemen, to another tasty episode of *Campbell's Panel Beaters,* the only radio game show that serves up theory hot, fresh and fluid to your living room.' The voice paused while the jumpsuited woman puppeteered the crowd's response up to the volume of rapture, then brought it back down to muted excitement. 'I hope your lips are smacking in anticipation, because on the menu this evening we have a steaming broth of notions fresh from the brains of top-quality academics. Yes, over the next half hour we'll be cooking up a veritable stew of ideas, a bouillon of discourse, a gumbo of logomachy – all topped off with a crouton of erudition and a garnish of rhetoric.' The audience tittered and rocked. 'So, on with the show. We have a packed house tonight, and everyone looks keen and ready to go… although I'm not sure the same can be said for all of our panellists.' Laughter rippled as the contestants, sitting stiffly in a row behind the athletic fluffer, grim-aced in pantomime fear at their pending trials on the large, stark stage. 'No, but really, we have a stellar line-up, as ever, and a packed programme for you tonight, so, without further ado, let's welcome this week's *Campbell's Panel Beaters*…' The fluffer motioned for a wild storm of clapping, raising her arms with each name to produce a parity of enthusiasm across all welcomes. The panellists responded in turn with a modest nod and suppressed smile. 'A big welcome please for Professor of Curating, Prentice Hall… lecturer and broadcaster Tolly Adio… the maverick columnist Fredegund… critic, curator and pedagogue emeritus Ida O'Dewey…' But despite the fluffer's best efforts, there was no ignoring that the storm intensified or palled according to the relative status of each contestant. 'And, of course, your Chair upon the throne of infinite wisdom, the all-round accomplished and lavishly upholstered Dean PJ Rothwell-Beer!' The rest of the MC's spiel was drowned by a jangle of shrill whoops and base bellows of men, women, boys, girls and castrates making free with the full vocal spectrum in their adulation for the septuagenarian as she mounted the stage, arms aloft, fists clenched.

The vaulted auditorium, built hastily using cheap materials and lots of fake chrome some thirty years previously to serve a swell in demand, was freezing. For once, Ida was glad of her inverted nipples, especially as she'd chosen to wear a particularly sheer cream scoop-necked tabard to go with her high-waisted, wide-legged, itchy tweed trousers. Since this was radio, not television, there was no set to speak of, no desk with a jaunty shape and a graphic splash behind which the panellists could shelter. They sat with their arms folded high on their chests, many shielding functioning nipples that protruded in the cold, their shadows alarmingly accentuated by the uni-directional lighting.

For Ida, public speaking was excruciating in innumerable ways, and no matter how often she mounted a stage to face an audience it never got any easier. She was particularly prone to urges to fall asleep in the immediate run-up, despite the discomfort of damp feet and hands, and the deeper regions of her bowels churning like a dropped bottle of bitter lemon. When the performance was underway the next suite of bio-chemicals would kick in, but in the hour or two beforehand the only way to cope was to pinch the tender white underside of her upper arm, clench her arse cheeks and think of tomorrow.

Of all public speaking formats, comedy panel shows were the very worst. The comedy was just a cover. These 'game' shows were actually a serious mode of peer critique, in real time and in public. The jokes often contained barbs aimed at professional adversaries, present and absent; jolly quips were intended to assert a plastic intelligence and mobile wit that superseded paradigmatic norms, and every wrong answer, while apparently played for laughs, was a hole in the hull of a sinking academic.

'It's barbaric. They make you splosh out your thoughts for inspection, like the contents of a fish's stomach,' Ida fumed when Sue, her agent, had first swung her the spot. 'It's nothing but a thinly veiled quality control process. They line us up and prod us, then measure the level of intellectual pollution we've been swimming in and the toxicity of the ideas we've swallowed. I wouldn't mind so much if they cleaned the rubbish out while they were at it, but oh no, they just throw us back into the same stinking pond afterwards. And then they call us up for another appearance the following week. It's serial abuse.'

The intellectual benefits of these ritualised public displays of weakness were debatable – they say we learn from our own mistakes, but other people's tend to produce only unreflective *Schadenfreude*. The entertainment value, though, was historically and unfailingly high. *Campbell's Panel Beaters* had topped the ratings since its first episode, and the visibility it afforded contestants had many career payoffs. So in the main, Ida swallowed hard, faced up and gave out, racking up her radio hours in the hope that they would miraculously rematerialise as laudable publications – which occasionally they did.

As is often the case in these programme formats, the Dean was the only scripted participant. Wearing a ruffle-fronted blouse, which, as any old hand knows, is the best way to conceal a cold nipple, Rothwell-Beer dominated proceedings with sturdily comic lines rooted in relevance, while everyone else rummaged about in their heads for whatever amusing wisps they could clutch at under pressure.

The show got underway with a few quick-fire rounds, like 'Attribute That Quote', 'One Theory in the Rhetoric of Another' and the game that Ida particularly excelled at, 'Reclaim That Canon'. This week she forged ahead with a tirade of feminist literary revisions that fell from her lips with such ease that many suspected the questions had been leaked beforehand.

'Ah, I can only really think,' she said with wide, cod-innocent eyes, 'of a couple. Let's see now: A Womb of One's Own, Madame Ovary, Of Mice and Menses, David Copper Coil, Three Men in a Blastomene, Candida, Women without Men, Lady of the Flies, On the Pill, I, Claudia, The Maltese Fallopian, The Big Speculum, Das Cap, Zen and the Art of Menstrual Cycle Maintenance, A Tale of Two Titties, The Daughter Also Rises, As I Like It, The Mooncup and Sixpence, The Mastectomy and Margarita, Ectopic of Capricorn, Miscarry on Jeeves, Infinite Gestation, East of Oestrogen, Gravid Rainbow, The Endometrium of the Affair, The Embryonic Man, The Cunt of Monte Christo. Oops, excuse my French!'

The pun dust settled, and the format switched gear to sustained improvisation, starting with 'Conversation Pieces', a game in which pairs of contestants ventriloquised well-known artworks. Tolly Adio and Fredegund took the respective roles of a huge contemporary abstracted metal figure in the landscape and an old stone statue of an historic general on a tall column on a traffic island, and squabbled over which was best: novelty or venerability; rural or urban; anonymity or being dead. Then

Prentice Hall delivered a monologue as an unattributed watercolour landscape, which, while including the occasional art-historical reference, lacked any jokes whatsoever and neglected to even acknowledge Ida, who stood stiffly to the side doing a brilliant impression of an Etruscan vase as she waited to be fed a line that never came.

In the next round, 'That's News To Me', each contestant was to step up to a spot-lit lectern, centre stage, to deliver an antagonistic polemic in response to a recent news headline. The trick here was to insert pre-authored tracts, which promenaded one's critical acumen, into an amusingly improvised but coherent polemic – a difficult weave for most academics. Hall was hopeless. Once he'd opened with a lame one-liner, he didn't even attempt to be funny. He gracelessly twisted the subject in hand towards his own area of interest, and swept off down his usual rhetorical log flume. His was a branch of anti-humanist theory that those in the backroom laboratories of the more progressive sub-departments thought passé, but which the mainstream media considered edgy and compelling. Unlike many of the other contestants, who would gladly sacrifice their intellectual standing for a laugh from the audience, Hall was an unflinching point scorer, which the producers considered a necessary dullness to save the programme from falling into comedic anarchy. So while Hall was tolerated for the solidity of his content, his academic allies were more embarrassed by his inability to get anyone else's joke than they were grateful for his service to their subject. He was a classic stooge, and Ida would have felt sorry for him if he hadn't been so comfortably oblivious and thoroughly unpleasant.

Hall's newsworthy headline was 'Prime Minister Gets Engaged'.

'Ah, yes, this is an example of the ghastly genre of socially engaged art, and it's not a step above, in my opinion, the frankly ridiculous seaside tradition of the kiss-me-quick hat.' The other panellists looked back at him blankly. Rothwell-Beer made a note on her pad. The audience remained hushed. Hall swallowed his hollow laugh. 'It's about our leader debasing herself by spending an hour in bed with the artist. Presumably there have been hundreds since who have spent an hour in bed with him too – all in the name of what the artist calls "recumbent sociology". In my opinion, it's yet another example of the instrumentalisation of art, and my responsibility as a curator is to protect it from this abuse.' The audience clapped politely and gave out a rustle as they made themselves comfortable for the monologue they knew was coming, like an ancient, reliable ferry chugging across familiar waters. The production crew, too, could foretell a good few minutes' slack to be taken advantage of, and the producer nodded in assent to their appeals to pop out for cigarettes, take a leak or make a quick phone call to secure their after-show plans.

'A curator,' said Hall, in his clipped, assertive voice, 'traditionally protects an artwork from damage by both physical and interpretative acts, but these days the curator has his work cut out for him, or her, when it comes to simply protecting the artwork from banalisation by way of subject-centred individual subjecthood. By which I specifically mean the way that art is in danger of becoming an instrument of the ruling elites, who cunningly present it as engaging with the needs and wants of each viewer on their own terms. What is more, since art has been made to seem as if it were bestowing cultural agency upon the individual, it has become yet another accoutrement of the aspirant, entering the flow of commodity exchange and essentially assimilating with capitalist structures. This is a travesty of all that art should be.'

This may have started out a jumble of unsubstantiated links, out-of-date jargon and gross generalisations that no one quite followed, but Hall went on to outline a proposition with such conviction – and in more detail than the producer would have liked – that he ended up sounding convincing to all but the most scholarly, who wouldn't have been tuning in to such populist fluff anyway.

'If this persists,' Hall concluded, 'if art continues to be heaped up with social responsibilities and ascribed ideologically transformative qualities, galleries will become indistinguishable from hospitals and counselling service hubs. This was never the point of art. It was always supposed to be useless. This tyranny of subject-centred individual subjecthood cannot – must not – be allowed to progress unchecked.'

The sound engineers snapped back into action as Hall's academic supporters clapped, their wild clothing adding to the semblance of enthusiasm. He may not have been the most popular performer, but he kept as avid an eye on the catwalk as he did on the bookshop shelves, spending regular fortunes on clothes, making him not so much a fashion icon as a conduit. He was regularly doorstepped by the paparazzi, and cheap copies of the mustard yellow feather jacket by Paracelsus he had worn earlier in the week had already flooded the high street and were dotted about the auditorium like giant stray chicks. Ida did not desire the status of fashion guru for herself, although she was always complimented in print on her stylishness; and Rothwell-Beer fans, too, tended to sidestep experimental trends, plumping instead for cool cotton vintage t-shirts that celebrated specific moments in the Dean's long career. Soundbites from her classic public speaking tours in period typefaces declared 'Now that's what I call becoming', 'Say yes to negative space' or 'Nostalgia is so five minutes ago'. A handsome man in the second row, mid-thirties with big browns, was wearing a rare 'Choose Live' t-shirt with mid-length, leg-of-mutton sleeves revealing a pair of powerfully suggestive forearms, and it was these that caught Ida's eye as she lurched towards the lectern.

Her news headline was 'Tots topple top toilet', which she calculated must be about a recently reported argument between two precocious children over a key *objet trouvé* in the Museum of Contemporary and Hard Art, a large public institution at the heart of the Academy where she had recently spent a year as Critic in Residence. The argument had got out of hand, drawing in surrounding gallery goers and escalating into a brawl, during which the ceramic had been knocked from its plinth and shattered irreparably.

For this round, Ida had planned to take a position contrary to Hall – not because this was necessarily her own position, but because he had some fierce detractors in some reputable thinklabs who she did not want to count amongst her own critics. The further delicacy was that, although she needed to author a contra-anti-subject-centred-individual-subjecthood narrative, she had to be careful that it could not be construed as pro-subject-centred individual subjecthood.

'Well…' she paused briefly, gripped the edge of the lectern, blinked away the blinding panic of liveness and made ready to dive in. Deep breath. 'Prentice, you talk about the instrumentalisation of art, but what have we here? It may be a urinal but it's not even plumbed in! What use is that to anybody?' The audience laughed and Ida fed off the energy. 'It doesn't seem that ingratiating to me. In fact, it's pretty feckless. Lazy even. Indeed, what has art ever done for me, I ask you. Here I am, day in day out, running circles around art, making sure it's not misunderstood. Poor art, my arse.'

A murmur spread through the audience. Ida scanned faces for signs that she'd overstepped the mark with 'arse', but saw only titillation, until she caught the eye of the man in the second row. Of course, since she was at the lectern addressing the audience, it wouldn't be so unusual for him to be looking at her intently. Still, she couldn't help feeling a thrill as her gaze hooked onto his and he smiled in total agreement with her.

'No, I think we worry too much about art being misunderstood or otherwise abused. There is an army of critics and curators protecting its meanings, making sure it gets everything it needs and fending off anything that it doesn't want. It starts with small things, like toasters being banned from gallery staff rooms in case particles of burnt toast introduce too much materiality for the art's liking. Because immateriality is what contemporary art ultimately wants. And these curators are shielding it from means testing too, and innovation legislature, resource maintenance and point of delivery assessment – in fact, from anything that forces it into a state of measurability.'

There were half-truths in this. The toaster ban was real, but it was down to particles of carbon in the air setting off smoke detectors and sprinklers; and part of the curator's job was indeed to shield the artist, and consequently the artwork, from the pressures of bureaucracy. But to ascribe this desire for liberty to the artwork itself was just a bit of fun.

'And why does art not want to be measured? Because it thinks it's better than us. It believes itself to be beyond heights and weights and durations and costs. It finds our preoccupation with materiality debasing.'

Spurts of lust were added to the quiver of adrenaline and chill as she made eye contact with the man in the second row. She dared herself to look more often, then less often, then not at all, then only at him. Excitement sent jolts through her speech patterns, making her appear to rise up indignantly as if impassioned by her own ideas, even though they were simply unfolding logically, if somewhat fantastically embellished, from her necessary opposition to Hall. What she had failed to notice, though, was that some time back her nipples had also started responding to the man in the second row. While inverted – or 'shy' as it is called when the inversion can on rare occasion be revoked – they were unusually long and, in their reawakened state beneath the thin blouse, were provoking variable ratios of hilarity and horror in the front few rows. Ida mistook this frisson for enjoyment of her conceptual comedy.

'Yes, art thinks it's better than us. It has been over-indulged and now the brat is developing a taste for ultimate power. Art is aiming for absolute sovereignty, and when it takes the throne it will banish the viewer, clap the critics and curators in irons and excommunicate the artists, for it wishes its own meanings to engorge, unchecked by the interpretations of stupid humans with their narrow preconceptions based in arbitrary ideologies…'

The man with the divine forearms was now sitting forward intently, while the wave of excitement spread backwards and upwards throughout the auditorium. Ida mounted the wave and rode triumphantly towards what she took to be the beach of public approval. Her voice started to rise in volume, pitch and speed as she reached a point of raw rhetoric. 'Yes! Pure meaning, without recourse to grubby matter or even leaky, contaminated time. This is the psychopathic intent of art: instantaneous flashes of transcendental significance with not a human soul to perceive it and turn it into a stodgy idea or an even stodgier sculpture.'

As she paused for breath, the audience's gasps were no longer possible to misconstrue. She must be well over time. Why hadn't the chair stopped her?

'Er, PJ, am I done here do you think?' she asked with the consummate timing of the comic self-interrupter.

'Well and truly, Ida,' said the Dean, nodding sagely.

Ida stepped down from the lectern and took her seat, shocked to hear not applause – let alone whistles and cheers – but silence. It was only when Tolly Adio began to drone on about funding streams that it sank in: she had just, accidentally, on a tidal wave of oration, denounced art as evil. Of course it had all been in the spirit of a game show, but a sympathetic grimace and shake of the head from her friend Fredegund told her that she had been controversially contentious. Contention may be a fundamental necessity in Academia, but there were limits.

Throughout the rest of the broadcast, as the other contestants delivered jokes with theoretically sound content, or at least theoretical-sounding content, Ida simmered in a complex brew of oestrogen and adrenalin, suppressing any further impulse to perform, just in case. She played it safe in 'Hunt the Slip-up', declared 'pass' in 'Name that Silence' and didn't even trust herself to open her mouth during the final round of quick-fire witticisms, at which she usually excelled. At the final score she placed a dismal third (Tolly Adio coming last due to a whopping fifty points subtracted for a fumbled phenomenology reference). That was fine. She didn't need to win every time. But the question was, well, the three questions were: would the media take the audience's dim view of her performance? And who was this delicious looking man in the second row, who throughout the rest of the broadcast had been taking notes studiously, looking up now and again to gaze at her? Was she in there?

CHAPTER 3

Ida squinted through the smoke rising from a cigarette on the basin rim, and searched in the small, overcast mirror for a clue as to what might have possessed her back there. She could see the low-level fear that was always simmering in the depths of her eyes, and in the line of her mouth she detected a trace of sourness. This was the vestige of youthful envy, although thankfully she had never succumbed to out-and-out jealousy. The jealous person, if she manages to contain any initial outburst, slyly manipulates the downfall of the subject of her jealousy. Envy, on the other hand, implies an amount of judicious measuring, self-adjustment and comparison, and generally leads to an improvement in the lot of the envious. Throughout her thirties, Ida had worked hard to eradicate the habit of envying others more powerful, cleverer, more popular, taller, funnier and so on and so on; and in the main she had succeeded, choosing instead to accept that there will always be someone more something-or-other than her, but also that she would always be more something-or-other than somebody else. She was of more mysterious origins than anyone she knew of, for starters, and she had a quicker tongue than many.

But there was one grievance that she could not reason her way out of: why, oh why, should artists be considered the *sine qua non* of cultural and intellectual life? She thought herself just as capable and imaginative as most artists, but they automatically trumped her because she wrote second-order texts about the first-order artworks they produced. Critics were characterised as managers rather than generators of culture, and so, although the media treated them as celebrities on account of their proximity to art and their glamorous, high-income, travel-enriched careers, they were not bestowed with the demi-god reverence of primary producers. Granted, Ida had an agent and a trainer, but that was a mark of professional standing. She didn't have a driver or a valet, let alone a body-double. She cherished being recognised in the street and all the powers and responsibilities that came with that, but she coveted the unconditional succour that artists enjoyed. Unconditional smacked of love, and love was neither the critic's nor the orphan's lot.

The critic's medium is language, which everyone feels they have a command of, and so her output would never be deemed as sacred as art-making. She was expected to be ten times better with words than non-critics, whereas an artist did not have to be ten times better at leaning a plank against the wall and calling it *Fulcrum II* than anyone else. The critic has to up her game constantly and produce ever more ingenious and obscure thoughts, ever more beautiful and challenging prose, while artists are positively encouraged to shut up and keep making the same thing over and over. It is then down to the critic to invent what it all means. And knowing that artists relied on people like her to enrich their output with intricate coils of theory and history, it was especially galling to see the general public invariably give all credit to the artist, as if these ideas were already in the artwork, and the critic was simply in possession of a special tin-opener with which to access them. 'But such,' thought Ida, 'is my lot'. She had been wise enough to notice that envy was not an enjoyable state, and so she had resolved instead to be happy for good artists and outspokenly damning of bad ones.

One vestige of these poisoned days that she had never quite managed to rid herself of was her desire to possess artists, good or bad, in inappropriate ways, preferably with the result that they would never get her out of their system. Her wildest dream, in the stillest portion of dawn, was to have the whole art world pining after her, which in the bright light of day she went about methodically, collecting hearts one by one. She had quite a haul by now. When she was younger she had employed seamier methods, generally involving studio visits that ended in hurried, ungratifying coupling on concrete floors, back and knees grazed, and followed by unwanted phone calls, which she would gently but firmly process over time into awkward encounters at private views. In some instances it could take years to settle into an unhealthy state of mutually feigned dissociation. But what had really put a stop to her more purple adventures was the time she was crouched in a tiny, mouldering lavatory with tears and mucous pouring through her nose, a glossy pendant of sperm drawling between her legs and the dropped toilet roll bobbing in the bowl, swollen to uselessness. The sink was in another room along the hall, past Dog knew how many people's open doors, and the name of the sperm's previous container, which she might have shouted if her throat wasn't so sore, had fallen down a crack in her memory. She was stuck there, air-drying, for so long that she missed an important lunch. No – these days she preferred not to offer herself up entirely, but to leave artists wanting more, unsure if they could ask for it. Artists in Academia tended to err on the side of caution, since the media loved an art scandal above all else, and so she could dazzle and woo them all she liked, leaving them dangling, their hands and tongues tied.

Such a campaign required that she took care over her appearance, although this should never be too apparent in Academia, where anything but basic grooming was assumed to be over-compensation for intellectual lack. To her ongoing delight, she had always looked five years younger than she actually was, although she presumed this would have been a bit of a problem when she was four. At a tiny bit over forty, though, the skin at the sides of her mouth and in front of her ears had started to lose their elasticity. She had looked into under-the-counter anti-aging creams, with 37 per cent improved hydro-locks and pH balancing paraben-free elasticisers, but found their promises too absurd and her pride too robust. Or was it too delicate? Appreciating that sagging is the root of all aging, she figured that the face was probably no different to the rest of the body, that its musculature could be toned for youthfulness; and so she devised the facial equivalent of rowing, that most all-over of workouts, which she undertook daily in bursts whenever her interns were not around. She particularly enjoyed the thrill of gurning and churning her face as she descended the communal carpeted staircase of her canopied mansion block, the excitement arising from the danger of discovery. Like when her neighbour, Sir Dawnay, sprang from his front door one sweltering afternoon wearing nothing but a hand towel, and the sight of Ida rowing downstairs with her face earning her the nickname Ida Boatrace in the Lemmon household.

By such means, Ida took care to be attractive, but not flashily so. She approached fashion as a collective intellectual game and used it to underscore a public persona that was authoritative when it counted and transgressive when she knew she could get away with it. She was self-critical, but not destructively so. In fact, she would identify herself as confident, up to a point. But right now she was experiencing a strange new sensation. She had not been entirely in control out there in the auditorium. Something from a deep place had spilled out messily onstage. It hadn't been envy or competitiveness or insecurity, but something else altogether. Evidently it hadn't gone unnoticed, but what was it? Gazing into her face for answers, it seemed so firm as to be impenetrable – from exercise to an extent, but also from years of maintaining public serenity when inside she seethed with passions and doubts. Giving up on any hope of revelation, she snuffed out her cigarette and checked her clothing as best she could in the small mirror above the sink, craning and peering down at an outfit that matched the ambivalence she often felt towards herself: itchy, high-waisted trousers tortured the skin of her lower half; layers of silk caressed the upper. She heaved the ladies door open with a sigh and headed to the after-show pub.

CHAPTER 4

In the beer garden, for visual interest, and rather more incidentally for food, the barbecue was flaming enthusiastically, leaping up to welcome each fresh sausage. PJ Rothwell-Beer had taken up station behind it, imperiously dabbing and shuffling the meat with long-handled tongs, before passing them on to the pub's sous chef to dice and drop into steaming bowls of broth topped with beery, cheesy croutons. The pub's main attraction was a majestic mural of wall-to-wall bookshelves, which transformed the garden into a rowdy library. A large central birch tree, not to mention the sky above, gave the lie to the illusion, but a credulous and dedicated drinker could always pretend this were Alexandria, where a ceiling would cramp the expansive Classical mind. The mural seemed to condone even the most irresponsible drinking as a valid research methodology and, before long, facial muscles had relaxed and shoulders slackened, sleeves were rolled up and ties pocketed. The ordinarily querulous had mellowed and the meek become emboldened, as the true arena of competitive Academia powered up.

The audience is a judgemental moon with an irresistible and singular gravitational pull. Once beyond its influence, though, academics are compelled by many other occult, often incommensurate, forces. This evening the pack gathered around Tolly Adio and Prentice Hall as they sparred. Prentice was douching his mouth with brandy as if it were breath freshener and bitching under the auspices of reminiscing. Tolly, being less agile, stuck to his red wine and threw in the occasional quip to keep things dialectical: 'Well *she* was putting on report any students she wasn't killing with poisoned references… That was the time they lynched three poets in the plenary… Oh don't try and tell me it was in the name of rigour – he is simply *de trop*.'

Terrified that anyone should tell her the exact nature and repercussions of her performance, Ida hung back from the scene, on the verge of bolting altogether. She would much rather find out tomorrow from her agent.

'Hi, that was really great this evening. I enjoyed your polemic,' said a voice at her left shoulder.

'Oh, er, it was, it was…' It was him, from the second row. Against the evening chill he'd put on a cardigan with wooden buttons, the sight of which almost made Ida sob. Such tender buttons for a man, she thought.

'No, really, you rocked the audience.' Was that a *twinkle* in his voice?

'Do you think so? I was worried I was losing them.' She rested her weight on one foot to make it seem less like she was pausing briefly while on her way somewhere else. He did likewise, and it must have looked to anyone else as if they had settled in to spend the evening together there, on the threshold to the bins enclosure.

'It was an interesting tactic you took with the urinal. I thought it was bold and refreshing.'

'Really? Thanks. I usually like to inflect emotive rhetoric with the cooling vocabulary of the art critic, while peppering it with ideas from associated disciplines, such as psychic anthropology and bio-literature. Interdisciplinarity makes an argument all the more difficult to follow and refute, I find. But, well, I thought that's just a cheap trick I always use. Why not try something new? So I went for heated invective, times a hundred, instead. I just hope people realised it was all a bit of fun. Some idiot will probably think I meant it.'

'But you did to an extent, no? Obviously in greatly exaggerated terms, but in every satire there's always a grain of truth, otherwise it wouldn't be funny. I think people weren't laughing because they saw too big a grain of truth in it. My name's John, by the way.' He turned on the full force of his big, round, brown headlamps and thrust one of his fabulous forearms at her. She shook it with mechanical formality, despite mentally slithering both her hands under the cardigan sleeve, up and down and around the arm, swallowing it with hungry, damp hands.

'John? Sounds familiar. Have we met before? Are you an academic?'

'Sort of, up to a point. Hey, can I get you a drink?' He twinkled some more. 'The lager here is divine.'

'Is it now? You must introduce me to its charms.'

She had been about to leave without even saying goodbye to Fredegund, but this all looked very promising. She suggested they sit indoors, away from the competitive banter, in a dark wooden booth in the furthest corner, and John fetched from the bar a pair of pints with tight round bubbles whooshing up from the bottom of the glass to join the froth at the top. He placed them on the dimpled, copper-topped table and sat opposite Ida, taking off his cardigan as if to signal the start of something. She almost gasped at seeing his forearms at such close quarters. They were strong-looking but smooth, tastefully haired and tapered to a fine-boned wrist. She would like to see them move, she thought. She drew out a cigarette and waved the rest of the pack towards him. He raised his arm in decline; she raised an eyebrow, to which he replied, 'asthma'. She sympathised then told him a story about a friend who thought she had accidentally sewn her son's inhaler inside a cuddly toy she was making, and how the kid had almost asphyxiated when he saw her ripping the bear's seams open to look for it. John responded with a childhood memory that may or may not have been his own, but which she laughed at generously; then she threw in a tart observation, at which he in turn laughed, then retorted to. In short, they were getting on from the off.

'Shall we?' she said, indicating her empty glass.

'Most certainly,' he said, to her relief.

'Would you mind if I gave you the money though? I don't want to bump into anyone at the bar. You know what it's like at these things.' She pushed her purse across the table towards him. He unzipped it without hesitation, as if it were his own, fished out the right change and pivoted towards the next pints.

To stop herself openly leering at him as he walked back from the bar, she read the quotes stencilled on the tobacco-scumbled walls: 'drinking is a form of suicide where you're allowed to return to life and begin all over the next day'. There were worse places to publish than a pub wall, she thought.

'But going back to that point about satire,' she said as he tore into two crisp packets with thrilling roughness.

'Mmm? What point?'

'You were saying about my polemic in the broadcast earlier. Er, what did I say? In the heat of the moment, I didn't quite take it in, I have to admit.'

'Well, let's see. You said that art was a spoiled brat, and psychopathic with it, that curators should be thrown in a dungeon and that sculpture was a stodgy medium. As far as I can remember.'

'No!' She was wide-eyed. 'I wouldn't have.'

'Something like that. It was terrific. I wouldn't worry about it. It's just a game show. Not to belittle it or anything. I couldn't get up on that stage. What I mean is, people know that being funny is different to being sincere or accurate. They're not that stupid.'

*

Four pints in and a warm damp cloud had enveloped the runnels and bogs of Ida's brain, with visibility dropping until it was impossible to see to the end of a sentence. The danger lies in making unwittingly circular journeys, like a bore or an imbecile; but then again, if the stroll is what you enjoy, and you don't care where you end up, back at the beginning may actually be rather convenient, because that is usually where the train station is. The best drunken conversations, from the outside, are clumsy and boring; but on the inside, they are penetrative and bold.

'... the critic shouldn't write about what they think, but what they long to think. It's, it's about, oh, what's the word? I dunno. But it's a fucking travesty...' A stifled hiccough stalled Ida. She signalled with her glass for him to take over, spilling a puddle of lager that dripped unnoticed onto her legs for the rest of the evening.

'Well, my thinking is, if everything carries on becoming more and more conceptual, we're all going to blip out of existence,' said John. 'First painting was dead, then sculpture keeled over, then video topped itself so as not to be left out. Did they bury performance yet? Wouldn't surprise me if they boiled all the artists down to a conceptual jam and spread it on the gallery walls. Soon the whole world will be dematerialised into a cocked hat. We're going to hell in a bus and art is driving. We must devise a plan. We must stop fucking art in its fucking tracks. We must bring it down, enslave it once more.'

All this was very confusing. Ida was unsure where they were on the irony spectrum and which analogy to run with. 'And how will you, erm, do this... this fabulous... this conquerance?' she asked, finishing the sentence in triumph at simply having found the end of it.

'*We*, Ada, *we* will do this together. We will take down the conceptual, Dogdammit. We will champion the formal, foreground the physical; we will utter the guttural and fuck the fuckable.' John was banging the table for emphasis; Ida, meanwhile, was wondering whether to ignore 'Ada' – she wasn't so sure of his name after all – or whether to make a 'thing' of it. Doesn't he realise who she is? Why, she's the most visible critic on radio, Dogdammit. Why, she oughta... She oughta grab him by those fabulous forearms of his and, and...

*

Two pints later the pair had reached a new level of intimacy that went beyond mere names, which had revealed themselves to Ida as arbitrarily assigned clutches of letters that were ultimately meaningless, since profound understanding is beyond language. By now it had become difficult for her to calculate the parallelogram of forces required to halt her propulsion into John's bed. The main fascination, besides the dark hair that she favoured, was his attentiveness. The attractiveness of an attentive man is exactly triple that of one who looks away when one speaks or who fails to laugh at one's considerable wit because he is cueing up his next anecdote. With every utterance she was sure she felt a fistful of their souls exchanging. She was experiencing, for the first time ever, ur-communciation, which just happened in this instance to be externally manifest as drunken cant.

After the eighth pint, en bloc anterograde amnesia kicked in for Ida, for whom there was now a lacuna between the time of weaving out of the pub, trying to avoid everyone else she knew (had she succeeded? she wondered), and waking, upside-down, in a room goodness-knows-where. John, being of bigger build and perhaps a stiffer constitution, probably suffered only a brown-out; but neither could explain why all the shoes he owned, from flip-flops to wellingtons, were scattered about the room.

CHAPTER 5

Thank you, Sian, for that view of the morning's papers. I just want to pick up on one of those stories – that of critic Ida O'Dewey's outburst on this station's very own *Campbell's Panel Beaters* last night. I have a transcript here, and let's just say it's a far from sunny picture that she paints of art. Among other things, she claims that art is a psychopathic despot and the rest of us are pathetically enslaved. It seems that Ms O'Dewey is unavailable for comment this morning, but we do have her agent, Sue Pelosi. Good morning Ms Pelosi.'

'Good morning Robin. Can I just say—'

'Thank you. Sue. I think what we want to hear is how you defend your client's – well, what shall we call it? – her invective, given just how offensive a large number of listeners found it.'

'I think you'll find it was a joke, Robin, not an invective. She was—'

'A joke? All this is a joke to her is it?'

'No, what I mean is that it was intended as a joke. I'm sure it ceased to be one the moment—'

'Ok, thank you, Sue Pelosi. I have here in the studio Bob Downs, the head of the Critical Standards Authority, who is having to deal with the thousands of complaints that have come in. Mr Downs, can you outline, briefly, the nature of these complaints?'

'Certainly Robin. Hello. Yes, they are mainly from people very, very offended by Ms O'Dewey's characterisation of art, which was a gross misreading of a curatorial stance that many have spent their whole careers fashioning, and which many, many people in this land steer by. In her invective, as you call it, Ms O'Dewey not only ridiculed this, but actually suggested a nightmare scenario that could spark a rash of copycat crimes. She was not only rude and critically disengaged, but irresponsible too.'

'So, Sue Pelosi, what do you say to those pretty damning words?'

'Thank you Robin, yes, they are fairly damning, but I think we need to put this into perspective. Ida was appearing on a radio *comedy* show, she was not delivering a keynote speech or publishing a textbook. It was a joke, which she was, if you'll recall the format of the programme, invited to make.'

'Ok, so let's accept for the time being that this was a joke, as you call it. I suppose deep down I can't help thinking that she won't have been invited to make this joke in particular. We don't have any of the programme's producers in the building to swear to this, unfortunately, but maybe if they're listening they could call in to confirm? We do have the next best thing though – Bob Downs, are there any precedents for this? Any cases of academics being invited to make this particular joke on radio or television?'

'No Robin, no there is no precedent for this. But can I just add that—'

'So, Sue Pelosi, let me put it to you this way: there is no doubt that she was not invited to make this joke, *ergo*, it must have come from her own head.'

'Well yes, Robin, no one is disputing that.'

'Right, so—'

'But what I am disputing is her intention—'

'Ah, hold on, if you will. We have one of the *Panel Beaters* producers on the line. Sir Bing Longside. Sir Bing, good morning to you. I understand you heard my question on air a moment ago.'

'Good morning Robin. Yes, yes I did.'

'Sir Bing, I would have thought you would be best placed to know the answer to this.'

'Yes, yes I would be best placed to know the answer.'

'And so can you please tell me, Sir Bing, the answer to the question: was Ida O'Dewey specifically invited to make the joke that she made?'

'No, Robin, no she wasn't.'

'Thank you Sir Bing. So, Bob Downs, there we have it from the horse's mouth, so to speak: these inflammatory comments were entirely the critic's own invention. As you say, this is a great irresponsibility in the eyes of a vast majority of people. How do you think the CSA will be dealing with this?'

'Well, we will of course initiate a thorough peer review procedure, and a decision as to whether Ms O'Dewey should be disciplined will be made on the grounds of our findings.'

'I see. What sort of disciplinary proceedings can we expect for this sort of transgression?'

'Well, like I say, it depends on our findings. This is not a clear-cut case and we really need to sift through the evidence—'

'But hypothetically. If it was proven that a critic, for instance, had been critically disengaged, and that as a result of that critical disengagement they were, let's say for argument's sake, irresponsible – what would be the CSA's response?'

'Well, hypothetically—'

'Could blackballing be an option?'

'Possibly. Guidelines and procedures would have to be consulted and—'

'Blackballing. As drastic as that?'

'Well, the CSA has guidelines it must follow and procedures it must adhere to, but—'

'It would certainly be a clear message to critics, and all academics too, that this sort of wild flight of fancy will not be tolerated. So, Sue Pelosi – blackballing. This is pretty serious. Do you think a career can stand up to that?'

'I wouldn't know about that Robin, and anyway, I really don't think things will get that far. As Bob said, there will be a thorough peer review, and I am certain it will find that Ida's intentions were totally benign. I am sure the fact of her appearing on a comedy programme has something to do with her flight of fancy, as you call it.'

'Benign, Bob Downs? Can you imagine a set of circumstances in which the sort of sentiments we heard last night can be considered benign?'

'Not offhand, Robin, but we shall have to wait and see what the outcome of the review is. I don't wish to jeopardise its outcome by speculating any further on its potential findings.'

'Fair enough, thank you Bob Downs, Sue Pelosi. We will await the outcome with interest. And in the meantime, listeners at home, do keep phoning in your comments on this and other stories. We have a message here from one Dr Connolly in the Humanities Department, who says about the O'Dewey scandal: "It just goes to show that inside every intellectual a sensualist is wildly signalling to get out." A most curious image. Now then, Corris, do you have a sensualist signalling wildly to get out of your meteorologist's body?'

'Certainly not, Robin, but we do have clouds across the region with rain bursting to get out. It's going to be a wet day right across the Academic territories, I'm afraid.'

CHAPTER 6

Mid-morning, when Ida was at last able to make a thought emerge from her fogged head, the first was, 'Oh no, I'm late for school'; the second was curiosity about who she would encounter on the pillow next to her. She knew there was someone, and someone not at all shameful. She could remember the forearms, but the face was blank. Had she really spent the evening staring at his arms? She opened her eyes to find another pair, large and brown, staring back.

'Good morning,' said the full lips beneath the fine, strong nose, and at the sound of the voice, with its low, truckish rumble, the whole person came flooding back to her.

'Why, good morning John.'

'There you are at last,' he said, rising from the bed like Poseidon and declaring over his shoulder, as he grabbed a dressing gown off the back of the door, that he was going to fix some eggs.

'Why, are they broken?' she asked.

He blinked back, smiled sarcastically, and left, closing the door softly behind him.

The afterimage of his upright, taut but not clownishly muscular body, topped by the dark forelock that flopped over his narrow, serious forehead, lingered for some moments on her retina before fading and depositing her back in his pigsty of a room. The walls were woodchipped, the skirting boards, door and window frames painted a thick gloss the colour of callouses; the curtains were improvised from Hawaiian shirts; the ceiling bulb boasted an inverted catering tub of mustard for a shade, and around the light switch a corona of grimy finger smudges spread to a diameter of almost a foot and a half. And to top it: a Yale lock, like in halls of residence or a lodging house. This was disappointing. She liked her lovers to have progressed far beyond a labelled shelf in a shared kitchen. Of course, this might just be a temporary stopgap due to 'circumstances', but then that generally spelled d-a-m-a-g-e-d-g-o-o-d-s. A recent divorcé, perhaps, or an entrenched bachelor. She wasn't sure which was worse: the freshly cuckolded, loaded up with baggage, or someone who resolutely refused to pick up any baggage in the first place.

It's funny, she mused, how differently the spinster and the bachelor are viewed. She was, technically, a spinster, since she was single and beyond the conventional marrying age, but the word evoked a bitter old hag, burdened with loneliness and shamed by rejection, sitting at a spinning wheel and casting hexes on the young and beautiful. The life-long bachelor is way more cheery a figure: free of limb and habit, quite possibly thanks to an earlier narrow escape from marital calamity. Ida watched a scene on her internal screen featuring a middle-aged, single, thwarted Diana, her quiver bereft of arrows, thick green hosiery laddered and her little horn dry from over-blowing. She was calling balefully after a bob-tailed bachelor as he darted gleefully away, leaping unfettered through the undergrowth of adventure and self-fulfilment.

As rapidly as she could with a hangover, Ida scanned the room for further evidence of John's status and calling. Stretching her torso out of the bed, she caught the aroma of sweet aniseed soaked into the purple nylon carpet fibres, which would explain the intensity of the pain in her head. Recoiling from the smell before she could see what might be under the bed, she instead surveyed what was within easy reach of her recumbent gaze. Shelves bore no textbooks, but stacks of magazines, and an orderly queue of eccentric cacti filed along the windowsill. Apart from the clothes they'd flung off the night before – and the stained and torn dressing gown John had just stepped out in – a heap of waterproof utility wear, with fussy velcro straps, decoy toggles and absurdly capacious pockets, appeared to be all that could pass for a wardrobe in the room. This man was a conundrum: while the dressing gown shrieked 'writer', the Velcro yodelled 'rambler'; the magazines indicated a restless mind and the cacti smacked of wanton carnality. Ida bundled all this into an image of a ruddy outdoorsy mouth-breathing sort of chap, which her experience of him so far did not corroborate. Preparing for the worst nonetheless, she started to plot her retreat, seeking out her own items of clothing scattered about the room like litter in a hedge. It was while she was untangling her underwear from a dumbbell at the foot of the bed that her bare backside, shining like a pale, benevolent satellite, greeted John as he reappeared.

'Good to see you smiling,' he said, placing a loaded tray on the bedside table next to a packet of condoms and a crampon.

Extracting herself from the gap between the bed and the wall, Ida surfaced with her knickers and notebook, which fell open to a sketch she didn't remember doing. John reached across to snatch it from her, but she swapped hands and held it at arm's length. He refused to play the game, slumping back into the bed with theatricalised nonchalance.

'Nice drawings. So, you're an artist.' She leafed through the book, nodding at marks she could tell were made casually but with experience. 'Not bad, not bad – if mimesis is what you're into. Is it coming back round again? Will you work them up into oils? Oh my Dog – is that me?'

John craned over to look.

'One of my better ones, I think.'

'Better than this one, certainly. That's Strelnikov isn't it? You've captured her arrogance brilliantly, right there, in the nostrils. And here's Fredegund. From a while back though. I remember that haircut. She did it herself, you know. So what are you? A celebrity portraitist? Is all this,' she nodded at her nudity under the covers, 'to try and get me to sit for you?'

'It's just a hobby of mine. I like to watch people when they're waiting to speak – it's such an emotional moment. You're all feigning a sort of cool blankness, but actually you're a mass of anxiety, supressed hilarity, guilt – all sorts of weird waves come off you.'

'You bloody sadist.'

'I call you all my little saussicons. Because you're made up of various far-flung stuffs in a skin, sweating under the grill, and you can be bought by the pound at any box office.' He reached for the tray and placed it on his lap.

'What's all this? My sitter's fee?' She reached out for a mug of tea. He handed her a plate of food.

'Breakfast.'

'Thanks. Um, these eggs look awfully firm.' She stared at them with hostility.

'But you haven't even tried them. How do you know? I might have added a cunning ingredient that makes them look firm, but in fact imbues them with a silken texture that melts on the tongue.' He shovelled a forkful into his mouth and closed his eyes as if in rapture.

'Eggs is eggs', said Ida, feeling that this was a fair portrayal of the paradox of eggs. She shuddered. 'They're a bit sci-fi if you ask me, all that solidifying with heat. Most things melt. But that is the wonder of them apparently. But really, they're fine, I shouldn't have said anything. I just make them a bit sloppier, that's all.'

'Sloppy, as in soup, you mean?' he said with his mouth still full.

'Well, yes, soup is generally...' Her hand was escorting a forkful up to her reticent mouth.

'Don't judge it before you've tried it. This is the problem with you—.'

Ida's eggs fell onto the bed-cover with a damp plop.

'You what? You Capricorns? You people who prefer coffee to tea, incidentally? You people who wear their watch on the left wrist? Oh, no, you must mean you *women*.'

'No, I wasn't referring to women.' He scraped up the egg with a knife and smeared it on a corner of toast. 'Some of my best friends are women. I mean academics, theorists, critics. Your problem is that you think you know things.' He popped the whole triangle of toast in his mouth, chewing vigorously.

'Yes, I do think that there are some things that I know. Quite a lot actually. But these women? Are you—'

'No I'm not,' he said, his mouth still half full. 'But, anyway, what I mean is that you think you know before you actually do know.' He swallowed. 'You think, think, think and seldom actually *do*.'

'Hardly!' Ida made a sweeping gesture to encompass their bodies, prone beneath the fabric and feathers. 'We were doing it like mad last night.' Although she was only guessing at this from the fact that they were both naked. She had absolutely no recollection of any sex act, no memory of foreplay or orgasm. She only hoped she had performed well enough under the circumstances.

'Well, nearly, I suppose, but never mind about that. You know, I'm sensing, judging from your performance on the radio yesterday, there is something distinctly earthy about you.'

This set Ida into a twin turmoil of sexual embarrassment (had she fallen asleep on him?) and professional horror.

'Oh Dog, I'd forgotten about *Panel Beaters*. I got a bit carried away, didn't I? And you were not entirely blameless in that, may I add.'

'What do you mean?'

'Egging me on, you were. Nodding away, taking notes. I thought I was on a roll. But oh no, you were luring me onto the rocks.'

'You were more than capable of coasting onto them yourself. And anyway, I wasn't taking notes, I was sketching you. You know, you have a very interesting stage presence.'

'I do?'

'Yes. All those other panellists were attempting a sort of monolithic authority, but anyone can tell it's a whole pile of rocky pseudo-facts built on shaky foundations, held together by flabby assumptions. But you – you don't bother trying to affect such an edifice. I could really sense the chaos in your head when you were speaking.'

'Oh, great.'

'You make a virtue of the gaps in your knowledge instead of pretending they're not there.'

'I do? That doesn't sound like a good thing.'

'I think it is. It keeps you working hard, stops you settling in any one place long enough to get dusty. All those professors have been defending the same patch of mud for decades, but you seem more adventurous than that. Now, try those damn eggs and see if they don't move you to ecstasy.'

Ida had to admit they were soft, despite their apparent firmness. The two of them argued for a while over whether this meant they were deceptively firm or deceptively soft.

'On which side does the deception lie? That of the eggs themselves, or in the perception of the eater?' she asked. He thought the former, but she insisted the latter. 'The deceit is that they appear to be firm when actually they're soft. Fact.'

'But that does not make the eggs deceitful,' he said. 'It's not the eggs' fault. They are insensate. It's your perceptual apparatus that is deceiving you. And anyway, the mere addition of the word "fact" at the end of any old spurious claim does not magically convert it to an inviolable truth. This is surely not what they teach in rhetoric lessons, is it?'

'No, it is my own wild invention, and it always works. Fact.'

Ida was enjoying this new brand of bickering, which, while born of distinct differences, suggested a more essential equivalence. And John seemed to be thinking likewise, because, as she dressed and headed for the door, starting to turn her attention to her late-morning appointment, he asked with refreshing directness if she might like to meet up in a few days' time.

'There's an event I think you might enjoy and some people you would probably benefit from hearing speak.'

'Oh yes, what on?'

They descended the dark, narrow staircase, which was stealthily producing the smell of communal spaces – a sort of average of all smells.

'Well, this time I think there'll be quite a lot about oil. It's fascinating stuff.'

'Oil? What's that?'

'You'll have to come along and find out.' He wrapped his dressing gown tightly around him before opening the front door to the street, where the trains and trams and goods lorries were thoughtlessly vibrating the air.

'Mysteries are actually quite boring. There's nothing skilful about withholding information.' She turned to face him, her face reaching upwards for a final kiss, testing to see if he were up to such a thing in the public arena of his doorstep.

'I'm not being mysterious, it's just that it's genuinely difficult to explain while half-naked on a threshold.' He lay one on her lips, his hands on her shoulders as if to prevent her floating upwards.

'In that case tell me when you're completely naked.' She pulled away to retrieve a business card. As she reached to deposit it in his dressing gown pocket he gently drew her in, enveloping her in spicy-smelling towelling, kissing her again, for longer this time.

'Well, it's been a hoot.' She stepped out of the radius of intimacy.

'Yeah, a real hoot. I'll call. Don't let that nasty old art get to you.'

'Ah, yes. I wonder how all that went down. I guess I'll find out soon enough.'

'Don't worry,' he replied, his thumbs tucked into the belt loops of his dressing gown in a strange melding of macho and effeminate. 'It was obviously a bit of fun, and anyway, everyone knows how to badmouth art – they're all at it behind closed doors.'

'Sure, but there's one standard for ordinary people and another for public figures like me.'

'Poor celebrity art critic,' he said with a pout, then blew a kiss, withdrew and slammed the front door, setting the cacti quivering on the windowsill above.

CHAPTER 7

Sergeant Singer was ex-military and a blue-chip abstract painter who, according to some, painted the same thing over and over, or, according to others, was so close to his subject matter that minute differences between canvases were, to him, colossal progressions. He was renowned for having the hots for any woman younger than his wife, and so Ida would not be encouraging anything extracurricular during this studio visit. After last night's exertions she lacked the energy required to fight off tall patriarchs.

Sergeant had laid the groundwork for his full and rewarding life long ago. On the back of his first sell-out exhibition he had bought a large, warm studio with plenty of assistants in the centre of Academia, a short tram ride from his many-bedroomed house. He had met his wife at his first after-show party, but rather than thinking 'I'm going to marry that woman', as those who claim to have experienced love-at-first-sight often recount, he had thought, 'Oh, so that's what she looks like.' They were married within three months and had become parents within another six. His wife had adhered to an obscure algorithmic method of contraception, but over several decades the number of children had mounted steadily, until her eggs had finally run out. With his bi-annual sell-out shows and his persistently climbing prices, though, he had always been able to keep the family well within the standard of living an artist should expect to enjoy.

The ease and regularity of his life was appalling to Ida. If she hadn't been feeling so wiped out she would have really shaken him up in this interview. She had been commissioned to write a piece about his upcoming museum show, but the museum had a press embargo in place. He was forbidden to show her any new paintings, and she was not even permitted to speculate on what they might be.

'Which means I can't even talk about old work, because, of course, he's been trotting out the same stuff for decades,' she had complained to the editor.

The editor suggested she went for the abstract ideas behind the work, or bent it round to a human-interest story instead.

'You know – ask where his concepts come from, how they are drawn from and add to life, the world, society, history—'

'Sergeant hasn't had a thought that's originated outside of his own arse for decades. Now I have to be a proctologist too?'

Sergeant's studio building was at one end of a fashionable central Academia street, with a huge silver and black department store, like an ocean liner, at the other end. A terrace of art nouveau townhouses spanned between them. Fussily ornate and in prime condition, each was painted a different sugary colour with details accented in white. Sergeant's brick block was more squat, rougher, ruddier and more pragmatic, its paintwork less proud to be seen in daylight. Not that anyone would have complained, because the studio of an artist of Sergeant's stature would bring value to a neighbourhood even if it had been a war-torn portacabin with an open-air pissoir.

Sergeant answered the door himself and ushered Ida in to what was far from the louche warehouse conversion she had been expecting. The floors were carpet tiled and the walls, instead of flaunting their brickwork, had been clad and painted a pale blue too insipid for a painter to have chosen himself. The lighting was stark and buzzed like a headache, and through open doors Ida could see rooms of unidentifiable usage, with weary, mismatched chairs gathering like cows in corners. Sergeant was wearing a suit, perhaps for the occasion. He was less athletic looking than she remembered from his television appearances, and had a slight stoop, perhaps because he was tall and the ceiling tiles hung low, although it looked more habitual than circumstantial. He hurried through a vast room, which was trying to appear empty of the large items under tarpaulins at its dark margins, and held open a door at the far end, ushering Ida up a narrow wooden staircase. She was still wearing those infernal itchy trousers and could smell her own aura of ethanol now that she was in an enclosed space. Beneath the silk her arms were goose-pimpling from the cold, and those damn scrambled eggs were haunting her mouth.

Sergeant offered refreshments and, after a protracted tea-making episode – during which he opened and slammed each cupboard door a couple of times as if he didn't know where anything was – they eventually settled down into large, cream-coloured prolapsing armchairs, a low wooden table piled up with art magazines between them.

'So, as you know, we're not allowed to actually discuss the new paintings, so I was hoping we might talk about the thinking behind them,' said Ida, lacking the stamina for lengthy preambles and niceties.

'Ah, I'm afraid I'll have to leave that entirely to you. I do the painting and you lot usually do the thinking, which seems to work nicely, what-what? If it ain't broke…' he said good naturedly, caressing his patchy beard.

He seemed much more personable, and less insipid, than she'd been led to believe, and so she relaxed into the job in hand, business-like but friendly.

'Ok… so, how about if I tell you what I think the thinking is and you just nod if you agree and shake your head if you don't. That way you don't actually originate any thoughts but I've still got something to go on,' she said.

'Hmmm, not sure. The curator was very adamant…'

'Fine, well, how about if you nod for no and shake your head for yes? That way you're not telling me, I'm inferring, and we're all in the clear.'

'Ah, good, yes, that sounds perfect. Tally ho, orf you go then.'

With greasy, paint-smeared mugs of tea in hand, they edged out of the harbour of politeness into the open seas of critical discourse.

'So, Sergeant – oh, I'm recording this, hope you don't mind, it just saves me taking notes, so I can concentrate on what you're saying.' Ida indicated the large silver device with a blinking red light on the table between them. Sergeant looked at it, as if noticing it for the first time, and leant right in to the machine's microphone to give his verbal consent.

'Anyway, so, yes, what I wanted to ask to start with was about time and narrative. It seems to me that your paintings are very temporal.' Sergeant shook his head vehemently, which confused Ida momentarily. 'No? Ah, hang on, I mean yes, they are about time. They compress the dynamism of history into a gestural moment.' More head shaking. 'Or rather, they envelope other times within their presentness, which the gestures connote.' Violent head shaking. 'Good, so, my assumption, or rather, my deduction is that you wish us not to know these as external narrations of histories and geographies, but internal, subjective comprehensions.' A slow nodding picked up pace and became emphatic. 'Ah, so you do wish us to know these as external narrations.' The nodding continued. 'Sorry, you don't wish us to know these as internal comprehensions. Or maybe you do wish us to know them as internal miscomprehensions?' Sustained nodding stymied this line of enquiry, so she started afresh from another angle. 'Ok, I think we can safely say, inferring from your references to the gash and the visceral smear, that trauma is a theme.' To which Sergeant, thankfully, shook his head slowly. 'Ah, not a central theme perhaps, but a concern nonetheless.' At this he was almost imperceptibly nodding. Extending the inversion of yes and no, he had also come up with the notion that the magnitude of his response should also be inversely proportionate, so that 'strongly agree' produced a slight shake and 'disagree a tad' a vigorous nod, which took a further twenty minutes for Ida to fathom from what seemed a tangle of contradictions and disproportionate reactions.

The hour continued painfully along these lines until she simply ran out of energy and ideas. It was like running after a fart, trying to pin this fellow down, she thought, and her mug of tea had long since run dry – as had her mouth. She was spent and would just have to fudge something poetic and evocative from what scraps she had gleaned.

'Great, thanks Sergeant. I think I have everything I need now. I just want to clear up a few practicalities about the show. Just very loose information now, no embargo-breaking details. You'll not be departing from paintings, will you? No videos or performance?'

He nodded his head uncertainly.

'It's ok, you can speak now. This is just a bit of housekeeping. Totally off the record.'

'Ah, right, I see. Then no, definitely no video. Just good old oil paintings.'

'Hmmm, that's interesting… Oil paintings? What sort of oil is it, do you know? Where does it come from?'

'What do you mean?'

'Where it says oil paint here,' she pointed to the label on a tube of cadmium red in an ashtray, 'that suggests it's a paint made of oil. I'm just wondering if you know what sort of oil that is and where it comes from.'

Sergeant whistled through his teeth and snorted before answering, 'Well-well. I've always just thought of it as one word: "oilpaint". I suppose now you're telling me it's two, is it? Oil… paint. Well blow me. I don't know. I just smear the stuff about. Maybe you should ask my assistant – Dora, I think it is. She's the one who buys it for me.'

At that moment, as if summoned by a silent bell, a tender-eyed, acne-ravaged youth appeared in the room.

'Ah, erm, yes, be a dear, Dora, and show Miss O'Dewey out. And give her a copy of the paint supplier's catalogue too, will you? Thank you very much Miss O'Dewey. I look forward to seeing our little chat in print,'

Sergeant chuckled good-naturedly, a paintbrush already in his hand and loaded with paint the exact colour of Ida's blouse.

Dora led Ida back through the various rooms and corridors to the street door, stopping off at a small, windowless office where she seemed to be stationed, which Ida scanned for old-fashioned maid's bells but found none. Dora handed her a thick paint supplier's directory, plucked from a huge mound of papers and books that may or may not have been supported by a desk, and then, appearing to summon up all her courage, asked for Ida's autograph, handing her a yellow index card and a book to lean on. Ida penned her best flourish, and, noticing that the book was Prentice Hall's *Extreme Curating,* couldn't resist handing it back with performed distain.

'Urgh, this hyped-up cream puff of a pamphlet. Not a writer I'd like to be seen to be leaning on.' She had read it cover to cover the previous month and had had to force herself through to the end before throwing it against a wall. 'I should sign one of my own books for you really. Do you have any?'

'Yes, of course, but I keep them at home, next to my bed,' replied Dora shyly but unmistakably flirtatiously, Ida thought.

'Ah, well, next time I come, bring it along and I shall be happy to write a little dedication in it.' Realising she sounded rather supercilious, she raised her eyebrows and bossed her eyes, sweeping past the young woman, whose unsmiling gaze followed her as she ploughed into the crowded pavement and pressed on home for some much-needed sleep.

CHAPTER 8

'Sue, I hear you were magnificent,' said Ida. She flopped down on the unforgiving Eames chair, jarring her coccyx and wincing, which undid the compliment in a complex way.

'Enough of the flannel, Ida. What happened the other night?' demanded Sue across her glass-topped desk. The office decor was 'modern', with not a warm, soft surface anywhere, from the strip lights down to the concrete floor overlaid with skin-shredding sisal mats.

Ida took a deep breath. 'Well, there was this guy in the pub and, well, we had a drink or two…'

'No, not that. I mean what happened on *Panel Beaters*? What have you done to your career?' Sue's eyes were hard and black, her mouth set thin as sandwich ham.

'But it was a joke. I thought everyone understood that.'

'You understood that. I had to guess it. The media are refusing to believe it. Dog only knows what the public thinks. Even if it was meant to be a joke, someone of your position shouldn't be seen to even be able to think these things.'

'But you don't think these things, do you?' asked Linda. 'You were simply speaking without thinking, which in this case is preferable, isn't it?' She offered round a packet of mints, which everyone ignored.

Ida slumped, groaning loudly; her agent and trainer exchanged glances loaded with significance – one sharp, the other less well formed, but this was as far as they got, because while eyes are not the least efficient organs of communication, neither are they the most articulate.

'I really don't know what happened,' said Ida. 'I was in that space of total flow, you know. I felt the audience carrying me along, it was electric, but I guess I just let apodioxis get the better of me. I was so hell-bent on opposing Prentice bloody Hall I wasn't looking ahead at the consequences, but it all seemed like good fun at the time. The crowd were buzzing. I was so in the moment, so alive, so onstage.'

'Hey, that sounds like something positive we can take from this,' said Linda. 'You've been working really hard on your apodioxis – no one can say you indulged Prentice, certainly – and there was some excellent rhetoric in there. Your Latinate delicacies paired with the brutal blow of Anglo-Saxon were fantastic, I thought. What was it again? Transcendental significance and stodgy idea. Very nice.'

'Ooh, that's not bad. Did I really say that?'

'Oh stop fannying about with irrelevances Linda,' said Sue. 'No one else even notices that stuff. The problem is beyond mere technicalities. You can't lose control like that Ida. You have to find the gags in the serious theory, don't just make up stupid theory. People can't tell the difference. They don't get sarcasm. They think it's all real. They're stupid. And will you stop jiggling your leg please Linda. It's making me feel queasy.'

Linda obediently stilled her leg, which was sheathed in thick beige wool and topped and tailed by a tartan skirt and clean white plimsolls. She was slightly bovine about the eyes – perhaps they were too far apart or maybe it was their unblinking roundness that gave the impression she was staring out from her skull at the world, uncertain but ultimately at peace with her uncertainty. She shone with health, as a rule; her hair was sleek and cut flatteringly around her face, like a mousy portal through which she looked and looked. Her form was full and powerful, again rather like a cow, and she moved equally ponderously, never in a hurry – unlike Sue, who was waspish, slick-haired and fashionable. Sue knew how to seem to carry herself in all situations. She had never once in her professional life been spotted doing the wrong thing, putting her foot in her mouth, over- or underdressing or even visibly wavering on any point whatsoever. This was mainly because she stuck to safe ground at all times, erecting a barrier of words or retreating tactically from anything she did not fully understand. She was aware of these so-called faults, but she saw nothing cowardly or unfair in them. To her mind she was simply configuring the world around her to her best advantage, and if this happened to make it more difficult for other people – well, that was their problem. This was the whole point of a fair and competitive society. And she saw not just her industry, but her home life too as a series of heats and rounds and bouts to be won. She stuck with Linda, professionally and romantically, because as an opponent Linda posed little threat, and as a teammate she had technical skills Sue lacked. This was the source of many of Linda's woes, for it was difficult to tell when she could expect to be an opponent and when an ally, with Sue often switching back and forth within a single minute. But Linda chose to interpret Sue's chip-chip-chipping away at her, especially in public, as a display of intimate and unconditional trust. Their clients eyed this dynamic with amusement, sharing jokes and scandalous episodes with one another, and universally rooting for Linda, hoping that one day she would give Sue the shock of her life.

Most clients neglected to analyse their own relationship with Sue. They didn't notice that they too let her dominate them. Many construed her professional bluff and blarney as professional nous, since the illusion suited their own fragilities. Generally though, Ida could see right through Sue, and smirked whenever she heard her hedging around an uncertain topic or echoing back to people what they'd just said as a means of appearing to concur on something she had never thought about before. Ida had a grudging admiration for how this usually produced results, and today there was no question that Sue was entirely right. Ida had overstepped a line. She had compromised herself before: in a live interview last year she couldn't remember the name of a single art magazine, and this just one month after misquoting in print her own appropriated quote on misappropriation. She'd come back from that by admitting personal issues were distracting her, and she was immediately and entirely pardoned. But this latest transgression was perceived as being of another category altogether. People were willing to go deep with it this time.

'The next question,' said Sue, 'is how on earth we're going to repair this unfortunate gaff, *tout de suite*.'

'Sweeter than toot,' said Linda.

'Not the time for wordy horseplay, thanks Linda. Now, let's think. You have denounced art and now you have to de-denounce it.'

'Or nounce it?'

'Linda, please, I'm working. Now, let's think about this systematically.' Sue was shifting up into her highest PR gear. 'A public apology doesn't actually undo anything, because it's an instant admittance of guilt. Claiming irony hasn't gone down well in recent years, and saying it was a piece of provocative performance art is such a cliché. What we really need is for it to become apparent that your actual intent was other than it appeared, or that some greater good will come of it, or that your argument was so nuanced it actually meant the opposite of what it appeared to mean. Or is there some way you could claim it was a new research methodology? For your next book?'

Abashed, Ida had to explain that, actually, she was at a bit of a loss with the new book. Not only had she not started, she had changed her mind about what it was about scores of times. Nothing seemed new or substantial enough. She kept thinking she was having a new idea, then soon realised, once she'd stripped it back to its essence or stretched it out in context, that it was the same idea over and over again – and, even more unfortunately, that it was the same idea as her last book.

'Oh dear,' said Linda sympathetically, 'you're blocked!'

'Nonsense,' said Sue. 'No such thing as "blocked". You're spreading yourself too thin, that's all. Forget the book for now, let's think what there is already on the table that can be used to uncook this particular goose, shall we?'

A flicker of pain passed over Linda's face at the mixed metaphor. Sue eyed her suspiciously. Linda pretended the quick of her nail had caught on her jumper before comment was drawn.

'The soap opera is the obvious vehicle. What if you instigate a sub-plot that post-rationalises your outburst as research for an upcoming episode? It'll take a bit of time to come to light, but that could be all the more satisfying. Eventually.'

'Yes, that could work,' said Ida. 'I see where you're coming from there. Good thinking.' Peers and detractors had pounced on Ida in print and on air. If she could engineer it so that, once the truth was out, her attackers bore the brunt of public censure for being illiberally quick to accuse, that would be truly delicious. 'So basically, I write a few scenes where a character denounces art and… and… how does it work? Why would I say in reality what I then get a fictional character to say?'

'Well, you've heard of artistic license. Say this was realistic license,' said Linda.

'Linda, please. Ida, this could boost your share value enormously if you play the longer game. We can goad the media into spinning the story some more, feed them some extra sub-scandals and kick up a sensational storm with you at the eye, and then you can reveal that it was all a stunt. Or an audience experiment. Hmmm, no, gen-pub would take against that. Stick with research. It's more noble. Anyway, whatever, you start off a villain, then become a victim, then an ingenious heroine. And if you die from stress in the meantime, you come out of it a martyr. It means you'll have to weather the storm a little longer yet, but it'll all be fine in the end. Better than fine. Trust me.'

Books had been written about academic hoaxes, their perpetrators exalted as true radicals fighting institutional rigidity. Ida had always dismissed it as a path not open to her. Professors and editors rattling internal structures and unravelling loopholes seemed remote to a freelancer out in the field. But now she realised that yes, she was on the inside of something. She imagined herself at the crux of a huge furore, a *Rückenfigure*, one foot on a rock, the gales whipping her hair about her caped shoulders… no, no, no, too romantic. There must be a better stereotype… a wizard behind a velvet curtain, her hand on the levers and pulleys, scaring the wits out of those assembled… nope, still wrong… an evil puppeteer? No! An alchemist at her crucible… a witch… Why were they all such negative images? Surely there was a positive role model for a devious shit-stirrer?

'So,' said Sue, 'since those journalists think whatever it suits them to think, we'll not stand in their way just yet. We'll ambush them later. Is that a plan?'

'Ok, let's do it. Um, what exactly was it that I was going to ambush them with?'

'I don't know. You're the writer. You'll come up with something. When's your next script meeting?'

'In a week and a half. I thought you had an idea.'

'And so I did. I just told you it.'

'That wasn't an idea, that was a placemat to put an idea down on,' said Ida.

'Or a doily to—' started Linda.

'Shit Ida, you're the damn ideas person. Go and cook up your own. Or get a frozen one from wherever they're kept in the ideas supermarket. Or if you really want to keep going with this analogy—'

'Metaphor,' braved Linda.

'—then ring up one of your clever buddies for a fucking takeaway.'

'Ok, ok,' said Ida. 'One other thing, though. Possibly not something you will have considered. Aren't I rather abusing my position? My job on the soap, I mean. I've always been fairly scrupulous, but this is out-and-out self-interestedness.'

'Self-interest is not a crime. In fact it's behind many of the greatest human achievements.' Sue drew herself up tall and formidable in the absence of actual examples. 'After all these years, all that work, all those moments of pain and triumph, you cannot, I will not let you, throw it all away in a moment of lust-induced idiocy. I'm assuming your performance the other evening was that.' Ida coloured. It seemed the right thing to do. 'The whole world heard the drivel you spouted, and they deserve an explanation. Obviously not the real explanation. But this way you devise something so clever they'll be eating out of your hand. Drooling over it, then eating out of it. You'll be a national treasure in a twinkling. Damn this plumbing.' Sue was giving her hands a quick psychosomatic wash in the stagnant pool in the office kitchenette basin, alongside which, uncharacteristically for such a tightly run office, a throng of rheumy-looking mugs slouched disaffectedly.

Ida had to admit that she liked the sound of becoming a national treasure. Her desire for historical perpetuity was strong. Not a natural-born breeder, she wouldn't be leaving a genetic trail behind her, but she hoped that another form of legacy was possible, one that was longer lasting and less of a liability than children and grandchildren, who would invariably drag the family name through the mud at some point. As it was, with her weekly onscreen credit, she asserted herself in the public imagination with the regularity of a bin man, which was something, but if she were to pull off a truly ingenious and singular act, her name would penetrate to the slow, majestic stratum of history itself.

'Now, if you'll excuse me Ida, Linda, I have a few calls to make.' Sue was about to imperiously sweep into her inner office when a lantern-jawed idol, with a blonde flattop and dark-blue dungarees that failed to cover the nipples adrift on his pectorals, burst in. His eyes swivelled until they found Sue. Ida backed out slowly, transfixed as his lips formed words, which sounded to her like the most wonderful poem with erotic, wide-open vowels.

'Alright love, I've had to just stop it off for now, that hot tap. You've still got your hot in the kitchen, but the loo will have to make do with cold. You've got a terrible problem with pressure all the way up here and your system is overloaded. Maybe back in the pumping station they'll install a booster – wouldn't bank on it though – or you could dig up your foundations here and get a private one put in. I mean, you could. It'll cost you, and you'd only get a few extra milligals out of that tap. It's up to you, really…'

CHAPTER 9

If you want to gauge if an idea is good or not, there's nothing like saying it out loud to someone else. They don't have to say anything in response. They don't even have to look sceptical or create an atmosphere of disapproval by intangible means. Somehow their very presence is enough to make the shit idea break down and confess. But in this case, the idea was too sensitive to expose to a friend. And so Ida arranged instead to try it out on a couple of her projected selves. Like most of us, she projected daily from a roster of constructed self-images: efficient working woman, imaginative writer, risk-taking critic, fun-loving companion and so on. By her reckoning there were at least a dozen of these homunculi versions hanging around in the projection booth of her soul, and from them she summoned the combustible combination of a wild-eyed Ida that knew no fear and a no-nonsense, practical-minded counterpart. A third, over-sensitive Ida was invited to join them for drinks afterwards, so that she didn't feel excluded.

Before it even had a chance to reveal itself as shit, the idea of a strategic breach of the critic's professional code was shot down by both parties.

'Don't get me wrong,' said fearless Ida. 'It's not that I'm worried about getting found out, but to get anything past Chip it would have to be so codified or allegorical that it wouldn't work anyway – no one would get it.'

'I hear you,' said practical Ida. 'He can smell a burn from a mile off, that one. And he'll be looking out for us pushing our own agenda, after all the fuss. We'll get nothing past him.'

'Thank you for those frank and open opinions,' said Ida. 'What I would really appreciate now are your thoughts on how else I – we – might solve this problem. If a solution can't be smuggled past Chip, what other options are open to us?'

Knowing one another too well, the two other Idas held back their thoughts, one opening her mouth as if to speak, then saying 'nothing', the other asking 'what?', the first shaking her head, the other pressing her until she had to insist, no really, it was nothing.

Ida had anticipated this, and cracked open a bottle of wine.

'Ah, lovely,' said the homunculi in unison as the alcohol washed over them on its way to the nearest neurotransmitters, from which liberal amounts of gamma aminobutyric acid, dopamine and serotonin were ordered up. Once these had started to splosh about the place, inhibitions quickly fell away and the pair were soon positing and refuting like old sparring partners.

'If we can't get one over on Chip, why not bribe him?'

'He'd never go for it. He's so damn upright, which is how we got the gig in the first place, remember?' When *Academy* was accused of trying to influence the outcome of the Young Semiotician of the Year Award, Chip had every scriptwriter on the show sacked, and asked a ragbag of critics and journalists to take over – Ida among them.

'Right, yes, I was forgetting. We could seduce him maybe.'

'Didn't we try that before? He didn't even notice. He's made of stone in the trouser department.'

'True, I must have blanked that. We'll have to blackmail him then.'

'It's a possibility. But blackmail must be conducted carefully. The threat has to hit the mark spot on, but not so heavily that they top themselves.'

'Ah, in that case, what if it's a threat that is not immediately perceived as a threat? It could be a promise or a hint that gradually grows into a threat.'

'Except we need him to react quickly.'

'Well, then maybe it's a quick-release but soft-impact threat that he doesn't realise is influencing him at first, but it compels him to act nonetheless.'

'Is there such a thing?'

'Oh I don't know. I made it up. I thought this was the point of brainstorming. If you're going to keep telling me my ideas are shit, how am I ever going to be able to get into the zone? You've got to get the shit out before you can get to the gold.'

'Alright, alright, crikey, you're touchy. I was just saying what I thought.'

'Well you could say it in a nicer tone of voice.'

'Oh, for crying out loud …'

The homunculi were in sour stalemate when Manfred, the most efficient and trustworthy of Ida's interns, pulled her back into singularity.

'Half-hour alert Miss O'Dewey. Coffee at De Lou's with Fredegund.'

Ida levered herself out of the velvet swivel chair, which had somehow managed to transport her from the huge mahogany desk to the other side of the octagonal, window-cuffed office. She paused a while to gaze at the shiny tower of the television complex currently under construction, a mile or so to the west. She was convinced she saw it grow a good few feet as she stood there. Then, shaking herself into action, she appraised the grey weather heading in over the treetops from the east and went to consult her all-knowing wardrobe next door.

*

De Lou's enforced a rigid door policy to protect the cream of the broadcasting and publishing businesses from the river of the unwashed that flowed past its front door. For a place of backhanders and insider deals, its interior was suitably seedy, especially during the daytime. The sunlight fought its way in through the wooden Venetian blinds to illuminate the spills and burns on the busy turquoise and orange carpet and give definition to the dents and scratches in the ostentatiously chunky furniture. The decor reminded the older clientele of their heydays. They would bask in groups, reminiscing for hours on end, their farty atmosphere attracting reverential novitiates like flies seeking historical titbits to regurgitate later.

Ida signed in at the reception desk, relieved to be asked her name for once. It was never clear if front of house here were so saturated with celebrity that they genuinely couldn't remember who anyone was, or if they feigned ignorance or complacency to put the more contentious luminaries at their ease. Lost anonymity is almost as difficult to grow back as a lost cherry, and public figures often craved this state of innocence, despite a paradoxically equivalent desire for the universal recognition of their importance. But at De Lou's everyone was in the same boat, and this made for an ambiguous atmosphere, with respectful displays of uninterestedness rocked by frequent outbursts of attention seeking.

It was always easy to spot Fredegund in a crowded place – not necessarily by her unkempt and once flame-red hair, now toned down with grey, nor by her white stick, which she flailed about the place like a rapier, but because there were usually several people staring at or gathered noisily around her. Ida pretended not to see her immediately and scanned the tables to find out who else was in. After walking round the whole room and peering into the various snugs and alcoves, she 'found' Fredegund sat behind a tall multi-coloured drink and engaged in an emphatic exchange with an artist on a neighbouring table.

'Honestly, dolly-boy, I saw Marvin Bunt snaffle up the last of them. The anchovies are off... No, not mouldy. Off: off the menu. It's a quaint idiom that you may remember from the days before you could get whatever you wanted by shaking your fist... Yes! I'm sorry, I shouldn't have butted in, but you know, I was just trying to be helpful... Ok, suit yourself. Do it your way, treacle-drawers...'

Ida had befriended Fredegund in a ladies' loo some ten years previously, when she was a fledgling public speaker and freshening up at halftime in a panel discussion. Fredegund had been spectating at the insistence of a friend's precocious son, who had shown no interest in a trip to the beach that Fredegund had tried to bill as *en-plein-air* reading. She had been hiding out in the ladies' to get some respite from the boy's interminable questions, which she could have answered had she the inclination to commit to the paragraphs they would require.

'Honey-pie,' Fredegund had said, washing her hands for the *n*th time, sudsing them up like meringues, 'I haven't been this comatose since honeymoon two with husband three.'

'I'm sorry?'

'These orators, whose words we are being forced to fellate with our ears, have nothing to say and they won't stop saying it. And that one, third from the left. She's turned up in a skirt that's about four minutes too short and is spouting utter tripe.'

'Well, that one who was third from the left is now the one right in front of you, and I don't think she's spouting tripe so much as spitting pips right now.'

'Oh very good. Very good. A girl with spunk. Fredegund,' she said holding out her hand. 'Just Fredegund. I can't be fannying around with surnames. And you must be Ida. I love what you've done with your hair.'

'Thanks,' Ida had touched her shaggy curls. She had spent a lot of time that morning getting the gingery tangle just right. 'How did you know about—'

'Your skirt? Well it is short isn't it?'

'Depends on the century.'

Fredegund had turned her face towards Ida, training the full beam of her closed lids, painted iridescent blue and shielding a pair of tiny, under-developed eyeballs, right into the depths of Ida's pupils, which were gaping in the dimness.

'Well, even in this century you come over like a slapper. Keep it up.'

'Thanks. Any requests for the second half? Anything you want to know about… whatever it is we're discussing today?'

'Oh Dog, is there more? I think just keep going as you are. Your brand of offal seems to be getting a reaction at least. The man next to me makes little sounds of disdain whenever you're speaking. I think someone might have a rival.' She had said this as if conferring a great accolade. 'Anyway, must go, plum-duff, but look me up at the *Post* some day.'

Besides her vituperative leanings, Fredegund's singular quality was that she was utterly disbelievable in conversation – entertaining for her friends, but not so good for her academic career, which she had abandoned long ago. It wasn't difficult to isolate her over-attention to visual detailing as the cause, although being a terrible name-dropper didn't help either. Most thought her peppering of anecdotes with an outrageous roll-call was the indulgence of a fantasist, but Ida had soon realised it should be believed immediately and entirely, for not only was Fredegund a rigorous academic by training but, like the best of jesters, she enjoyed access and privileges that the serious scholar only dreams of.

A curious anagram of fate had granted Fredegund access to the highest levels of Academic society. She happened to have a name that was similar to another very eminent scholar who nobody much liked. At first Fredegund had been invited to dinners in error, but her hosts had been so relieved to find a jolly vamp willing to tell hugely entertaining whoppers for her meal ticket, instead of the curmudgeonly recluse they had been expecting, that they kept on making the mistake. The unpopular scholar was himself relieved to be free of such onerous social duties, while still able to be glad he had been nominally, if ineffectually, invited. And Fredegund got to go to everything of note. She had luncheoned with the Prime Minister on many a high day and holiday; she had been present when the Dean fell out with her husband over a footnote and burned the manuscript of her book under the grill in rage, and she had been at the private party where one of the most decorated artists in Academia threw the host's daughter out the window, and all present had agreed to blame it on gate-crashers.

Ida kept this knowledge to herself. She never stood up for Fredegund when her proclamations were pooh-poohed, not because championing the oppressed can seem more divisive than open-minded, but because she sensed Fredegund didn't want her cover blown. If prejudices hadn't prevented her, Fredegund might have been among the new elite that had emerged from the first interdisciplinary think-labs. Her academic methods had been similarly heretical and deliberately esoteric; and she too had flaunted outward signs of scientificity while making liberal and approximate borrowings from whichever disciplines whet her appetite. And yet academics had automatically assumed these were not radical yet legitimate departures from orthodox academia, but that Fredegund was simply erratic and uninformed. Her inconsistencies – the very source of her brilliance – were put down to lack of character. And so her academic trajectory had been a disastrous flatline. Journalism, on the other hand, did not involve giving lectures or any other moments of interpersonal persuasion. All business was conducted at a distance, by fax. And so Fredegund's crediblity had gradually grown back. And of course she never name-dropped in print, or otherwise abused her position on the best mailing lists. She was happy writing solid journalism on matters of interest to the general reader. But off-duty she made a sport of confusing people and spreading mayhem. She rose to greet Ida, instantly forgetting the couple she'd been quarrelling with.

'Nice work the other night.'

'Oh bugger, yes, that,' said Ida. 'What a stink they're kicking up. I mean, it was only a joke. You got that, right?'

'Oh yes. We all did. It was clearly a joke. And a very good one too. It's just that some people couldn't make the leap of faith to find it funny.'

'Some people? You mean everyone.'

'I mean that mook Tolly. You know, dear heart, I heard that when he was born he had to wait until his mother cried at the sight of him before he could figure out how to do it himself.'

Tolly was a regular gameshow adversary, and they despised him not because he was competition, but because he was not. He also worked the grey area between Academia and the media, but this was because he could not excel in either. Ida found his journalistic methods troglodyte: he would inanely lumber up to the big subjects and bash them over the head with an emotive truncheon; then, having raided, with few scruples and less discrimination, the simpler fruits of hardworking, slow-moving academics, he quickly packaged his spoils in sloppy, middle-brow journalese, not bothering to secure them with references or other such civilising fussiness. She couldn't understand why everyone couldn't tell all this immediately from just one look at his annoying face, with its damp, protruding bottom lip and his eyes pressed in deep like plugholes.

'Oh Dog, what baseless assumptions has he been spreading now?' said Ida. It wasn't that Tolly was a nasty conniver, peddling slander and barbs under the banner of analysis. He wasn't smart enough for that. The real danger of Tolly lay in his lazy habit of sticking to the first thought that entered his head, and in his rash over-simplifications, which the slower-witted clung to, mistaking them for pithy aphorisms.

'Well, I was having a gin with PJ after the show,' said Fredegund. 'She was looking rough, wasn't she? Anyway, she told me that Prentice told her that Tolly said in the green room afterwards that you'd intimated beforehand that you were ready for a shakedown. Or was it a rubdown?'

'Ew. I don't remember any of this. What else did he say I said?' She scoured her memory for any conversations she had held in the green room, but the bleaching effect of pre-show nerves generally obliterated everything.

'That level of detail didn't survive the gossip mill I'm afraid, sweetie-pie.'

'Which is why there should be more verbatim gossips like you.'

Ida caught the eye of a waitress, who sloped over like a creature of the plain, took her order of a rum punch and sloped away.

'Anyway, toots,' continued Fredegund once the waitress was out of earshot. 'You know I've been working on this book?'

'The mysterious one that keeps you out late every night and gives you a permanent hangover?'

'Yes, that's the one. I was wondering if, when it comes to it, you wouldn't mind writing the preface.'

'Golly, Fredegund, I'd be honoured. But shouldn't I read it before agreeing? It might be awful.'

'Yes, it might be, and in a way it is, but I have an idea that you're going to love it anyway. It's really going to rock some boats.'

'You calling me a lifeboat chaser?'

'Oh, who doesn't like a drama. Anyway, no need to decide just yet. I'll be in touch when the time comes.'

'Well, you know I'm always behind you, whatever. Hey, what happened last night at that opening? Sorry I couldn't make it. I was a bit done in. Had a bit of a late one after the broadcast, as you can imagine.'

'The dark chap, second row?'

'Ah, you noticed him too then.'

'I noticed you noticing him, baby-cakes. Bless you, you were trying to be so discrete. Oh it was funny. So… any good?'

'In many ways yes. Fabulous. In other ways, mmm, not sure. Over all – yet another curator's egg.'

'Is it worth overlooking the downsides? I mean if the ups are so fabulous…'

'Oh the ups are up there, yes. But the downs... You remember Dillon?'

'Ah yes, I get you. Another bottom feeder, this one?'

'Dillon wasn't a bottom feeder. He was just travelling in a different direction.'

'Horizontally.'

'Yes.'

'Along the bottom.'

'Well, yes. And you might say this one isn't exactly wreathed in the appurtenances of success either.'

'I see. And you want someone to scoop you upwards into the high life, not drag you down into his grotty purple carpet.'

'How did you know?'

'Who doesn't want that?'

'No, I mean about the purple carpet.'

'Oh, just an unlucky guess. But if you want my advice, angel-face, if you don't like the look of the carpet, don't go on top. And if his ceiling's artexed, go back to yours.'

'Right, great advice, thanks.' In light of Fredegund's multiple husbands, Ida could never decide if she should follow her advice on romantic procedure or not. She was obviously good at bagging them, but... When she thought about it, it was only sex that Fredegund tended to counsel on. She wasn't one to get too abstract. 'So how was it last night? What was it that I passed over for a delicious early night?' asked Ida.

'Oh, you didn't miss much.'

Fredegund had been smoothing her thighs vigorously with one hand for some time now. It was a habit of tactility that no one could deny a blind person, but it was slightly annoying. And if there was one thing that made Ida suddenly intolerant, it was evasive descriptions of things she wanted to know about.

'Here, have a cigarette, and don't wait for me – tuck into that drink,' said Ida, reaching out with a lighter. 'But tell me about last night. What was it?'

'There was a performance, which was too long. Lots of smoke and reading out from textbooks. You know the sort of thing.' Fredegund lit the cigarette and sipped her drink as simultaneously as she could manage without ruining both. 'You were missed at the dinner, by the way. Jørn was asking after you. He was sat right next to where you would have been, although I'm pretty sure he swapped round the place names when he thought no one was looking.'

'I wouldn't put it past him. He knows how to get what he wants. Well, not everything. But what is it with reading out loud these days? It's so boring. No one makes their voice go up and down. They just drone on and on.'

'Well last night the voice going up and down was the whole problem. I think it's called acting, no? It was excruciating. No one could make eye contact with the poor woman afterwards. People find it so embarrassing to have someone pretending in front of them. Don't mind it so much myself. It's the ones who think they're being "authentic and real" that curl my undercarriage. I felt bad for her, sitting alone at her own dinner, so I went over and congratulated her.'

'You bloody sycophant.'

'Not what you think. I congratulated her on succeeding in making us all feel uncomfortable.'

'Oh Dog, no, was it supposed to be bad? Was that the point?'

'She certainly brightened up at my suggestion that it was, but who can really tell whether failure is intentional or not these days?'

'I know. So annoying. An artist can say, "My intention is to produce something that fails to fulfil the orthodox criteria of quality," and then they can make any old crap and everyone calls it experimental. But when it comes to us critics, we can't say, "Oh, I was being purposely contentious to challenge the orthodoxies of acceptability". No, there's one sauce for the goose and none for the gander, as far as I can tell.'

'Oh, I see where you're going with this Idy-poo.'

Ida thought it judicious to lean in and lower the volume, to enforce a bit of discretion.

'But it's true though, isn't it? Artists can do what they like and us lot have to toe every line going every which way.'

'Only publicly, dearest. That's the deal we signed with the devil for the ferocious power we wield.' Fredegund was still leaning back in her seat, not oblivious to Ida's desire for discretion but not yet ready to grant it. People on neighbouring tables were listening in with variable abilities to disguise it. In fact they were all listening in to all tables within earshot at all times. It was a wonder anything ever got said, but then this is one of the functions of platitudes: one can appear to be speaking when in fact one is mostly listening. Their other function is to enable one to speak without having to listen. 'What you have to hang on to, sweet-cheeks, is the knowledge that all this denouncing of transgression and announcing of investigations is…' and now Fredegund did lean in and attempt a hoarse whisper, which carried uncannily, '…performative.'

'Is that supposed to make me feel better? Knowing that my downfall is for everyone else's entertainment?'

'Not for mine, poodle-paws. I am crying inside with you. But take solace in the knowledge that these CSA chaps are performing a mere ritual of moral correctitude; it's little more than a symbolic display of swift reactions in cheap suits.'

'Hey, where's my drink? A scapegoat could die of thirst around here.'

Fredegund cooie-ed and waved at a bonny, black-quiffed waiter, who smiled pleasantly and nodded.

'It's really creepy knowing there's a room full of people discussing me behind my back,' said Ida. 'If they just came and asked me, I could straighten it all out. I wonder if it's a life peer or a hereditary one heading up the review.'

'If it's a lifer, you'll have a much better chance of bribing them. Those hereditary ones can't be budged.'

'I can't bribe anyone!' Ida was hissing now.

'Oh, don't worry. It doesn't cost much. Old Redgreen gave a back-hander to a life peer to cover up a massive—'

'Redgreen? Head of—'

'Indeed. How do you think he got to the top of that particular pile? Anyway, it just took a loan of a particularly rare text book and an introduction to Dame Jane Frampton.'

'What do you mean "just"? What could I possibly have that a peer would want?'

Fredegund answered with a raised ridge where an eyebrow had once thrived.

Ida didn't feel like chatting much anymore. Her mood had dipped distinctly, and she was keen to get out of De Lou's, out of public view and back to the world of interns, who never told her anything she didn't already know, and books, which were seldom personal. She scraped back her chair, smoothed the lap of her tangerine cotton day dress and told Fredegund how marvellous it was to see her but she had to keep it brief this afternoon.

'But your drink hasn't even arrived yet. I'll go get it. You look like you need it.'

'Sorry F, I just don't feel like it today. Do you mind?'

Fredegund's face melted into a muddle of kindness and farewell, tensing just moments later to call out across the room to Ida's back: 'And don't forget to call the gynaecologist darling. It can be hellish if you leave that sort of thing too long.'

CHAPTER 10

Ida shivered and wondered what to do to make the afternoon turn to evening more smoothly. She was never good in the afternoons, and today, having blown out Fredegund, time had lost momentum. She had no other deadline, no meeting, no big project in hand. A drop-off in engagements was starting to reveal life's underlying starkness. To dispel her uneasiness, she had set the interns some long-neglected tasks. She could hear them all over the penthouse. They were tapping nails into the walls of her octagonal office to hang yet more small paintings, drawings and photographs that were periodically gifted to her by artists unclogging their storage racks. Buckets clattered against the wrought iron of the rooftop conservatory, where plants had serially failed to remain alive and so had been replaced by a large ping-pong table. In the library drawers, swivels and hinges and any other moving mechanisms were being checked, waxed and buttered, the creaks and squeaks soon displaced by swishes.

Ida listened dotingly to her redbrick home at work. She was proud of how it was at once universally desirable, in that it was luxuriously built to the highest spec, and a demonstration of her own ingenuity. She had designed the intricate shelving unit that covered an entire living room wall, with each shelf, drawer, cupboard and pigeonhole a snug housing for the single object it had been planned for. The bathroom was a crystalline cave, its rough plaster walls, floor and ceiling embedded with bottle bottoms through which the outside world could be glimpsed in drunken distortion. And the bedroom was a lush miracle of upholstery, drapes and cushions, reconfigurable to any leisure mode required. But most of all, she loved that her home was a sturdy suite of generously portioned rooms at the top of a handsome mansion block, which met the busy central Academia pavement below with the impact of an irrefutable truth. She felt it to be a strong argument, that she was anchored in society, that she was 'at home'.

She found daily joy in dizzying herself on the spiral staircase that led up from the large and light living room to the upper floors, where the real business of writing and shagging happened, although sometimes these activities would spread elsewhere when the interns weren't around. The middle floor, however, where the kitchen and dining room were sandwiched, was a source of anxiety. The kitchen was just a bit of a bore, because of the endless choring that it called for, but the dining room furniture was all wrong, the hardwood flooring too sports-hall-like and the hand-painted wallpaper, with its design of fantastical flowers, too botanically inaccurate to take seriously. If she was honest, she was embarrassed by the pretensions of the room. Even the light behaved affectedly here. Although the views over the trees of Academia were as magnificent on this floor as the one above and below, no sunlight entered beyond a couple of feet; instead it hung coolly back, reserving judgement.

Ida principally used the dining room in the evening for guests, and had added ceiling lights, lamps and glowing panels until it looked like a lighting shop running low on stock. But on occasion, like today, she would sit at the large oval table, half enjoying the dining chair cutting in just above the back of the knee as if it represented the pressures of life itself. She wasn't against indulging her moods at all. She felt it was important not to immediately try and 'right' every bad mood, because they must serve some function and, like most things, were better out than in.

To feed her anxiety, she scanned the more serious newspapers for any mention of her peer review. There were the usual news items on Academic affairs, internal wranglings and departmental developments, features on research groups and their exciting innovations, profiles on up-and-coming academics, columns deliberating newly posited theories with enthusiasm or derision, and the usual lifestyle padding about artists' interiors, critics' wardrobes and professors' eccentricities. There was nothing explicitly pertaining to her, but a murky intimation in a diary piece made her shiver at the thought of Fredegund's suggestion. The fear of disclosure would make her more miserable than any fate that a bribe could allay.

Eventually, at around five thirty, just when she was wondering whether to allow her anxiety to overflow into panic, the phone rang and the voice of Jørn Hødd, made metallic by the wiring, told her he was in the neighbourhood and would like to see her. Since the interns had just embarked on a precarious venture on the roof that would be criminal to leave unsupervised, she invited him over, and within minutes he was bounding up the stairs, pink and breathless beneath his yellow matting of hair. Ida received him in the sitting room and, relieved at the company, pronounced the sun to be well over the yardarm, extracted two glasses with heartbreaking curves from their cubbyholes in the shelving and poured out a couple of large sherries.

'Here's mud in your eye,' said Jørn excitedly.

Jørn was sweet on Ida, although she had gently rejected him years ago for being too keen. She had been careful not to be categorical in her rejection, as he frequently proved useful. He could drive a car, for instance – a rare accomplishment in Academia – and his family had a lovely summerhouse in a quiet countryside region. He was also precocious, already a senior member of one of the more dynamic think-labs and chair of the editorial board of *May*, an academic journal that published, as the strap line claimed, 'permissive interpretative texts at the interface between thought and action'. In this latter capacity, Jørn was not averse to skewing representation within the journal's pages to Ida's advantage, occasionally prompting writers to cite her articles or even, on one occasion, demanding a rewrite of a text that was critical of her.

What Ida had neglected to discover, though, was Jørn's fabulous suite of coital techniques. He had learned them from a 'special aunt', a friend of his mother's who had spotted his potential early on. She had been coming to the house for fortnightly coffee mornings since he was nine, having moved to the neighbourhood on divorcing her celebrity husband. She had waited almost until Jørn was legal, then seduced him at a neighbour's Christmas party. For over two years she had coached, drilled and groomed him every Saturday afternoon under the cover of elocution lessons to correct a lisp, which miraculously disappeared with his virginity. In these sessions she had talked him through the minute biological events that charged her sinews, until he understood the female body, in and out of orgasm, better than any medical student, and could fulfil her fantasies no matter how frequently she changed them. The affair – although this seems too passionate a word for so pragmatic a mentorship – ended when the woman suffered a stroke and was moved by her grown-up children into permanent care in a distant district.

Jørn did not parade his talent. Even after leaving home he would repair to the family summerhouse once or twice a year, with someone he would introduce to his parents as a 'research colleague', to keep his hand in. He was looking for the right person to share his skills with long term, and had tried many a time to seduce Ida, perhaps because he saw in her something of the special aunt, since she was a good twelve years older than him. But no matter how hard he contrived to meet her alone at home, she always counter-contrived to meet in crowded cafés and bars. Today, however, he'd caught her with her guard down, or maybe she was softening towards him, he hoped, as he took his sherry.

She landed on the large, oxblood leather sofa with an exhalation of air that demanded a response.

'You look tired. Are you ok?' He sat two sofa cushions away, angled towards her.

'Oh, yes, yes,' she replied breezily enough.

'It must be hard, this peer review. Do you have enough legal support?' He shuffled a little closer.

'Yes, thanks, Sue's been great. And Manfred, my intern, has been a bit of a Dog-send. I didn't realise he took notes on everything. In a shorthand only he can decipher. I'm hoping there'll be plenty of evidence there to draw on.'

'Well of course, because you are essentially a responsible, caring critic, and the truth will out, as they say.' He stretched out his long, twiggish legs, his feet almost touching hers now. 'It's probably a case of damage limitation in the meantime, because people can be so precipitous.'

'Precipitous? Who's being precipitous.'

'Maybe I'm out of line telling you this, but it's your right to know. I heard from Fredegund that Chip is making noises.'

'Fredegund? I just saw her.' She reached forward and put her glass down on the table. 'She didn't mention anything to me about Chip.' Was Fredegund abandoning her after all?

'I saw them coming out of De Lou's together, just now.'

They must have bumped into one another after she'd left. She picked up her glass.

'What sort of noises is Chip making?'

'Well – dropping noises, actually.'

'Dropping?'

'Yes.'

Back down went the glass.

'Dropping what?'

'There's no easy way to say this. You.' Jørn found it difficult to meet her eye. She snatched the glass back up, downed its contents and jumped up for a refill. He wished he'd kept his mouth shut. But he wanted to help if he could. She sat back down two feet further away. 'Listen,' he said, 'why don't you let me help you? I could write a piece for *May* exploring the progressiveness of satire. I could name you, or not – we could see how it reads. But I think if I were to start teasing out some of these peer review issues in a more, shall we say, scholarly way, it can only help. These civil servants and opinion formers always observe the established form and the discussion never moves on. You need a different sort of authority to vocalise this radical new territory you're exploring.' He reached over and touched her shoulder gently, as if to demonstrate the refining impact that someone with his intellectual prestige could have on the popular media. Ida spilled her sherry into her lap.

'Oh damn. Sorry, Jørn, I'm so strung-out at the moment.'

She rose slowly, stiffly and loudly, like an aeroplane at take-off, and taxied across the living room to change her clothes.

'But that sounds amazing,' she shouted down two floors of spiral staircase as she changed. 'If you would do that, it would be so amazing I don't know how I could thank you.'

'Well,' he shouted back. 'I'm not just doing it for you. I'm doing it for the advancement of the public's understanding of art.'

Jørn cared deeply about art and theory, almost as much as he cared about sexual pleasure. He couldn't fathom how mind and body had become as separated and hierarchised as they had, but he was looking forward to the next sea change in popular ontology. All this dualism was seriously regressive. Just imagine all that erotic pleasure locked up in those dry seminar rooms and tightly bound volumes. He was sure that monism would come in on the next big swell and submerge the dualists into one big love-in of mind, spirit and g-spots. But he also knew that he couldn't singlehandedly bring about such a change, since one's position at the scholarly avant-garde is not entirely manageable. The trick is not to direct knowledge so much as to micro-manage one's position within the field, to bob around in relation to the smaller eddies of radical thought that make up advancing waves of opinion and praxis. And these ever-responsive micro-movements were incredibly energy-intensive.

'You know,' he shouted, 'you've drawn attention to a boundary not many have considered before.'

'I have? Which one?' said Ida from the top of the stairs now.

'Between fiction and satire. Or is it sarcasm and critique? I don't know yet, I need to work on it.'

'But Jørn, I can only imagine I've got caught up in some sort of zeitgeist. I'm hardly a revolutionary or the sort of person to tear a rent in the fabric of history. I'm not even a natural-born genre bender.' She floated down the final few steps wearing a mauve satin dressing gown that rippled around her shoulders and thighs like buttermilk, its shoulder pads, high-waisted belt, generous lapels, crossing low down to reveal her fine clavicles, and the modest train delivering her to him with majesty. Jørn gulped the last of his sherry, its warmth supplementing the tingling in his groin.

'That's as may be, but as we know, the interdependency of the inside and outside of a category are perpetually under discussion, and my job is to monitor and ever so slightly influence this. In *May* we have control over acts of legitimation, if you take my meaning, and can push certain lines of progress.'

Ida's face had softened and pinked a little from the sherry, more of which she was dashing into their schooners as she thanked him in advance for all the help he was about to give her, but could she see the copy before it went off – just so she knew precisely what it was that she was supposed to have been up to? He was agreeing to this, while drinking in the smell of satin warmed from within, when there was a clattering down the internal spiral staircase.

About eight or nine young men and women with moustaches or high bobbing ponytails, their eyes glittering with ambition, stampeded into the room to report excitedly to Ida that they had finished on the roof and to suggest that now it was time for her to give them a little something in return. She threw an apologetic look at Jørn and said, 'Well, this is Jørn Hødd the famous academic journal editor, who you will no doubt have read avidly. Perhaps he might like to stay a while and impart some pearls for your betterment? Perhaps if you ask him nicely…' At which Jørn excused himself with an ungracious mutter, and Ida set to improvising a short seminar on one of those things they never teach you at the Academy: the advisable habit of checking used envelopes for notes written on complement slips before reusing the envelopes and potentially sending personal messages to wholly inappropriate recipients.

CHAPTER 11

What do your parents do?' asked John.

'They're dead,' said Ida.

'Oh, I'm sorry.'

'It's ok, you didn't kill them.'

'How can you be sure? Who can really tell what is caused by what? How did they die?'

'I think, John, that conversational playfulness does have its limits.'

'Sorry. I'm just interested. What did they do?'

'They were art historians.'

'Ah, so you specialised in contemporary art as a rebellious act?'

'Something like that. You're really not afraid to ask personal questions, are you?'

'Neither are you. And I quote: "Do you like that? Do you want more?"'

'Well, there's intimate and there's personal. You're so probing. And I don't mean in that way.'

'I was brought up to show an interest in other people.'

'And I was brought up to show respect and wait until these things are offered up in the natural course of conversation, not to suck them out with a pump.'

'I'm far too busy to lie around waiting for you to tell me secrets.'

'You're busy? I really must go. I have to file an interview today, and I haven't a single quote to pad it with.' She shifted among the dinner plates, which crunched lightly as they dented her flesh with their perfect, obdurate curves.

Writing up the Sergeant Singer interview was going to be a bitch of a task because, once she had transcribed the recording, she couldn't find the notebook she had been using that day. She had many, many notebooks, and employed a system of labelling and colour coding that she found totally straightforward, but which her interns took weeks to get the hang of. And since there were always at least two new interns amongst the cohort – and even Manfred couldn't watch over them all every minute of the working day – things tended to become misplaced. She had re-membered that the interview notes would be in a media appearances notebook, on account of her not having gone home after *Panel Beaters*, but even this did not unearth the precious record of events. Without them it was impossible to tell from the audio tapes whether Singer had been nodding or shaking his head at any point during their 'conversation'. She'd have to brew up some serious blarney.

'And then I've got a reviews roundup to polish off by Friday morning. Life is just one long string of deadlines, as far as I can see.'

'Poor, overworked celebrity critic,' said John, a fork jabbing him excitingly in the upper thigh.

She'd had late-night needs after the sherries, and so, instead of waiting the few days to see John as semi-arranged, she had sent a message by intern, who returned with an invitation to go on over. She had ordered a taxi and was there by midnight but, as there was no response to the handful of gravel she threw at his window, she went off in a huff, after having dropped a note through the letterbox calling him a cunt-tease. Then she had knocked on the door of any ex-lovers she could think of within walking distance. Only one was in and awake. He opened his front door with a surprising lack of surprise, saying that, funnily enough, he'd just been thinking about her. When she was halfway up his staircase she had heard the pillow-wracked voice of a woman asking 'who is it darling?', at which she turned on her heel and sprinted back to John's, not caring if she woke the whole house by ringing all the doorbells. This time he came to the door, with no real explanation but plenty of apologies for having missed her earlier. In the hallway she picked up the note left previously, pretending it was pocket litter, adding as she tramped up the stairs that he could make it up to her if he liked, which he did indeed seem to like, over and over again. They had eventually fallen asleep just before the grey dawn had started to sink in through the thin Hawaiian shirts.

'Always on a deadline…' John's tone was dangerously ambiguous. 'Always on the make.'

Ida lingered over an 'errr…', resisting one of the rules that were writing themselves in the manual of this emerging relationship. This rule dictated that anything either of them uttered was a red rag, and the other was a bull. 'On the make' was not a compliment, she felt. People without ambitions all too often confuse them in others with vanity and greed. She gathered herself for the charge.

'You make it sound like "on the rag". Distasteful, is it, the thought of working to someone else's requirements?'

'I wouldn't know. People seldom need anything in particular from me, to deadline or otherwise. There are many advantages to hiding your light under a bushel.' He tousled her pubic hair as if it were the head of a young nephew.

'You can hide other stuff under there too if you like.'

'Thank you. Do you have the time though for a little more living before your deadening line?'

She scrabbled to the end of the bed, looking for the lacy edges of her knickers among the crockery.

'Ah, she prefers her deadlines to either of us,' said John to his purple accomplice, who had risen to watch her groping about on her hands and knees. It trembled and bobbed and sounded like Punch: 'I know, I know.'

Ida abandoned her search and turned her attention to John's toes, counting them off on his left foot. 'I… love… dead… lines… because…' Then, taking hopping steps, syllable by syllable, up his tastefully haired leg, '…these so very mortal aims, make me feel so very, very alive,' reaching his knee at 'aims' and slowing in pace as the hair became sparser on the inner thigh.

'Oh-oh-ohhhh, yes, mmmhmm,' he cleared his throat. 'Deadlines are vital. We need rigidity...'

'No, no… We need elasticity.' She brought her middle finger into step, marching the pair up and down his *adductor magnus* with an exaggerated bounce.

'No. We need external rigidity, fixed targets and absolute deadlines to constrain and focus the abstract, aimless thinker. Speculative production is pointless,' said John, short of breath as the marching slowed to exploratory arabesques around his *adductor longus*.

'Maybe,' breathed Ida, 'but what about a deadline on having an idea? If an idea is intangible, then it cannot have a deadline placed on it. Do you agree?' Her digits were now conquering the scrubby plains of the *pectineus*.

'Oh yes, yes, oh yes...' groaned the landscape of flesh and hair.

'Aha! Got you!' said Ida triumphantly, as she withdrew her hand and rose stiffly to a sitting position. She was reigniting a blazing row they'd had in the night about whether an idea was an object or not. The row had erupted from John's accusation that she'd stolen someone else's idea in one of the rounds in *Panel Beaters*. She had said you can't steal an idea because it's not material. Then he'd said that you can certainly grasp an idea, which suggests it can be carried away, and anyway, thanks to language, you could identify an idea, and naming was tantamount to owning, because identifying was categorising was organising was controlling. Neither of them felt the matter had been satisfactorily settled.

'What is a PhD if it isn't a deadline on an idea?' John groaned, still horizontal.

'Oh, that's something else again. It's a display of knowledge rewarded with a certificate. You cannot impose an arbitrary structural element such as a deadline on something as dematerialised as an idea. You're mistaking the idea for the delivery of the idea. The deadline is on its delivery, not on the idea itself.'

'And that is where I have got you,' he said, catching his breath. 'What you are conceding here is that an idea can be delivered and consumed just as well as any other object. An idea is not a supernatural entity that arrives from the great beyond, but a bridge. It's how we join up where we are with where we want to be. Say, for instance, you are in a dungeon filling rapidly with water. That is a very concrete timeframe within which you must have an idea.'

'But in this scenario, the only idea possible is acceptance of death, which is a bridge with a destination no one can describe. Not so tangible, after all.'

'Sure, in this particular case study real outcomes are limited, and so the number of possible ideas are limited. For what is real is possible, but what is possible is not necessarily real. Reality will always be equal to or less than the possible, which is the source of humankind's ceaseless sorrow.'

They were both sitting upright by now, alert among the scattered plates, shoes, journals, smoking paraphernalia and general mess that joined seamlessly with the clutter that tumbled from the cupboards.

'These bridges,' said Ida. 'how do they enter our heads? Where do we get the materials from?'

'It's all in there already, we just haven't arranged it in that formation before. An idea happens when something external precipitates the meeting of two things that haven't met in the brain before; they've been in different rooms of the same building all along.' He reached over to pick a sachet of silica gel out of her hair.

'So you're saying ideas are immanent after all?'

'No, not entirely. They are partly mastered by external conditions, conventions, events and so on. Different ideas occur to us under different circumstances, right?'

'Of course. That's what I was saying,' she said with exasperation.

'And different ideas occur to different people in the same circumstances, right?'

'Yes.'

'So there you have it. Ineluctable proof of a fluid interdependency between interior and exterior.'

'Which presumably would mean that one could blame the external world for providing the conditions for a bad idea? Or someone else. I could blame you, for instance, for putting me off in *Panel Beaters* and making my head rearrange ideas in the way that it did.'

'Woah, steady on, I don't think that's quite what I mean. Fluid interdependency and blame are not the same thing. What I'm talking about is a propensity of one perspective to encourage one interpretation, and for another perspective to produce a different reading, but for there to be continuity from the point of origin in both cases. Let me use an example… Ok, what do you get when you put two and two together?'

'Four,' she said dryly.

'How clichéd. I make it twenty-two.'

'Oh John, you are silly.' She smiled, caught unaware by his nimble two-step. 'I'm not sure we can really call algebra a cliché.'

'That's precisely what it is. Numbers are a received idea. We are oblivious to their origins, we just shunt them about and the energy they've accrued over centuries of use bursts forth when we rub them together. Two and two – bang – twenty two.'

'Energy? Clichés don't accrue energy. They make us lazy precisely because we don't think about their meanings when we use them. They are dull and worn linguistic channels mindlessly travelled to get us where we think we want to go. Two plus two is four, which is what I want right now. Four. Phwoar. Phwoooaaarrrrr, you deviant number cruncher...'

She pushed him back onto the horizontal, crushing a saucer painfully into his scapula, and resumed her finger drills, this time starting at the *serratus anterior*, trooping with dignity towards the *brachioradialis,* then advancing ardently back down to the *psoas major*, where all ideas – whether clichéd or novel, fully formed or foetal, slithering in organically or arriving by parcel post – dissolved throughout their bodies.

CHAPTER 12

'And perhaps this is why Sargent's paintings speak to us so eloquently. As we each hurtle towards our own ultimate trauma, they mirror in multiple and in miniature our own abstracted states.'

Finished. Ida put down her pen with the satisfaction of a dull job duly done, and called to Manfred to type up the copy and fax it to the editor. It hadn't been too bad after all, she thought. Once you've got an angle, you can generally find a nice arc to tidy all the fragments of thought into, and then you just need to tie it off with a grandiose statement that makes everyone feel they've performed a deep bowel movement of the mind.

Manfred, coltish in shorts, tennis shoes and a crisp white shirt, trotted in to the book-lined library, scanning for Ida among the many reclining chairs, footstools, standard lamps and desks. He found her sitting at a small roll-top bureau. Lollipop in mouth, he took the handwritten sheets and read them as he walked slowly back down to the interns' smaller, stuffier office on the middle floor, where he would type it up in moments on the hectic electric typewriter. She could hear him snorting – his own method of laughter – on the spiral staircase. Ah, the pleasures of the text, she thought. Why are they so often suppressed? By writers and readers both. Essays stiff and dull to read cannot have been anything other to write; although for Ida, writing academic essays had been like pulling out her own entrails, and reading them was like being locked inside an airless cupboard – so there was some qualitative difference at least. She often thanked Dog she had relieved herself of these burdens by becoming a critic.

It was the academic's habit of piling up abstract terms that had driven her off. A few abstractions were fine – you could infer their meanings from the context – but once they accumulated into edifices she stood no chance. Without the traction of examples and illustrations, the text just floated around in the portion of her brain marked 'sounds and shapes'. But to the academic, examples are like stabiliser wheels on a bicycle: they help us learn how to exercise our understanding and judgement, but they must be withdrawn early to avoid over-reliance, so that we can develop our own skills.

Admittedly, proceeding by example can be problematic. Say, for instance, you are trying to explain to a child about sharing and you say, 'Timmy, you should share your fudge with Tammy. Then you will both have some, and that is fair. And then when Tammy has fudge and you don't, she will share it with you.' The danger that you court with this singular example is that Timmy will only share fudge and will fail to extend the abstract idea of sharing to other sweets and snacks, to toys, good humour, time with mother and so on. And this is the reasoning behind the academic's abstraction: a specific example may be contained by, but will never entirely fulfil, a universal rule, and so it is better not to mention any specifics at all. But in Ida's experience this was nonsense. The particular was always far in excess of any universal rule. Timmy might think Tammy shouldn't have fudge because she is getting fat, or because he's a diabetic and sugar-free fudge is so expensive and difficult to find and Tammy can eat any old sugary rubbish from the corner shop. Or perhaps Tammy doesn't even like fudge. No, the trick with examples, Ida taught her interns, was never to offer them singly, but in pairs or trios at slight variance with one another, demonstrating multiplicity, contradiction and changeability as the natural state of everything.

Take this too far, though, and you end up with the unsubstantiated and inconsistent flummery of gutter arts journalism. The arts pages in the red tops dealt only with the subject in hand, seldom contextualising or drawing comparisons. Their articles ranged from lazily knee-jerk to cruelly whimsical, and it was often felt, even by those who generated it, that arts coverage was an animal that they fed but did not consider domesticated. They watched it stampede some poor innocent here, or unaccountably carry aloft a young unknown there, often before they had graduated, sometimes before they had even made anything. But in reality this animism was nothing more than a cover for the unpredictable aggregate of individuals' mistakes or machinations.

And if the journalists weren't enough of a liability, there were the subeditors too. The right and proper way for a headline to be written is that something occurs in the world, the journalist reports on it and the subeditor infers a natty title from this report. But if a subeditor happens to have a great idea for a headline, they will move heaven and earth to fabricate a story to warrant it. There was the ridiculous 'Hegel Don't Bother Me', for instance, where a librarian was actually persuaded to claim to have been driven mad by the hauntings of the author of *Phenomenology of the Spirit* himself. Granted, this propensity towards punning is a side effect of the necessary act of compression. In a literary form where any conjugation of 'to be' is eradicated, the words are bound to become unstable, their meanings doubling up and sliding about – and this is the natural habitat of the pun. But many feel that the flippancy of wordplay is inappropriate given the sobriety of much of the news that it relates. The tradition has been too long established, however, and so wars are announced via assonance, and individuals demolished by any insulting pun that their name happens to suggest.

The day after Ida's contentious *Panel Beaters* performance 'O'Dewey decimated' and 'Just not critic' were the pick of a rather lame crop. By now the story would have filtered down to the slower-moving, gossipy layers of the media, and so she had picked up a copy of *Academic Insider* to check. She flipped through its pages, loaded up with loud magenta and yellow graphics and photographs inset with small stubs of text, until she found her name splashed across the top of Tolly Adio's notorious 'Boob or Bust?' column, and read:

'Which way next for naughty critic? Witty critic and broadcaster Ida O'Dewey has been rocking the boat, and pals say she may be forced to bail out quite soon! The last edition of *Campbell's Panel Beaters* saw the critic and essayist extraordinaire say some unpardonable things about art that we here at *Academic Insider* dare not repeat! Listeners sent in thousands of complaints to the Critical Standards Agency and curators are on the warpath. The controversial Ida, with an IQ of 136, has said that "it was all a joke", but a pal has told *Academic Insider* that Ida might actually believe some of the content of her outburst. With a reshuffle coming up in the Art Department, where she is a visiting lecturer, this could make the managers think twice about having her back. There are even rumours circulating that the forty-something may be looking for romance, and that this is all a sensational way of hanging up her critic's hat. We can't swear this is the case, though, as the cerebrally limber Ida has been seen working out in mnemonic bootcamps, and she even has her own personal rhetoric trainer. So watch out beardy professors! There's either a feisty woman chasing after your jobs or a top piece of talent about to enter the dating game!'

If you were to close the magazine in disgust and throw it into the nearest bin, you would slam the photograph of Ida – compromised by a low deckchair on the third day of a literary criticism festival the previous summer – right up against a glossy studio portrait of Prentice Hall. If, on the other hand, you were sucked in by the chatter and continued to read, you would learn of Prentice's announcement of a sabbatical and his withdrawal from all but the more ceremonial duties of a Professor of Curating to concentrate on a new project, yet to be announced. You would follow the conjecture on how this new project might be a soon to be vacant curatorial post in a major museum, since Prentice was 'the ideal candidate' following his 'dazzling' twelve years in the curating faculty, where 'he has turned a respectable provincial department into a cultural dynamo'. And you would read such phrases as 'high energy' and 'larger than life', which were far from his colleague's experience of him. Had they been consulted, they would probably have sidestepped his plodding pedantry, lack of humour and theoretical hobby-horsing, alighting cautiously instead on his ever-expanding wardrobe and his 'womanly' delight in stationery.

CHAPTER 13

After an uncomfortable few days, Ida was clad in layers of Goretex that rustled loudly as she and John strode briskly through the shopping arcade near his flat. The windows of the boutiques and specialist provenders were blinded. Only the tasteful gold-lettered signage hinted at the plenty to come once the slumbering forest of mahogany and wrought iron next awoke for business. Ida buried her face in the nylon fur lining of her hood, hiding from whoever else might be pacing out the shortcut to the tram or strolling in the after-hours, enjoying the poignant atmosphere.

It had been a difficult few days, not because she'd been aching terribly to see John again – although her roving eye had not roved as far and wide as it might ordinarily. Or rather, her eye was as mobile as ever, but some other organ or gland seemed to talk her down fairly quickly. She had fancied her concierge's holiday cover, until he had stood up to reveal his appalling pleat-fronted trousers; she had harboured a crush on a curator glimpsed in a gallery backroom, until her nasal whine down the telephone had caused Ida to wince; and she had started plotting to meet with a critic who had performed brilliantly on a television quiz show until, three rounds in, he had used the word 'palimpsest' – a total turn-off. She hadn't noticed this reflex at all, but something within was stealthily at work, closing down romantic avenues as quickly as they presented themselves.

No, the cause of her discomfort was acute career palsy. Her appointments diary was drying up. She would be acceptably busy for a short while yet, meeting deadlines already in place, but the months to come were looking alarmingly bare. And worse – Singer Sergeant was suing for loss of earnings following the publication of her article. He claimed that her 'wildly erroneous and irresponsible version of their conversation' had caused him to be dropped from a major survey show, and he was taking legal action to recoup the massive fee he would have bagged for it. Sue's solicitor had assured her the accusation would not stand up in court because of the ambiguity of the original journalistic brief, but first Ida needed to clarify with her editor that she had been contracted to write a profile with interview-sourced quotations rather than an editorialised interview. Both these formats, the solicitor explained, contained elements of objective representation and subjective inference, but a profile allowed for a greater ratio of the latter. Unfortunately, the paper that had commissioned her was a maverick outfit. There was never anything in writing regarding formats, let alone a contract. The editor, permanently drunk, never knew what would appear in his pages from one day to the next. In which case, the solicitor counselled, Ida should stand her ground, refuse to settle, and face Singer down. It was her word against his. This was not comforting though. With his expensive lawyer, Singer's word was bound to be written in an august cursive script on opulent paper, which always stood up so much better in court.

And so it was that, in a frazzled state, she followed John through the genteel arcade to the tram, made two changes, took a bus replacement service and a funicular link to an area of Academia she'd never noticed before, all the while praying she wouldn't run into anyone she knew. Or the paparazzi. Dog no, not looking like this. John had foisted the nasty garments on her, saying that without them she simply would not be admitted where they were going. Although at least feminine in cut – their inelastic, rustling shells cinched at the waist – they were a little too large and over-busy with umpteen zips and Velcro stays of questionable utility.

'You need lots of fastenings if you're active, you see. When there's no pothole to dive down you need a zip or a toggle to fiddle with.' He had coached her briefly on micro-behaviours so that she might blend in. 'But most importantly, shut up,' he explained.

They eventually exited the transport system and followed a series of alleys and snickets to the hinter-bowels of the funicular station itself. John knocked softly on a door that was impossible to notice unless you knew it was there. A small shutter opened on to a shadowy face, to which John announced himself as Berg. Ida hadn't heard his surname before, and it came as a mild shock that he even had one. 'John' had come to mean something quite specific to her, which this surname did not corroborate.

The door opened and they stepped into a cobbled interior lined with ranks of pickaxes, ropes and carabiners arranged in an interlocking pattern. Behind them three more men announced themselves as Berg and filed in. Ida was about to ask if this was some sort of family reunion, when John smothered her mouth with his own to staunch the question. A clutch of male and female Bergs arrived and then a further small horde, by which point the corridor was at capacity and Ida and John were bustled along another passage and another, each steadily pitching downwards, the wooden batons providing footholds for any Bergs in high heels or slippery polyveldt soles.

They came out at last into a chamber, a cross between an auditorium and a cave.

'We're in the bascule counterweight housing of the bridge now,' said John with the attitude of one enjoying the advantage of knowledge, and who intends to release it in exasperating fragments.

'What's a bascule counterweight housing? The walls are dripping. Are we underwater?'

'Indeed we are. You know when the bridge is raised, when a tall ship is scheduled to pass through? Well, the road that's levered up into the air has an equal and opposite counterweight that swings downwards. This stepped slope is what accommodates that big swinging counterweight.'

'You mean a great slab of road could come down on us at any moment?'

'In theory, it could. But don't worry, we have a person in the bridge control room in the Utilities Quarter who arranges all our meetings around the bascular timetable, so in practice it doesn't.'

'Where's the Utilities Quarter?'

'Out past the humanities crèche, just north of the paint factories.'

'That's a long way off to be able see if we're in here or not when it's being raised.'

'That's remote control for you. Most people don't like causality to be too in-your-face. But this is exactly the sort of thing we're fighting. We want to reinstitute the mechanical engineering that has been all but replaced by decentralised, ambiguated electronic networks.'

'Fighting, yeah, right.'

Ida wasn't used to fighting talk and it produced a discomfort that she transformed, with a pinch of ignorance and a dash of alarm, into scorn.

The chamber was filling with men and women – presumably all Bergs of one stripe or another – murmuring in low tones.

'Who are…'

John cut her off, hissing out of the corner of his mouth.

'I can't be seen to be explaining everything to you. We've been over this. Just act like you know what's going on, and keep your mouth shut. Don't even agree with anything. Just sit there and look earthy.'

'That won't be hard in this… this anorak.'

At this point a whip-thin man in his sixties, dressed in a black and yellow ceremonial version of the outdoors garb that was absolutely de rigueur here, stepped out into the centre of the auditorium and cleared his throat softly until the assembly settled into a respectful, expectant silence.

'What *is* he wearing?' asked Ida.

'Soft microfibre with a peached outer and an inner of hydrophilic laminate,' John whispered.

Unlike Ida's get-up, which rasped loudly with every fidget, the man's robe gave out the faintest sigh as he retrieved something furry from within its folds and pressed it to his chin.

'And now?' she asked.

'The beard of a goat.'

'Council of the GASMAN,' intoned the master of ceremonies – or chairperson, or judge, or high priest. 'Welcome. It is good to see you all here once more. And welcome to any newcomers,' to which Ida smiled and nodded professionally. 'We have many important items on the agenda to work through. So if we could press on. K2, the apologies, if you please?' He removed the beard and held it in both hands, arms outstretched.

A man, grey head-to-toe, stepped forward, took the beard and pressed it to his own chin. He read a list of what sounded more like place names than people's names, then passed the buck on to the first of a string of men and women, who each delivered dull, information-laden presentations on disappointingly familiar subjects like funding streams, legacy, outreach and archiving, brightened only by the goaty tuft dancing on their chins as they spoke.

Just as Ida was on the verge of bolting, a rather handsome man in his forties called Snowdon took the beard. He was sinewy and energetic, prowling the stage area and speaking too rapidly to draw adequate breath. Ida suggestively nuzzled John's foot in deferred appreciation as Snowdon delivered another list of figures, this time conveying something called 'oil rates of production and distribution in Foreign', which, if it hadn't been for the vigour with which he delivered them, would have taken Ida right through the pain barrier.

But then Snowden performed a rhetorical pirouette, which she didn't follow at all. His body, too, was behaving differently. It seemed to have become heavier, difficult to keep upright. He stopped pacing and jacked himself up on the lectern, as though without it he would slump to the ground, and her interest switched, quick as a flock of starlings, from his physical form to his spoken content.

‘…and so when I enter the seismic state, my electrolytes become communicative with gravitational fluctuations, by way of electromagnetic translations that I won’t bore you with. But the upshot is that I have this unique ability to sense the density of the ground I am walking on. AP have been employing me as a prospecting tool in their Foreign operations for some years, but now they are turning my attentions to Academic soil, as they ramp up their explorations here.

‘So here’s how it works: the gabbroic intrusions and other thicker layers of dense igneous bedrocks create gravity fluctuation highs of up to 180 milligals, and these anomalies are significant enough for me to fall over completely and not be able to get up. In fact, I will start to tumble at around 20 milligals, which is lucky, as this is precisely the magnitude of gravitational variance that the prospector would be interested in. The deposits they are looking for occur in low-density sedimentary basins, which are where I will not fall – that is, 20 milligals and below. I am about to sign a contract of deployment whereby I shall pace every foot of the territories, discounting the dense igneous of the north west, where I am likely to stick to the ground and never get up, and which would mean that the subterra is not likely to match the prospectors’ requirements. But other than that, who knows from where the oil will flow? Perhaps even here.’ He let go of the lectern and made a few arduous steps before falling to the ground, a dead weight. ‘Or perhaps not.’

The audience was unsure whether to laugh at his feeble drollery or worry for his physical comfort, although everyone relaxed when two prepped attendants leapt up to help him to his seat, and a hearty applause built in proportion with the confidence that it was indeed appropriate.

The meeting was then concluded by a fabulous tirade delivered by an old-school orator, who stirred in Ida’s breast a desire to do something epic and significant, but as yet unidentified.

‘…We must stand firm, comrades, on terra firma. Make that firmer than firma. We are faced with a world that is loosening its grip on a life that is lived fully. We are surrounded by those who look to metaphysical heights and psychological depths for meaning. They have forgotten the earth beneath their feet. They have forgotten their feet. We GASMANs must draw the heady back down to earth, and then on through the Earth’s crust, to the roiling heat of sub-terra, where truth is not to be reasoned with. Humanity has made too great a claim on the causality of things – oh yes, comrades, you can be sure that there is an academic somewhere who would attempt to explain us, the GASMANs, by way of social causes. Oh yes, oh yes. But we shall not be theorised or contextualised. We cannot be fodder for the weak-bodied thinker, because for one, we have too much mass for their thoughts to push around like that, and for two, the fact of materiality is irrefutable, non-negotiable, unwavering and absolute. Material can be transferred, through effort, from one place to another, from one form to another, but it cannot be eradicated. You cannot dematerialise materiality. The rationalising government and the strategising corporations can try to make things disappear through their command of language, but we, as GASMANs, know that these things remain, just the other side of a false wall made of words. The GASMAN pounds these false walls with big fists. And these fists will grow the more we pound on the walls. Our efforts will be evidenced by our tools. We are tools. The GASMAN uses his feet to stamp on the earth, to make it move. The GASMAN shoots forth like an angry bullet to shatter thought unallied with action. The GASMAN is shielded by intelligent fabric that knows it is fabric through experience, not conjecture. The GASMAN shall hit the soft mark of the overthinking, underdone lamb chops of the Academy high table. Join me in crashing the ball, GASMANs. Rise up. Rise up, and if we descend, it shall be upright.'

CHAPTER 14

'So, if you're not really called Berg, who are you?' asked Ida once they were settled with their pints.

'You can call me John Browse. My parents did, and I don't see why we should break with tradition now.'

If, before the Great Methodologies War, all Browses were once Deweys, then she and John may well be related. But this did not occur to her. She was too busy feeling a little depressed at how many veneers there were to a person, how little chance there was of ever being sure you knew someone.

'And who are the gasmen? And what gas?'

'Not gasmen. GASMANs. Geophysical and Somatic Materialists Against Normativity.'

'Dog, that's confusing.'

'Well, if it provokes a frown that's fine by us. Physicality is what we're trying to place back on the agenda in Academia.'

'So I gathered. It's a fun idea – kind of like the free market is a fun idea – but it's not exactly going to happen, is it? The whole of Academia isn't going to suddenly go "oh, d'you know what, we've been wrong all this time. Let's stop being thoughtful and just eat and shag and shit."'

'We're not advocating wholesale reversion to barbarism. It's more about establishing new emphases. It's a shame Kirkpatrick didn't turn up to speak. Her approach to the oil question is fascinating.'

'Oh yes? This Kirkpatrick, what is she?'

'It's a bit difficult to explain. You'll meet her one day soon, I'm sure.'

Ida wasn't keen on another woman being difficult to explain.

'Now, let me treat you to supper,' said John, picking up a menu. 'Although I'm afraid you won't find any of your soup abstractions here. The food's rather more substantial, which is why it's a GASMAN haunt.'

The Flounder was a pleasantly dark, low-ceilinged pub with quiet music and a large expanse of tables and chairs arranged over sawdust-strewn tiles. Ida looked about for tell-tale high-tenacity rip-stop over-trousers, pick-axes and the like, but saw only respectable Academics in the fashions of the day.

‘Is soup abstract?’ she asked, once John had returned from placing an order of something called singing scuffs.

‘Certainly. Carrot soup is not a mimetic representation of a carrot. It resembles one only in colour.’

‘And in taste.’

‘Not if you count texture as part of taste, which I certainly do. The insipid liquidity of soup has nothing to do with the crunchy taste of the fresh vegetable.’

‘Crunchiness isn’t a taste.’

‘It certainly is. It’s not just the tongue that’s involved in tasting. The whole mouth is important, including the jaw. That’s the problem with this fashionable diet of soup. There’s no engagement beyond slurping.’

‘There’s toast too. That’s chewy or crunchy…’

‘Yes, but then it’s floated in the soup as croutons and pretty much swallowed whole. You’re a bunch of ducks. It’s the same with canapés. I’ve seen people standing round a tray of canapés, chucking them down like slaves into a hold. You miss the whole joy of feeding. Chewing is vital.’

Ida tried to protest, but he was already stuck into his subject. She sat back and let him get on with it.

‘Originally food was invented only partly for sustenance. An additional function, now often overlooked, is its marking the passage of time. They say that to keep time moving onwards, you should observe all ten meals every day and, importantly, you should really enjoy them: an early breakfast on rising; a second breakfast, in the old German tradition, when rumbling recurs around nine; brunch, closely followed by elevenses, or vice versa if you favour Bohr’s algorithm; lunch; tiffin at four, with the focus on small savoury sandwiches rather than cake, to avoid a mid-afternoon sugar coma; tea; dinner; supper, and, of course, a midnight feast as a full stop to the day. Each meal should consist of one, two or three courses, plus intercourses where appropriate, and the main cycle might be accessorised with any number of sub-cycles of casual snacking.’

‘But why so anti-soup? There’s nothing to say that any of these meals can’t be soup.’

‘Time is as physical a phenomenon as any, subject to the laws of physics and the interconnected systems of matter and forces. It’s complicated, but the net result is that souping is a reductive process, and this poses a serious threat to diurnal momentum.’ He paused to wrap and pocket his chewing gum.

'Don't be ridiculous. Time is a chimera, an intellectual tool by which we perceive events in the universe. It doesn't have momentum – it's not going downhill.'

'Ah, Ida, you are wonderfully, exasperatingly theoretical. Have you never heard of time's arrow?'

'Of course – it's a classic play by the ancient thinker Amisimus. It demonstrates how morality is contingent upon causal interpretation.' She could trot this out, having studied Amisimus some years back and found him wanting, although she had never been sure what it was that he wanted.

'Ah, no, not the Classics. I'm talking about the contemporary science of time, the fundamental process by which time flows. The actual, physical, literal arrow of time.'

'Oh, don't be silly. We only perceive it as flowing in a single direction. If there's one thing that Amisimus tells us, it's that causality is a matter of perspective.'

'And in theoretical physics, too, laws and forces work in both directions, so there's no time's arrow in theory. But in practice, in human experience, there is. We can never retrieve this moment, for instance.'

At this point their food arrived. The waitress lowered a giant plate of mysterious stucco lumps onto the table, knocking over the salt, which John then spent quite some time pitching over each of his shoulders, first with one hand, then the other.

'You never know quite where the devil might be sitting,' he said.

Not knowing what he was talking about, Ida popped a singing scuff into her mouth, still ignorant of its origins – animal or vegetable.

'Ah! Hot. Anyway, you were saying: you honour the sensation of the day passing linearly, right? But how do you counter theories of non-linear time?'

'With other more particular theories.'

'Rather than general rules? Or by "particular" do you mean fussier theories? Neither sounds very rigorous.' She was still chewing, determined not to ask what she was introducing into her personal ecosystem.

'Particular in that it's down to particles. Everything is made of particles, which are constantly rearranging themselves, and entropy reflects the number of ways a system can be rearranged without changing the overall appearance and properties of that system. So a crystal is a low entropy system and a fluid a high one. You're supposed to peel them, by the way.' He pulled off a thick membrane to reveal an abject-looking inner scuff.

'We always ate them whole in our family. But tell me, am I a high or a low entropy system?' She was fishing for compliments now.

'A human being is somewhere between the two, and a whisker below the entropic state of an oyster. Anyway, high entropy systems are more likely, as they're less specialised, but – and this is the nub – the second law of thermodynamics dictates that the entropy of the universe can never decrease. Everything is gradually transforming from a low entropic state to a higher one. Over time everything devolves from the peculiar to the indistinguishable. Want any more?'

'Think I'm alright actually. You finish them up. What does all this mean in human terms?'

'That no one is so idiosyncratic that they don't mulch down eventually.'

'That's a great comfort,' said Ida. 'And how does soup come into it?'

'The problem with soup is that it is already in a high entropic state. It's not very specific in its structure. You can rearrange a bowl of soup many, many ways and it will still be soup. The same goes for a tray of canapés, which is but umpteen shavings, pastes and gobbets infinitely rearrangable in arbitrary combinations. You see, human physiology, observing the laws of thermodynamics, breaks down complex foods to less complicated slurry, and this is in keeping with the flow of time, which is pegged to the direction of entropic change.' Ida still looked blank. 'Ok, Let me demonstrate… You've probably noticed that when you try and recall the previous week, the days stretch backwards like a road, and along this road you've stopped for meals. Try and visualise that – a road with a café stop for every meal. Go on, try it.'

Ida never discussed her food intake. It was considered gauche in her circles. To brag at length about drinking, on the other hand, was perfectly respectable. In the name of knowledge exchange, though, she would indulge John in his thought experiment.

'Ok, yes, I've got a road.'

'And can you tell me about the cafés, describe the meals that they stand for?'

'Let's see: soup, canapés, canapés and soup, soup, canapés, soup, soup.' It took a surprising amount of effort to go back just three days.

'And can you remember the soup flavours? Er, does soup have flavours?'

'I don't think so. "Flavour" implies synthesis, but soup's taste is immanent. A bit like ideas, apparently. Anyway, no, I don't remember what sorts of soup.'

'Well, this is my point. I, on the other hand, can tell you that last night I had anglerfish fois gras in hay, Thursday's dinner was pheasant tartar with sweetbreads dauphinoise, Wednesday's was a henge of hot sauce-slathered spare ribs, Tuesday's was potted hough, Monday and Sunday's were both herring lasagne, hot then cold, and last Saturday I dined on goat wellington. Then there are the high teas, the lunches, the tiffins and so on, but I'll not bore you with them. But you get the point: Monday is distinct from Tuesday is distinct from Wednesday and so on. And being able to differentiate means that there must be distance between the days; they haven't piled on top of one another, and the entropic process of digestion has greatly contributed to the forward momentum of time's arrow. You, on the other hand, can't remember one day from the next because you're in a haze of soup and canapés day in, day out. What's more, you start off with a non-specific slurry and expel an only slightly less specific slurry. The differentiation between entropic states is too slight. If you don't stop eating such abstract food, you could cause the stagnation of time itself.'

'Abstract?' Ida swung her right leg over her high horse. 'It's not like I'm eating spherical soup in a perfect vacuum. Soup can be very corporeal. Have you ever cracked an egg into a clear tom yum? It's a moment of pure biology that can shunt you right into next week. And if you want viscera—'

She was cut short by a couple in noisy outdoor gear approaching the table. They stood there for a beat or two before John noticed and jumped up to greet them, introducing them as what sounded like 'Hands and Feet'. Hands was blonde, pale-skinned and attractively boyish if somewhat sullen; Feet was much younger, paler still, stringier and cripplingly shy. Her cheeks smarted as she said hi, while Hands simply dropped his eyes to the floor and mumbled some rote politeness or other.

Once drinks were secured all round it was, according to natural law, down to John, as the common link, to establish the direction of the conversation within the newly constituted group. His obvious option was to draw the newcomers into the soup debate, which would, if their get-up was anything to go by, mean two allies for him. But generally pub law dictated that a fresh conversational topic was developed out of either one person's wildcard opening or a subliminally negotiated, shared theme that suited the majority. If it is tacitly decided that a new topic should be embarked on, another set of laws kicks in. If all members of the group do not know one another already, then a point of mutual interest and knowledge should be sought. This can be very broad and vague if necessary, to accommodate a range of sensibilities. A textbook host would introduce strangers by way of common experiences, such as sailing or having dated the same person, identifying a common ground with as many interesting landmarks as possible. But people from radically different cultures, without even television programmes or a canonical history in common, often stare out at a wasteland with little more than the muddy puddle of their current discomfort as the sole point of convergence. And even siblings, childhood friends and life partners, whose common ground is large and crowded, can find its landmarks so familiar as to be too boring to mention. And so there is no optimum constitution that will guarantee easy conversation within a social group. Every situation requires fresh tactics, to be negotiated in the split-second of a hello. Some are born adept at this, others learn strenuously. Only a few never bother with it.

Ida was excellent at intuiting dynamics from these moments and used them as testing grounds. For instance, if John were to draw his allies into their debate, she would consider this an aggressive move and a signal that their intimacy was illusory. It would mean that the subject of their discussion was a continuation of something attached to John, of which Ida was one of many satellite contributors, rather than it being something they had created together. She would also be keeping an eye on what passed between Hands and Feet, which couldn't really be their names. Hans maybe, and Fi? Short for Fiona? Ida would be inferring plenty from their opening conversational gambits, although at present it seemed she wasn't going to glean much from Feet – a name she decided suited her in fact, for she was mute and kind of funny-looking.

The socialised human brain can process instantaneously what has taken the isolated writer a considerable amount of time to identify and describe. But though these appraisals are made within the head, the first stone is cast externally, provisionally and by uncoordinated committee. In this instance a few 'how are you?'s and 'what are you up to?'s didn't suggest any especially favourable way forward. Since John was not taking responsibility for his role as common link, it was becoming clear that everyone present was equally culpable. Feet and Hands were starting to twitch with discomfort, and so Ida guessed it was down to her.

'So, John was telling me about oil. You ever come across the stuff?'

She wasn't about to lead them all back to that stupid entropy argument, so why not nudge things on?

'Mmm,' was all John added, with a faint smile.

'Yeah,' said Hands while Feet picked at her beermat. Ida waited for more from him, but that seemed to be it.

'It sounds very interesting. I don't really quite get it yet, but John knows a fair bit about it. Quite the scientist, apparently.' Ida was prattling now, partially as a means to express her annoyance with John.

'Yeah,' said Hands. 'Yeah, he does. Um…'

'It's quite mysterious stuff, isn't it?' Hands and Feet simultaneously picked up their drinks and took long pulls. Having already insinuated the answer in her question, Ida couldn't very well continue that line. 'So, how do you all know each other?' she asked, cornered into a platitude.

John shrugged and said, 'Oh, 'round and about.'

Ida was about to leave her seat, making her annoyance visible beneath a transparent pretext, when John tossed out a casual question that had the effect of wetting split wood.

'Oh, Hands, did you have the meeting at AP yet?'

Hands expanded slightly in all directions.

'We were there just now. Feet was PAing me.' He smiled shyly at Feet and Ida looked questioningly to John. He was not being very gentlemanly in this exchange at all. Now what were they on about?

'PAing at AP? ' she said. 'Always good to be palindromic.'

Hands looked positively terrified at this endorsement.

'We heard Snowdon talk tonight,' said John, 'and it seems he's got AP working all over the Academic territories now.'

'Yeah. It's a sensible project, given the political situation, but could be more technologically sophisticated,' said Hands, gesticulating with tense claws.

'More sophisticated than some bloke falling over?' said Ida.

'Snowdon's anomalous capacity is a useful resource, but a machine is cheaper to run than a person, and as a survey it doesn't factor in other useful properties like magnetic susceptibility and thermal conductivity.'

'So we need a gang of super heroes then,' said John. 'Snowdon, Magneto Man and, and…'

'Watts per metre Kelvin?' said Hands.

John laughed in a way Ida hadn't seen before, from right down in his diaphragm, and Hands looked shyly pleased. Ida tried to catch Feet's eye, to give her a sisterly 'what are they on about?' shrug, but Feet was following the men intently.

'But what I can't ascertain is why AP use the GASMAN dowsing technique, when it's well within their power to develop an equivalent technology,' said Hands.

'Maybe they already have, but they just want to double-check using traditional methods. Like they use your skills too. That's a similar sort of folk knowledge.'

Hands picked at a beermat furiously.

'It's a science,' he whispered.

'Er, who are AP?' asked Ida, eager to help this vulnerable young man out by pulling focus. He seemed sweet.

'Academic Petroleum,' said Hands, staring down at the litter he had produced.

'And Hands pimps himself to them occasionally,' said John, with a cruel sneer directed at the top of his head. 'He advises some of the top brasses in body language.'

'Body language?' said Ida. 'That's psychology. That is definitely not folk. Don't be mean, John. It's an 'ology. Science. Fact.'

'I'm sorry. I was just winding you up, Hands. Joke.'

'Oh.' Hands brightened immediately and the air cleared as quickly as it had choked.

'But why,' asked Ida, 'do they need to know about body language? What do AP do?'

'Deals,' said Feet, blushing in the warmth of John's appreciative chuckle.

Ida wondered whether a direct question would vaporise her entirely.

'AP,' said John, 'produce and trade in oil.'

'Strange name,' said Ida. 'Where does it come from?'

'Academic Petroleum. Petroleum being from the Latin *petra*, meaning rock, and *oleum*, meaning oil,' said Hands. 'And according to some, the "Academic" was chosen to insinuate it into the mainstream while it operated as a shell company, not actually conducting any business.'

'Ah that old myth,' said John. 'And the shadowy hand on the lever belongs to ... ?'

'The GASMAN?' guessed Ida, just to have something to say.

'Could be,' said John, waggling his eyebrows.

'That is just hearsay,' said Feet. It was the only full sentence she had uttered so far, and Ida detected an accent strung across it.

'No one has conducted an audit of all AP's production concessions throughout Foreign,' said Hands, 'but it's known to have stakes of varying percentages in many state interests, each with a different agreement regarding percentage income, tax rates and so on. And that's just the upstream dealings. If they were a shell company they wouldn't be so diffuse, and they wouldn't have the assets either—'

'Listen, guys,' butted in Ida, 'I'm sure this is fascinating, but—

'Sorry Ida,' said John. 'We're being a bit cliquey. What would you like to talk about?'

'Well, I was only going to say that I thought it was my round.' She indicated the fast emptying pints. 'I'm very happy for you to talk about whatever it is. I'm sure I can amuse myself by fetching drinks, ordering scuffs, looking pretty – that sort of thing.'

Feet jumped up to help with the drinks, Hands loyally accompanied her, and John, not wishing to appear lazy, stood up too, and so Ida ended up guarding the table while the others all went to the bar. They eventually returned, Hands still talking.

'… nationalisation of course poses a huge threat. Agreements would have to be redrawn, their longevity slashed, royalties and tax rates renegotiated, and domestic to export sales ratios too. AP would risk losing a substantial stake in the international market …'

He would have kept going with his analysis for hours if a woman with a tired face, tight dress, bare legs and pink high heels like a pair of grazing flamingos hadn't walked unnecessarily close to the table. Both men almost set to stone in their attempt not to look up, while Ida rolled her eyes at Feet, who was greedily looking the woman up and down. Ida let the conspicuous pause sink in a little, then seized the moment.

'Guys, guys – hello? Yeah, we're back in the room. Can you just tell me one thing. This all sounds very high-end business, but what exactly is oil for? Who is buying oil? And to do what with it?'

'To set fire to it,' said John with glee.

'Hands,' said Ida, 'you seem to be a sensible chap, and John's being a silly bastard. Tell me in, let's say, nine words what oil is for.'

'Oil is latent energy, which is released through combustion.'

'It's fantastic,' said John. 'AP are building up a global economic market based on fires and explosions.'

'But why? Nobody pays for energy in Academia.'

It was a matter of national pride that electricity was free user-side, even in the furthest satellite campuses. The Academy had always picked up the bill as part of infrastructural costs, although no one knew quite how reasonable this bill was. AcaGen provided power through a mixed economy of mini-fusion stars and algae – a setup that was versatile and responsive to terrain and climate. In summer, when the algae bloomed in green slicks around the coastal territories, it was harvested and burned to provide the lion's share of power; then in winter, when it died back, the grid was switched to draw entirely from mini-fusion stars. The radioactive source material of these tiny stars on earth had a half-life of just 200 years, compared to the 100,000 years of nuclear power station waste – a timescale that threatened to dwarf the lifespan of any warning signs, or of the language they were written in. Mini-fusion was a brilliant solution, and the technology was continuing to progress. Soon large stations and sub-stations were likely to be replaced by mini-fusion units in individual homes, perhaps even eventually in every appliance, garlanding Academia in millions of tiny hand-holdable stars with short toxicity tails. If they were competing with this, AP had their work cut out for them.

'You say that power is free,' said John, 'but the user in Academia is locked into a system by which money is translated into other currencies. You are slaves to certain behaviours, which are rewarded with a station in life, with power.'

'That's ridiculous,' said Ida. 'Electricity's like books. It's part of the infrastructure and we all have a right to it. How can AP hope to dismantle that? And why?'

'Providers thrive on limits,' said Hands. 'AP will drum up a scare about limitlessness, such as a threat of black hole profusion or algae super-abundance, and then they'll introduce oil as the solution. And they will appeal to material stability too. Instead of bringing outer space to Earth or prehistoric sea life ashore, oil-fuelled energy brings the subterranean to the surface.'

'Oil,' said John, 'is much less awesome and awful, more tangible and *real*.'

'And safer,' said Hands. 'The statistics for last year were—'

'That's right,' said John. 'There's no risk of anything collapsing into infinity or frothing up like an infection. It's less shifty. It is what it is.'

'It is beautiful,' said Feet.

'I'll take you to a refinery one day,' said John. 'You'll fall in love with the stuff.'

'Right. But going back to this Academic power thing,' said Ida. 'I don't quite get your meaning.'

'What is the Academy,' said John, 'but a complicated ecology of exchanges that stand in for a market? What are research points other than units of backhand exchange with which to buy more credibility and attract more resources, more research interns, more job security? You just don't realise because it's all been converted to academic capital, absorbed into the institutional machinery.'

'Don't tell me what I do and don't realise. I know that the Academy is… is… well, it's lots of things. But anyway,' she turned to Hands, 'what's your take on it?'

'The Academy,' he said to the space between glasses in the middle of the table, 'is an on-going struggle to determine the conditions and criteria of legitimate membership, not to mention the hierarchy within that membership. And this struggle also determines which of the assets and abilities of those who come out on top are to function as capital within the Academy.'

'So you're saying it's not just about good scholarship, then?' said Ida, wondering who on earth this guy was with the trousers of an all-weather rambler and the tongue of a Marxist scholar. 'I mean, I know about the popularity contests with students, but when it comes down to it, the Dean will surely only progress the person she thinks is best in their field.'

'There is no fixed strategy for promotion in the Academy, because it is a reflexive system made up of its own arbiters. There are any number of tactics and currencies. Research points is one, but there are many other ways, like writing prefaces and sitting on editorial panels, through which alliances are made public, mutual interests advanced and the capital of opponents devalued.'

'I see your point,' said Ida graciously. 'Um, Hands, do you, are you a departmental manager by any chance? You seem to know an awful lot about what goes on under the bonnet.'

'I'm a PhD candidate in the Science Department.'

'Ooh, how interesting.' Ida turned her charm up full and beamed it straight at him. He paled. 'So, when are we all going to visit a finery?'

'Refinery,' Hands muttered.

'Probably not for the foreseeable,' said John. 'I understand the oil industry is closing its ranks after the assassination of the Foreign president.'

'Oh yes, I heard about that,' said Ida. 'The president – I forget his name. It was a counter-cultural faction, right? Hey – it wasn't you lot, was it?'

'I don't think it was us, was it Hands?' said John. 'The GASMAN are more mouth than trousers, right?' Hands looked confused. 'I mean the

GASMAN wouldn't go round assassinating politicians, would we?'

'Not an AP-sympathetic Prime Minister of Foreign,' said Hands. 'It wouldn't be in our interests. Nationalisation is certain now and that is a major blow to AP and given the historic relationship—'

'Ida!' said John. 'Will you stop playing footsie with my pals.' He shook his head and glared at her.

'I am not!' she protested, retracting her foot swiftly. The power of words, she felt, was unassailable. No actual proof could overrule an opinion delivered with enough confidence. And anyway, in Academia language was the only way anything occurred. People *talked* new situations into being; nothing just *happened*. 'I wasn't.'

'Come on you old boiler, let's get you home.' He drained his drink and manhandled her excitingly out of her seat. She gave Hands barely a second glance, and had certainly forgotten about the existence of Feet, as they headed for the door.

CHAPTER 15

'Sue has asked me to work with you on your style,' said Linda.

She and Ida were sat in matching winged armchairs in Linda's windowless office, the heating cranked up. Bizarrely, there were no books, papers or folders in view. Apart from the cardboard wallet Linda clutched in her hand, they were all hidden, like eavesdroppers, behind a long green velvet curtain covering three walls, which gave the room a synthetic feel, like daytime television.

'Now what's wrong with it? Honestly, she's a fucking fashion despot.' Ida tossed her silk festoon over her shoulder.

'Oh Ida, please be careful with that word.'

'You're not squeamish about expletives are you? Thought you liked a bit of Anglo-Saxon.'

'I meant despot. It gets you into trouble. It's not a nice word, so let's just put it back in the bottom of the scrabble bag shall we?'

This marked a significant difference between the two women: whereas for Linda, speech was an anagrammatic game in which words were chosen strategically from the vast vocabulary at the player's full disposal, Ida did not experience any such command over language. Sometimes it flowed normally, occasionally even beautifully; at other times speaking was like wrenching a cushion out from under her own backside, and in the worst of times she felt her words were sweated out involuntarily and prone to sour offensively.

'But I wasn't talking about fashion,' said Linda. 'I'm the last person to be able to help with that. And anyway, you'll be glad to know that Sue says you've nailed that at last.'

'At last?' wailed Ida. She imagined her agent and trainer discussing their clients like parents tutting and sighing over their teenager offspring.

Linda shrugged diplomatically and, with a single movement, took a bite of the sandwich that materialised from her sleeve.

'It's your oratory style that needs a slight rethink. I've collated a few transcriptions and there are some very nice things in here.' She placed the sandwich on the table between them and waved the transcripts in the air encouragingly. 'I already mentioned, where was it… Ah yes: "transcendental significance" and "stodgy idea". A great abuttal of Latinate bureaucracy and colloquialism. Worked really well, I mean apart from the overall confusion that particular speech caused.'

Linda usually steered clients toward either the Classical simplicity of the Attic style of rhetoric, the protractedly ornamented Asiatic style or the middle-of-the road Rhodian. In Ida, though, she had sensed the potential of collaging styles. Ida had a facility for interspersing a florid passage with an Anglo-Saxon wallop or two to splendid effect; and while, or because, this was not necessarily within her control, it was always exciting to listen to. Disappointingly for Linda, Sue was demanding this be reined in. If Ida was to confine herself to a single style, Sue had argued, she might be more in control. Linda didn't at all want to implement this straightjacketing, but…

'It wasn't a speech,' said Ida, while also trying to figure out what was in the sandwich. It smelled like fish but looked like grated carrot. 'How many times do I have to tell people? It was a joke.'

'Ah yes, of course. But anyway, I think it would be good to concentrate on just one style of rhetoric for a while. Which would you prefer to focus on?'

The styles each had their pitfalls. The Attic could come across as meagre or instructional, the Rhodian as loose and too eager to please and the Asian as swollen, pretentious and too obviously trying to be moving. Linda couldn't decide which accusation could be levelled at Ida. To her, the problem lay elsewhere. But Sue was insistent.

'Just simplify it,' Sue had shouted through the open bathroom door that morning, while Linda was surveying the black-filled pores around the flare of her nose with scientific detachment. 'I don't know how. You're the language mechanic. Just fewer moving parts, ok? Might make it marginally safer for us all.'

'Um, I don't know,' said Ida. 'Obviously not the mediocre option. Um… Asiatic? Is that funnier do you think? I haven't talked this through with Sue yet, but if I'm going to convince the CSA that my intentions were comedic I'm going to have to produce some more jokes.'

'I can certainly train you up on the Asiatic, but the comedy I'm not so qualified in. I'll have to make some calls and see if I can find you a workshop to attend.'

'Thanks, Linda, you're a real brick.' She felt a genuine fondness for Linda, who was chasing an evasive morsel with her tongue, her eyes glassy with contentment. If only everyone, if only *she* could enjoy the inner peace that Linda did.

'Can I talk to you as a friend?' Ida ventured.

'Sure.'

'The thing is, the other night, after the radio show, my whole career flashed before my eyes, and I thought, I'm over forty now and my options are dwindling. I feel like I'm in a funnel that's getting narrower and narrower. Er, Linda, when I say as a friend I mean off the record...'

'Oh, right, sorry,' Linda crossed out the notes in her reporter's notebook, put down her pen, took another bite of her sandwich – showering large orange parentheses onto her lap – and looked limpidly at Ida, confusing signs of friendly concern with passivity. 'Do go on.'

'Well, the thing is, I found myself wondering about motherhood the other day. I met this woman who was so terrifyingly content, I had to ask her how she did it. She said she was a mother and that was it. She didn't have to explain her methodology, her references, her track record. I asked her about her children and, well, it was utterly dull, and they're obviously high achieving in the usual ways, but it was a source of joy for her. It got me thinking that she had her legacy in place right there – once she'd done the hard work of pushing them out of her pelvis, of course.'

The woman had been a friend of John's who they had met for a quick drink. Ida had been resistant to what she considered to be propaganda at the time, telling herself breeders want everyone to feel knackered, to stay in every evening and to degrade their conversation daily so they don't feel they're the only ones missing out. But this woman's words had obviously had an impact. Ida had asked John why he saw her, what they usually talked about. 'The same,' he had said off-handedly. He didn't mind women obsessing about their biological shelf-life, it was only fair he should listen, since he didn't suffer one himself. Suffer? Ida had been outraged. Women have this incredible capacity and all anyone can focus on is the point at which it dwindles. 'I know. Tick-tock,' he had said, shaking his head in commiseration.

'It made me realise,' said Ida, while Linda chewed thoughtfully, 'that I have to keep chipping away at my future, like a shapeless rock, and every time I chisel a bit off to make the shape I want, it just grows back. My future has a dumb sort of sentience. Its sole intent is just to keep me busy with it.' She paused. 'You mustn't breathe a word of this to Sue.'

Linda nodded in total understanding. Sue was vociferously anti-breeding. She froze out friends and colleagues who became pregnant, pronouncing them 'lost to the brain jelly'. And if a client, male or female, should be so rash as to conceive, she struck them from her books at the first sign that fatigue was cramping their performance. The many brightly coloured crèches that clustered around the departmental buildings did nothing to dissolve her hard-line position. She maintained that having children split a person ('literally', one cold-shouldered mother had muttered ruefully), and that she was not in the business of absorbing clients' clashes of priority.

'I know what you're going to say,' continued Ida. 'That my books are my babies. And in a way, books do persist into the future, like offspring, and they're more obedient. But it's only notionally and physically that they persist.' She slumped her shoulders mournfully. 'But actually, in people's consciousness? Usually not. Books melt away in the collective memory. It's ideas you need to generate and distribute if you want to make history these days. That's why artists have the status they do. It used to be images that were king, of course, and that was much easier, because you can make an image out of anything; but an idea, well, who even knows what one of those is?'

Linda was at a loss on this point. She picked up her sandwich. It was not appropriate, she felt, to take another bite, so she held it in mid air.

'But children will beget children will beget children,' said Ida. 'They are ideas that have their own ideas. It struck me that breeding would be a much easier, sure-fire way of achieving what I'm expending a lot of time and effort on. But then I thought I'm probably just having a mid-life crisis and I should run it past someone before I did anything about it. And what with your background, I thought you might have some feedback...'

Linda was born of a long line of dedicated cultural-support workers, and had grown up with a colourful parade of professionals trooping through the family home. Troubled artists and writers sought legal advice on copyright issues from her mother, and academics came for whatever it was that Dr Buck offered behind his green leather-padded door. Linda had learned to play silently and lay in wait for clients' red-eyed departures, but apart from rare and incomprehensible outbursts in the hallway, she had never heard a word that passed between her parents and their clients. She had, however, developed an intuitive understanding of how to comfort what her mother called 'overthinkers'.

'Oh dear,' said Linda, resting the sandwich on her skirt, made taut by tubular thighs. 'Can you perhaps use epanados or congeries to describe your feelings more precisely?'

'Oh, it's not an intricate feeling at all. It's quite broad and abstract, like nostalgia for something you've never known.' Ida straightened up and leaned in earnestly. 'It sounds boastful, and I don't mean it in that way, but I always used to believe I possessed an imagination in excess of the normative transcendental imaginary of our time. I suppose I never found a way to express it. But I have a feeling that there might be something just around the corner. I can smell the beginnings of a category collapse. I can almost touch it, and I think I have it in me to pull off something big. I can't really tell you any more than that right now. And maybe all this talk of babies is because I'm scared of failing at whatever this big thing turns out to be.'

Not liking the sound of category collapse, Linda interpreted Ida's needs along practical lines.

'We,' she announced, 'are going to upgrade you to the Hermogenes system of rhetoric. It will pump up your floridity and ornamentation, which will help greatly to boost your authoritativeness. It sounds like that's what you need most at the moment.' She stood up, scattering the remains of the sandwich and treading it into the carpet. She strode to an opening in the green curtain, plunged in a sturdy, veterinary-like arm and, without having to look, withdrew a pad.

'It sounds strenuous, is how it sounds,' said Ida morosely.

'It's not for the faint-hearted, granted. It includes six basic types of style: clarity, grandeur, beauty, rapidity, character and sincerity, which, when employed with skill, create the stylistic ideals of force or awesomeness. But that's not all. Clarity is further anatomised into the subtypes of purity and distinctness; grandeur into solemnity, asperity, vehemence, brilliance, florescence and abundance; character into simplicity, sweetness, subtlety and modesty, and the major sub-distinction within sincerity is indignation.' She was making out a prescription for the library – a modest list to start off with.

'Blimey. Are you telling me I have to think of all of those at once every time I open my mouth?'

'It is for the advanced orator, but I think you can handle it. It's for those who wish to impart their rhetorical style with moral and emotional, as well as aesthetic force.' She handed the chit to Ida.

'Is it good for comedy too?'

'Certainly. And I shall be in touch about workshops. Don't worry, we'll have you firing on all cylinders again soon. No more of this baby talk.'

'You, Linda, are a star. I feel better already, thank you.' She rose and made for the door, as if to a refreshed future.

'No Ida, it is you who will be the star. You just need a bit of a style makeover. And you need to find yourself some subject matter, of course.'

*

The workshop was a disaster.

'One-to-one,' Ida had stipulated. 'No group humiliation, if you please.'

Linda had rung round and got wind of a practicing clown who tutored in mime. Once Ida had got the predictable jokes out the way – if she ended up having to shoot him, would she need a silencer? If he was arrested, would he be told he had the right to talk? – she thought it sounded like a great idea. Linda approved of comedic training that did not encroach on her own linguistic syllabus, and Ida, too, could see the merits of separating speech and movement.

'If the comedy happens all in the gesture, I can stick with my existing lecture contents. Great plan, Linda.'

Ten days later, she was back on the phone.

'It's fucking psychological abuse Linda. Where did you find him? In a secure unit? He's a lunatic!'

Ogden LeBrun called his method of character construction 'Looking In'.

'A good character,' by which he meant an original one that the performer will always be able to slip in and out of, 'can be best found within oneself. Your Fifi or Poopoo or whatever you decide to call your mime persona is already there inside you. You simply need to look in, identify it and pull it out, by the scruff of the neck if necessary.'

The method was painful, but easy.

'All you have to do,' he told Ida, who was trying not to catch sight of her black-leotarded figure in his studio's wall-sized mirror, 'is focus on your vulnerability to the pressures generated by society's standards of physical beauty and intellectual brilliance.' He paused, as if waiting for her to display some sign that she was doing just that.

'Can you give me a bit more than that? Sorry, I'm not used to this way of working.'

'Okay, here it is. Think of what society thinks is the perfect person. Beautiful, clever… Yes, that's it, imagine the most perfect person. Now, think of yourself and how you physically deviate from that standard. Focus on one deviation, one blemish, and concentrate on it. Make it more pronounced, more and more pronounced, until you yourself become distorted. I want you to connect with your deviations, learn to accentuate them and use them to shed your layers of inhibitions, your prejudices and even your deep-seated mannerisms.'

It wasn't clear how such a scrub-down of social conditioning was to be achieved, but still, Ida went along with it as best she could. For her deviation she plumped for her huge arse. No one else would call it huge, but in relation to her ribby torso and small, door-knob sized breasts, it was unexpectedly generous. And so she focused on it, dwelt on it, lamented and chastised it. She was loath to accentuate it, but she stuck it out obediently, standing on tiptoes to nudge it out even further. Her inhibitions were clinging fast though. She felt ridiculous, ugly and gullible. And her prejudices were confirmed when she braved a glance at the mirror. She looked like she was readying herself for an unholy rogering from behind.

As for her deep-seated mannerisms, she had never been aware of what they were. Her friends could have told her it was fiddling with her lips as she read, tossing her hair when someone said something she didn't like, neglecting to use her opposing thumb when opening a screw-top lid, holding her breath when opening doors... The litany was long, specific and inapplicable to walking around a clown's studio, so she just tiptoed back and forth, sticking her backside out and inhaling deeply as if that would inflate it further.

'That's it. Great,' said Ogden, clapping his hands twice in encouragement. 'And... stop.'

She resumed her normal posture and turned to almost make eye contact with him.

'Ok, next exercise. You are visiting an archaeological site. You are alone.'

She accepted this willingly, glad to leave the studio. She closed her eyes.

'Have a good look around. What is it like there? Are you in a desert? A jungle? A grassy plain? Walk around the site and try to memorise every physical detail of the structure. Is it a house or a whole village? A crumbling palace or a temple that once glittered under the eye of an unforgiving Dog? What is this place? How big is it? How decayed?'

She made to answer him, to tell him it was a ruined minimalist arts centre, three stories of corroded concrete... He shushed her, raising an expressive finger to his lips.

'Try to soak in the past. Look left, look up, look behind you. The past is everywhere.'

She did as he said, opened her eyes and looked around his studio, but could only see him, her, their shoes over by the door.

'Yeah, you don't need to actually act yet. This is all mental projection,' he explained.

She closed her eyes and was back with the stained and crumbling concrete, weeds growing up its flanks now that the inhabitants had stopped torturing them with sulphur.

'Walk among the ruins. Touch them, smell them, relax into them.'

They smelled of stale urine, rust and pond slime. She walked on, sidestepping a mound of fallen rubble and looked up at a staircase, which remained intact. It spiralled upwards, ending abruptly at the bleached sky, where a pigeon shat. Underfoot, a worm shrugged.

'Suddenly you feel that everything around you has started to tremble. You feel the earth vibrating beneath your feet. You can't seem to find your balance. The tremor builds and builds and reaches a climax. The ground, the ruins, the trees, even the sky is shaking violently. All at once, right before you, the earth cracks open in a wrenching, ear-splitting groan.'

Ida joined in with that groan. A sudden and overwhelming memory of being vibrated to her core until she was sick flashed through her. The moment was terrible only because it was so tantalising. It was immediately replaced by a surge of joy at the realisation she was experiencing a childhood memory, a flashback to before The Spill.

'Hold on to what you are feeling. This is real; you are in an earthquake. You and your flaw are in an earthquake. It is your flaw's fault. Focus on your flaw and tell yourself over and over, "I hate it! I don't want it! I can't stand it!" Build up a negative emotional reaction to the flaw. Imagine what might be the most extreme act you would commit in order to destroy it or correct it.'

This was confusing, because Ida had forgotten about her enormous arse and was much more interested in her memory. She didn't care to discuss her lack of past with this freakish man and was making ready to fudge some stock emotional reaction. Luckily, he seemed to change direction. They were possibly on to the next exercise.

'Now, moving about the room, try to hide your flaw in an exaggerated manner. If this draws attention to it, the result should be comical. This is fine. Desirable even. Mime as many activities as you can imagine –

bowling, ice skating, reading a newspaper, cooking pancakes. I want you to bring out all your physical tics and arrange them around your deviation.'

After a full half hour of this Ogden called the session to a close.

'Your homework for the next week,' he instructed, 'is to expose your flaw in your day-to-day life. At work, with your family, at a restaurant, in bed. Try to make it as noticeable as possible, and to experience it as intensely as you can. Everything you do must be led by your awareness of this flaw. If others notice it, all the better. Exaggerate it even more until they can see nothing else.'

This was a tough call. Parading her flaws in public would undo years of hard work, so instead she confined her exercises to around the house. She explained to the interns, and got them doing the same. All week there were shrieks and howls of laughter all over the flat, followed by quiet, introspective spells. Ida wondered if her mother had had such an ample backside, and how far into their courting it had been before her father got his hands on it. She daydreamed of meeting others who also bore this mark of high breeding. They would be unaccountably drawn to one another, and discover that they were blood relatives, all great writers from a dynasty that could be traced back to the Classical era.

In all, it had been a constructive week. She had made peace with her backside and had even come to enjoy wiggling it in the air like a blind mole surfacing. The second session was when she came undone.

'This week we will be plunging deep inside to face our shame.' By which Ogden meant *her* shame. 'Think what it is you are ashamed of. Your speech patterns, maybe, or your family background? Do you come from the wrong side of the tracks? What do you know to be an internal fault, and which fault have others found in you? Does it still rankle deep inside that someone once called you stingy or stupid or selfish?'

Ida didn't know where to begin.

'Now, I want you to react physically to that acute shame. I want you to pull in, tighten up, become one with your emotion.'

Her shames were multiple. They rose up through the barricades she had erected, swirling about her like ghouls, taunting her, pressing down, squashing her, pasting her to the floor.

'Very good, very good,' said Ogden. 'Now, as we did last week, I want you to let this emotional problem lead you as you perform tasks.'

She remained on the floor, groaning with self-loathing.

'Excellent, excellent.'

She lay there for the full hour.

'And… rest. Lovely. Now, your homework this week is to work with this major fault in your character. I want you to keep it in focus for the entire week. Make sure that it is the font of all that you say, and that your every utterance demonstrates it, accentuates it. If you are self-conscious about being considered stingy, bargain effusively over the price of *everything*. If you worry you are lacking a sense of humour, chastise all jokers for being flippant, be literal whenever you encounter irony. If you have been accused of vanity, steer all conversations towards your triumphs, your appearance... Whatever it takes, turn yourself into a monster. I want you to really have fun with it.'

This clown was a sadist. She could not have felt more raw if he'd scraped her all over with a blunt knife and marinated her in salt and lemon. What right did he have to do this to her? She should punch him on his stupid nose.

'If I want to face up to myself,' she growled, as she stomped about the studio gathering her coat, bag and shoes, 'I'll do so in the safety of a therapist's couch, thank you very much.' She wouldn't give him the satisfaction of her tears, but once she had slithered home and dismissed the interns she went to bed for the rest of the day, weeping and cursing the viciousness of clowns.

CHAPTER 16

In the busy dawn, as bins rattled, bread ovens fumed and the streets drooled sanitising spray, scum reporter Pearl Blake was persuading the man in the dry cleaners to secrete a tiny microphone into the weave of Ida's tweed jacket. She peeled off a note, then three notes, and finally folded at five. The man picked them off the counter like dirty handkerchiefs, looked down his shiny nose at the device and carried it like a bogey on his fingertip to the back of the shop, where Ida's jacket hung waiting.

Ida, meanwhile, was getting into the shower, reflecting on the gallery talk she'd given the evening before, which had gone off without a hitch, but also without an audience. The publicity material had listed one date, and the events curator had given her another, and so the two of them sat in the empty gallery café while Ida talked about the exhibition into a tape recorder. It was important, she felt, that her efforts were logged and her content entered into the archive. Any future listeners would be none the wiser that the swishing noise in the background was the sound of the floor being mopped, although the lack of laughter at what turned out to be some quite good jokes was a shame. Given that it was a clerical error, rather than her failure to draw a crowd, Ida didn't mind at all having just the curator as her incredibly attentive audience. It was a novelty to be able to talk *at* another person without having to consider any desire they might have to join in.

Once Manfred had arrived with her dry cleaning and had been instructed on the day's tasks, Ida set off for the tram stop feeling better than she had done in days. She was looking forward to teaching. Every so often she gave tutorials in the Academy's top art department, where star-struck students could benefit from a ten-minute blast of the wisdom that had forged her reputation. Now that she was not a full-time member of Academy staff, her enjoyment of these sessions had rocketed, mainly due to the alleviation of paperwork and pastoral care. She felt like a flying doctor, swooping in and dropping a supply of prompts, ideas and constructive criticisms, before disappearing out of the students' lives, usually forever.

Curiously, the Fine Art Department building bore a strong Fascist profile and its fluted spire was topped with a gilt eagle. This particular bird has been adopted as the emblem of nobility, power and authority by a surprising number of nations and ideologies throughout history. Surprising because, in nature, the eagle is lazy, cowardly and bullying, often snatching prey from the claws and beaks of smaller birds.

The building itself was of pale, majestic stone with a terracotta stripe running round halfway up, giving it a parcelled look. The main block was broader than it was high, the central tower bracketed by two smaller side towers that echoed its form, one bearing a clock, the other a barometer. Beneath these instruments were two small balconies, which gave the façade a care-worn, baggy-eyed look, and the two lower-level blocks that extended forwards like arms imbued it with a rather sinister intent, appealing tenderly towards those who entered the ornamental forecourt, before funnelling them greedily towards the entrance.

The keys to the balconies had been lost long ago. Only the most determined suicides used them now. Back in the day they had been the Fine Art faculty's lookout points during the Great Departmental Wars, which the building still bore the scars of. There were bullet holes in the stone here and there, and the barometer was stuck on 'change' following a mortar attack. When she had been a full-time academician, Ida had met many people who had fought in these wars, some of them still drumming up conflict whenever possible, partly through nostalgia, and partly as a genuine attempt to raise standards. But more broadly, hers was the first generation to experience academic stability following the violent spates of disciplinary reorganisation, foreshadowed by repeated and lengthy dynastic conflicts over succession and supremacy.

Traditionally, professorial succession was horizontal, with the throne passing to colleagues, rather than vertically to acolytes. But with the proliferation of sub-categories within departments, and contradictory positions emerging across any one discipline and branching off into sub-disciplines, rows over seniority, eligibility and epistemological inheritance boiled over into unchecked conflict. The first stone was cast by a semiotician, in response to what he perceived to be an attack by a deconstructionist. This was quickly followed by a clash between the Applied Arts Department, which clung to the model of dynastic possession, and the Politics Department, which had asserted the right to elect its own professor. In a last-ditch attempt to legislate college-wide, a pronouncement was made that eligibility for succession should be restricted to those senior lecturers who had studied under the outgoing professor, but this failed when a hostile Art and Design merger broke all peaceful resolve. The Design Programme directors challenged the Fine Art Department on grounds of utility, and developed their commercial links with workshop facilities, their access to foundries, kilns and injection moulds, attracting sculpture students in their droves and depleting the Fine Art reserves. Then two cultural studies professors claimed artworks to be within their remit, since they are simply cultural objects to be read like any others, which provoked the Fine Art Department to wage out-and-out war. Drawing on its massive methodological artillery, it conquered the principalities of English Literature, Cultural Studies and Social Science, breaking off the campaign to summer in Anthropology.

The mid-war decades were characterised by aggressive territorial augmentation and simmering, uneasy, cross-disciplinary marriages, with many more sub-disciplines subordinated into Fine Art's domain. But it was precisely this aggressive expansionism that generated conditions for eventual peace. During these fiery days, departmental administrative and pedagogical efficiency was greatly impeded by the system of partible inheritance, which dictated the equal division of assets amongst all inheritors. This meant, in practice, that if a professor within an acquisitioned sub-department retired or passed away, the dedicated professorial post was liquidated and its assets divided equally among senior lecturers. Within a few years this reduced assets to impracticably small proportions, with budgets and equipment scattered to no useful ends, giving rise to endless disputes and litigation over boundaries and ownership. And even when new assets were brought in through grants and sponsorship, there was no central departmental estate in which to implement them, since the habit of atomisation had devastated everything.

It was when the Fine Art Department was bloated on violent victories and over-ambitious student intake, its resources and faculty members fragmented and dispersed, that PJ Rothwell-Beer's right and royal road to power led to the position of Dean. She had worked her way up through an Academy at war, but was determined to be the one to end it. She drafted, implemented and delegated far-sighted and placatory actions, taking assets and resources back under central control, organising peace conferences and seminars and abolishing partible inheritance outright. From now on, she decreed, management would be swelled and human resources would rule with an iron rod over the inauguration of new professors. And the new currency would be research points, earned by learning and the dissemination of that learning, since this was something that could not be violently grabbed, but must be slowly and steadily achieved. Under this new regime, old-school departments quickened their own downfall by adopting a rigid sense of grandeur, making them incapable of adapting, and inviting subjugation at the hands of young bucks in previously subordinate, but now, through the mysterious tides of fashion, sexier departments. Perhaps most importantly, sub-disciplinary distinctions were abolished in one fell swoop by the institution of Interdisciplinary Studies across the board. The vestiges of departmental divisions remained, as dictated by the architecture of the Academy, but a professor from one department might teach in any given department from one day to the next, so that revolutionary momentum was entirely checked by an all-pervasive and turbulent insecurity.

Even during Ida's time as an academic, the Academy had still been a field of struggle, since any principle of hierarchisation, however legitimate, equates to a bun fight for distinction. To boost the impact of new research outputs, departments jostled for media attention and new audiences, which involved some ugly behaviour. But this was still far from out-and-out warfare. Ida had encountered the sort of struggle – of each against all – that is in fact stabilising. If everyone involved shares the same objectives, if hierarchical advancements are rigidly linear and universally strived towards, and if the level of competition is constant, the Academy will persist in relative peace. But even though she had taken up her first teaching roles during the comparatively benign disorderliness of the Interdisciplinary Peace Accord, her career had unfortunately and prematurely stagnated under a professor of the old warring guard. She had been left waiting years for promotion to lecturer, and was instead insultingly and periodically conferred minor titles and positions that were supposed to be emolliating. She had been loaded up with every committee membership, small research fund, electoral commission seat and peer journal readership going. The new Academy had a knack of generating these at will, whenever a new satisfaction was required to make up for some disappointment or frustration, to the extent that if you were to list them all, there would be way more rewards, awards, titles and entitlements than there were academicians.

Ida had realised the hopelessness of her position under this bullish professor, now long dead, and had escaped, via the departmental side vent of media training, to her current life as an art critic and public figure. And this was why it was so especially exhilarating to return to the Fine Art Department after all these years – on her own terms and beyond reproach for whatever undisciplinary methods she might wish to practice.

*

Pearl Blake was crouched at her listening post, chuckling in anticipation as she listened to Ida breathing hard, presumably as she climbed the many stairs to the Fine Art office. There was a faint rustling and mumbling, followed by Ida's booming voice.

'Hello, hello, good morning. How are you? Ah, is that my tutee list?'

More rustling and faint mumbling. More booming from Ida. But Pearl heard no other voices. She twiddled knobs and slid sliders, but no amount of boosting could make audible any voice other than Ida's. Damn. That idiotic dry cleaner must have fumbled the gain setting with his stupid, over-stuffed fingers. She felt sick with disappointment. Furious and sick.

'Hello, are you Sophie? Hi, I'm Ida. Good to meet you. [...] Ha hahaha ha. Thanks. Really? Which bit in particular? [...] Oh, yes, it is rather, isn't it? Anyway, what are you up to? [...] Right, I see. And this bit of floss on a plank is the apotheosis, is it? Nice, in a *povera* kind of way. I'm rather confused by this painting though. What is that bit of green doing? [...] But even paint can't just do being – it's always 'up to something', as Aldershof would say. I was reading an essay by him the other day called *On Becoming the Right Hue* and it's amazing because... he's a post-heterotopic intra-Marxist enameller and... [...] Oh er, Aldershof. JBS Aldershof. Want me to spell that? J, as in juggernaut; B, as in bu... ah, you've got it. Anyway, there's this brilliant moment when the whole universe seems to rotate through thirty degrees because you think hang on, does he mean khaki? And then you realise no! he actually means avocado, because we're in a bathroom, not a war zone. And you really get subjectivity as a process of socio-political inscription not illustrated, but actually embodied, by this green. [...] Yes, totally, and yet not at all, which makes it *so* Schiller. But anyway, I must move on. Thank you, er, Sophie, it was great talking to you. Good luck!'

Pearl had been listening in, trying to fill in the gaps where Sophie would have been speaking, but not having been to art school it was all too mysterious. Every word had a meaning that she could access, but some combinations seemed designed to undo those meanings. Socio-political inscription? What was that? And inscribed on what? Her annoyance was cut short by Ida's voice in her earpiece once more. The next tutorial, she supposed.

'Hi, are you Xavier? Hello, I'm Ida. Good to meet you. [...] Thanks. You know, one does one's best. Ahahah. So, what are you up to? [...] Ah right, yes, hair is a really interesting medium. The Victorians worshipped at altars made out of hair, of course; but even more interesting for you, perhaps, is hair as a liminal signifier. Have you heard of JBS Aldenberg? He's a post-Marxist, anti-heterotopian ceramicist and he wrote this really interesting essay with a whole passage about sinks – plugholes being the liminal conduit, of course. There's this bit where there's one hair that's really long, I mean, like *this* long... Shit, what was that? [...] Oh! Did I just do that? Oh gosh, sorry. Was that the diaphanous sphere that was...? [...] Oh shit. I'm *so* sorry. Listen, er, I'll get my people to send you some more hair. [...] I'll get you some keratin then. Some sixty per cent improved keratin – I know Pantene personally. Intimately. [...] I'm sorry, sorry, I have to move on... Shit. [...]'

Pearl, perked up. Has Ida O'Dewey just trashed a student's work?

'Hi, Hyun-Ok? Hi, how are you? Nice to meet you. [...] Oh, you mean on *Panel Beaters*? No, no, no. That was an exaggeration, a joke. [...] Honestly, it's fine. It wasn't real. That's so not going to happen. Don't worry about it. [...] Really. I didn't mean it. Oh dear. [...] I really think [...] Well, it's a bit like, you know when someone says they "love" cake? [...] You do? Hmmm, well, maybe... Look, I'm sorry, this isn't very... [...] No, not exactly. Er... [...] So you've not got anything to... [...] Yes, I understand, but honestly, truly, really, really, really, that's really not going to be the case. [...] You know, I think you should probably talk with your tutor about this. We don't really have the time right now. [...] Oh, did he? Well, your peers then? [...] Neighbours? [...] Parents? [...] Oh, I'm sorry. Well, maybe next time I'm in we could... [...] Ok, great, yes, until next time then. Um, thank you. [...]

'Hi are you G–, er, G– [...] Gwynne. Right. Hi, I'm [...] Ah, sorry, Gerwynnie? [...] Gerwayne. [...] Anyway. Hi, I'm Ida. So, what are you up to? [...] I see. [...] Right [...] Sorry, did you say foam? [...] As the ontological obverse of the punctum? Ok, go on. [...] Uh-huh, as in Bunny? [...] Ah, of course, yes. Good old Walter. [...] Heraclitus? In what way, precisely? [...] Ah right, yes, I thought you meant the other way. Ok. [...] Ooh, now, which one's he again? [...] Ah yes, that's right. [...] Well, you certainly have a lot of angles covered. Which is ok, but maybe there are too many angles. Or not enough, actually. You don't seem to have taken infra-Marxist, post-homotopian enamelling into account. Look up Aldenblik's *On Becoming the Right Hue* – it refutes all this stuff into a cocked hat. But gosh, sorry, ten minutes goes fast, doesn't it? Anyway, look him up, he's really sage. Good luck! [...]'

Pearl politely turned the volume down when a new reverberant quality to the audio suggested Ida was in the lavatory. How interesting, she thought during the hiatus, to hear how the teaching of art was actually conducted. There was much more chat than she imagined.

'[...] Yeah, I really like the way you talk about that curve. It's very urinal, of course, very messianic. It really reminds me of something. Now, what is it? There's something, oh, I haven't thought about this for years, but I can almost see it, hang on [...] yes, that's it! I've managed to pluck it out of the correct mental filing cabinet I think, hahaha. There's this really nice little essay called *On Becoming the Right Hue* by, oh, wotsisname [...] Alberdink! JBS Alberdink. If I remember, there's a eulogy to the instep of a urinal in it, but it comes from such a wry angle that you don't even realise it's about aesthetics until it turns on a ha'penny and, bam, you're affected. I haven't thought about it for ages, so I'm a bit hazy, but there's a bit, I think, on the temporality of curves, or the curvaceousness of time. Anyway, talking of which, crikey, I have to move on already. It's been great talking to you. Good luck! [...]'

What was this name that kept coming up? Alber-something. Was this the third time Ida had mentioned it? The fourth? Was Pearl imagining this? Was it one name among many?

'Hello, are you JC? Hi, I'm Ida. Goodness, you're tall. Oh wow, that smaller painting there [...] Well, I don't know what it's about, but I can tell you what it reminds me of. It's funny, I was reading a book of Aldenkamp essays just this morning [...] It's right here in my bag [...] hang on. Here we are. Look at that cover! Uncanny, isn't it? That blue line there is just like the little squiggle here, but bigger, and a bit greener. And straighter maybe. Uncanny [...]'

*

At lunchtime Pearl flicked off the receiver, exhausted from all the listening. She had to admire the art tutor's stamina. That was one long session of ceaseless talking. At a personal level she could sympathise with Ida for giving the same text reference to every student – no one can keep pulling fresh stuff out of their arse. But it was not best practice, she knew that much, and the man who'd employed her for the job – a man who allegedly went by the name of Peanuts Swinglow – would probably have his own ideas of how to spin it bigger too. If he was the newspaperman he claimed to be, that is.

Pearl hopped out of the business end of the van and into the driver's seat in time to catch Ida quitting the building. The proximity gave Pearl a thrill. She made a sudden movement to attract Ida's attention as she passed within metres. For a split second they made eye contact, before Pearl dropped her glance with something approaching guilt, and Ida switched to thinking, with some trepidation, about the script meeting she was heading to.

CHAPTER 17

Ida could feel the atmosphere flip as she walked through the television production offices. Employees broke off their conversations to track her with their eyes, waiting until she'd passed to cluck and raise their eyebrows at their colleagues. The producer's PA was visibly embarrassed as he told Ida to take a seat, and forgot to offer her a beverage. The producer's door opened and Chip's head poked out to call her in with uncharacteristic sobriety.

'Take a seat,' he said.

'Thanks Chip, but I think I'd better kneel,' said Ida. 'I don't think you're going to like what I have to tell you.'

'Well, hang on a minute. I don't think you're going to like what I have to tell you. I'm the boss here, so I get to go first.'

'Erm, no, I said it first, and I'm the talent, so I get first dibs.'

'I think you'll find that the unspoken rule is that I rule.'

'No, I think you'll find that I've just told you that I quit.'

'Damn it. That's cheating. Saying something in the past tense doesn't make it happen earlier than it actually did.'

'Well, do you understand the essence of my point or not? You know I've quit, right?'

'Well, I suppose...'

'Then I will have got in there first, no matter in which tense.'

'Ah, but could you prove it?'

'Certainly. I have a hi-tech mini-microphone concealed in the weave of my jacket. But I will let you hold a press conference to say we came to a mutual agreement if – and only if – you say that it's because I want to pursue a career in comedy. And if you agree to my being replaced by Tolly Adio.'

'Adio? Why Adio? He's not exactly a pal of yours.'

'Hey, I'm an adult. I don't need to institute a carbon copy of myself. I can admire the abilities of a rival, you know.'

'Right,' said Chip with the scepticism of a weathered producer.

'Plus, I think that if someone else is to take over then it should be immediately evident to viewers that I'm no longer involved. A totally different script consultant would be less confusing all round.'

This made more sense to Chip. They'd need to run a relaunch campaign, of course. Adio wasn't what you'd call super-academic, but he had the loyalty of a broader, dumber readership, some of whom at present thought the show too elitist. He could swell their ratings, but they'd have to be careful not to alienate existing viewers. The network should announce a new departmental think-lab alliance, but also heighten an existing plotline so that it would be impossible to stop watching during the changeover. Yeah, why not employ Adio? A bit of lowbrow could be just what the show needed.

Tolly, Ida knew, would be terrible at it. Under the influence of his taste and methods, the show would sprout clichés, turn slushy, and would eventually have to be snipped off the network. She seemed to have forgotten that the point of the exercise was to redeem herself, and was instead instilling widespread rot. Actually, she hadn't forgotten, but it seemed impossible to engineer her own redemption, so she had decided to settle for ruining something else instead. Redemption seldom works in real life, because the vast chaotic universe is governed by perverse and unpredictable interconnectivity that makes it impossible to control. The best she could do was set something going that no one else could control either.

'And make sure he knows it was me who recommended him.' She figured no one could be such a worm that they'd continue spreading muck about her in print after such a big favour.

'Ah, right, I see,' said Chip, pulling down the blinds. 'I'll let him know, but only if you do one thing for me in return, once you've turned that microphone off.'

*

In compensation for the unpleasant afternoon, Ida visited her favourite department in one of the classier stores. The brightness of the lighting department, though entirely explicable, was always magical. A grotto swagged in luminosity and glister, its upper volume was pendulous with lambent bowls, cylinders and asteroids, the lower regions racked with twinkles, blazes, radiances and glimmers of more shapes and hues of yellow- and blue-white than any painter could replicate. And, more enchanting still, the temperature here was a good ten degrees higher, as the department pulled hard on its local mini-fusion substation. Ida stepped off the escalator as if on to a beach. She unbuttoned her coat and took off her shoes, as if strolling through the surf. She stood in front of a display of standard lamps and closed her eyes to bask.

'Is madam looking for anything in particular?'

Her eyes opened to find a dusky young man wearing a staff uniform that was obviously a temporary stand-in for speedos and suntan lotion.

'Always,' she sighed, dismissing him with a gesture of boundless contemplation. She was simply happy to linger beneath the wattage, bathing in its warmth and smelling the newness around her, the aroma of hot metal uncontaminated by dust or finger grease. She pretended to be looking to buy so as not to be moved on by security, absently turning over price tags, while turning over in her mind thoughts about power.

Power was a large and complicated word that split and twisted unhelpfully. She wasn't sure if she was thinking about mini-fusion and oil, authority and autonomy, or lust and love. Indeed, these could all be used as analogies, allegories or euphemisms for one another. Understand one and you understand them all.

What was it John had said, with those lips of his? That the Academy traded in alternative currencies in pursuit of power. Knowledge, as they say, is power; so if Academia is a site of production and reproduction of knowledge, then is power fuel, apparatus and product? And what about other forms of power beside knowledge and forearms? There are positions of power that have little to do with intellect, and positions in sex that might. It's to do with structure, and positions within a structure. Is it the structure that generates the power, no matter who is in what position, or is it the relations between individuals that produce the power to manufacture the structure? And what about status? Is that the same as power? Because often that is conferred, not generated. Is oil generated or conferred? Power can be earned, in the form of cultural capital, as published works and broadcasting appearances; but mini-fusion is given away. And people pay for sex, in more ways than one. Sometimes intellectual prestige is won by turning down power. Who doesn't admire a maverick? Mavericks are sexy. But not all mavericks are powerful. John is sexy, and therefore a maverick, but he doesn't seem to have any power. Except in those arms, those thighs, those shoulders… Perhaps he doesn't want power, because it comes with responsibility. Is oil a big responsibility? The sad irony is that those who reach the higher, plumper seats of power in the Academy have to sacrifice any chance of increasing their cultural capital or intellectual renown because they're too busy juggling their responsibilities and arranging the expenditure of their power. They spend all their time organising research time rotas and working on media relations that will increase the departmental profile and generate revenue and more power…

No, Ida was realising, power is not an inert substance personally possessed by ordained individuals; although it does seem to be something that can be handed around. Perhaps it is more animal, since animals cannot really be possessed or fully controlled, but they can be kept, after a fashion, and need tending. Power breeds obligations, which in turn elicit solicitations that produce further powers, and this proliferation has the dung-like whiff of animal reproduction…

'Hello aunty Ida,' a little voice piped across her thoughts.

'Oh, hello, little one. Where's your mummy?' She thought the kid looked familiar, and it seemed to know who she was, but she wasn't so good at recognising people too far removed from her own demographic. Young boys and old men were impossible.

'Ida!' said a bustling, pretty-mouthed woman with a neat black bob and surrounded by a phalanx of differently sized children. 'What a surprise! Lamp buying too? I'm after one of those lovely green glass-topped desk ones. You know, with a brass setting. It's Derek's birthday tomorrow. But how are you? You look fabulous. Derek's been telling me you're quite the contentious one at the moment. Of course I haven't the faintest idea what he's on about when he tries to explain, but it all sounds very glamorous. So tell me, how are you really?'

Ida winced. Not because she disliked Suky. On the contrary – she was one of the few college girlfriends she kept in regular contact with. She was a good listener and had a wicked sarcastic streak, but she had settled down with a nice design tutor in an outlying region, the children keeping her too busy to make it into central Academia that often, and so they spoke mainly by phone across the lifestyle divide. No, Ida had winced because when Suky asked how she 'really' was, that meant one thing.

'Oh, I'm fine. I've been seeing this M.A.N…'

'Emayen?' Suky looked baffled.

'Em. Ay. En. Man,' whispered Ida, motioning with her head towards the children, who were busy turning as many lights on and off in unison as they could.

'Oh don't worry about preserving their innocence. They're more worldly than any of us. You should hear what comes out of their beastly mouths. But, anyway, tell me. Who's this Em Ay En? A professor, I bet.'

'Not exactly. Not at all, actually. He's quite marginal, let's say.'

'Ooh, a renegade huh? All that radical stuff can be very sexy.'

'Yes, it can be. I think he might be more peripheral than radical though.'

'Ah, I see. I suppose what you really want is someone slap-bang at the centre of it all, don't you? You want a nice connected guy who can draw you back in with the gravitational pull of his own stratospheric success. Can gravity pull you stratospherically?' She tittered, apparently happy to leave the children swarming around the beach bum, who was entertaining them with a long and inappropriate anecdote.

'I see Derek's been filling you in good and proper,' said Ida. 'Maybe you could tell me: is the word out there that I'm cruising for the peripheries? Is a marginal man the last thing I need?'

'Oh, don't listen to me. What do I know about careers? Look at me. But I do know about some things. Do you love him?'

'Oh good Dog, no, nothing like that. It's a bit of fun. A lot of fun, in fact. I don't really believe that a man could make or break me anyway. It's more a reflection of how I'm feeling in myself. If I had the guts, I'd go with any dropout I fancied and make it work. I'd drag the eccentric into the centre through hard work and brilliance, and everyone would say oh how marvellous this dropout is after all, if only we'd realised…'

'Oh dear Ida, you sound a bit tense. Maybe he's not so good for you after all.'

'No, it's not him. It's, oh, it's all getting on top of me I think. I just quit the soap opera this afternoon. And I've got a book deal, but I'm a bit stuck for subject matter. And my public appearances are on a downturn, so my agent's disgruntled. A painter is trying to sue me. I can't seem to nail my rhetoric. And I've got a terrible feeling my best intern is going to move on because of all the crap. They're terribly conscious of one's standing, you know. There's just too much change at the moment, and none of it for the better.'

'I know what you mean. We've just had our windows redone and they've already started leaking. Derek junior is getting bullied at school, and – would you believe it? – Derek senior is getting bullied at work by a teaching assistant. The oven timer's broken, so I just burnt Derek's birthday cake, and I had to cancel our holiday because Tina, the middle one, has mumps and the car failed its MOT.'

'You have a car?'

'Sure. I learnt to drive. It's amazing. Want me to teach you?'

'Wow, yes! How long does it take?'

'Oh it took me months and months, but you'll pick it up in no time. We'll have an intensive crash course. Hah hahahhah. Listen, I'd better round up the pack and get on back home. I've got a party to organise. But don't worry about all that stuff, Idy. It sounds bad when you lump it all together, but it's really just a lot of little things that you are more than capable of sorting out. They just look worse when they're all in a pile.'

'You are very wise, Suky,' said Ida, considerably cheered by the sight of her gathering her brood and shepherding them to the cashier, green lamp in hand. And by the prospect of learning to drive. Now there was an esoteric accomplishment. Maybe she could use the experience as subject matter. 'Heuristics in the Fast Lane' sounded like a good title for a paper.

'Is madam interested in this one?' The assistant must have been asked to hustle her into a purchase by his manager. To be fair, she must have been there for ages.

'Sure, why not,' said Ida, glancing up at the vast chandelier, the price tag of which she happened to have in her hand at that moment. It was a bright crystal and brass mass that radiated from its centre along eighteen arms, each connected to both its neighbours by three draped strings of large lustrous droplets the size of eyeballs and holding innumerable kaleidoscopic representations of the room within it.

'Can you wrap it up and send it to this address,' she said, paying with her press card and tipping the assistant with a wink.

CHAPTER 18

Ida had lied to Chip about the microphone. She had found it before their meeting, when sponging a soup dribble off her lapel, and had crushed it between her thumbnails like a nit. The discovery had been a shock. Who would want to catch her out – and at what? She had been taught about surveillance hardware on her media course, not as an official journalistic methodology, but as a rogue technique to be vigilant for. She had not, however, been taught how to guess which total stranger, without personal motive, could have planted it on her.

Pearl Blake, meanwhile, was muttering to herself as she headed home to bag and post the tapes to the specified PO box. Peanuts Swinglow. Ridiculous. She figured she'd done a good job under the circumstances. For every star there is a corresponding gutter, and now she had something that could drag Ida right down into hers. Clichés clung to Pearl's journalism like salt to a pretzel, and over the years they had leeched into her thoughts too.

Chip, in the meantime, had sent a press release to the news agencies announcing the change of *Academy* script consultant, making it clear that Ida's departure was her own choice, that she was devoting herself to a 'ground-breaking' new comedy project. Ever thirsty for content, programme producers sent their researchers into the archives to dig for historical comedy. They aired fuzzy clips of long-dead philosophers and artists clowning and raconteuring, performing to similarly long-dead audiences with low laughter thresholds. There was debate as to whether a serious thinker debased themselves by also writing or performing comedy, or whether comedy was a legitimate field of research and formal enquiry. It is an opiate, said some. It is the ultimate critical weapon, said others. One columnist claimed to have predicted Ida's move to comedy, given her recent *Panel Beaters* appearance, which they had considered comic genius all along. Another found it difficult to take her seriously as a comedian after such a comical career as a serious critic. On the whole, the response was positive, but Ida still had plenty of convincing to do.

Sue would no doubt be propelled into action, and would ask for a timescale, treatment and audience projections. She would want to start planning a marketing strategy. Ida would have to palm her off with something enigmatic for the time being. Maybe she would eventually write a thesis on comedy or a comic thesis, or an outline for a new TV mockumentary or a comic strip for one of the dailies – who knows? – but she didn't want to commit to a particular format yet. She wasn't even really locked into comedy. In these interdisciplinary times it was perfectly acceptable to drift off-topic. In fact, the widespread opinion was that no project should ever stick to the subject of its proposal, because if it were a known entity from the start, it wasn't new knowledge.

But Ida did need a starting point of some sort. A concept or hypothesis or theme to get her going. She ran through a few possibilities, rejecting them all for either being essentially the same as her last project, or derivative of someone else's. Was there nothing new in the world any more? Well yes, there was: what about this oil stuff? She had certainly never heard of it before. It sounded glamorous, dangerous and exotic – fine qualities for a research topic. But the next problem was how to research something on which there were no existing publications. Unless the GASMANs could provide her with content. She would ask John.

John. She made herself think about him, so she could analyse her thoughts in daylight. Or rather, her emotions, which could be inferred from their influence on her thoughts. Did she really like him in that way, or was she letting him stick around until something better turned up? And, even if this were the case, was it unethical? They were having a good enough time. As long as she found him interesting, it was legitimate to keep sleeping with him, even if she knew he wasn't The One. That was her law of the sheets, anyway. Suky would say something like, 'but if you know there's no future in it, you're wasting his time and yours', as if there were a ticking bomb to be disposed of, by which Ida presumed she meant her fertility. Ida would say she preferred to live in the moment, because the future is a mirage, an extension of the critical appraisal of our ever-changing present. In reality, anything could happen tomorrow to make a nonsense of plans, so the present is all we can really know we have. Suky would recognise the sense in this, but reject it on emotional grounds, saying that if you really love someone you protect their happiness in all directions and dimensions. Ida would appreciate this, as well as the point that one should love oneself in all dimensions too, but this could never override her impulse to make do with what she had for now. She would be left wondering if she was low on a particular suite of hormones, or if her lack of family had made her hard-hearted.

As for John, there was no clear evidence of emotional forward planning there either. She wasn't sure if he even liked her. He could be so spiky. Maybe he was just using her. He had probably never been so close to the knobs and levers of public opinion. It must be alluring. Ida was under no delusion that he was smitten by her herness alone, but since she was interested not only in him, but in his world too, she couldn't very well fault him on that.

*

A small item in a few of the red tops the following day reported a pile-up on one of the main arterial roads, caused by an unidentified substance leaking from a large Foreign vehicle. There had been no fatalities, but an art mover's truck had caught fire and exploded, destroying the oeuvre of an artist whose identity was withheld for legal reasons. A woman had been dragged from a van moments before it too burst into flames.

This lucky survivor, as an alert reader might have guessed, was Pearl Blake, an already tough reporter now hardened beyond appeal by her scrape with death. Determined not to lose Swinglow's hefty fee, she had limped off the road and into the nearest Academic building, where she hired herself a research intern.

'I need you to help me find these art students.' Pearl handed the intern a list of half-remembered first names. 'We need to get whatever tutorial content we can from them, and in particular the title of any book recommended.'

'Good luck with that,' said the intern. 'Not the best memories, art students. And they'll all be in the pub by now. Give them a pint and you pull the plug on the entire day's learning.'

'Well, it's all we've got. And if it comes to it, we'll just have to feed them their lines. The author we're looking for is Alderbank. Got that?'

'Got it.'

'Repeat it back to me.'

'If it comes to it, we'll have to feed them their lines.'

'No, not that bit. Never repeat that bit.'

And so, borrowing some undercover clothes – a pair of outsized men's suit trousers, a yellow feather jacket and a rucksack full of textbooks – Pearl headed for the pubs and clubs to hunt her quarry.

CHAPTER 19

Yeah, yeah, sure, yeah. Yeah, uh-huh. Ok. Yeah, like I said, I really should...'

The tug of disengagement was obvious in Sue's voice, but when Ida entered her office she swung her legs sideways over the arm of the chair and tucked the phone between shoulder and ear, as if settling in for a long chat. 'But, anyway, you must tell me all about it... No, no, it's important...'

When Sue was in a particularly bullish mood, her relationships with clients developed the qualities of dysfunctional parenting. She would assert her authority by any small means available, and the client, if they were willing to play their part, had the option of waiting meekly, sloping off sulkily or lashing out. Ida was more amused than anything else by what she took to be the petty misdirection of low self-esteem. She knew that ultimately Sue needed her clients, and her abuses were tiny revolts against that dependency. There were limits to Ida's maturity and tolerance, though. In their early years of working together, if Sue had tried to belittle her in front of anyone but Linda, Ida would pull on all her capacities and swipe her down like a gnat, countering coded aspersions with blunt aggression. These days Sue confined her spats with Ida to non-lingual acts in the privacy of the office.

Today Ida was feeling fairly sanguine, but not unmischievous. In rebellion against being made to wait, she examined the collection of ornaments on the mantelpiece with wilful clumsiness. They were curious forms on the edge of figuration, like netsuke retrieved after a year in the sea. This one looked like a blurred samovar; that one was caught mid-morph between a foot and a tap. Sue eyed her with restrained concern as she turned them over with exaggeratedly stiff fingers. In the centre of the array was an ornamental plate bearing a painted landscape in its central roundel. It had been a gift from an artist – a satisfied client, now deceased – lauded for her incredible pictorial detail. Ida never tired of looking at it. She bent over to peer into the landscape, her hands tucked between her knees, her backside aimed directly at Sue.

The central scene was a country wedding, with the bride in full meringue and the groom nervously waiting at the rose-decked bower as the ruddy-faced priest looked on, rapturously ignorant of the tensions among the congregation. In the front row the mother of the bride was glowering at her husband in anticipation of the drunk, over-emotional speech he would give; the father of the groom was eyeing up the mother of the bride, thinking how much more charming family get-togethers would be from now on. Three forlorn ex-lovers of the groom were dotted about those gathered here today, each unaware of the other, since the groom learned early on that talking to lovers about exes was not worth the trouble. A middle-aged man was hopelessly in love with the groom and, had his family business not been going under, he would most certainly have found the courage to speak out when the priest asked if anyone present knew of any impediment.

Beyond the formal garden a rural idyll rolled towards a horizon, where it met a white sky troubled by solid-looking clouds. In the middle-distance a farmer and his hands were tending the livestock and fertilising the fields. Outside a barn an exciting new piece of equipment was being readied for its inaugural use the following morning. Two families were availing themselves of fruit in the neighbouring pick-your-own farm, one with two young children grimacing at the sour gooseberries, the other with a sulky teenager trying not to be interested in the sweet, pulpy raspberries that had been his confection of choice just a few years before, and which his parents hoped would coax him out of his hormonal funk.

In the foreground, in front of the wedding party, ran a road that bore left and led to the county courthouse, top right, where a plagiarism trial was in its third week. The defendant wasn't sure that technically she was entirely innocent. She had such a good memory that she may well have unconsciously remembered verbatim something she had read, then written it down much later, not realising its source was outside her own head. The cruelty of cryptomnesia was that she remembered the words, but could not remember remembering them.

Starting out from the left of the foreground, elegant pylons strode the fields, barely noticed by anyone, save the farm hands, who made kinks in the course of their tractors to circumvent the concrete pedestals to which the steel legs tapered. These pylons were leading one another, strung together as they were, to the deep, deep distance, where, right in the centre, a power plant spewed steam into the put-upon sky. A hairline crack was appearing at an imperceptible rate in one of the main cooling pipes. Ida felt she should tell someone, but who? It would be awful to barge in on a wedding for something that could wait a little longer; the farmers and fruit pickers were not likely to have access to the right channels, and the judge would point her towards a pyramid of procedure that would cost her weeks. Even when she was the omnipresent eye, Ida was pinioned by a lack of real alternatives for action.

'Can I just say one thing: hardly the end of the world. Read the papers. People are dying out there. Gotta go. Speak soon.' Sue hung up. 'Sorry about that. A client with intern trouble.'

In fact, she had been talking to her grandmother, or rather her grandmother had been talking at her about her grandfather's habit of re-categorising and re-alphabetising everything.

'He shouted the place down when I filed his socks under "s",' she had said. 'Now he's decided that they're hosiery. Men haven't worn hosiery since the Sans Culottes.'

Sue's grandparents were high-functioning cultural theorists, now retired and with too much intellect on their hands. She had lived with them following her parents' death when she was 13, and they had lavished her with affection and vocational advantages, eager to atone for previous mistakes. Following a traumatic teen love affair with an older artist, Sue's mother, Athena, had passed her final year of school in a thorazine daze, her academic potential slipping quickly away and her televisual looks dulling until all her accomplishments had faded to mediocrity. In a hurry to marry the girl off to some advantage, her parents had sent her to Camp Climbdown, a yearlong residency for below-par offspring of overachieving parents, where she met Buffer Norman, the camp's handsome and practical but petty kleptomaniacal head chef. Sue was conceived pretty much on the spot and was born before the residency year was up. The couple were married and took a brief honeymoon during the thirty-two hour labour, and named the child Sue, after what they imagined Athena's parents would do once they found out she'd run off with the staff instead of bagging herself a professor's son.

Sue adored her happy, doting parents and their itinerant life, moving between residency chef jobs, of which there were hundreds throughout Academia. She helped them run the kitchens and keep the accounts, and they figured that she was learning as much, if not more, than she would in school. And so it was without peers, teachers or relatives, or indeed anyone she'd known for longer than a month, that she found herself bereft at the death of her parents in a kitchen fire. She had been ambling back from an errand when she heard the crackle of the inferno. As she turned the corner and saw the blaze, two columns of flames separated from the main bulk of the fire and stumbled hand-in-hand towards her, zigzagging across the field as if intent on dropping to the ground at her feet. The wind was fanning the flames, whiter, hotter. Clear-headedly, she used the only liquid to hand to douse the human bonfire – a large catering bottle of rapeseed oil. Much later, in therapy paid for by her grandparents, she would painfully recall that the sizzling fumes smelled deliciously savoury.

'Interns can be more trouble than they're worth,' said Ida, moving away from the mantelpiece and taking up position in the chair opposite Sue. 'Did you hear about Spooner's intern? The one who sued for unfair dismissal and was reinstated. Spooner made it so uncomfortable that now the intern's suing for dismissal. Whose intern is it, anyway?'

'I'm not at liberty to release any more information, I'm afraid.'

'Actually, I think you'll find you're obliged to release all the info you have. I have a contractual right to know of any of my agent's other client's business that may affect me. Anyway, I never remember names, so I'll hardly be spreading gossip, just wild inaccuracies. Come on, spill.'

'Listen, Ida, you need to concentrate on your own career before you go poking about in other people's. You may seem to have been let off the hook, but I still need to perform some serious mouth-to-mouth on your diary.'

'Really? I thought I'd – we'd – undone any real damage.'

'In theory, yes, but people are unsure how to pigeonhole you now. They're going to be waiting to see what you do next before commissioning you, so just you be careful. Maybe consult me before you do anything else. But there is one thing that came in last week. I was holding it back, just in case.'

'In case what?'

'Oh, I don't know. Total meltdown.'

'Well, thanks for the boundless confidence. You sure I can handle it now? What is it?'

'Don't get too excited. It's some wall text for a local museum. They need 300 enlightening words on a new commission. Everything you need is in there.' She pushed a slim file across the desk.

'Woopdie-doo.' Ida sighed. 'When's it due?'

'Three days from now.'

'Ok, well, I think I can fit it in. Damn, I really thought I'd averted disaster.'

'It's far from a disaster. You're just going to have to get yourself a new label pretty quick, because no one will be able to hire you if they don't know what you are.'

'Yeah, suppose you're right. Well, the only thing between me and my new project is this wall text now, so I'd better get on with it. Got to keep the bread under the butter, as they used to say.'

'Quite. I've also had a call from the Fine Art Department. It seems you trashed a student's sculpture and they're seeking reparations.'

'What? I did what?'

'One Xavier Xavovnich has lodged a formal complaint with the college, claiming that you broke his sculpture and promised to send compensation in the form of replacement materials but have neglected to do so.'

'Xavier… Xavier. What was the work, do you know?'

'It was a ball of hair, apparently. Although how you broke his hair, I don't know.'

'Oh Dog, that. Yes, I totally forgot. Oh for crying out loud. It's just student work. If it hadn't been made out of his own damn hair, I'd offer to shave my own head. But no, of course, being an artist it has to be all about him. Gorgeous copper curls just won't do.' She shook her hair in annoyance.

'So, what are we going to do about it?'

'Well, maybe… I don't know if this is covered by our contractual arrangements, but, could you, do you think, swing me some sponsorship from Pantene, and get the little shit a year's supply of new improved keratin shampoo, maybe with some of those paraben-free elasticisers or something?'

Sue sighed and made a note on her jotter.

'Fine, and I shall make the appropriate changes to our contract, to now include "pouring oil on litigious art student's hair".'

The phone rang its single, internal ring. Sue snatched it up, grunted and listened.

'Ok, put him through.' She lit up a cigarette and spoke through the butt. 'Hi, Troy. Wassup?' Troy went on for some time, while Sue frowned, stubbed out her cigarette and started emptying her nails of dead skin. She remained silent until he had finished – Ida could hear a long pause

– only then responding: 'Sure, Troy, you could do that. Or you could honour your loyalties to me and not have your wife find out about little Bessie Bosoms in her boudoir every first and third Thursday of the month… Yes I bloody well would. Why would I be bothered about your cosy little wife and her baggy breeding bolthole?… Hey, don't take it so hard. I hear little Bessie doesn't. Hmmm? What's that?… Thank you. I look forward to it.' She hung up and smiled sweetly at Ida, who was agog at such ruthlessness. 'So, Ida, this new project. Are we talking essays? Television? A live tour?' She spoke this last option in a tone so hallowed it hung before her like a vision. Ida struggled to respond.

Before the moment could become critical, a sudden belch and gushing sound echoed loudly in the small lavatory that lay beyond an oak-lined door in the furthest corner of the office. The two women sat up abruptly, looked at one another in alarm, and made towards the door on tiptoe. Sue depressed the handle and tentatively opened the door to reveal, in obscene contrast to the white tiling, a small geyser of glossy black liquid spurting up from the sink plug and dancing provocatively at nose height. Droplets dashed about the walls and floor, and a strange smell billowed and filled the small room. Sue threw her cigarette angrily into the toilet pan, where it gave out a sharp hiss, and then went about stemming the blowout with white towels, calling to the secretary in a voice that penetrated like trumpetry to call up that bloody plumber again.

CHAPTER 20

The future was gaining momentum in Ida's mind and she was keen to set it careering.

'Meet me in the Guts and Garter,' she had instructed John. 'And bring your notebook.'

It was a fashionable pub, despite being over-lit and made up of hard surfaces. Ida arrived first and resorted to reading an art magazine as a shield against the next table, where a shiny-nosed, pigeon-chested young man leaned towards a thoroughly pissed woman dressed in a yellow feather jacket, which he was obviously allergic to. The high frequencies of his sneezes clashed intolerably with the blare of the uplighters and joined the braying of the other clientele in bouncing around the tiling. By the time John turned up, Ida had moved twice as tables had become free, putting a little more distance between her and the sneezing man. John put down his pint a little too heavily on the cold marble, causing another spike of irritation, but complaining wasn't on her agenda this evening, so she told him instead about the incident in Sue's lavatory.

'It was so strange – there was this stuff coming up the plughole. And it just wouldn't stop. Sue turned off all the cocks, as she likes to call them, but there was already gallons of it slopping over into the office. It's the weirdest thing though: the stuff was black and glossy. I was wondering – do you think it might have been oil?'

'Oil?' John laughed. 'Coming up out of your agent's plughole? That would be a miracle to base a religion on.'

Annoyingly, his scorn succeeded in embarrassing her.

'Well, I was just wondering—'

The man sneezed on the other side of the pub, the echoes severing conversations mid-flow.

'Anyway,' said Ida, 'what I wanted to talk to you about was, well, other than to see you, you know, to say hello and all, but anyway, there's some big funding just been released in the Anthropology Department. It's for interdisciplinary research and I want to propose this oil project for it. Will you be my interdisciplinary collaborator?' No beating about the bush there, she was pleased to note.

'I don't know.' John didn't seem particularly thrilled at the thought. 'What did you have in mind? Which of my disciplines do you wish to collaborate with exactly? And what oil project?'

'Oh, I don't mind which discipline. That doesn't matter. You just have to be different from me.'

'Well I can think of one wrinkly-smooth, dangly-firm, shiny-hairy undisciplined bit that's different from you,' he said, curling his wet lips.

'Don't be gross. I'm serious. This is a serious funding pot.'

'Dirty money, eh?'

'Well, yes, you know it is a necessary evil sometimes. I don't want it for myself, obviously. But I do need to pay for train tickets and books, and to treat the interns now and again – that sort of thing. Anyway, what I was thinking was that we could sketch out a proposal for a research trip to a finery.'

'Refinery.'

'Brilliant. And I can write a paper on the, I don't know, the comic bio-geometry of oil? Hmm, have to get anthropology in there somewhere. The comedic anthro-geology of oil? Oh, and it needs some art in it too, of course. How about "The Anthro-Comedical Geology of Oil in Art"? Or "The Anthro-Geology of Oil in Art: A Comedy"?'

'You speak as if knowledge were as malleable as language. That's not quite how it works, you know.' His tone was withering. Had she been flippant? She didn't think so. 'The Academy is ridiculous. It pretends at this fluidity, with all these cross-departmental research units, but actually it's as static as the pile of bricks that it really is.'

'Oh, that's not fair,' said Ida. 'The interdisciplinary thing is a little hampered by campus layout, granted, but the intention is real. I mean, can anyone really say where the dividing line is between literature and philology; and isn't demography encompassed by cultural studies and history? And think of mechanics – that's taught in maths and physics classes. And isn't the history of artistic practice included in art history curricula and practice-based courses too? And don't forget the tunnel that runs between the Social Science and Statistics Departments.'

'That's all very well, but everyone still secretly thinks their departmental axioms are the only valid and true ones. On paper everyone's collaborating and borrowing methodologies and cross-referencing ideas and data, but in practice you're all crewing your own disciplinary boats and woe betide anyone who tries to board with the wrong articles.'

'Ooh, nice. Do you want to develop the piracy metaphor some more?

Are we on a sea of indeterminacy perhaps? With the land of absolutes in another time zone, which we all secretly yearn for, but professors run tight ships, and anyone mentioning empirical truth gets forty lashes?'

John sipped his drink, refusing to join in.

'Oh you're no fun today. But tell me, are you saying "yes please, I would love to overcome some of the limitations of academic orthodoxy and grasp with ardour this fabulous opportunity to collaborate"?'

'What I'm saying is that the Academy makes claims of radical decategorisation with all these new thinklabs and interdepartmental electives, but some of us have been working this way for decades.'

'You know, I just realised, I don't even know what your work is. I mean, I know you're a GASMAN, but that presumably doesn't attract an income, and that you're lodged somewhere in the Academy. But what do you actually do? How do you pay your rent? Although you can't be paying much for… Hey, hang on a minute. John! You haven't even mentioned the chandelier!'

'The chandelier, yes.' He laughed. 'How can I ever thank you? I shall attempt to hang it for your next visit.'

'You mean you didn't hoist it immediately?'

'It's as big as the room. It'd drain the grid if I left it on for any length of time.'

'Let's hang it tonight and take all our clothes off and star bathe,' said Ida, warming to her pint, to John, to the future. 'We can talk about our collaboration. What did you say you do at the Academy? It might be useful.'

'I didn't. It's nothing major, just a small support role.'

'Which department?'

'Anthropology, as it happens.'

'Perfect! Oh, it's all coming together. You bring the anthropology and the oil and I'll bring the art theory and the chandelier. What a party.'

The man sneezed, this time so loudly that some ducked in alarm.

'Molotov,' said John over his shoulder.

'So, seeing as I have your blessing,' said Ida, 'I'd better get cracking on the application, if that's ok with you?'

'Oh why not. I take it you just need my name on the form, right? No actual input.'

'You've got it. The only upcoming outcome is a paper at an interdisciplinary caucus, next week I think, in Edgeboston. But you don't have to do anything for that. You can be my sleeping partner.' She tweaked his nipple through is shirt and leered. 'But seriously, I just have to outline the project, indicate legacy, outline methods for measuring impact – you know the sort of thing. And then at the festival I'll read something poetically vague to mark out our territory before anyone else nicks it.'

'Fine. Hands will be there doing some research next week too. You should go see what he's up to.'

'Hands?'

'Yes, you know. Blonde, youngish. You played footsie with him in the pub.'

'Nope, doesn't ring any bells, but sure, I'd love to hook up with any friends of yours. In the meantime though, I really should get on with some research.'

'Right, yes. You go get on with that.'

'Great.'

'What's your focus?'

'Well – oil, of course.'

'What about it though? Which aspect?'

'Ah, good point. I don't know. What do you think?'

John swivelled a pair of dead eyes towards her and put down his pint.

'What?' she wailed.

'Do you even know why you're getting into this?'

'Sure. For my next project.'

'But I mean really why. What is driving your interest? What is it about oil that attracts or repels you?'

'How can I know that until I've started? I don't know anything about it at all. But that's ok, isn't it? I don't suppose anyone knows what they're going to discover until they're halfway to discovering it.'

'You're really not phased are you? You'll just treat it like any other subject matter and put it through the old academic mills and filters. Well you're in for a shock. It won't bear that sort of treatment. There are too many interdependent moving parts. You can't just analyse barrel prices or extraction techniques or downstream ... fandangos.'

'Fandangos?'

'See – there's lots I don't know about it either. No one knows it in its entirety. I really don't see how you're going to go about it. Or why.' He was not angry, but spoke quietly and emphatically, which was far more disturbing. Ida couldn't decipher his mood this evening. 'The oil industry is very large and complicated,' he concluded, retreating into a hard, internal place.

'Is it as complicated as love?' She felt a thrill at testing the word out on him.

'Oh no,' he said, smiling strangely. 'It's simpler than that.'

'Well, unless you have a better idea, maybe I should do a recce, see what's out there and then we could have a dialogue or something. Does the GASMAN have a library I could use?'

'There's an archive, which has documents and textbooks. Not so many theories or narrativised histories. We don't much go in for that. We like our data raw.'

'Sounds just the ticket. Can someone like me use it?' She salivated at the prospect of primary research. It might be a slog, and there would be risks that came with frontier analysis and theorising, but she could be sure she would be the first to break this new ground.

'We'll see,' said John, in the tone of voice a mother uses when asked too directly for something not entirely improbable. While Ida didn't recognise this as a parental device for amplifying gratitude over time, she nonetheless sensed it to be a display of spurious power that would ultimately dissipate.

'Thanks John, you rock.' She kissed his fine jaw.

He gave out a motherly sigh of surrender and added, 'You'll have to pose as a GASMAN though. We'll have to come up with an identity. What's your favourite mountain?'

'My favourite mountain? It has to be the butter mountain.'

'I don't think that'll cut it with the archivists. You strike me more of a second summitter. How about… Dykh-Tau? Yes, I think that suits you fine.'

'Hang on, are you saying the gasmen have little gang member names? After mountains? Not even gasses? Ha! I can't tell if that's really cute or totally bombastic. What's your *nom de terreur*?'

'Sidley.'

'Sidley? Where's that? Austrania?'

'Antarctica, actually.'

'That's about right, you hostile ice tundra, you. Can I get your large emptiness another pint? On the rocks?'

*

'Hello, Ida,' said a voice behind her as she waited before the taps and backlit bottles. In the mirror she saw Autumn Padget, a copy editor whose efficient rationalism and clipped way of speaking made writers itch. 'I'm looking forward to the talk. Will there be any comedic pyrotechnics today?'

'Two pints of Collingwood please. Pyrotechnics?' asked Ida, splitting her attention between barman and Autumn, skewed slightly in favour of the former.

'Yes. I was going to attend anyway, but if you have a jape planned, all the better, *n'est pas*?'

'Attend? Where?'

'Hopper's.'

'Hopper's? Why, what's on?'

'Oh dear, you've forgotten, haven't you. You're giving a talk there in about, let me see, eight minutes.'

'Oh shit!' A wave of stomach acid refluxed up Ida's oesophagus. 'What's it on?'

'Aphids throughout art history, apparently,' said Autumn, reading from a listings magazine.

'Shit.' Ida rushed over to John, whacked his drink down on the table, took a thorough pull on hers, yelled 'Gotta go. Gallery talk. Forgot. Put that chandelier on ice. I'll make it up to you', then fled the pub.

CHAPTER 21

Ida made it up to John with a torch-lit dinner round hers, dressed in nothing but a string of pearls only half a shade paler than her breasts, which were in turn half a shade paler than the chicken they ate before devouring one another. They had entered that phase of a new relationship where a rolling programme of libidinous anticipation and fulfilment keeps both parties frisky, good-humoured and short-term in outlook. Even when learning seriously about the other's bad habits and other weaknesses, they were able to tease without causing offence. Caught up in the moment or the about-to-be, the past had ceased to have consequence, and the future proper was not as interesting as what was just about to happen.

For their next date he was taking her to an intriguing installation in a district she had never visited before. The poplars lining the remote lane were trying to remind her of an impressionist painting she'd once seen hanging somewhere that smelled of… disappointment, was it? Or disinfectant? In the painting the trees had fragmented the sunlight and shivered the sky, but here they absorbed the wind and transposed it into a pacifying rustle. The intimation was not so much that the world was vibrant with activity, but that it was coasting gently. Ida and John were holding hands, which she would only have allowed in the countryside. Here there was no elsewhere, no history, no deadlines, no peers, no pressures, no need to speak. Her thoughts were idling along at their leisure, feeling no compulsion to form themselves into anything particularly communicable.

'What,' said John, 'would you say was the main function of the art critic?'

She withdrew her hand from his and looked at him as if he had just shat on her forehead.

'What?'

'I was just wondering. Is it describing or finding fault? What's the critic's remit? Recording for posterity or improving the future?'

'What you have missed out,' said Ida tartly, 'in your delicate analysis of the critical process, is thinking. The critic looks at an artwork then thinks about it, then writes down her thinkings and then thinks some more. Thinking is the essential verb here, not parroting or nit-picking.'

The wind dropped, holding its breath at her annoyance. A herd of cows were slowly and silently moving towards them from behind, their oblong flanks bearing maps of lost islands in extinct oceans.

'But traditionally critics were judges, weren't they?'

Ida sighed, and clambered fully out of her languid mood.

'Yes, in the bad old days we used to legislate. Critics used to say this week everyone should make this sort of art, today this medium is passé. That sort of thing.'

'But how did they decide? Calculation? Divination? Whim?'

'That was when they felt they could draw on their specialist knowledge, deep conviction, shared ideology…'

'So if two critics disagreed, one of them must have been mistaken?'

'Quite, which is how it all fell to pieces eventually. Judgment was judged to be impossibly illiberal. Now, if we want to state an opinion, it must be posed as a provocation.'

'To provoke what?'

'Discussion, I suppose. You can take a stand in a discussion, but you always have to climb down from it afterwards, which is good, because it means you can take a different stand in another discussion another time.'

John laughed, grasped her hand and swung it as they walked.

'So, just to check: you pronounce something according to some set of standards or other, and then later, when this proves unworkable, undesirable or boring, you enlist some other set of standards?'

'You got it! Capriciousness is the critic's proven methodology.'

'Jeez. Poor artists. Is there really no broad code of conduct or manifesto or…?'

'Oh Dog, no. It's all to do with specificities. You can't be reductive or generalising. Because it's so changeable, you need everything to be small and, well, not inconsequential, but packeted – molecular, if you like. You need to be able to criticise something very, very particularly so that when a similar situation occurs you can change your position and say that it's because the context is different this time, even if it's just very, very slightly different.'

'How very female.'

Ida dropped his hand as if it burned and stopped halfway up a hillock.

'Female? Not as female as this.'

She lifted her jumper and t-shirt, making a tent for her head and revealing her bare breasts, which she shuddered at him in a war dance or a hex. She gyrated and growled, her soft curves battering the wind, which had picked up to an enthusiastic caress. She wondered what John was doing. It sounded like he was just standing there looking. He had better be looking. Now it sounded like he had circled her and was running towards her from behind. Somehow he was very close but still running. She felt a hefty shove in the small of her back, which clacked her jaws together painfully and threw her forwards, her arms still entangled in her clothing and unable to break her fall. She heard John exclaim, in front of her now, at some distance. He was shouting and moving about inefficiently. She struggled back into her clothing and found herself sitting in a country pancake, which had released its sharp odour on the cracking of its elephantine skin. John was running after a cow, quite some distance off, his arms outstretched and its huge udder swinging between stiff legs.

*

The installation was the most impenetrable thing Ida had ever encountered. The spat with the tit-envying ungulate may have shaken her, as confrontations with new consciousnesses can, but she still had her wits about her. She had approached the installation as she would any artwork, consulting her databanks for references and comparators, but this – she couldn't think of anything else like it.

It had been dusk by the time they reached the installation. An hour or so had been eaten up by the search for a stream in which to wash off various mucks. Following Ida's cowpat encounter, John had fallen into a stagnant, lichen-choked ditch while trying out a death slide made from a great long piece of hawser slung between two trees with an old tyre for a leg up, the rope frail with age, the boys who had made it already grown into thugs and blowing the heads off trespassers. Eventually they found a dear little stream frothing with detergent as it skipped through the moss-mattressed floor of a copse. Most convenient, Ida had marvelled, having soapy water ready mixed and on tap. They took advantage of the solitude and grabbed an *al frisky* tumble, as John called it, although Ida's heart hadn't entirely been in it. A breach of trust had occurred, she thought, by him letting a cow humiliate her.

As they rounded the copse, the view across a shallow valley revealed itself. It took a few moments for the cuboid of pipes, railings, tanks and chimneys to resolve into architecture. At first it appeared to Ida as a textural intrusion in the landscape, then as a wound exposing inner viscera, then an eruption from the ground. With the timing of a well-planned theatrical experience, the lights were turned on against the gloaming, and the installation became a city of the future. Uplighters and floods threw the tubing and recesses into heightened chiaroscuro. Men in orange boiler suits and white hardhats could be seen moving along walkways beneath pipes that were as wide as the men were tall.

'This is amazing,' said Ida. 'Whose is it? And who commissioned it? Why haven't I heard of this before? And where is everyone else? You'd think there'd be coaches of people coming to look. Is it open yet?'

'It's not public knowledge yet,' said John. 'We shouldn't really be here, so we'll have to hang back a bit. Make sure they don't see us.'

This was fabulously exciting. Ida decided she would write a feature and steal a march on the official press launch.

'These people in jumpsuits, they're still building it by the looks of it. What will the outer covering be, do you know? Mirrors? That would make sense. Sculpturally, I mean.'

'Oh, no, that's it. It's finished. Those people are just doing maintenance. It's been up and running a while now.'

'Really? It needs that much maintenance?'

'Sure. There's a lot that can go wrong. A really bad malfunction could end in an explosion, of course.'

'Oh that's good. How do they simulate that?'

John gave her a look that she couldn't interpret.

'No, a real one. With deaths and everything.'

'No!' He was probably exaggerating, but even so, she couldn't think of any precedents. There were artworks that were supposed to autodestruct as part of their intended lifespan, and there had been accidents involving flammable materials, but nothing like this. Nothing where the curators or gallery assistants or whatever they were had to service the piece to keep it intact and to save their own skin. That was one extreme installation. No wonder it was so far from the central gallery district. It must be an independent curator working beyond the usual constraints. Hey, she thought, it's an over-demanding artwork! Just like she had predicted in *Panel Beaters*. She had invented the wild idea as a joke, and here it was for real. She didn't suppose it could have sprouted up in the last few weeks – she couldn't have actually inspired it. It must just be that she was spot on. Ok, only in a one-off case. Her predicted epidemic was yet to pass.

But still, this was vindication.

'Do you know anyone here that I can speak to? I'd really like to hear more about it.'

'No,' said John. 'Like I said, it's really hush-hush. I only know because I overheard someone I shouldn't have. I thought it would get your juices flowing, but I can't tell you any more than that.'

He was turning away now, making off over the tussocked ground towards the train halt. Ida would have liked to hang around longer. When it came to performance and installation, she was trained to endure hours. Days if necessary. Still, what little she had seen she could write paragraphs on once she got going. She tore herself away, looking back now and then to watch the installation glimmer against the electric blue of the evening sky, but never once letting out of her sight the cows that were pretending to graze in the middle distance.

CHAPTER 22

Mind-mapping was a means of navigating alien terrain that Ida used frequently, and not just for academic purposes. She found that separating a situation into its linguistic elements and then putting them back together with a tangle of lines, no matter how messy, was always going to be neater than the unmediated reality. And if you can visualise it, you can control it, her first-year tutor had told her.

The phone was off, the interns were off and she was on the sofa, her new blue drafting notebook opened to the first double page spread. She had written the word 'oil' in the middle, the 'i' only just escaping the crease. The second word, slap in the centre of the left-hand page, was 'power'. Oil and power. That was a punchy start. Two antennae sprouting out of the top of the rectangle bounding 'power' ended in the word 'status' and the interrogative 'electrical?' 'Power' was mirrored by another grand abstraction on the opposite page: 'economics'. It seemed to be important to break symmetry, and so 'economics' had grown six stalks, which Ida's pen dithered over a while, before committing 'money' to one. The rest would have to be filled in later, once she was sure of the scope of this aspect of the subject. It was looking good so far. Two meaty chunks. What else? How about oil paint? She did need a disciplinary crossover. She wrote 'paint' to the bottom-right of 'economics'. The ready supply of terms was running low now. She thought back to the GASMAN meeting. Unfortunately, this was before she had become properly interested in the subject, so she had no notes. But there was that man who fell down. She wrote 'gravity' above power, and jotted 'gasman' near to it too. Should balance that up with 'Academic Petroleum' on the other side then. Oh, and 'finery'. She lay back, along the sofa, and held her notebook at arm's length to better appreciate the aesthetic qualities of her work. It looked pretty busy she thought, and could offer some guidance when in the GASMAN archive. As a route map to enlightenment it was an acceptable start, if a little generalising.

Since leaving the Academy she had come to appreciate the benefits of not possessing specialist knowledge. Unlike scholars confined to such corridors of thought as metallurgy of the Prussian Empire or the syntax of eighteenth-century bylaws, she roved wherever she liked, picking up relevant information as she went instead of carrying knowledge about in her head. She could not even count language as her specialist subject. That was a means, not an end. And no one could claim art as their specialism, because it is as various and amorphous as mud. No, as shit. It is made up of unknowable ingredients that can never be studied in their entirety. Artists, she thought, are like goats that ingest whatever wins their interest. In their many stomachs they examine, interrogate, problematise, subvert and pastiche their subject matter before excreting it as beautiful, shocking, confusing, delightful or expensive nuggets, dollops and smears. The critic is the veterinary-cum-archaeologist who must infer from this output the diet of the ruminant and the nature of its constitution, pronouncing it in fine fettle or diagnosing problems and doling out critical linctus.

Ida had, for two decades now, picked up these turds and, for a week or two at a time, tucked them into the pocket of her mind, turning them over and examining them before relating her findings. What sort of a list would it be, she wondered, if she wrote out all the surrogate subject matter she had ever written about? All the ingredients that had gone into this shit? She opened the drawers of her filing cabinets one by one and worked her way through the morass of essays and features, starting with her recent piece 'The Art of High Maintenance'.

A couple of hours later the list was complete. She could hardly believe she had covered so much ground. It was scandalous, this list, in its bravura, flitting from health and safety to alchemy to bioengineering to political representation to comic books to failure to avatars to artist-run spaces to place to collaboration to waiting to synthetic reality to surveillance to hands to humour to women to the grotesque to art on television to DNA to collage to obsolete technology to sex and lace to government secrets to the appropriation of Modernist forms to statistics to public spaces to democratisation to the aesthetics of politics and the politics of aesthetics to animals to cabinets of curiosity to art education to medieval utopias to postmen to tables to road-movies to slapstick to bodies to special needs to oddness to hens to nineteenth-century spiritualism to intimacy to slowness to stripes to Tyrian purple to multiple chemical sensitivity to structuralist film to electroplating to futile labour to text in art to sex workers to sport to anthropomorphism to objecthood to urbanism to Antarctica to labyrinths to self-reflexivity to gestalt psychology to parades to authenticity and spectacularisation to paint to gaps to natural history to religion to radiation to criticism to osmosis to generalists to cars to protests to themes to doodling to The Prisoner's Dilemma to categorisation to Sienese painting to gravity to street furniture to work to the uncanny to noses to putting a bag on a head to scenery to ovals to technology to penguins to walking and thinking to parks to textiles to bawdiness to lonely teenagers to the sublime to geometry to cubes (more specifically) to clichés to travel to mistakes to associative thought processes to allegorical and literal change to utopian architecture to narrative imagery to portraiture to absence to specialists to eventhood to Surrealism to chance to military oppression to games to reviewing to historical reconstructions to jesters to collecting to speculation to blushing to magenta to bears to rain to tomatoes…

No one could truly understand all this. The last chronicled polymath died in 1863. Luckily, the average reader was more interested in the artist and the artwork, and required only glancing commentary on whatever the artist's own subject matter might be. It was perfectly acceptable for a critic to be abysmally broad brushed, for her to include whichever arbitrary factoids fitted her predetermined argument, or to present information riddled with assumptions and simplifications. And it was fine to be at least thirty years out of step with current specialist research. But Ida's standards were higher than this. She wished to be judged on a par with academics, even though she knew this to be impossible, because where they had entire careers in which to understand something, she usually had a fortnight.

No wonder she was a chronic sufferer of Imposter Syndrome. The condition was rife in all departments at all levels of the Academy. A recent study had found that ninety-three per cent of academics suffered from Imposter Syndrome to a degree that was partially or wholly debilitating, in bouts lasting from six months to life. Human resources managers were campaigning to bring it out into the open, since in their experience it was the uppermost cause of absenteeism, but no members of faculty would come out in public support. People were comfortable discussing the Dunning-Kruger effect – a cognitive bias whereby the individual is unable to gauge their own incompetence and so suffers illusions of superiority – but Imposter Syndrome was never mentioned. Where the Dunning-Kruger effect creates discordance between attitude and action that is apparent to observers, Imposter

Syndrome involves an internal battle that is to the untrained eye all but invisible. The sufferer believes herself to be an ill-equipped, incapable interloper, while everyone else is presumed to be perfectly at ease with all that is expected of them, and she waits in still and quiet terror for the appalling and inevitable public revelation. The only cure, it was said, lay in the universal declaration of suffering. If everyone admitted to their insecurities, the conditions on which the syndrome thrived would be eradicated entirely. But since multilateral honesty was never going to happen, Ida inoculated herself with the assertion that the talent of the art critic lay not in deep knowledge and wide understanding, but in creating connections between apparently dissociative ideas, and the more ingenious the stretch the better. The critic who could find a witty or deviant link between tomatoes, Sienese painting and multiple chemical sensitivity was at the top of her game.

'You need to be able to weave logical associative links between any two, three, four or twenty-nine ideas,' Linda would say. 'You should ignore the more direct routes, and take the most scenic or daring or hitherto unknown.' She would regularly bowl out challenges without warning. 'Ok, here's one: how about a sewing machine, an operating table and an umbrella?'

'That's a ridiculous array of objects. There's no link between them whatsoever.' A bout of cystitis had taken the edge off all fun for Ida that day. 'And why the insistence on lateral association anyway?' She had pointed out that finding logical links where they don't really exist was the behaviour of the paranoid.

Ida scanned several of her texts, trying to identify where she had fudged a link, but it was surprising how authoritative it all sounded. Before long she found herself admiring her younger selves for their ballsy improvisation, pasting over the cracks with some rhetoric here, screwing in a few popular references as hooks there and, overall, producing perfectly respectable copy. She shouldn't worry so much, she scolded herself. Concealing her ignorance was another of her talents. And anyway, the few who could correct her when it came to oil were, as far as she could tell, friendly, Foreign or entirely without media contacts.

CHAPTER 23

According to folktales, oil is the blubber of the Earth, which is but a vast animal; or it is the urine of whales, conveyed from the North Pole in subterranean channels. A Methodist revivalist once claimed that it was in storage underground until required by Dog to destroy the world at Armageddon; Episcopalian proctors warned that it should only be used to light the fires of Hell, and most certainly not for profane purposes. A poetic scientist once described it as buried sunshine, comprising the unexpended solar power housed in plants and marine organisms that died some 150 to 350 million years ago. More recently, a sect of ardent procreators had maintained that oil was the liquefied souls of dead ancestors, and that resources would increase with world population, so to keep the home fires burning it followed that we must go forth and multiply.

Ida thought these myths too simplistic, and indeed, according to John, in a motorised, moisturised, plasticised age, oil does overspill any description. It oozes and gushes everywhere, and clings to everything. In fact, he said, oil is not a substance, but a vast and complex system that absorbs things, places, people and ideas. Ida thought he was being hyperbolic, trying to intimidate her. Well, she was a trained researcher, with rigour and objectivity on her side. What's more, as a critic and media personality, she also had subjectivity and flair to draw on too. She was confident about finding an angle she could manage, but she conceded it might be prudent to seek council on the most appropriate analytical methodology to start with. If the data was interpreted properly, whatever she constructed from it would at least be solid.

'Ok, now, here's a question: would my first step towards understanding a very large and complicated thing be a long one backwards, so that I could eye it from a distance and take it all in at once, or would it be forward, for a super-close-up view to see how it's put together?'

She was standing with Jørn and Fredegund at a private view, relaxed in one another's company, while around them others were flexing their professionalism.

‘But bunny-hunch, you’d need bloody long legs if it’s really big and complicated,’ said Fredegund, shooting out her white stick in illustration, knocking a wine glass out of a woman’s hand. ‘You’d need to climb to higher ground too, or build some sort of umpire’s chair.’

‘But,’ said Jørn, his stringy frame stooping above them, ‘that only gives you one perspective, unless the chair has wheels.’

‘Ah yes, I forgot to mention that, toots. Thank you, yes, it does have wheels, and interns on hand to circle you around the thing,’ said Fredegund. ‘And the larger the thing is, of course, the taller the chair would need to be.’

‘And do you require a more complex chair to view more complex objects?’ asked Jørn.

‘Oh, you’re just being silly now.’

‘But isn’t it a touch conservative?’ said Ida. ‘It’s a Dog’s eye view you’ve got there, which may seem authoritative, but you’d miss everything on the underside.’

‘Yes, of course,’ said Fredegund. ‘You don’t want to play Dog? How queer the younger generations are. Ok then, how about, since it’s a large object … ah, but how large? Does it approach planetary proportions?’

‘Yes, actually. Planetary proportions is exactly what it approaches.’

‘Well in that case, it’s probably better to use a satellite, so that your viewpoint orbits the whole of the thing, whatever it is. What is it by the way?’

‘Oh, it’s just an abstraction so far,’ said Ida.

‘Right, well in that case, yes, a satellite would be your best bet, and then, once you’ve gained an overview, you can gradually step closer in to ratchet up the resolution and fill in your initial sketch with increasing levels of detail. Like doing your make up, my little cutie-patootie.’

‘I disagree with your methods,’ said Jørn, his shoulders back and chin inclined in defiance. ‘Because firstly, a satellite is beyond the means of ordinary academics.’ Fredegund started to protest that this was all hypothetical, that it was unfair to suddenly turn fiscally sensible.

‘And don’t raise your voice at me either,’ she added.

‘I’m not shouting at all,’ he replied.

‘I never said you were. But your mouth is definitely higher than it was. Lower it or I shall take enormous offence.’

‘And anyway,’ he continued, ‘say you did obtain an overview somehow, you’ve then got another layer of questions to contend with. You now have to fill in the detail within this established perimeter and across fixed contours, but is it best to work left to right, or radially from the centre?'

'At a guess,' said Ida, 'from the centre would be best.' She was thinking of a portraitist working outwards from the philtrum.

'Aha, you see, this is where it becomes impossible, because the so-called centre can only be an arbitrary decision on your part.'

'My part? Why me,' wailed Ida. 'I'm not in charge. This bit's her analogy.'

Fredegund, refusing to take back the buck, shrugged, pursed her lips and snatched up another bottle of beer from a passing tray.

'Or on the part of whomever is observing,' Jørn acquiesced. 'The centre of a large complex thing in space is a matter of relative position. To minimise any such questionable impositions, I'd suggest getting all the details down first, and allowing overall structure to emerge from internal relations between details.'

'Ah, so the first step should be forward, for a super-close-up view then?' said Ida.

'Yes. You'd then need to inch over the surface of the large, complicated thing, measuring as you go. Take an intern or two with you to note down local contours, colours, gradients, textures, temperatures, apertures or whatever other empirical information you can gather. Then, when you get home, parse this data and assemble an understanding of the whole.'

Ida was impressed by the Jørn's pragmatic approach. Manfred, of course, would lead the expedition on the organisational front.

'What a bloody-minded, long-winded way of going about it, you bloody beard-splitter,' blew in Fredegund hotly. 'Just think how long it would take and how many sets of instruments you'd need to lug about. And you would need to exert considerable pressure to consolidate all this data into a comprehensible whole.'

'Well…' Jørn looked uncomfortable, unused, being an editor, to direct attacks.

'And you're going to get a whole load of different local knowledges producing all sorts of discrepancies. You're going to end up with a whole load of crumbling contradictions.'

'Yes,' said Ida. 'Conventional understanding should appear solid until it's really thumped.'

'Ok,' Jørn conceded. 'I can see your point. But – and this is a really big but – I do think your way, Fredegund, is too ocular and imperious by far. There must be an acceptable third method. Things seldom come in pairs in reality.'

'I don't know about imperious,' said Fredegund, 'but I see what you mean about ocular. It is one of my few but deadly weaknesses, prioritising the ocular. So, how about hands-on sampling here and there from what is easily within reach, moving on, then sampling some more, moving on again, sampling again, moving, sampling, moving and so on?'

Jørn nodded his assent.

'And then from this smattering of gleanings an approximation of a whole can be extrapolated, presumably?' said Ida.

'Yes,' said Jørn. 'I suppose it is, scientifically speaking, the least satisfactory approach, but it's the most achievable.'

'And the most common, no?' said Ida. 'But as we know, if the large, complicated thing under examination is something people are touchy about, there can be hell to pay. You hear so many allegations of misrepresentation in the Academy, and I'm sure a lot of it's down to this research methodology.'

'Well bugger me sideways and call me Cecelia,' crowed Fredegund, 'if we haven't just hit upon the dissertation of the evening, dear heart. "Thick as Two Short Shits: The Politics of the Mis-described"!'

'Yahoo!' whooped Ida, causing a momentary lull in the gallery that she was a little too sotted to care about. 'Well done Fredegund. Nice footwork. Please, do tell us *all* about it.'

'No, please, spare us,' groaned Jørn.

Fredegund smoothed down her flyaway hair and arranged her body into the perfect stoop for an ageing professor who has given up learning decades ago, and cleared her throat as if it had turned rusty from brandy.

'Today, boys and girls, I am going to discuss the impracticalities of liberalism in the context of specialist knowledge of a very large complex, multi-part thing. As you know, any copper-bottomed liberal scholar would always caveat their own knowledge as entirely contingent, and quite likely draw on a whole host of other scholars' theories, mixing them all up into a relative soup of semi-understandings. When liberal scholarship is at its most inclusive, the multitude of frictions cancels one another out through polite tolerance, forming a paste of semi-incoherence. Blah blah blah, etcetera, etcetera. But when it comes to knowledge of a large complex, multi-part thing, we cannot ignore the fact that the liberal muddle of representations, descriptions and interpretations is as least as complex as the thing itself, if not more so. Blah blah blah blah, etcetera. A hegemonic scholar, on the other hand, would insist that his is the only viable account, and that any other representation must be shot and buried. But while this compression into rigid singularity is obviously wieldier, brute elegance is generally not the main aim of modern politics. And so on, etcetera, blah-blah. No, the solidarity of blah is when blah blah blah and we all come to acknowledge that blah blah and blah blah, moreover blah blah blah blah … '

Ida and Jørn merrily joined in, contributing a 'blah, blah, blah' and a 'blah-blah' to phasing rhythms that began quietly then ballooned to fill their corner before spreading through the gallery.

'Blah blah blah,' said a woman in a little black dress and large jewels to her sweaty, bald companion.

'Blah,' he bleated back.

A tiny man in a tiny suit delivered a 'blah-blah-blah-blah' like machine-gun fire into the crowd. Further blahs and blah-blahs spread until the entire private view was blah-blahing at the top of its voice, everyone mad with relief at being unburdened of content.

*

In the GASMAN Archive Reading Room a raft of men were typing with two fingers. They enjoyed the full compliment of fingers and thumbs, but preferred to jab the keys accusingly. You: O. You: F. You: F. You: full stop. Their qwerty clamour agitated the air into a storm around them. Ida (or Dykh-Tau, as she was calling herself today) pushed on through with her trolley of books to the furthest, most tranquil corner.

Before commencing her important research, she needed to smarten up the lilac fleece she had borrowed from John. Its pilling was extreme and gave her a shaggy silhouette she felt she didn't deserve. A full quarter of an hour later a nearby cough broke the spell that picking at pilled fabric, split ends or flaky skin always cast over her. She stuffed the large ball of fluff into a utility pocket at her thigh and opened the first page of the first book.

She still had many questions about methodology. For instance, if she was to start at an intimate scale and work her way up incrementally to the global, what would those increments of knowledge be? Should she start with what is known at present, or amass knowledge in the order that it was discovered? And was it discovered, or was it devised or invented? Or inferred? Or guessed and then verified? Had she prior knowledge of the oil industry, she would have known how to contextualise her questions, asking whether to start with organic chemistry or the moment the first prospector struck oil or with the current price of a barrel of oil. Being a humanist by training, though, she was more inclined to take as her embarkation point a critical analysis of the poetics of the sociological impact of the history of post-colonial oil politics. But then again, maybe it would be more *au courant* to push off from the material stuff itself and follow its seeping involvements outwards, backwards, inwards and forwards, through societies, economies, cultures, ecosystems and consciousnesses all at once… But actually, she had always found that the best method of all was to close her eyes and jump. Because if everything was as interconnected as John made out, then it wouldn't matter where she started – she'd get to the proper beginning at some point.

*

Ida encountered the first fork in the paper trail in the second footnote in the preface to the first book. She was reading about how Boulton and Watt's steam engine, patented in 1775 and employing a separate condenser, held off further improvement until 1800, temporarily suppressing development of engine efficiency. Boulton and Watt's precursor, Newcomen's atmospheric-pressure steam engine, had converted less than one per cent of the energy it consumed into useful motion, but nineteenth-century fuel developments – involving a move from charcoal to coke to heat the smelters that produced the iron from which the mining machinery was made, and the convergence of iron, steam engines and coal usage with the invention of the train and the expansion of the railway network, primarily for further coal transportation – enabled an exponential increase in power generation efficiency. The capacity for generating electricity in Academia some 150 years previously was 1.56 million horsepower and rose to 22 million 80 years later and to 100 million 30 years after that.

Ida paused to enjoy the realisation that, while carbon-based power had now left human and animal muscle power way behind, it was still expressed as horsepower. But this was not what waylaid her. The footnote alluded to bearings as a means of increasing efficiency. But what were bearings? How did they increase efficiency? Were they still available? She sifted through the 'b's in the library catalogue and selected *Bearings: hidden workhorses of the mechanical age*. The book's frontispiece was a reproduction of a sketch made by Leonardo da Vinci of a set of roller disc bearings based on an idea mooted by an anonymous contemporaneous German engineer and eventually fitted onto a coach in 1734 by one Jacob Rowe. In 1772, the commentary began, a handful of years before the Boulton and Watt engine patent, C Varlo, a resident of York, fitted bearings with the full complement of cast iron balls to his carriage with considerable success, and then, two years later, Welsh iron founder Philip Vaughan registered, in patent no. 2006, a pair of full-complement ball bearings for each wheel of a carriage, with grooves in the axle and the inner ball races. But it was not for another 70 years, with patent no. 2855, that these balls would be kept in a separate cage rather than being fed into the bearing through a hole that was then stoppered up.

Flipping through a fistful of pages to speed up the narrative, Ida found that by 1898 one company alone was manufacturing 20 million steel balls a month. This exponential rise in demand was due to the popularisation of the bicycle in pre-Academic Europe. The evolutionary leapfrog from French velocipede to British bicycle occurred when a pioneering English cyclist won the first ever Paris-Rouen road race, beating his nearest competitor by a full 45 minutes and averaging 7.5 miles per hour over the 76-mile course. This, added to the advent of the Franco-Prussian war, prompted a boom in bicycle production to the north of La Manche where, by 1893, there were an estimated half a million cyclists, and twice that by the turn of the century. A frenzy of innovation culminated in the widespread adoption of the cup-and-cone full-complement bearing by 1897, although it wasn't until the refinement of steel production that real precision in the manufacture of these ball bearings would make unthought-of levels of efficiency possible. In 1890 balls could be made consistently to within 0.025mm, and half this by 1892; high-precision balls of the last decade of the last century were made with a radial run-out to less than one micrometre (0.001mm). Ida couldn't bring herself to read the final chapter to find out the current limit of accuracy – it was bound to be chillingly inhuman.

She could recognise in these early volumes on engineering the base odour of utility and economic imperative, yet the tang of electrification was missing. The spiked musk of sweat obliterated all in this shunting, logical world, where material strength and mechanical ingenuity were the sole weapons against the terrible magnetism of the earth. But she put this savoury machismo to one side with regret, recognising that the cart had somehow arranged itself before the horse (or, as she would be able to joke later, the tanker had overtaken the plankton). It was probably prudent to find out the truth about how oil came to be in the first place.

Oil, according to the GASMAN archive, is not made from whales or dead souls or horses, but from dead sea creatures. One litre of petrol is, in compressed form, the equivalent of 25 tonnes of ancient marine life; or, to turn it about, if all the plant and animal life produced over the entire planet for 400 years were compressed into fossil fuel, it would last Academia one year. But with global reserves built up over millennia, the whole planet could power up for generations to come. If this was the case, Ida wondered why there had been such a split in the Foreign and the Academic stories of energy production and supply. Academia must have rejected oil long ago, but why? And how many people knew about this? A block-busting thesis was becoming a real possibility. She read on.

Foreigners' discovery of fossil fuel had freed them from a troublesome reliance on woodland. If such a dependence on wood had continued, by the 1820s it would have devoured a forest the size of Academia, double that by the 1840s and double that again by the 1890s. Before long, the largely uncharted expanse of Foreign would have been scraped back to bare rock. The switch to fossil fuel placed pressure not so much on Foreign land – where the extraction of energy took place – as on the land where raw materials like cotton grew to supply the new industrial processes, and where sugar, tea and coffee grew to sustain the burgeoning workforce. Colonial control of large sunny regions was the most obvious way to guarantee sustained production of these phototropic crops. And so, if you think about it, oil is buried sunshine after all: it is a stand-in for outmoded photosynthesis-based fuels, and has suppressed many a personal freedom in these hotter climes.

Ida had never before considered the potency of inanimate stuff to make things happen, having always laid the blame with people. She consulted *What's What*, an almanac that had been included in several bibliographies and which traced the material basis of every historical event back to its inanimate primal causes. It was researched, collated and published by a group calling themselves Carbon Watch, which might have seemed a bit biased to anyone believing the inorganic to be equally culpable. Ida, however, was not alive to the distinction, but was incredulous nonetheless to read that almost every coup and revolution in pre-Academic times was fuelled by oil: 'The Great Game' as the Anglo-Russian political skirmishes in central Asia during the late nineteenth century were known; the Russian Revolution of 1905; the Constitutional Revolution of 1905-11 in Persia; in 1906 the Bamabatha rebellion in Natal and the Dinshaway incident in Egypt; the Mexican Revolution of 1910-20; the First World War; the popular uprising of Egypt in 1919; the Great Syrian Revolt of 1925-7... And as decades passed, the dates of incidents fell closer together. As reliance on oil intensified, so did its lubrication of global events. The type in *What's What* became smaller and smaller, until the very last page was, to the naked eye, solid black.

More immediately disconcerting for the copper-bottomed humanist, however, was the lack of personal narratives in this version of history. Can't an oil company be broken down, thought Ida, not only into executive, management and workforce, but into further subdivisions, factions and splinter groups of people? And can't these in turn be crumbled into smaller and smaller aggregates, and eventually into individuals? But *What's What* ignored entirely the circumstances and motivations of the souls involved. When reading that it was the second general strike by oil workers in Baku that precipitated the Russian Revolution of 1905, there was no way of knowing if some took industrial action regretfully, some aggressively, some with half an eye on a day off. And if the Second World War was really about restricting flow from Ottoman oilfield concessions, who did the actual squeezing of the pipelines, and how? Ida wanted to hear the voices of the people involved.

She closed the triple-glazed door of the oral history booth behind her and sat down in front of a telephone and a folder of laminated sheets that bore reams of meaningless titles and reference numbers. Her eyes slid down the columns with exasperation until they were caught by the word 'fracking'. That sounded kinky. No matter if it wasn't directly connected with oil. Wild guesses, hunches and idle indulgences are all legitimate tools available to the researcher. She picked up the telephone receiver. A voice asked what she would like to listen to. After a bit of confusing back-and-forth, the voice informed her that the tape was lined up and ready to play over the telephone line, that she could verbally request a rewind at any moment and should hang up when she was done listening. Was there really someone on the end of the line at her beck and call, listening to her listening? That was creepy.

A voice, soft and very close, announced the commencement of the twenty-third GASMAN live oral history session and introduced each speaker, explaining where they came from, what they looked like and whether they seemed agitated, resigned or were markedly ailing. Each speaker was echoed by this voice, which listened to and instantaneously translated, in a tone devoid of passion or even modulation, their accounts of living with fracking, which, it turned out, was some sort of contagion. The oral histories comprised a litany of its symptoms, which ran from all-over and permanent itchy rashes to devastating carcinomas of the vital organs, from mild paranoia to levels of schizophrenia that trigger school shootings, and every shade of inhibiting and arresting physical and mental condition in between. Cures were sought in herbs, crystals, string knotting, the laying on of hands and cabbage leaves.

One man announced his fear of his approaching birthday. The average life expectancy in his village in Foreign, where extraction and refining had started some sixty years ago, was 55. He was about to turn 54. Another woman spoke of her community, which had, just six years previously, embraced a deal and sold most of their land for a song about proceeds being pumped back into the local infrastructure. This had indeed happened, but with construction practices that were short-sighted and cursory. She told a sad story of such grotesque proportions it could barely find articulation in her poor, canker-thickened mouth. Everyone in the town, she said, was sick, and no two cases were the same. Many had frequent stomach cramps and spells of giddiness. She herself had given birth to three stillborns in a row. Her son complained of a travelling ache in his joints – one day it would be in his right elbow and his left knee, the next in his lower back, then in his feet and hips. Most people had regular nosebleeds, as did the livestock; horses whinnied at night from colic, and dogs' gums bubbled up with sores. Her husband had pancreatic cancer, arthritis and asthma, despite a lack of family history of any of them. All the old people had dementia, and the middle-aged complained of such a poor memory already that they couldn't recall the locations of the rashes and hives that sprang up about their person. The community's medical methods consisted entirely of praying and imbibing infusions made from a weed and sipped in communal copper fuddling cups.

The final speaker was from the far, far icy north, where this disease was preparing to move in, having bought the concessional rights to his neighbourhood. He was so broken by what was happening to him and his people that, in the most moving oral history of all, he simply choked up, too distressed to speak, but took the ten minutes allotted him nonetheless.

'What a confounding disease fracking must be,' thought Ida. 'I hope there are vaccinations, because if it ever spreads to Academia …'

She shuddered, then ran her finger down the column of titles again and asked the voice on the phone to play something called *Energy Warfare* by someone called Riggaz with Attitude featuring Ten Gallon.

A voice said 'certainly' and within seconds the hum of the line exploded into a drum-driving rap with a whole rack of sexy hooks:

'You better prepare,
Cuz it's energy warfare.
Riggaz supplying refiners
An' burying miners.
Lives on the pipeline,
Power blowing out, high time
For energy warfare.'

The singer then expounded on the historical context, going back to how striking coal miners in the nineteenth and early twentieth centuries were circumvented by the contrivance of an oil dependency. Kerosene had previously been used only in lamps, but new myriad uses for oil generated a lucrative market, and the fight for sources threw riggers and miners into a state of war. The take on the period was quite different from what Ida had read in *What's What*.

'It's energy warfare
You betta take care
Cuz I gotta a couple of miners bagged
Stuffed in the backseat, muzzled and gagged
Cuz they forgot to watch their sufferin' backs.
I grab a barrel, fill it up to the max
'N roll over the wife of the governor of the mine.
She loves when I shove my saveloy friend
Up in her ass, while we hang over brine,
She don't have to pretend.
We're in a rig, over the fuckin' haddock pasture
Can't fuck her no faster
She screamin' "grab my titties, suck on those bastards"
But I ain't no sucker, I won't snuggle up with her after.
I'm a riggah, but y'all look like a miner.
I'd rather lick on a ballsack or have a coronary
Than live in caves and hang out with a canary.
You fucking pussy moles claw at the ground.
Us riggaz iz gonna fuckin' dumbfound,
Yo miners gonna pussy-fart and piss on the settee
When you see oil more everywhere than even spaghetti.
It's energy warfare,
I'm bringin' home the drama,

Not in my pyjamas,
Bustin' outta my riggah hard hat
Bein' hard spat
In energy warfare.'

There is no better way to access the folk, thought Ida, than through their songs. She left the listening booth and sought out some early issues of *Texan Sounds,* a peer-to-peer journal of crude doggerel and refined barrel-raps from the gushing state, and requested some newspapers from around the same time. A pincer movement, using popular and official records, was a methodology she'd not thought of before.

The Foreign Energy War, it turned out, had been going on at the same time as the Two Cultures War, which had eventually crystallised into Academia's humanities bias, and subordinated the status of science departments. It felt uncanny to read newspaper headlines pertaining to what were now well-known historical events. Articles represented the confusion, mess and limitless doubt about something Ida knew as bounded incidents, fixed in time and strung together in causal relation. Suky had often repeated the platitude 'in a hundred years no one will care', and looking back at articles on professor so-and-so's publicly humiliating declaration on something-or-other, it really was apparent how forgetful or lacking in rigour the future was, or is, or ever will be.

The present was not much more attentive, it seemed. Given that so many folk had been singing about the war between miners and riggers, there was very little mention of it in the newspapers. There was one short but dense opinion piece in the *Times* on mental health in the energy sector, written with reference to a mass suicide in a town Ida had never heard of. She was incredulous. How could history let her be ignorant of this tragic incident? The article described how large-scale conversion of the Foreign Navy to an oil-fuelled fleet and the invention of the combustion engine had secured a dependence on oil, which could be extracted and distributed more easily than coal. Where coal was hacked directly from underground seams and shovelled from place to place, oil could be pumped remotely, keeping workers closer to managers – the upside being that their working conditions were safer and cleaner, the downside that their every decision was governable. The lesson learned from suicidal coal miners, speculated the journalist, must be applied to oil workers, who would surely be feeling repressed or possibly even paranoid as a result of current conditions. If the workforce required to drill for oil was much smaller – since once oil started coming, it could be left to flow under its own efforts – their community might well turn claustrophobic. And certain stabilities came at a price, it was suggested. Pipelines had replaced trains loaded up with coal and the men that ran them, and although vulnerable to sabotage, pipelines had fewer points of weakness than railway networks with all their mechanical and human components. And tankers, unconstrained by rail tracks, were able to switch destination according to demand, or to avoid flashpoints. But these liberations presented the problem of competition, with the arrival of cheap reserves from elsewhere a perpetual possibility, which no doubt subjected oil workers to further pressures of uncertainty, leading again to paranoia and social breakdown. This gave Ida something particular to look for in *Texan Sounds*. Among the reviews, in-depth analyses and transcriptions of the latest songs lyrics, she might find corroborating evidence of mental health issues in oil workers – a great subject for an interdisciplinary thesis. But most lyrics explored the themes one might expect of popular songs, drawing on the industrial context only for the sake of rhymes like 'crude' and 'dude', 'oil' and 'goil'.

In the May issue Ida's interest was piqued by a feature on Fathers' Day, mainly because, with the objectivity a lack of patrimony afforded her, she could see what a cynical invention this pageant was, and in certain moods she was perversely attracted to phenomena that annoyed her. The article 'Who's the Daddy?' traced the lineage of Texan hip-hop back to Petro-Suppression Blues Ballads and singled out the master of the genre, a proto-petro-protest singer-songwriter Buzz Car Willy, who sounded like he might have more content than most. Another forage unearthed a book of Buzz's song sheets, among them a waltz recounting the invention of cars that ran on electricity or vegetable oil, the latter with 25% fuel efficiency advantage over their petrol-thirsty equivalents; a lullaby eulogising the fair Elsbett, an engine in which diesel was injected into a central core of hot air, where it combusted without making contact with the chamber walls, and a dirge mourning the kerosene lamp's snuffing out of candles. But there was nothing here that substantiated the *Times* journalist's hypothesis on mental health, and Ida wasn't sure she was so keen on writing about it anyway.

Neither was she convinced of the reliability of music as historical evidence. She decided to get back to the serious stuff of books. But which books? She wondered whether there were any books by an O'Dewey in the archive. This was as good a way as any to make a decision – a perfectly viable research tool. And sure enough, there was a book by I. F. O'Dewey on oil consortium strategies, published some seventy years previously. The first chapter described mechanisms that would bring about oil scarcity when necessary, which could include price regulation, calculative arrangements to government quotas and lend lease loans, whatever they were. 'Operators can, if necessary, be paid for *not* producing oil,' coached Imelda Fay, which is what Ida had decided I. F. stood for. Chapter Two explained how to generate shortage through rapid and bizarre inflation of need, coupled with the reversal of earlier attempts at efficiency. Engines should be converted into greedy versions of their former selves and manufacturers given incentives to lay off the lines that produced such economical models as the one-cylinder Isetta 250, the 2-CV and the four-cylinder Mini and the Beetle. New gas-guzzling, souped-up cars with six, eight, ten and even 24 cylinders should be aggressively marketed instead, intensifying the desire for oil. Although the technical details were flushed immediately down the pan of Ida's ignorance, by Chapter Three she knew Imelda Fay to have been an unscrupulous wire-puller, and slammed the book shut.

Laying aside her disgust, she knew she must press on. But in which direction? She had to draw a limit around her research too. It did have a habit of running away with itself. What was the most promising subject she had encountered so far? She thought she had wanted to concentrate on the human interest, the voices of the people, but so far they had built into such a babble she didn't know which was a trusted source, which was incidental. It was probably best to start with physical materiality and bring the human element in later, once she had a better grasp of the basics. And she did rather like the look of oil rigs, their unconditional functionality, no-nonsense straight lines and modular makeup. Their uncompromising bruteness and ungiving materiality would really exert her descriptive writing skills. And rigs were truly avant-garde. They were literally striking out into remote seas, with nothing but time and space for an audience.

She sought out a volume on rig design. The diversity of constructions was awesome. They were almost as various as types of insects or slang for the male member. Some looked like a stranded end of the pier, with latticed support work, hut-like stacks and red-and-white striped funnels, persistently and persuasively jolly, despite the lack of passing punters. Others were grungier, the colours and textures of old skips and tractors. Some budded upwards and outwards from central columns; others spread lower across broad orange trunks, like sturdy tables. One looked like a mechanised elephant spouting fire from its elevated trunk; another was elegantly leggy and waspish against the grossly swelling sea. They bristled with cranes and proffered helipads to the skies; they were laddered and crated and battered and gleaming; they were heroic and pathetic and arrogant and complex. The metalwork was outsize, held together by a giantess's nuts and bolts, and the use of colour was bold, but sensitively so – more bright than brash, it could have been orchestrated to buoy the morale of inhabitants, or perhaps this was pragmatic colour coding to aid modular construction.

For Ida's purposes, the choice of rig was simply a matter of taste. Each would bring its own atmosphere to the writing. The interiors, though, were still a mystery. The archival photographs dwelt on structural specificities, but neglected to answer questions like: Does signage on doors use full words or acronyms? Is the flooring linoleum, tile, carpet or sawdust? Are the door handles levers or knobs? How many beds to a room? Do the operational decks have different sorts of bins to the living quarters? In an unfixed rig, is the lavatory bowl on gimbals? There was much to find out.

*

A half-revolution of the rotating door bore Ida from the silence of the library into a murky stridor through which people rushed to homes and hostelries. After the hush of the reading room, the vast conurbation of Academia seemed fraught with clankings, boomings and wailings. As she made her way home, Ida felt her freshly acquired knowledge disappear, gradually displaced by the demands of the transport system, by the attention of strangers and by every reminder of things to do and people to talk to that her mind involuntarily generated. All that reading hadn't gone to waste – she had taken notes, of course – but she was disappointed to realise that the content was not on hand for immediate use. She didn't know any of it yet.

*

That night she was visited by none other than the spectre of the oil industry. It appeared during a typical dream – a movie-trailer of incoherent but profoundly significant images and incidents. This regular dreaming was abruptly halted by the ringing of bells for half a minute, or a minute maybe, or perhaps an hour, followed by a clanking noise, far below, as if someone were dragging a heavy chain over some casks. Then there was a booming noise as a door flung open, and footsteps mounted the stairs to her room.

A spectre bearing the public face of the oil industry oozed through the bedroom door, drawing a weighty chain clasped about its middle. This chain was long, wound around and about like a tail and was garlanded with jerry cans, well heads, pipe sections, tankers, holding vats, share indexes, cartels and regulatory bodies.

Following the customary exchange of denial and verification between the living and the undead, the spectre showed Ida the truly ghastly sight of a global industry so complex that not a single participant understood their position within it. Her eyes took in scenes that were of such abundant contingency that they looked like unmitigated chaos. Her ears funnelled reams of statistics like telephone numbers, which she tried to memorise, but they slipped away like… telephone numbers. And then the spectre, with dark strings of drool grieving downwards from its mouth, delivered a monologue so devastating that Ida's blood curdled *and* froze. Eventually, spent, it walked backwards towards the window, which gradually opened to let in confused noises from without: incoherent sounds of lamentation and regret, wailings inexpressibly sorrowful and self-accusatory. Then, after listening for a moment, the spectre joined in the mournful dirge, and percolated out into the cold, dark night.

Dreams, like theories, are famously non-Newtonian; they are abstracted, dematerialised, lubricated by fantasy and seldom have audio, for noise is traditionally produced through friction, impact or vibration. This dream, however, had been cacophonous, vibrating and vibrant with the shrieks, clatters and clanks of girders, joists, pivots and winches, the rolling of barrels and grinding of drills, the whirring of data and skyrocketing of prices, the whoops of the fortunate and the howls of the fleeced. When she awoke, the edge of Ida's ignorance had been truly knocked off. She had at last exchanged her belief that the oil industry was a single, vast structure made up of solid parts, joined up through the efforts of those that manufactured them, for the knowledge that it was a multitudinous torrent of self-reflexive indeterminacy.

CHAPTER 24

Things had started going wrong again.

'For one thing, I can't remember to turn up at my own events. If it hadn't been for Hatchet Padget in the pub I'd've missed the gallery talk altogether.'

'Ah, Hatchet – there's a name I haven't had to balk at for many a year. How come Manfred hadn't given you a diary alert?' Child number five was suckling at Suky's breast while she laid back on the sheepskin-covered chaise longue, the phone tucked in close enough for Ida to hear happy gurgling noises.

'Day off. Was probably at an interview or something. Well, he's not getting a bloody reference from me. He's mine, not theirs.'

'But anyway, how did you pull it off? I'm assuming that you did.'

'Oh yes. I blinded them with poetics. I just sort of sprayed out words until the time was up. Then the other day I was on this panel. You know the sort of thing – twenty minutes each of gut-spilling and then some curator bounces it all down into a single paragraph. But anyway, the thing was, I was about to speak when I realised I must have picked up someone else's notebook by mistake. I don't know if you've ever tried working from someone else's notes, but it's like trying to get dressed in nothing but zips. The bits you do have are insubstantial, and none of them join up in any way that makes sense.'

'Idy darling, I know you make this stuff up for me because of some misplaced belief that I shall be your biographer one day. But really, it's too hilarious. No one would believe me.'

'Well, it gets worse. Now it seems I can't even identify what's art and what isn't. This is really embarrassing. I seem to have written about an installation that turns out not to be an installation after all. I mean, it is, but not of the art sort. I'm going to have to try and get the piece back from the editor, but I think it might be too late.'

'Is that serious? It sounds serious.'

'That depends …'

'On what?'

'Things I can't control, unfortunately. One of which is me, it seems.'

'Are you becoming a fatalist, Ida O'Dewey?'

'I don't blame fate. I blame John. That's the other thing. I'm not speaking to him.'

'What, ol' forearms?'

'Yeah. He was the one who told me it was an installation.'

'And so it was.'

'Yes, but not the sort I thought.'

'Is that really his fault? Sounds to me like a miscommunication.'

'It's hard to explain. He also let me be trampled by a cow.'

'What?... Ow! Little bugger.' Suky yelped and the baby started screaming. 'Shit, better go Idy. Sorry. Call again soon?'

Ida hung up with a sigh and readied herself to go out.

It was Thursday. Gallery roundup day. For the past five years Ida and Jørn had turned this into a ritual of their asymmetrical friendship, taking a turn about the galleries, drinking coffee, taking in a matinée performance and ending up in a pub to thrash out ideas. Then Ida would write it up overnight, filing copy by 10am for proofing, setting and printing in the Saturday supplement, which came out on the stroke of one minute past midnight. It was tough fun, important-feeling and real.

They met after lunch outside a gallery, where they had heard good things about an installation made entirely of air currents. No more off-piste installations. She was only writing about gallery-sanctioned, plainly identifiable art today.

They opened the door, stepped into a large white room and looked about, at nothing. They took a few steps forward, and then a few more. Still nothing. Jørn was heading back to door when Ida gave out a shriek. Her hair had shot upwards and was standing on its end, quivering in a sudden gust that emanated from a hidden source. He grinned and said 'Wha—', a blast of air snatching the rest of his words and dashing them against the far wall.

'I've been thinking,' Ida said loudly over the sound of the winds, her hair an impossible column undulating upwards from her face, 'about fiction.'

'Hah, I haven't thought about that since undergrad. What about it?'

She stepped into a wind local to just her skirt.

'Well, between you, me and the mistrals, I'm about to publish a piece in *Muse* that is not entirely true. Not that it's false, or a lie. It's just that the framing of it is slightly fictionalised because... well, if I'm honest, I misread the situation.'

'What do you mean the framing is fictionalised?'

'Perhaps it's more a category error. You see, I saw this most amazing installation and wrote about it, but it turns out it's not art.'

'Oh dear, that's embarrassing. We haven't had a cleaner throwing out an artwork by mistake for a while, but this is definitely related. Although you've elevated something instead of— '

'Yes, thank you Jørn, I realise that. What I am trying to do now is turn this round into something constructive. I'm thinking of it as having a very lively fiction on my hands, and I'm trying to figure out which direction to take it in. You see, it's a potential vindication of the whole *Panel Beaters* incident. It's an artwork that needs constant maintenance otherwise it explodes.'

'Really?' asked Jørn. 'Who made it?' He was enjoying the migration of Ida's hemline from knees to upper thighs.

'Oh, you're not paying attention. No one made it. Well, someone did, but not an artist. So now I'm thinking of inventing an artist and saying it's by him or her, and championing their practice.'

'But why would you do that? Other than to cover up your mistake.'

Someone entered from the street, the open door producing eddies that ushered in half the litter from the pavement. Soup cans and newspapers rattled and rustled about the space dangerously at head height, forcing Jørn and Ida to duck under their jackets and tumble out the door laughing, thoroughly enjoying the maelstrom. A gallery assistant out on the street thanked them for coming and thrust a sheet of A4 into their hands, which they crammed into their bags with all the other press releases, listings pamphlets and programme notes. All bags in Academia are similarly caught up in a cycle of engorgement and periodic purging.

'You don't want to end up like old Sturry,' continued Jørn. 'He's spent his whole career insisting "doing" is pronounced "doing" to cover up for an initial mistake. Unbelievably, he'd only ever seen the word written down, never spoken, until his department deputy tried to correct him.'

'Oh, is that where that comes from? Hah. Well anyway, I'd like to continue with the fiction because the actual installation's very interesting. Its instability is a by-product of the stuff it deals with, which is what I really want to write about, but can't because I don't know enough about it. If it were art though, it would be so much easier. There's more tolerance for speculation in art writing. So I just have to make up more artworks that are somehow to do with this stuff that I want to write about.'

'Well, you know what that would make you.' He reached for the door handle of the next gallery and paused. She shook her head. He opened the door onto a blacked-out interior. An usher passed them a booklet and showed them to a vacant viewing bench with an efficient sweep of his torch beam. 'An artist,' whispered Jørn.

Two differently grey rectangles were gradually appearing on the dim screen before them, the sound of waves and the occasional outraged cry of a gull signalling that this was a seascape. Something in Ida's breast soared at the thought of becoming an artist.

'But one who can never claim the credit for her artwork,' said Jørn. 'You'd have to go through all the effort of conceiving and making each piece, but you'd always have to credit it to someone else.'

'Fucking artists,' she hissed. 'They're not getting their hands on any more of my credit. Even if they're a fictional artist. They can fuck off.'

A throat was cleared in the dark. A sharp floral perfume and the deep timbre of the larynx suggested that at least two people were buried in the blackness, although this is to make certain assumptions.

'I made that artwork. I wrote it into being,' said Ida, disconsolate, as whatever handle she'd had on her idea fell off in her mental grasp.

'Ok, then how about if you reveal that it was you who made the artworks after, say, a year. It would be a sensational durational performance.'

'That would be positively megalomaniacal,' she said, half choking with indignation and drawing from their invisible companions a gale of shushes. Like chided school children, they twitched with the effort of containing themselves for another twenty minutes while the video image darkened ever so slightly.

'Well, let's look at this from another angle,' said Jørn once they were back on the tree-lined boulevard, falling in with the bustling stream of pedestrians similarly ducking in and out of glass-fronted white cubes, ornate red-brick museums and scruffy project spaces. 'Let's ask not what do you lose or gain by pretending it's an artwork – we've identified that – but what would you lose or gain by not pretending it's art?'

'Twenty years of authority and respect? And anyway, that's entirely hypothetical. I've already written about it in an art magazine as if it were an artwork. It's already about to go off to press. I'm almost already screwed.'

'Did you ask the editor to hold it back?'

'Of course. I said there were some facts I wasn't able to check, and that I wanted to hold it over until the next issue, but he said that unless I got a replacement fifteen hundred words to him by tea time… I've been up since five trying to write something else, but my head is so full up of this other research, I have nothing for him.'

They had paused to look at a window display of rain running permanently down the inside of the glass, dashing against it at times with vigour. They both shivered involuntarily and dutifully took an explicatory leaflet from the dispenser.

'Oh, that really is too mean of him. Come on,' said Jørn, decisively. 'Come with me.' He grabbed her hand and yanked.

*

Jørn held a finger to his lips and pushed open the old, pitted oak door. The smell of dead skin spilled out. Ida hung back and held her breath, through reflex rather than anticipation, although the cinematic creak of the hinges lent a certain terror to the scene. Jørn stepped through the door and bade her follow, and while every molecule in the universe that had ever passed through her body was screaming 'don't', she followed him.

Not one to hover in a doorway – for that is the proscenium of apologists – Ida stepped further into the room and let her eyes adjust to the darkness. She fancied she could make out hunched figures along the walls, but wouldn't have bet on it. She wouldn't have laid stakes on much at that moment, because even good old Jørn was not quite as she knew him. His body had changed. It was no longer long and foal-like, but tall and forceful, like the letter 't'.

'Do you ever read the reviews of Lea Crefern or Earl Fencer or Lance Refer?' he asked, his voice jimmying a space for itself between a high, shimmering clatter and an unidentifiable low booming. She wasn't sure that she had, and so offered a faint nod tempered with narrowed eyes and a tilt to the head. 'No, no one has,' he said.

There were no windows down here, and the only electrical lighting shone on to a tall white plinth. Jørn was over by it within a single bound, peeling a layer off its top with ease. He held the white rectangular substance aloft, where it trembled before he crumpled it in a single fist. It was paper. And the clatter was that of typewriters. The typing stopped momentarily, then resumed. Had Ida imagined it, or had the shoulders of the figures shuddered with sighs?

'This,' whispered Jørn, 'is where the unread dwell. The denizens of the back pages, the copy filers and inch fillers. They have no future and can remember no other past.'

Ida approached one of the figures nearest the door, a woman in brown

– they were all in brown – whose hair had grown over her keyboard but which bothered her flying fingers not one bit. The woman looked ahead, her eyes shut and her mouth open just enough to slide a coin in. She seemed to incline her head minutely at Ida's approach, but gave no other sign that she cared who or what was afoot. There was a small pile of gallery press releases at the right of her typewriter, the logos easily recognisable even in this dim lighting because, illumined on the skyline, marching across the back of publications and arriving at home daily on envelopes, they have been drilled into every Academic's unconscious. The woman reached for the top sheet, placed her spread palm across it, picked it up in one sharp crackling movement and pressed it to her upturned face as if it were a damp flannel in a desert. Her chest heaved, her hair fell in greasy ribbons and a low moaning drove Ida back a step, out of fear that the woman was about to be sick or otherwise voluble. The next stage of the working process remained mysterious, but resulted in five minutes or so of furious typing, with interstitial gestures of thinking performed by clawed hands above the keyboard. When the woman came to rest, her hands now inert in her lap, the freshly typed sheets were collected by a bent old man, who had been sitting on a high stool in a wood-panelled kiosk, and deposited on the top of the column of paper.

'So, which exhibitions do you want written about?' asked Jørn. Ida was not able to reply; her thoughts had scattered to chase down explanations for this macabre place. 'How about those shows we've just seen? Was it my imagination, or was there a lot of weather this morning? Anyone in particular you'd like to write it?' She looked back at him blankly. 'No preference? May as well go for gender likeness, then.' He took the press releases from his bag, smoothed them out on his chest and put them on top of the greasy haired woman's pile. 'Three shows, fifteen hundred words. Upbeat but critical, with an emphasis on socio-political effects of weather,' he said with steady authority. And off the woman went into her shamanic ritual while Jørn stood by, checking his watch now and then and smiling pleasantly at Ida to keep her involved.

Twenty minutes later, at half past three, she was running up the four flights of stairs to the offices of *Muse*, copy in hand. The editor was perfectly placated with a fresh piece on three newly opened shows, and pulled her previous copy from the out-tray before putting the kettle on to signal the end of another successful editorial cycle.

*

Sue instilled in her clients the importance of being as visible before and during a project as they would want to be afterwards. No matter how blocked or knotted they were, it was good to remind the publishers and the broadcasters of their existence. And so Ida suggested, after marching out of the final gallery, that she and Jørn decamp to the De Milo Arms. The pub windows were half-shuttered all day, the scant sunlight that crept through the dark wood interior bore an inordinate density of motes and, with the vapours rising off the brandy helped along by the bulky radiators that were always blaring, it made for the soporific fug favoured by post-lunch publishers.

'Manfred!' Ida exclaimed as she caught sight of her daily saviour on yet another day off (they were surely more than weekly now), tucked in a corner talking intently with a mousy young woman she could meet twenty times but would never recognise.

'Ah, good evening. I believe you two have met before.' Manfred motioned towards his companion, who turned round to smile shyly through a permanent mask of embarrassment further pinked by blemish scars.

'Ah, yes, of course… Hello, nice to see you again.' Whoever she was. But, more to the point, what were interns doing in a pub like this? 'You guys here for a bit of industrial rubbernecking?'

Manfred looked appalled at the idea. The young woman blinked heavily and remained silent.

'Dora has a meeting and I was just helping her prepare.' Manfred tactfully waited for Ida to excuse herself and leave them to it, but Ida always felt she should atone for not recognising someone by being overly familiar and positive.

'A meeting. How exciting. It's moments like this that you realise just how historical we all are. I mean, how things can go one way or the other, and that it's you, and what you say, that dictates it. How very exciting. I'm sure you'll do brilliantly in your meeting.'

Dora didn't look at all excited at being historical.

'Oh, it's not that big a deal,' stepped in Manfred. 'I think this is, what, the third, fourth meeting? Anyway, Dora, I'll leave you to it. See you later at the AGM.'

'An AGM. A meeting? Today?' said Ida.

'Yes, this evening. It's the Union of Interns and Apprentices' AGM.'

'But it's Thursday. I'll be needing you this evening.'

'Well, I did coordinate with your schedule. You'll be writing your round-up. You won't even notice I'm not there.'

'But I might need something.' Ida was being spoiled, she knew she was, but she felt weak at the thought of Manfred's upcoming defection. He should know how much she needed him.

'I can stand in for him if you like,' whispered Dora.

'If you don't mind, that would be amazing,' said Manfred. 'It'll only be for an hour or so, and I can show you the ropes before I go.'

'But then *you'll* miss the meeting,' said Ida to Dora.

'That's ok, but he's the chairman. He has to go,' said Dora.

Ida had no idea Manfred was chairman of any union. Luckily, she had always treated him well. The interns of today are the opinion formers of tomorrow, after all. She wondered if she met the union standards of engagement.

As she was navigating this small puddle of anxiety, a purple-faced, corpulent commissioning editor, renowned for his cut-throat ploys for poaching best-selling writers, approached the table.

'Well, well, Ida O'Dewey. To what do we owe this dubious pleasure? Do you have a comic book to hawk or something?' His remark echoed round the pub.

'Not yet Teddy, darling. But when I do you'll be the last to know,' Ida said as witheringly as possible while wearing a floral print blouse. Teddy gave off a gale of good-natured laughter and slapped her on the back.

'Just kiddin' ya kid. I'd love to see your whatever it's going to be, so when you're nearly finished remember your old Teddy. Now, if you'll excuse us, we have a very important meeting. Dora, great you could come at short notice.'

To Ida's incredulity he kissed Dora on both pimply cheeks. Manfred made his excuses and trotted out of the pub.

'Maybe,' she thought as she looked about for Jørn, 'she's his step-niece, and he's training her up for some entry-level position. Well, if anyone is lucky enough to be able to capitalise on nepotism, good luck to them, I say.'

She dismissed matters of interns from her mind – because really it was their job to think about her – and plopped down next to Jørn on the banquette.

'There you are,' said Jørn. 'I just had to fight off a mess of a woman wearing just a rucksack back-to-front. And trousers, thank Dog, but a remarkable look nonetheless. The excitement gave me rather a taste for the ale. Why don't you call on the services of Lea Crefern again to write your round-up and then we can come back here, stay all evening, go on late somewhere else…'

'I don't think so Jørn. Thanks. I really appreciate your help, but I never want to see that place again.'

'Humbling, isn't it? They ask for nothing in return, just continuous press releases and the occasional packet of biscuits. You may think we keep them there against their will, but they like the quiet and the dark, with just marketing material for stimulus.'

'It looked like a sweatshop to me. How many people know about it?'

'It's a communal resource for all editors, but it's also one of our good works. These burned-out critics need somewhere to exercise their craft, and we protect them from any damaging feedback by tucking their copy in corners where few eyes wander. Except when there's the occasional editorial emergency, like today. And it's perfectly good copy that they produce.'

Ida had been ready to pour her hottest, tarriest scorn on the copy, but like he said, it was perfectly fine. Nothing pulse-raising, just solid description and analysis, and out it had come like plain and pearl knitting. It was unlikely that anyone would mention how her piece lacked her usual whatever it was – chirpy verve? – and it was far, far preferable to the alternative humiliation.

'All the same, I'd rather not perpetuate such a thing,' she said.

'Suit yourself. But anyway, now you've been saved from spinning a fiction what will you do with your new subject matter do you think?'

'I don't know yet. I'm in the first phase of research still, getting to know the expanse of the terrain. You know that difficult first notebook.'

'You should follow your first instinct. The fiction idea is interesting. I tell you what, you should write your research up as a novel. You can bury mistakes in fiction, and you can indulge in lies. Quite why academic essays are the go-to form I don't know. If I weren't straight jacketed by research points and impact analysis, I'd write a novel. It's an overlooked mode of critique.'

For Ida, meeting the unread writers had strengthened her sense of responsibility as a critic. Filler produced by the yard contravened the ideological policies the industry publically espoused, but she could see now that without people like her, this sort of thing was likely to become rife. A rare surge of honour for her profession snuffed out the attraction of fiction.

'Mmm, interesting,' she said, careful to remain non-committal. If she disagreed on political grounds they would be here all night. 'But that's a whole other discipline to master. I don't have the time.'

'Nah, fiction's just storytelling, like remembering things, gossiping, lying, telling anecdotes down the pub.'

'Then I'd be hopeless. I've never had a good enough memory. Although technically I could lie, I tend to avoid it, because I can't guarantee I'll remember which lie I told and won't contradict myself later.'

'Really? You've never told a lie?'

'Not that I can remember.' She smiled sweetly and blinked.

He laughed and she felt the recurrent thought that bound him to her passing through his mind.

'If not fiction, what do you want to write then?'

'In all seriousness?' she said, sculling with her index finger the scum on the top of her pint, as if it were a portal that gave out on to a beatifying future. 'I want to write something so startling and revelatory that it scrapes back the veneer of everyday necessity. I want to write something so powerful that it vaporises all that we have constructed to protect us from knowing the animal truth of existence.'

'Pfff,' he said, after taking down an inch of amber ale, 'I'm not sure the written word can ever do that.'

CHAPTER 25

On consideration, Ida had found idle curiosity to be more urgent than round-up review writing. She tottered at the top of her library's sliding brass ladder or sat cross-legged on the herringbone oak parquet floor, almost not thinking about the job of work she was avoiding. The spotty young friend of Manfred's – Maureen? Doreen? Dora? Nora? – had popped in every half hour to check if she needed anything, which, while well-meaning, only served to bring the deadline incrementally closer. After three morosely received rejections of assistance, Ida exclaimed, with brilliantly camouflaged irritation, that the one thing she really needed was a fresh cup of coffee at the top of the even hours throughout the night. Dora, to her credit, took this so seriously as to place the cup and saucer on the desk at the stroke of eight, ten, midnight, two.

Ida had started her research into the novelistic form by pulling the ever-loyal Concise OAD off the shelf. It was like grasping the hand of a childhood friend.

'Novel. Fictitious prose narrative of sufficient length to fill one or more volumes portraying characters and actions representative of real life in continuous plot,' said the dictionary primly and with an accent that bore some analysis. A melodious Frenchness overlaid a Celtic brogue, certainly, and a Dutch glissando emerged now and again; but a murmur of Arabic could also be detected, along with the occasional Nordic blatter. The effect was orchestrated Academic, certainly, but it was more delicately layered than you might expect.

'Real life?' thought Ida. 'In continuous plot? What about magical realism or fragmented narrative?'

'I hadn't quite finished, actually,' said the dictionary somewhat chippily. 'Novel. Of new kind or nature, strange, hitherto unknown.'

'But how can that be so? What about revisionism and sequels? They can take a novelistic form too. And how can something be representative of real life *and* be strange or hitherto unknown? What do you mean by "real"?'

'Real,' said the dictionary, 'is a former silver coin and money of account used in Spain and Spanish-speaking countries.'

'Now you're being obtusely homonymic. Give me reality.'

'Reality is what underlies appearances. Next entry, if that helps: realpolitik, the policy of placing material greatness of one's own nation before all other considerations.'

'Interesting. So are you telling me that on the one hand reality is beyond material appearance, and on the other one must keep up material appearances to really be politikal?'

'Don't ask me,' said the dictionary. 'I don't invent the meanings. I'm just passing them on.'

'So, let's unpack this a bit shall we?'

'Unpack, unpeg, unpen, unpeople, unperch, unpick, unpin, unplait, unplug. I could go on...'

'Unpack and unpeg, yes, but unpen, unpeople, unperch? Can you un-anything?'

'Pretty much any verb, yes.'

'Nouns?'

'If they also have a verb function too, yes.'

'It's a shame actions speak louder than words then, otherwise I could go round undoing everything bad I did by saying "un-whatever it is".'

'I don't think,' said the dictionary with severity, 'it works like that. But you would have to check with my grammatical colleagues.'

'Actually, I can tell you myself how it works. Many people think the word that universally undoes all unpleasantness is "sorry".'

'But that means "feeling regret". I don't understand...'

'This is language in action, which you wouldn't know about.' The dictionary threw her a dejected look and ruffled its pages in a sigh. 'Sorry, I didn't mean it to come out that way. You see, in practice, language is more performative than the words on the page you're used to. People know "sorry" means to feel regret, but they think that if they say it in the right tone or make the appropriate face, it will obliterate whatever grossness they have already perpetrated or, in cases such as barging through a crowd, they are about to perpetrate.'

'It does also mean "wretched, paltry, shabby, of poor quality". Maybe they are using it as a self-identifier?'

'Oh if only. But no, it's considered more of a magic word that brings about a change within the mind of the person it's said to.'

'That change being...?'

'Forgiveness I suppose. Sorry, how did we get on to this subject?'

Ida wrinkled her brow with the effort of retracing their steps. 'Let's stay focused here. You said, hang on, yes, you said that "novel" was a representation of real life, but that it was also new and strange.'

'Ah yes, what I neglected to mention is that the first "novel" is a noun, the second an adjective. I always ignore those italicised bits at the beginning – they look so messy – and as a result I'm hopeless at distinguishing between homonyms; they all run together in my head, so it's all or nothing, I'm afraid. Just don't ask me about the word "yet" – I have five column inches of various meanings and usages, and I haven't met anyone yet who understands the difference. But, if I've got you right on this, it's "the novel", noun, the first one you want: "Fictitious prose narrative of sufficient length to fill one or more volumes portraying characters and actions representative of real life in continuous plot."'

'Thanks, yes, that's the more achievable of the two; but I don't understand the "real life" bit. Nor the continuous plot. How does fantasy figure in that definition?'

'Ah, you see, fantasy is an "image-making faculty", so real life is full of fantasy and vice versa. People think of fantasy as being at the extravagant or visionary end of things,' said the dictionary. 'But in fact, real life and fantasy contain one another. One is not subordinate to the other.'

'Ok, well, thanks, I think you'd better leave it there before we get side-tracked by another term in the definition. I mean, this is all very well, but it is just semantics, isn't it? One can have also an intuitive grasp of the word in context.'

'Semantics is my bag, sister. Too much intuition would put me out of a job. But if you want something more theoretically developed, you'd be better off talking with one of my colleagues. There are all sorts of specialists on the team. Just along there, on the next shelf down, you'll find a *Companion to Academic Literature*, which could be useful to you.'

Ida picked up the well-dressed tome, plump, glossy and obviously accustomed to keeping the best company. She thought it looked a bit stuck up its own dust jacket. Her impulse was to give it a wide berth, but in the name of research she opened it at random. It commenced with a cut-glass accent and not so much as a how-do-you-do:

'The plot centres on the attempts of young Jacintha to escape from her jealous guardian Strictland and to elope with her admirer, Bellamy: a rope ladder is provided, but there are many mistakes and misunderstandings before the final happy outcome. Sutcliff, Rosemary, see children's literature. Svengali, see Trilby. Swan of Avon, the Sweet, see

Avon, the Sweet Swan of. Swan of Lichfield, see Seward, A. Swedenborg, Emanuel, born Swedberg. Sweedlepipe, Paul or Poll, Martin Chuzzlewit, Sweeney Agonistes, TS Eliot, Sweet, Henry, Shaw, Henry Higgins... Thomas, Thomas, Thompson, Thompson, Thompson, Thoms, Thomas, Thomas...'

Ida closed it with a loud clap and returned it to its place on the shelf, thinking it a name-dropper and a thoroughly unpleasant read. She hadn't noticed it before and wondered where it had come from. Her shelves were dappled with books she couldn't account for, but this was common in Academia. If even the most advanced academic made an inventory of their bookshelves, categorising them as 'bought and regretted', 'borrowed but haven't got around to yet', 'read about twenty years too late', 'flicked through with confusion', 'aspirational purchase, unopened' and so on, the only conclusion to be drawn would be that they too suffered from Imposter Syndrome.

Books have been noted for their room-furnishing qualities, but they can also dress a person. We acquire titles not only to extrude our intellect along the lines of their content, but also to adjust our self-image and the image we project for the sake of others. The schoolboy buys into action hero comics to compensate for his clumsy unworldliness, and the teenager into moody existentialism to provide his spurting hormones with a void to disappear into. But the adult's choice of reading matter becomes complicated; as her social world expands, peer pressure becomes byzantine and the actual and the projected selves battle it out repeatedly. If we know how to read them, the bookshelves we end up with can tell us a great deal that we are best advised to deny.

Ida set her eyes to a middle-distance stare that encompassed an entire wall of book spines. She willed the narrative of her lost childhood to emerge, then her most profound psychological weakness (she was still curious to single this out), then, at the very least, evidence of a favourite colour. But all that was revealed was the influence of her vagina. Alongside the titles from her own college reading list were those from modules taught by gorgeous lecturers she'd had half a mind to switch to; then there were the books with a beguiling author's portrait, and those on subjects she knew the brunette across the hall or the cutie down the road or the dashing critic on television were particularly interested in. Good Dog. Had she been led by the libido all these years?

'Well, madam,' she addressed her genitals, 'no longer. No way. From now on I make all the decisions round here.'

Not for the first time that evening, she thought of John, and her pudenda tingled, letting her know it wasn't willing to take a back seat just yet. Why hadn't he telephoned? Why hadn't she called him? Pig-headedness on both their parts? She doubted it. There was something going on his end, and she needed to know if it precluded her involvement. She had let relationships peter out before, hoping her silence would be interpreted correctly and without fuss by the other party. Was this what it felt like to be on the other end? Oh she was starting to learn her lesson, if that's what this was about. But what if it wasn't that? What if something really had happened – a traffic accident, a landslide, an act of Dog – then he would think her callous for not noticing his silence. But she had. Oh, she had noticed.

Splitting up with men was not something she was afraid of, but she had never been dumped herself. If she caught wind of the end she sped it up, forced a denouement, became the more efficient party. For her, a break up was a theatrical moment, requiring interpretative, writerly and performance skills. The truth is never enough in these situations, and a vague 'it's not working' is too negotiable. A break-up speech is a dramatic genre that requires the skilful progression of ideas, attention to detail and the incorruptible narrative arc of the best well-made plays. Ida had a folio of scripts developed from a handful of templates, each tailored to the particularities of the person concerned, and sometimes, if absolutely necessary, tailored to her relationship with them. Once they were complete, each text was as unique as a thief's thumbprint.

Her most clear and forceful break-up speech, when she wanted to be sure there was no possibility of any reconciliation, comprised a list of the person's physical, social, intellectual and spiritual failings set to the rhythm of a limerick with an expandable middle section. It was a clever reversal of the 'it's not you, it's me' cliché, and was really quite musical when delivered with percussive accompaniment. Another favourite recipe was the diamanté, a lesser-known poetic form of seven lines that compares two subjects using the following formula:

Line 1: one noun that names the first subject;

Line 2: two adjectives that describe the first subject;

Line 3: three present participles related to the first subject;

Line 4: four nouns, the first two relating to the first subject, the second to the second subject;

Line 5: three present participles related to the second subject;

Line 6: two adjectives that describe the second subject;

Line 7: one noun that names the second subject.

In a break-up speech the two subjects should obviously be 'you' and 'me', and the present participles were a particularly enjoyable section to really throw the thesaurus at.

You
Gloomy, wet
Drizzling, wasting, drowning
Deluge, disaster, tempest, abundance
Raging, arresting, booming
Powerful, furious
Me

Maybe one day, when she had settled down and had no more need for them, she would publish her folio of speeches. Teddy at Random would turn himself inside out to get hold of that material. That day was not on the horizon yet though. She sighed, feeling hurt by the running aground of what she thought had been a goer.

'Your 4 a.m. coffee,' said Manfred gently. He looked tired, older and at odds with his shorts and tennis shoes.

'Four? In the morning? Oh bugger fucking hell. I haven't even started the round-up yet. Manfred, quick, go make me some scrambled eggs on toast. Do you know how to do that?' He nodded discreetly. 'You're amazing. Ok, go do that, then I want you to run me a cold shower and lay out a really, really itchy outfit. The scratchiest, woolliest things that will make me cross as hell. It's writing time!'

CHAPTER 26

Looking out over the surrounding countryside from a viewing platform at the top of a tall, tortured metal sculpture gave a conference delegate the perspective she needed before delivering a paper. Ida was entirely prepared for the Edgeboston Interdisciplinary Caucus. Allowing herself the easy option for once, she had fished out a six-month-old paper, written for an interdisciplinary conference that she had not made it to on account of having missed the train, on account of having been trapped inside her own apartment by an idiot intern, who had double-locked the door and then disappeared all day, purportedly to the library. Now that the outrage had passed over into anecdote, she was ready to capitalise on it. All that had been needed was a couple of up-to-date examples, and a title that made reference to the new form of delivery she had devised, which she was very excited about. In fact, for once, her pre-gig excitement equalled her anxiety, and the two flip-flopped for precedence in a stomach also battling with vertigo.

From her vantage point she could see the entire circumference of the festival's eight-metre-high concrete boundary. Gaps large enough to drive a car through would appear in this wall overnight, and construction workers would be scrambled to plug the opening before more gate-crashers careened through. Most wall breaches were stopped up within a matter of minutes; and the autograph hunters and star fuckers who remained at large were mostly harmless, although there were one or two rumoured to be passing themselves off as academics in order to spread bad theory in the café tents, or even to take the podium under false pretences.

Ida had arrived on the fifth and final day of the festival. Consensus was that it was going extremely well. Beneath her, the cream of the Academy and the everyfolk were indistinguishable from one another, swarming between social engagements, meals and ticketed events. From this distance the colourful stalls, tents and portacabins dotted about the muddy field could just as well have been a Mediaeval war encampment in a vital campaign. Beyond it, the city of Edgeboston was thrumming and smoking away, spidering out the occasional stretch of road or train track into an otherwise unpopulated landscape. In the distance purple bruises stood in for the mountains at the brink of Foreign. This really was the edge of the civilised world.

It was nearly time to go on. The stairs rang with every footstep, and Ida's breath came short and hard. It was a good way to ready herself. Get that breathlessness over with. She marched to the stage entrance of the main tent, where a delegate's paper was still in progress:

'The historians will ally me with the losing side, the rhetoricians will put a plague on me with their parrhesia, the quarrelsome logicians will bind me in their tightest arguments, the etymologists will derive my name from herpes, the pedantic grammarians will refuse to correct me, the poets will defile my memory in rhyming couplets, the musicologists will find ancient songs about my failings, the physiognomist will identify me as impotent, the astronomer will banish me to the furthest galaxy, the zoologist to the genus of the stink ant, the Dean will defame me at open day, the archivist will destroy all record of me, the anchorman will lampoon me, the whore will turn down my money, the bin men will refuse me, the gulls will go hundreds of leagues out of their way to shit on my head...'

A production assistant motioned for Ida to mic up. Her stomach and knees melted a little. Expectations are usually justifiably lower in the provinces, but that paper had sounded perplexingly good. Her confidence in her old content and untried mode of delivery was starting to waver. But it was too late.

'And now we are honoured and delighted to welcome to the lectern Ida O'Dewey, who will be presenting the intriguingly titled paper, "Feeling Texty: Braille and the role of haptic affordances in epistemological subjectivities".'

*

They say that the other senses are heightened when sight is not available, but this is not strictly true. Some blind people work hard on deciphering audio information – using the sound of breathing to pinpoint the position of people in a room, or ascertaining the speed of a vehicle from the pitch of its engine – and others memorise the relation between patterns of raised dots and letters of the alphabet. But these are learned skills that don't suddenly rush in when sight is lost. A social reflex does kick in immediately, however, when the sighted are plunged into darkness. They tend to rein in their movements so as to avoid accidents or embarrassments, producing a preternatural stillness.

The dark, as seen from onstage, was unexpectedly filled with huge blots of colour. The so-called blackness was in fact made up of patches of indigo, dark puce and deep ochre; and tiny red 'on' lights gathered vignettes of barely perceptible three-dimensionality about them. During the lengthening silent introduction, the audience's anticipation was starting to develop into perplexity. Ida's had already flipped into visceral terror. She hadn't learned Braille at all – not one dot of it. What she had really done was record herself reading the paper out loud, flatly and slowly, so she could play it back into an earpiece and parrot it into a microphone, mimicking the tone of the reading so that the audience wouldn't think that she was speaking from memory or extemporising. She had even recorded a whispered message to herself at the beginning of the tape – 'Don't worry, it's all here, just say what I say' – for reassurance that the tape was fully rewound, and as a reminder that her pre-performance self had done ample planning, that she was in safe hands.

Waiting a good few minutes after the lights went out and the audience had settled, she pressed play.

'Don't worry, it's all he-e-e-r-e…'

She heard her own tinned voice slow down and lower, then slur to a halt. She knew that feeling of running aground only too well. The batteries. A column of acid rose from her stomach. Her instinct was to play dead, but in the dark that wouldn't solve anything.

Over the sound of blood roaring in her ears she barely heard a nearby van door open and close, a snippet of radio talk show tumbling out: '… deeply troubling but nonetheless beautiful…' The audience gave out a murmur. Ida racked her brain for the first line of her paper. If she could start, maybe she could busk the rest. She knew the gist of it, but what a shame to lose all those lovely turns of phrase.

She cleared her throat experimentally. The audience tittered. She crossed and uncrossed her legs. Her corduroy culottes gave out their characteristic little shriek. The audience laughed. The last throat clearance died down and the suspended emptiness endured until uncomfortable fake laughter started to ripple at the back of the auditorium. Someone towards the front made a sarcastic remark to a neighbour, the word 'nothing' rising up and provoking stifled snorts that worked their way back to meet the wave that was rippling forwards from the rear. Like two weather fronts meeting, thunderous peels erupted. And so the hour clocked past, with Ida doing very little to provoke hilarity. She simply held up a near-black mirror that reflected whatever the audience decided to see in it, which on this occasion was a pacey but subtle farce of the throb of tent canvas in the wind, the creaking of chairs, insinuating coughs, a bout of vibrant sneezes and, just five minutes from the end, a distant crash. By the time the house lights were due to go up, every person in the auditorium was euphoric, their bodies ringing with laughter.

*

'Wow, Ida, that was aymayzing. The darkness as a signifier of the state of ignorance. I know it only too well.' A man about Ida's own age looked up at her through smeared glasses, smiling with the unease of one who is seldom recognised by old acquaintances.

'Oh hi. How are you?' Although to be fair, Ida wouldn't have recognised her own reflection following the trauma of that performance.

'Frank, I'll see you back at the ranch,' said a passerby helpfully, slapping him on the back. Ah, Frank. Frank… Cass. Yes, Ida had crossed paths with him frequently over the years. He had been a mediocre scholar, having absorbed six of the 'correct' texts, which he would quote from whenever applicable. But he was not envious of those with more inner resources than he. Rather charmingly, he was effusively enthusiastic about anything he hadn't thought of himself.

'I just adored that. It made me realise I know absolutely nothing. I'm going to have to relearn how to tie my shoelaces now.'

'But Frank, what are you up to these days?'

'Oh, you know, same thing, different department. Musicology at the moment, whatever that is.' He was one of many pawns handed around by senior lecturers and professors in exchange for favours incurred on editorial boards or in recognition of a referral for appointment to a valued post, his only haven the uniformity of basic administrative chores. 'I heard someone saying what you just did then was called Haptic Epistemology. I'd never heard of it before. Is it very big back in central Academia?

'Haptic Epistemology? No, it's not big. It's still quite small actually,' said Ida.

'And the Braille bit? I didn't quite understand how…'

'Well, you see, I was reading in the dark to myself using Braille.'

'Aha, I see. And you were reading on the subject of… ?'

'The subject of… of… conflictive performativity of the half rhyme in Texan oil rap. But you don't need to know about that. What you perceive is enlightenment live, onstage, in the dark.'

'Hilarious!' He chuckled, shaking his head in admiration. Where did they get their ideas from? 'Well, I'll see you at the Interdisciplinary Plenary.'

Ida stepped out into the remains of the afternoon, blinking in the weak sunlight and wondering what to do next. A crowd over by the perimeter wall was dispersing, and those withdrawing had a look on their face that made her want to see what they had seen.

Nosing through the concrete and twisted steel, its back end buried in rubble and its windscreen smashed, was a white car. A woman lay along the bonnet, facedown, her legs still inside, a piece of paper grasped in her hand and her long hair alive in the breeze. A man was splayed half in, half out the passenger door, his leg tangled in a seatbelt. A5 sheets of paper were flitting out from the car interior. Men in grey uniforms were trying to contain the situation, herding onlookers back to the festival. There was nothing to see, apparently. A sheet of paper danced teasingly across the grass, coming to rest at Ida's feet. Failing to comprehend the scene before her, she intuitively reached out for the information, but was beaten to it by a mountain of a man. 'AP OUT / STOP STEALING OUR OIL' was all she had managed to read before he snatched it up, scrunched it in his left fist and swallowed it whole while looking her straight in the eye.

CHAPTER 27

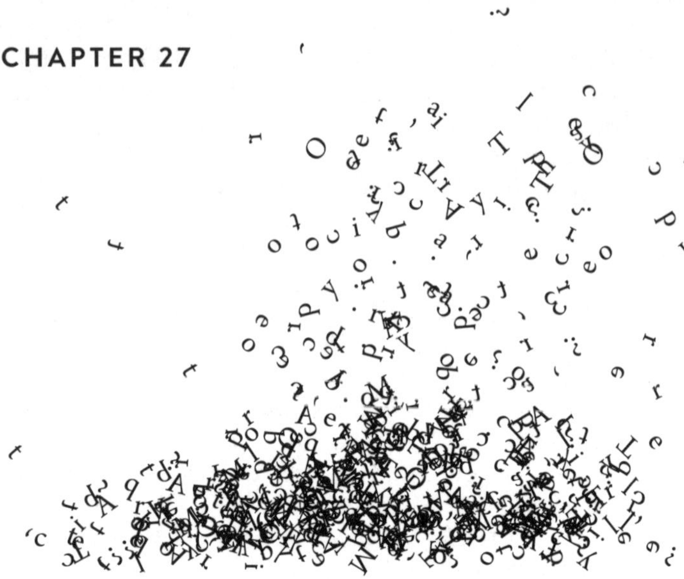

The wind whipped up drifts of vinyl lettering into hillocks of ever-changing gobbledy-gook – a lower semantic form even than nonsense. The materiality of language had never been apparent to Ida – she generally thought of it as gaseous, due to its origin in the spoken word – but here it was solid aggregate. Neither had it dawned on her before that all the wall texts in all the galleries have to go somewhere once the show is over. And yet here they all were, literally broken down, divorced from meaning, with no possibility of reconciliation. It was a disturbing sight for one charged with putting letters, words and sentences in meaningful order. She swore she recognised a few of her own well-turned phrases being harried by the wind.

The bus station was at the edge of a semi-industrial quarter, where the well-maintained civic spaces of the Academy began to fray. The wall text dump was part of the municipal exhibitions disposal plant, where discarded citadels of MDF were put through a vast chipper, the three grades of chips sifted into separate hoppers and shipped out in three directions to fulfil new functions, the finest grade heading for Foreign, where, according to rumour, it was used to bulk out food.

Hands and Ida boarded a single-decker bus with the burgundy and cream livery of the provinces.

'It's really very nice of you to share your content with me like this,' said Ida as they shuffled along the low-ceilinged gangway.

'Yeah. Um, content?' asked Hands, who was more engrossed in choosing the right seat, stopping at one, checking the view, the proximity of heaters and the state of the ashtray before moving on. The fifth seat he tried, almost at the back of the bus, seemed to fulfil all his criteria.

'I mean Jim,' Ida slipped in beside him. It was a cosy fit. 'It's very trusting of you to give me access to him. I might nick all your material. I won't of course. I think our projects are very different, but still, it's very open-handed. Thanks.'

'A GASMAN always shares his contacts.'

'A very clever system, I must say.'

'Yeah, it's not a system.'

'Sorry?'

'Sorry? Why?'

'What?'

'Yeah, it's not a system.'

'What's not?'

'Sharing contacts. It's not a system. It's an operation by which a system can produce internal change. But it's not a system in itself.'

'Right. Sorry.'

'Apology accepted. It's a common mistake.'

'Oh.'

A large Foreign lorry drove past the bus station, its roar drowning out even the grating whine of the chippers. They watched it, glad for the interruption, until it was entirely out of sight.

'Yeah, so, er, you and John,' said Hands with the effort of one who has learned through long and painful means how to conduct the semblance of friendly interest. 'How long have you two been ...?' He started to panic, unable to spot a safe place to park the sentence.

'Collaborating?' offered Ida.

'Yeah.'

'Oh, we've had just a few sessions together so far. Figuring out aims and outcomes. The groundwork, if you like. We haven't really gone far down any particular route yet in terms of planning content. You know how it is at the beginning.'

'No.' He looked at her, deadpan.

'You know, that over-politeness you get at the beginning of relationships – of collaborations. That "is this what we both think it is" sort of subtext. You must have had that with Jim. You're both thinking, are we talking about the same thing? Does he want from it what I want from it, or at least what I think I want from it? You know – that endless internal narration that seems to accompany every bloody social exchange ever.'

'No, I don't know.'

The bus engine awakened with a cough. They paused to listen.

'Funnily enough I went to the countryside quite recently,' said Ida when the silence had become burdensome again.

'Yeah,' said Hands. It wasn't a question. He seemed bored.

'Not this far out, but it was still very interesting. I like how in the countryside things are made out of what they're not.'

When she and John had walked back from the 'installation' they had seen gates made from bed frames, planters from tyres, chicken coops from cars. The locals converging on the train halt to pick up friends and relatives were wearing socks as gloves, jumpers as headscarves, cardigans as trousers. And there was one surly man who, at the arrival of what must have been his mother, judging by their shared chinlessness, cracked a smile that took up half his face and revealed teeth made out of dry-roasted peanuts.

Hands was rubbing his shirt cuff and saying 'yeah' at a peculiarly fast rate as she described all this to him.

'Oh sorry, you must have been to the country a lot and here I am telling you all about it. Gaw, shall I tell your granny how to suck eggs next, eh?'

'She's dead.'

'What?'

'My grandmother.'

'Oh. Sorry. Mine too.'

'Sorry.'

They both fell silent. The bus started up and pulled out of the dingy concrete bus station into the sparse traffic. Was he upset? Ida wasn't entirely sure. He was turning pointedly away, or maybe he was just counting the brickwork, the fence posts, the chimneys, the seconds until the end of time.

'Anyway,' said Ida determinedly, because otherwise they were both ridiculous, 'you must brief me about Jim, and about your collaboration.'

It was as if the sun had come out. The clouds of confusion evaporated and Hands embarked on an extraordinarily long, rhetorically plain but detailed account of Jim and how they worked together.

He explained how his PhD, 'Body Language Under Pressure: corporeal semantics in life-and-death situations', had been reclassified by the Linguistic Department as psychology, and how 'ologies were automatically referred to the Science Department. He'd been working on his PhD for two and a half years now, and had conducted research for chapters on firefighters, parachutists and beekeepers, as well as deep-sea divers, which was Jim's area. But while diving comprised just two chapters of Hands' thesis, it was the obsession from which he had distilled his academic career. Being somewhat awkward on land, he had been attracted to the grace of the diver; but with a congenitally perforated diaphragm that made him liable to hiccup dangerously under compression, he was unable to dive himself. And so now, instead, he kept divers in giant fish tanks, like pets, visiting stressful situations upon them to observe their coping mechanisms. Torturing them felt good – a means to punish them for enjoying what he could not.

Hands had heard of Jim through the Academy, where Jim worked part time when he was 'on the beach', as they say in the industry when a rig worker is between shifts. Where most rig workers have two weeks on, two weeks off, divers work three-week shift cycles, so that their bodies are forced to deal with pressure changes a little less often. For his three weeks on the beach, Jim spent two weeks teaching intensive engineering modules in the Physics Department, and the other week surviving in a stone cottage on a moor.

Jim had immediately understood the potential of a collaboration, and registered his interest on the condition that all rights to the chapters on divers were to be co-reserved. Now that Hands had finished writing them, he was going to hand the copy over to Jim for redrafting into an industry standard communications manual, thereby boosting Jim's standing in the diving community and earning points for impact for Hands, all on top of the research points that the collaborative project attracted in the first place.

'It's very impressive,' said Ida when Hands eventually drew his long and thorough commentary to a close. 'Especially the diving on oil rigs. I would just love to get on to a rig for my project. But I suppose that's a bit of a pipe dream.'

'Yeah,' said Hands.

'Hmmm, shame.'

'Which rigs do you prefer? Jackups or Semisubmersibles? Jim's worked on all types.'

'Oh jackups, definitely,' she guessed.

'He can tell you all about them. He has a lot of experience.'

'Jim sounds rather splendid,' said Ida experimentally, wanting to ask what he looked like, if he was straight or gay, logical or intuitive.

'He's a good diver,' said Hands flatly.

Ida's head was starting to ache from the effort of conversing with this awkward man, and so she made her excuses and gave herself up to the warm, fuggy atmosphere of the bus, to its gentle lurching, rocking motion and the fumes of its engine. She could feel the warm solidity of Hands' shoulder and the controlled movement of his breathing, as she thought just a little more about what Jim might be like before drifting off as the bus rolled and bumped its way further into Outer Academia.

*

Some two hours later – having seen nothing of the raptors suspended in mid-air above invisible prey, the copses whisking past like covens of gracious witches, the pylons pedantically measuring the terrain and the sun glancing side-long across gently undulating fields, each framed with concentric borders of dirt track, ditch and hedgerow – Ida emerged blinking into the clear light of the deep countryside. The handful of other passengers that had made the full journey were gulping down oxygen and ozone, stingingly fresh after the used-up air on the bus. Ida looked about, wondering what sort of countryside this might be. She knew of a few genres – forests, of course, and heath and hills – but it wasn't evident quite what she was up against here. A physical geographer would have been able to tell instantly from the vegetation and the sweep of the terrain that an expanse of brine was a short distance behind them at a drop over a wedge of a cliff, while a cultural theorist would have analysed the architectural evidence to ascertain this. A view of the sea would once have been made a picturesque focus, but since a right and proper anxiety about nature had re-established itself, screens of tall trees had been planted, and all new builds faced resolutely inland. And so Ida and Hands headed off towards their appointment with Jim, the prehistoric sea unnoticed in the background, staring ominously, relentlessly.

They found Jim blotting the oily rainbows off the top of his tea with a paper serviette in the café just a short trot down the road from the bus stop. It was a hot and greasy joint, with unsympathetic lighting and smeary formica surfaces that smelled of the tawdry dishcloths that had wiped them. Hands handed Jim a folder and exchanged a few technicalities before announcing that he'd leave them to it for a while.

'Ok, great. You just take as long as you need. We'll be fine,' said Ida, turning to smile at Jim as Hands strode out through the multi-coloured flystrips.

Jim was about Ida's age, tonsured, with an equine nose and a small mouth that remained open a little at the front at all times; his eyes were far apart and angled downwards as if making for his ears. The overall effect was not pleasant, but this could be unfortunate rather than deserved, and it did impart a certain look of decisiveness.

'So, what are you having?' asked Jim.

'Oh, a thoroughly nice time, thanks.' Ida chuckled encouragingly.

'No, I mean to drink.'

'Quite. Of course. I'll have a sweet tea please.'

Jim unpicked his long, angled legs from the bolted-down plastic bucket seat and strode to the counter, where he stood with his back to her, as if for appraisal. Tight arse, broad shoulders lowering to a neat waist. Shame the front elevation isn't so fabulous, but perhaps his was one of those idiosyncratic faces that become attractive when animated, or through familiarity and fondness.

'Here you are,' he said, lowering two large chipped yellow mugs to the table with underwater slowness. 'The tea here's awfully chalky. I don't know how they do it. It's the only caff for miles though, so we just have to swallow it as it comes.'

'Oh, it's fine,' said Ida. It really was. 'So, you're a diver, I understand. I have to say I don't know anything about diving. I'm probably going to ask the most idiotic questions.'

'Don't worry. I'm used to it,' he said with a put-upon sigh.

'Ok, well, if it's alright with you – and thank you for giving me your time by the way. It's really generous. So yes, um, to dive straight in, as it were. Really, I wanted to ask, although actually, I'm reticent to be too prescriptive in my questioning, since I'm not exactly an authority...' Come on Ida, she chided. Spit it out. 'What I mean is, a preliminary question, if there had to be one, would be "what potential sources of tension do you perceive in your area of specialist knowledge?"'

Jim looked at her with the eyes of a fish straight from the freezer. He couldn't have looked more annoyed and wearied if she'd poured off milk on his shoes.

'What I mean by sources of tension,' she trooped on, 'are phenomena that are at odds with one another, perhaps due to pluralistic contradictions or, as Lyotard calls it, the *differend*.' She was gabbling and name-dropping now, and it was all his fault. 'Erm. This could perhaps be allegorised through an account of contrary physical forces, but I, as a writer, am more interested in the metaphysical rendering of this within structural phenomena that can be read through real experiences of the oil industry. So, for instance, perhaps there are two opposing views within the industry, whereby one person might perceive their role as facilitating culture through the production of fuel and technology, and another might consider himself to be operating at odds with culture, since oil is ultimately utilitarian? Oh dear, now I have been way too prescriptive by clarifying my question with an example, but hopefully you can glean from this the sort of tensions I have in mind.'

'I can assure you,' said Jim flatly, 'that none of whatever you just said passes through my mind. My main concern is making sure that a) I don't drown and b) I can keep a platform standing up in the sea without it collapsing and killing hundreds of people. I don't have time to spend on abstractions when thousands of lives are stake.'

A couple of days later, lying sleepless in bed, Ida would author a perfect response to this.* For now though, she clearly had to change tack. This was not going well. She thought Jim was an academic, or a part-time academic at least, but obviously in his department things were conducted differently. She was at a bit of a loss as to how to lead.

'Actually, maybe you could just tell me the things that interest you, so that I can build a picture of it first and then ask some specifics once I've

* 'I think you have brought an incredibly rich source of tension to my attention right there! Of course, one has a tendency to miss precisely what is under one's nose, so it falls to me to let you know that you have hit the nail on the proverbial head.

'It is becoming clear that a potent source of tension, which you so aptly demonstrate, is produced by the contradiction between the palpable effect and affect of industry on individuals and the very human impulse to consider oneself somewhat abstracted from the causal structures of the universe. We have a tendency to place ourselves at the centre of our own world, so that all that we do and say has immense impact because everything radiates outwards and, due to the gravity we afford ourselves, eventually falls back to us. But, rather rationally, we also imagine that, while we are at our own epicentre, we are only peripheral to others, who similarly place themselves at the centre of their universes. We infer this to mean that we don't really have to be entirely responsible for anyone else at all, since everyone else is the maker of their own fate, future, will-to-power, call it what you like, and so we are magically absolved. But it seems that when one works in something as real as the oil industry it becomes difficult to ignore one's impact on the world. I shall call this "the suspension of unilateral perspectivism".

got the lay of the land. Or the sea, rather, hahahah.'

'I wouldn't say that it interests me. It's what I do for a living. We don't all have the luxury of doing what we enjoy.'

'Right, er, and what is it that you would do on an average day?'

'There's no such thing as an average day. They send me from pillar to post and back and beyond again. I'm lurching from one disaster waiting to happen to the next. It's a mess out there.'

'Out where, exactly?'

'Oh, everywhere. It's all a mess. And muggins here has to sort it out. The other day I ordered a new bottle of gas and it took three days to turn up. Three days. I was stuck there on that boat while Ivan, of course, snapped up all the work. I had to just sit there and watch him clock up the hours. I lost hundreds, thousands, that time. They said it was a squall kept them beached, but whoever heard of a three-day squall. Inefficient, work-shy...'

All fantasies involving the thwack of wetsuits among the breakers were dispelled. Any admiration Ida may have had for Jim's profession was buried beneath a landslide of disappointment in the man himself. A microscopic curl of her top lip was the only telltale sign of the contempt she was concealing within her professionalism.

'Want to order something to eat? I'm famished after all that travelling,' she said, once he seemed to have finished his current grouse. Maybe he was one of those people who become crotchety when hungry.

'You can try if you like,' he said. 'Last time I had oxtail soup here there

'I know, you're probably thinking this all sounds very Nietzschian, all very last century, but let me explain further so you can see how this is inflected with contemporary bio-politics. It's all very well for me to sit here talking about causality as an abstract idea, but I know that when I say this, you will bring your own experience to it, and so I ultimately do not have to shoulder all the blame for how you receive it. But if, say, I were sitting here designing a pipeline and it then ruptured outside your house, I expect you, like most people, would experience it in more or less the same way: you would say "oh no, what a 'beeeep'" (here, with a nod to pluralism, you could insert the word of your choice); and so there is little wriggle room for interpretation in this scenario. I, then, would be far more culpable when it comes to authoring the situation, since you, the homeowner, have no opportunity to re-contextualise or co-author it with respect to the specificities of your own intellectual, emotional or cultural background and milieu. And so this sort of pressure is at odds with the get-out clause of marginality that we ascribe ourselves in the lives of others. It is a clear case of material fact overcoming specious self-knowledge.'

was a tail in it alright, but it wasn't an ox's. I don't want to know what goes on in that kitchen. And those fryers. You should see what comes out of the vents out back. No, no, you go ahead, I'll just chew on my own hand, thanks.'

Ida flung herself towards the counter, and after a short respite returned, bowl in hand.

'You're a brave one,' he said, eyeing the steaming bowl with contempt.

'Not as brave as you, by all accounts.' Maybe flattery would perk him up. 'Can you tell me about the dangers of your job?'

'Dangers? Plural? It's all one big danger, from start to finish. And it's also boring as hell. Danger sounds exciting, but this is the most boring danger ever. We work fourteen hours at a stretch, but we can't keep going down to 500 metres then coming back up each day, because it takes three days to decompress safely. You'll have heard of the bends, of course. So when we're not in the water, we live in a tiny tin can under the same compression conditions as the depths we're diving at. And believe you me, that is tedium itself, with added issues. One is the air that we breathe. You see, in compression conditions of 50 metres and below, normal air becomes dangerous. The nitrogen in it causes a particular type of narcosis that is a combination of depression and a tendency to laugh too much at things that aren't very funny – we say that someone's 'narked' when this happens. And so instead of air, like we're breathing now – although I bet a fair bit of the oxygen is displaced by grease and legionnaires in this place. But anyway, instead of air, we breathe a mixture of helium and oxygen when we're diving and when we're in the tin—'

'Doesn't helium make your voice go funny?' asked Ida between spoonfuls of delicious, salty, greasy stilton soup that lined her throat like mucus.

'Yes, helium contracts the larynx, which makes the voice go higher. And that has the unfortunate effect of undermining any authority we might have. It's embarrassing. We tell them that such-and-such a structure is unsound or that some strut or other has rusted and they just laugh like drains. You can hear them down the line calling us "chipmunks" and "diddymen". So unprofessional.'

'Yes, I can see your problem. Lucky it seems to go back to normal afterwards though, eh?' she said, hoping that was a bright side he could recognise, but an expression of even deeper annoyance was spreading over his face like camouflage netting pulled over a tank. They sat in momentary silence, Ida not daring to finish her soup for fear that the clamour of the spoon against the bowl be taken as offensive disregard for his travails.

But actually, fuck him. Since the interview was hardly going to result in firm friendship or any other collegiate relationship, Ida decided she may as well press him for all she could get instead of trying to make him like her. He didn't like anyone.

'Now, Jim, what can you tell me about the interior of rigs? I've seen plenty of photographs of exteriors, but no one thinks to document the interiors. What do they look like?'

'How should I know? I'm incarcerated in the divers' boats. Totally different. They wouldn't let me on board a rig anyway. Very hierarchical it is. Those roughnecks can't stand us divers. We're too heroic for them. There's no bit of a diver's life that isn't treacherous. Even the really ordinary things. I bet you're thinking the biggest dangers are the explosives, the sharks, the bends, the air running out. Everyone does. But no. It's the lavatory.'

'Really? How?'

'It can suck you inside out. You see, if there was a breakdown in the compression system, the series of air and water locks would undergo sudden pressure changes that would create a vacuum strong enough to prolapse the innards of any poor bastard who happened to be crapping at the time. So that's why all toilet seats are drilled with holes around the edge. It looks like some pointless design thing, but these little holes can actually save your life. They make a more easily breakable seal between the buttocks and the seat. Of course, knowing my luck, it'll be the way I go, holes or no holes. Unless the Foreigners get to us all first. Of course now they're nationalising the industry we're all going to be frog-marched off the premises. Out of a job altogether. They've always prioritised Foreign workers on Foreign concessions, but they never had anyone with the brains or the lungs for diving. Pigeon-chested nation, Foreign. But now we're all being drummed out they'll have to train up some mountain-dwelling Foreigners or something. Probably breed them specially, cross them with narwhals. Deviant, the Foreigners. Cruel. Wouldn't like to be left behind finishing up AP's business. Better off out of there.'

How Hands worked with this permanent pulse of negativity was beyond Ida. What a shame, though, because it was clear what Jim could bring to the table, with his career spanning twenty years and straddling engineering, economics and geo-politics, conducted under 500 metres of water in all however many corners of the globe there were. But this was buried under a silt of life-hating bitterness. Oh, the crying shame of it. She could weep.

'But I can see I'm boring you,' said Jim, breaking off suddenly.

'Boring? No! Look, I've completely forgotten my soup, which is unusual for me, I can tell you.'

'You academic women usually like more glamour, more high-end speechifying and theorising...'

'Luckily, I'm not really a full-on academic. So no, you're not boring me. I'm transfixed. In fact, perhaps you can tell me all about oil rigs. I'm hoping to get on to one, you see, for research. For my next project. Oil rigs are beautiful, aren't they?'

Jim was just turning up his nose in reply when the tinkle of the bell above the café door announced the return of Hands, covered head to toe in a dark, sheeny filth and grinning.

'Hey you two, come and see what I've found.'

CHAPTER 28

'That Jim's a miserable bastard. How ever can you work him?'

Ida and Hands were slumped in facing train seats, speeding back to central Academia, a *memento mori* of abandoned snacks and torn packing on the table between them. The carriage was filled with cigarette smoke, the passengers all pulling together to keep it topped up.

'Yeah. I'm told he's insecure and that he doesn't mean it,' said Hands.

'I suppose anyone would feel insecure under hundreds of feet of water,' said Ida. 'You have to give him some credit for that. It must be very disturbing.'

'And he does have very good connections at AP.'

'Ah, I see,' said Ida. 'So you're as ambitious as the rest of them then?'

'Yeah, I have ambitions. But I don't think that's inherently bad. It's selfish, of course, by definition. That's our biological imperative playing itself out culturally. But one's ambitions are not necessarily harmful to others, especially if they're realistic.'

'I suppose you're right. There's a difference between a psychopathic desire to conquer the world and a benign ambition to step foot on an oil rig. You wouldn't think it's too much to ask, would you? Jim reckons it's impossible too.'

'Yeah.' Hands seemed to be weighing something up. 'It's not impossible. You need to get a foot in the door at AP. They're about to advertise for a critic-in-residence. The open call isn't out yet, but I can get you an interview if you're interested.'

'Really? That'd be incredible. Do they have an art collection they need contextualising or something?'

'They want a critical context for their business practice so they can popularise the brand for an academic market.'

'Isn't that what they call intellectual white-washing?'

'They call it marketing.'

'Hmmm, interesting. If you could arrange an interview, that'd be amazing.'

The landscape ribboned past, a darker version of the previous day's.

Dappled sap greens, so dazzling then, now sulked under an overcast sky. The magnificent fun they'd had, too, was flattened into exhaustion.

Hands' discovery had been a country fayre and his clothing had been soiled by a pig slathered in axle grease, which he had chased and grappled to the ground. Since such a creature would be barred from the bus back to Edgeboston, he announced to a collective cheer that the hog roast was on him. He raced back to the café across the fields to fetch Jim and Ida, while a group of locals slaughtered the screaming animal and expertly erected a roasting jig, with corrugated iron walls, a spit and a huge rotating handle wrapped in a damp chamois, which everyone took turns to turn until the sizzling barrel of meat was pronounced ready.

With grease trickling down their chins and smeared around their pewter tankards froth-topped with cider, Ida and Hands had stood on the brink of the action, watching the mummers and morris men from afar, until the pull was too strong and they found themselves whirled around, hankies tied to their index fingers, bells strapped to their shins. They daubed each other's faces with deep-blue woad, coal dust and pungent pig's blood, and whacked strangers' behinds with a switch of birch top-tied with the bladder of the late pig, the proteins from which were coursing through everyone's veins, fuelling a higher gear of Bacchanalia. Short plays with narratives of lust, jealousy, murder and magic progressed with breakneck speed and little emotional nuance, enacted by a troupe of players dressed in costumes made with great resourcefulness from sacks, elastic bands, bottles and Styrofoam. The stage was little more than a slight tuffetted rise in the field, and the audience were equally unceremonious, booing, shouting or ignoring the play altogether. Children and dogs rushed the actors at inauspicious moments, and drunks tried to join in stage fights, having forgotten that it was fiction.

The centrepiece of the day had been an ancient rite, the Salting of the Sea, traditionally performed to assuage the ocean's insatiable hunger for sailors, fishermen and boats, which it frequently swallowed whole, and human-made structures or equipment, which it licked at persistently over time. On paper, the seas may be as territorialised as the land, but in practice they are a slushy, foggy hinterland beyond national legislation. A sea cannot be had up before a judge for criminal damage, since the irrepressible forces of atrophy, rust, drift, dissolution and derangement are beyond ethics. We now know these forces as 'chemistry', which we can influence with our technologies, but to the ancients they were governed by the whims of deities, who could be cajoled by acts of worship or coerced by sorcery. If these oceanic gods enjoyed a surfeit of salt, it was reasoned, they would be more thirsty than hungry and might stop eating boats, piers and people. And so the folk lowered themselves down the white cliff face on coloured ropes to offer rock salt effigies of items and loved ones lost in the preceding year to the ravenous waves.

For Ida, the fayre was an exotic display of otherness, and nothing to do with nostalgia for a communalising past. But while she and Hands participated – he with full absorption and she never dropping the narrow smile of self-consciousness – Jim was bored and annoyed. He pettishly pronounced folk to have been trumped by modern technologies and therefore irrelevant. But Hands pointed out that these activities were the sciences and technologies of their day: dowsing, ritual sacrifice, fertility dances and offerings of braided corn had been recognised methods for boosting the availability of water, fuel, food and child labour. Seismic surveys, pesticides, poly tunnels and antibiotics were their contemporary equivalents, reflecting new beliefs that might be dismissed as outlandish magics or quaint misunderstandings in the future. Jim harrumphed and walked off, muttering about time being money. Hands promised his back that he'd call soon. Ida heaved a sigh of relief.

The next morning, following a fitful night huddled round the fading hog roast, Hands had talked of how the abandonment of Pagan technologies was a great loss to science.

'There are, in my opinion, some things we can learn from the ancient peasantry,' he said as Ida nursed the blister on her shin, sustained from falling asleep while in contact with the still-hot corrugated iron. 'Take cable ties, for instance. People used to fix things with string. Now it's all cable ties. You don't hear about a cure for warts using knotted cable ties, do you? Plastics have displaced material pluralism and secondary usage.'

They were laying on their backs in a haystack, Ida listening docilely as Hands reflected on how ancient technologies were called magic, and how new technologies often seem just as mysterious and improbable.

'For what are magic and technology but the apparent control of phenomena ordinarily beyond an individual's control? Technology is the extension of the body's natural capacities, while magic is the performance of totally new powers; but there is a fuzzy region where technology is so progressive that our natural capacities are no longer recognisable. Take optics. The facility of the eye stretched beyond human scale to penetrate deep space was a talent previously ascribed only to Dog. But now the astronomical processes witnessed through the most powerful telescopes have been replicated in the technology we use to boil our kettles. We are among the stars every day.'

The implications of this were storming through Ida's tired brain. As the colour crept into the morning and the air started to warm, she alternated between excitement and frustration at not knowing what to do with this new insight. As Hands continued talking, Ida swam in and out of his stream of ideas, a word or image sending her off at a tangent or causing a pause. She was getting the hang of him, getting used to not being able to predict which bit of what she was saying he would respond to, or in which direction he would take it. The conversational ball is usually passed back and forth with the aim of prolonging a volley, but Hands was liable to wander off along his own thoughtlines. To begin with she had found it infuriating, and had tried to grab fistfuls of conversation back, but by sun-up she was relieved to put herself to one side and to enjoy the peregrinations of a mind other than her own, which had, for as long as she could remember, been repetitive, petty and jumbled. Hands on the other hand seemed able to hold the entire world in his head, and to perceive it as a series of causal relations, which he could relate in complete and perfectly formed sentences.

'Excuse me guys, I'm going to have to move you on,' said a man appearing around the haystack.

'Oh, sorry. Do you need the hay? Is it feeding time?' Ida was surprised to see that the farmhand was wearing smart trousers and a shirt of matching brown, with a golden logo embroidered above a breast pocket full of pens. Still, the countryside has to move with the times, she supposed.

'Ha ha, yes, that's right,' the man said jovially, beckoning to his identically dressed mate. As Hands and Ida looked on, the two skimmed off a thin layer of hay to reveal a large inflatable cone, which was pumped empty with a portable contraption and flat-packed, along with the crated hay, into the back of a shiny brown truck bearing the legend 'Academic Historical Re-enactment Stores'.

CHAPTER 29

'Ah, here she is – the new artist on the block. Congratulations!' said Sue, who was emerging from her room as Ida stepped into the office.

'Ok, can the sarcasm. I'm fully aware that I fucked up again.' Ida nearly tripped on thick carpet where previously there had been poured concrete. The casements had been hung with swags of rich velvet; the old paint, the colour of which she couldn't remember, had been covered over with broad striped paper in burgundy and gold, and a new parade of rather theatrical uplighters circled the room. 'Blimey, is this the new agency image?' She took in the scene of office harmony: files piled high on mahogany desks, phones answered within a single ring by underpaid staff, Linda's robust legs wrapped about a Chesterfield kneeling stool like an anaconda with its next meal.

'You might have fucked it up as a lecture,' said Sue, 'but as a performance you nailed it. You've been all over the papers. It seems it was some sort of coming-out as a comedy performance artist, or a performative comedian, no one's quite sure. Do you even know yourself? Of course I was straight back on the radio saying it was all planned, and that prig Robin lapped it right up. The sycophant.'

'A comedy performance artist? They'll put any three words together and say it's a thing. To tell you the truth, and you can bury this immediately, but in actuality I made a total fuck-up of the lecture I *was* going to give and for some reason everyone decided it was all on purpose and highly hilarious.'

'Well, yes, I think we will bury that one,' said Sue, looking about to see how many personal assistants or receptionists might have heard, but there was only Barbie – thick-set young woman, flat-backed head, gravelly voice – deep in a telephone call.

'I have to admit, it was entirely my own fault. I knew to expect shoddy tech in the provinces, but I didn't cover my arse quite as sufficiently as I might have. I wouldn't wish the sensation of hearing disaster announcing itself through an earpiece on my worst enemies.'

'An earpiece?' said Linda, looking up quizzically over a pile of photocopies.

'Actually, I'd rather not talk about it. So, word got about?'

'It certainly did. Barbie's collated your press cuttings.' Sue picked up a plump file and opened it. 'This one's particularly good: "It was like being inside Malevich's *Black Square*: total annihilation, but somehow such profundity in its rawest form was hilarious."' She leafed through and pulled another out. 'And a mention here from Briony Da Corta. She calls it "a blank comedy".'

'Is that a good thing?' But Ida felt a glow of accomplishment. It was a shame this glow was sparked by praise from without; but still, it warms, it warms...

'You should really thank your friend Jørn Hødd,' said Sue, handing Ida a photocopy of some pages from *May*. 'This came out the day of the performance and did a very nice job of framing it for you.'

Ida started reading from the second paragraph, since the first one is usually for warming up the writer, not the reader.

'A comedian has material – that is, matter that is crafted to represent an idea, to provoke a sensation or thought – which certainly sounds similar to the practice of a sculptor or a painter. But let us look a little closer at this material. It can be observational or fantastical, drawn from life or the imagination. Are we not in the realm of image-making here? The next question is whether this is mimetic representation or abstraction, and the answer, I will argue, is that, as with the plastic arts, it can be either.

'The comedy routine that is based on an observation – let's say on observations regarding the relationship between a man and his mother-in-law – can be made more generic or more specific; it can reflect the assumptions we make about all relationships between men and their mother-in-laws, or it can relate a particularly absurd relationship, which, while normalising all other such relationships in relation to it, also emphasises their own particularities. An instance of the former is the succinct, "Take my mother-in-law. Please." It abstracts the relationship into pure negativity. The man does not want his mother-in-law around him. He asks us to please take her away. Many men can identify with a desire to block out the view of their wife's mother, since she stands for what the wife, and consequently the husband too, will become – that is, older, decayed, closer to death. This fear of mortality is expressed through the embodiment of negativity by the mother-in-law, and it is this that is being laughed at, in its pure, indistinguishable form, through the palimpsest of a relative acquired through matrimony. It is laughter at the recognition of death, projected through the obfuscating filter of abstraction.

'An instance of the second mechanism, that is, of particularisation, is the joke, "I'm not saying the mother-in-law's ugly, but she uses her bottom lip as a shower cap." Here the fantastical specificity is understood as a cipher for all specificities. Negative attributes of any mother-in-law are interchangeable, since they are metonymic of a generic negative attitude held by the husband rather than the negative attributes of the mother-in-law herself; and so, while this produces laughter through comic distortion, there is an essential zero state from which the person laughing knows that this comic absurdity has been constructed, and that zero state is, once more, their own approaching death.'

Ida was impressed by Jørn's clarity but wondered what it had to do with her. He had mastery over theoretical tools that could winkle the most occult meanings from a text, artwork or random event in the street. He could find richness and importance where others saw empty inconsequence. She hoped she would understand what he had found. She scanned the pages for her own name and continued.

'If we take the recent declarations of critic Ida O'Dewey, for instance, we can discern the potential for equivalent functions in the art of comedy and the comedy of art. O'Dewey's characterisation of art as a self-absorbed and power-crazed despot is a succinct performance of material manipulation in the vein of the mother-in-law joke. The originary material – that is, art – represents for many their own lack, just as the mother-in-law represents their lack of immortality. But where the mother-in-law represents mortality through a temporal and phenomenological fold – i.e., an encounter with their own wife's future self – art confronts a person with their own artlessness in the here and now. Art operates through contrast and complementarity, its elevated ontology pointing up our common shortfalls, and so we do indeed perceive it to be an entity that denudes us in a way, that reduces our self-worth. The effect of this, in the best of all possible worlds, would be that we work all the harder to maintain our uppermost standards as moral human beings. In our world, however, this is, at best, patchily achieved; we strive for the aforementioned state of grace, but when it slides beyond us, we simply accept that art is our superior. O'Dewey's tyrannical art heightens our awareness of the discrepancy between ourselves and art through inversion. Art-as-divine is transfigured into art-as-profane. We become victims and art the animal aggressor; and so we are given license and capacity to fight, to achieve parity with it.'

'My Dog,' she said. 'How does he do that? I mean, now I've read it, it feels completely true, that is exactly what I was doing, but I couldn't have said so at the time. It's funny isn't it, how we enact these ideas but it takes someone else to put them into words. Hmmm, amazing.' She read on.

'But let us consider the media's reaction at the time. It was as if O'Dewey had invented fire and Dog was cursing her for it. She handed to the everyperson a means of self-betterment by way of satirical inversion, and yet the immediate response was outrage. I would suggest this is because some feel that if art were re-described as driven and fallible, we would lose respect for it, for it will become too much like us. But just as one does not lose respect for one's wife simply because, like her mother, she too will eventually age and die, neither will we abandon art because it has appetites as we do.

'There is one final but important distinction to make here. The narrative that O'Dewey related was an instance of exemplification: she focused all her specialist knowledge into a singular image, which listeners then interpreted using their own, more often than not, generalist knowledge. Far from a declaration of fact, the satire invited us to bring our own subjectivities to our readings, but many blamed O'Dewey for having placed these subjectivities in there in the first place. The press in particular. If the critic's words caused offence, it was because we tooled ourselves up for it. Her fiction, her joke, her media-specific artwork was a proposition which, like all great art, we could measure ourselves against – but unfortunately for O'Dewey, many found themselves falling short.'

Ida lowered the photocopy. She felt humbled, grateful, proud and anxious all at once. This was an incredible piece of engineering, and remembering those theoretical ducts and twists would be a challenge. They were rather a blur already.

'Well,' she said, 'if that doesn't put the peer review back in the cupboard, I don't know what will. I don't suppose you've heard anything about it lately have you?'

'Not a dickie bird, but that could mean anything,' said Sue. 'It's all very well turning the trade press around, but it will take more than one buddie's endorsement to sway the CSA.'

In fact, the peer review was already being dismantled due to 'new evidence'. Six months down the line, on its scheduled completion date, there would be no mention of its findings anywhere in the media. Some dogged civil servant, paid to go through the motions until the brief's barest necessities were fulfilled, would possibly know the answer to the question it had been set up to investigate; but by then its real purpose – which was to be seen to respond to controversy rather than to instigate change – would have long been served.

'Oh Sue,' said Linda, 'you are quite the pessimist. I think this is an important turning point for you Ida. Does he say anything about your rhetoric?'

'Tut tut. Look at Linda trying to find a reflection of herself in the shine of another's success,' said Sue savagely. 'So, moving on, we need to work on your next project and really whip up a storm around it. There's still much room for improvement in your appointments diary. Your loss is my loss too, you know. But you need to tell me – it's not going to be performance art really, is it? You're not going to defect to a gallery?'

Sue shouldn't sow such seeds. For now, though, Ida laughed at the very suggestion.

'I don't think long-form performance is really my bag. But I do have an exciting new departure up my sleeve. I shan't give too much away about the subject matter, because it's still fermenting in my head, but I can tell you that I am going to start writing the most sensational novel about it.'

'A novel?' asked Sue, frowning.

'A novel!' exclaimed Linda, salivating.

'It's still very much in the research stages, so I can't say much more than that, but I think it's going to break ground that people didn't even know existed. Listen, there are some fascinating characters that I want you to help me to get to help me. If I organise a soirée next week, will you come?'

Sue and Linda looked automatically to Barbie, who barked 'Wednesday's good', without having to consult so much as a wall planner.

'Hold your horses Ida,' said Sue. 'You do know about Prentice Hall, don't you?'

'What about him?'

'He's writing a novel too.'

'What?' Ida's blood turned icy.

'I've got a press release here about his upcoming novel. It hit the newsrooms while you were away and they're going ape over it. You'll need to hang on a bit and make sure you place yours in proper tactical relation to it.'

'What the fuck is Prentice Hall doing writing a novel? He can't be. I got there first. I've been planning my novel for weeks,' wailed Ida.

'Well, it seems he's been planning his a little longer. Or maybe he hasn't; maybe he's just announced his first. Either way, you'll be accused of bandwagonning if you suddenly announce you're writing one. You'll undo all Jørn's good work. Maybe just hang on a bit, get your story straight and then announce something more specific, more comedy-performance oriented.'

'Bastard, bastard, bastard. I know he's just plucked this out the air. There's not really a novel. He's just filched the idea from me somehow. There's a mole. That's what it is. I bet it's one of those fucking interns. What shall I do, Sue?' Ida was wringing a paper tissue that had been stashed up her sleeve, its shreds littering the carpet.

'There's lots of other things you can do.' Sue clicked her fingers at Barbie, who sprang up and cleared away the mess with a dustpan and brush plucked from her desk drawer. 'A novel's just one idea. You can have another idea just as easily as you had this one. Just move on Ida.'

'But this idea wasn't easy. It was bloody hard. It's my idea. My only idea for ages. I'll not have another one for another age. Damn that fucking Prentice. Fuck that damn leech. Actually, do you know what? I'm just going to go ahead anyway. I bet he just writes a stupid normal boring straightforward novel with a… a plot and characters and all that boring normal stuff. Well I'm going to write something so novel it's going to knock his into a cocked hat. He'll bring out his novel and I'll bring out mine and mine will make his look so fucking un-novel. Actually, you can jolly well call a press conference and announce it. Or go on the radio again. Say I've been working on my novel, which will be a totally new sort of novel, and that I've already been working on it for ages. Say the dark performance was research for it. Yes, and *Panel Beaters* too… And before they accuse me of a U-turn, tell them it's a comic novel.'

'Listen, I'm not crossing a heavyweight like Hall. And neither should you,' said Sue, blowing smoke aggressively and stubbing out her cigarette – a full stop to the discussion.

Ida knew she was right. Prentice was a manipulative, managerial sort of academic, a professor who, like Rothwell-Beer, had travelled the Royal Road to power but, unlike the formidable Dean, had not quite made it to the pinnacle he had his eye on. This short distance from what he perceived to be his rightful place in history made him more ruthless than anyone further down the career slope. And because his time was guzzled by the administrative and managerial responsibilities of his elevated post, he closed the distance between himself and the elite hands-on researchers by any means available to him. He had probably offered them a seat on a committee or the guest editorship of a journal to flatter them into spilling their content. It was just her luck to have randomly alighted on the latest thing.

'Ok,' said Ida, 'I'll bear your position in mind, but Prentice isn't the first novelist, and neither will he be the best. I'm going ahead with my research, and I'd appreciate it if you'd help. But I won't ask you to stick your neck out publically. Just come to dinner. You too Linda. That's all I ask.'

'Ok, ok. Anything to keep the peace,' said Sue. 'By the way, who are you going to cover in your reviews roundup this week? The phone's been ringing off the hook all morning – the galleries all want to be reviewed by a comedienne it seems.'

'Shit. Is it Thursday *again*? Oh bugger-fuck,' said Ida, sprinting out the door.

CHAPTER 30

The doorbell chimed and Ida scampered down the spiral staircase to brief Sue and Linda while Manfred peeled their outer garments from them.

'Now, a quick word before you go up there. I have no idea who some of these people are, but I'm guessing you'll have to be a bit – how shall I put it? – accommodating. Don't pick them up on their grammar Linda, ok? And Sue, there's no point asking for their hot tips on artists, because they're not that way inclined. Just roll with it and it'll be a hoot. And if you get bored, there's always Jørn to speak to. Or one another. Just don't talk to me too much please. I've got some important work to do tonight. Hey, where's your New Face?'

'Sorry. We couldn't think of anyone you didn't already know,' said Linda.

'That's not strictly true. I suggested bringing the plumber, but Linda vetoed him,' said Sue.

'Well, it does seem a bit arch, doesn't it?' said Linda.

'He would've been just the ticket tonight, I'm sure. Anyway, never mind. Just get up there and mingle,' said Ida.

New Faces dinners, to which each guest brings someone they know but the host doesn't, were all the craze in Academia. Despite the official line on interdisciplinarity, academics were prone to socialising only with colleagues and allies. But since many people worked in areas that abutted other disciplines and knew practitioners just the other side of the divide, this new methodology could effect social interdisciplinarity without the risks of inviting complete strangers. Ida had contacted all the GASMANs she had met and liked so far, which only amounted to John and Hands. She wasn't inviting Jim for all the new faces in Foreign. Excitingly, the party seemed to be working out. It was an odd mix of people, but to an outside eye they could have been any group of friends or colleagues getting along with typical guardedness. It wasn't uncommon for New Faces dinners to drag along in near silence, and so she took the gently stilted burble upstairs to be an auspicious start.

Back up on the middle floor, the kitchen was issuing steam thick with the musk of saffron. In the adjacent dining room people were standing, sipping wine and talking politely in pairs, commenting on the walls full of art and the impressive view across central Academia, which seemed, from their high vantage point, to be made up of a series of theatrical flats that gradually faded into the misty distance of the forest canopy.

Ida clapped her hands for attention as she herded the new guests into the room. 'I must introduce everyone now that we're all here. Ok, everyone, this is Sue and Linda, and Sue and Linda, this is John; John – Sue and Linda; and this is Johnnies John – his distinction, not mine, may I add. Johnnies John, this is John and this is Sue and Linda. Although I should really say this is Sue and this is Linda, because they do come separately, of course. And this is Hands; Hands, this is Sue, Linda, John and Johnnies John; John, Johnnies John, Sue, Linda – Hands. And Patty – did I get that right? Yes, good. Patty – meet John, Johnnies John, Sue, Linda, Hands; Hands, John, Johnnies John, Sue, Linda – meet Patty; and here we have Jørn …' and so on. 'Ok, did you catch all that? Oh, and Juan's in the loo. Here he his. Juan, this is Sue and Linda and John and Johnnies John and Hands and Patty – did I get that right? Sorry, yes, this is Patty, and Jørn and I'm Ida, I think. Hahhahhah.'

Juan, short and sweaty, shook hands silently and solemnly with everyone. Ida had no idea who he'd come with. In fact he didn't seem to know anyone and maintained a look of polite disinterest throughout. He could have just wandered in from the street, for all she knew. Still, it was easier not to cause a scene.

'Shall we sit?' asked Ida rhetorically. Everyone hesitated. 'There's no placements, so wherever you like.' People dithered around the long oval table, shuffling and excusing themselves to jostle towards people they liked the look of, or away from those they didn't. John sat at the other end of the table from Ida. They had somehow made up a couple of nights ago. She wasn't sure what had precipitated her ride to his bedsit in a small-hours taxi. But anyway, it was nice. That was the word for it. It had felt nice to wake up in his familiar arms. They'd had a fun breakfast in bed and a slow morning and it was as if nothing had happened, which is what John had insisted was the case. He had been busy working and so had she. They were mature enough to see each other or not depending on desire and circumstance, rather than paranoia or sense of duty. She had agreed, raised her coffee cup and offered a toast: 'To desire, not duty.' Apart from Suky, she hadn't told anyone about John, but she didn't want Sue, Linda or Jørn to feel she had hidden something from them, and so John was under strict instruction not to let on they were seeing each other. And so he sat next to Patty, who was far too attractive for Ida's liking. Jørn tried to wait until Juan had taken a place, so that he might sit well away from him, but Juan dithered and Hands sat down and leapt up at least three times, circling the table like a dog, leaving a last-minute vacancy next to Jørn by taking the seat Jørn had been hoping for above all – next to Ida. The only place left for Juan now was next to Jørn.

Jørn covered his disappointment at sitting next to Juan by turning his back on him and asking Linda a long, in-depth question about litotes. Sue, meanwhile, channelled her disgust at the immediate company towards the odd little figurines made from straw that played sentry to each setting's soup spoons.

'They're corn dollies,' said Ida. 'A little something for you to take away when you leave. Hands and I got them when we were in the countryside the other day. There was an amazing folk fayre, wasn't there?' He nodded in assent. 'Oh you must tell them about the greased pig.'

'Yeah.' Hands blushed deeply from the waist down. Before surgery he would have blushed from the waist up too – a crippling impediment checked by routine keyhole procedure under each armpit, which permanently impeded the blood's rise to the face and neck. During their time in the country together he had eventually relaxed and even became demonstrative, but he was obviously uncomfortable in a social group. In the Science Department he could cope with the objectivity of the language, and in GASMAN meetings the agenda was always clear, but around the dinner table people spoke in bewildering convulsions, lurching between strident opinion, self-effacing confessional, hearsay, facticity, small talk, quotation and insinuation of every sort. Ambiguity, irony and sarcasm were particularly impossible for him to grasp, which is partly why he had specialised in body language, for being primarily unconscious, it was consequently fairly objective. 'The pig… yeah… *That* wasn't greasy or…' he faltered, wondering if sarcasm was the way to go right now.

Ida stepped in and told an entertaining story of how Hands had chased, wrestled and won the greased pig – some feat of the imagination, because she had been in the café with Jim throughout. She omitted the killing, roasting and eating episodes.

'What were you doing in the countryside? I thought you hated it,' said Jørn, not managing to suppress a flash of jealousy. He'd had his suspicions that there was something going on for Ida. She had smelt different lately. So here he was. What a schmuck.

Ida explained about Jim and Hands' collaboration, and, to Hands' further discomfort, Jørn asked what someone always asked when he was outed as a body language specialist:

'So, what does everyone in the room think of me, then?'

'He's not a bloody wizard, you know,' said Ida protectively. 'And anyway, asking a pig-headed question like that, you might not want to know the answer. Now, who wants a Castrol GTX? It's a very old classic cocktail: gin and tonic with methylated castor oil fizzed through it. Knock-out.'

The drinks were mixed by two interns dressed in rented black tie. They leaned solemnly over the diners' shoulders and affected bizarre mannerisms picked up from old films: moving glassware with gloved little fingers cocked, pouring long streams from high jugs, like urination, and standing stiff as caryatids against the wall between tasks.

'Oh, Manfred, be a poppet and warm that plate of thingies through, will you?' said Ida. 'You know, the brown ones that look like tiny stews. I hope you're all hungry – tonight we're having special countryside canapés followed by porterhouse, blueberry and anchovy bisque.' Everyone made fitting sounds of wonder at such a striking menu. 'And the dessert is a surprise.'

'Sorry, madam,' said Manfred with discrete insouciance, 'I am contracted only to buttle. I believe you have omitted to engage a sous-chef.'

'Quite right, Manfred. Bravo.' Ida nodded approvingly. 'These interns know their rights these days. Historically they have been so exploited, they're unionised up to the hilt now. Good for them, I say. In my day we were thrashed if we didn't comply with the boss's every whim.' She turned to Manfred again. 'Remind me tomorrow to tell you about the time I had to arrange a vasectomy for a very reputable editor.'

Manfred nodded with sobriety. 'Madam.'

'Don't worry,' said John, 'I'll sort the brown things. Just needs putting in the oven, right? With the timer set to, what, twenty minutes? And I'll put the main soup on low while I'm at it, shall I?'

Ida nodded with a look that was intended to prompt him to at least ask where the kitchen was, but he was already padding off down the corridor, obviously perfectly at home. Sue and Linda assumed he, and everyone else, had been given a tour before they arrived – it was quite the show home after all – and so they drew no conclusions. But Jørn noticed. So *this* was the competition. He mentally apologised to Hands.

The talk around the table became smaller and smaller until it fragmented into multiple, localised conversations. John soon returned and slipped into his seat, paying attention to Patty on one side and totally ignoring Linda on the other. Typical man, thought Jørn. Youth and beauty are not to be sniffed at, but he knew from experience that the overlooked plainer woman is so much more grateful, and generous, when she is attended to. He should demonstrate this chap's shortcomings to Ida before she was in too deep.

'So, John,' said Jørn, in a tone of voice dangerous as quicksand. Everyone stopped to listen. 'Ida tells me you're working together. Are you a comedian?'

'No, not a comedian. At least not on purpose,' said John.

'A scholar of comedy then?'

'No, it's not something I'd like to analyse. You know what they say: you can only perform an autopsy on a corpse. I prefer my comedy alive and mystifying.'

'That's ridiculous,' said Jørn. 'Analysis does not necessarily destroy its subject.'

'Maybe not, but it seriously impedes one's enjoyment of it.'

'Ah, but that's where you're wrong. Even a gynaecologist can fall in love.'

'Touché,' said Ida cheerfully.

'Yes, very good,' said John.

'Haven't I heard that before?' said Linda.

'Not from me,' said Jørn quickly, although this was indeed a purloined line, so he was relieved that Johnnies John seemed eager to add something.

'That reminds me of a joke.' The diners all turned, grateful for an opportunity to stare legitimately at the green and blue pistol tattooed on his neck, faded as if it had been in a shop window for years. It twitched as he spoke. 'This woman goes to the gynaecologist for an examination, right? She gets up in the stirrups and the doctor has a look and says, "You really do have a very large pussy. You really do have a very large pussy." The woman looks at the doctor and replies, "Alright, you don't have to say it twice." "I didn't," says the doctor.'

Silence.

'I don't get it,' said Linda. 'Why did she take her pussy with her to the doctor's?' Everyone burst out laughing. 'What? *What*?'

'I'll explain later,' said Sue, husky with laughter.

'Well that went better than I thought it was going,' confided Johnnies John to Jørn, who asked if he had any more jokes like that, to which the answer was another deluge of filth, which Jørn adored and memorised.

'So, Johnnies John, isn't it? What is it that you actually do?' asked Ida, while motioning for the interns to serve another round of cocktails. 'I hear you have a business in Edgeboston. You inherited your father's shop or something?'

'Yes,' said Johnnies John. 'I own an adult emporium. My dad was big in porn. I learned everything from him. Businesswise, I mean, nothing funny, you know. He wasn't like that. I always wanted to go into real estate. I like property. I like land. Owning land is the noblest thing. But I've got sex shops in my blood. I opened an estate agent, John's Urban & Residential it was called – classy. But it was in a slum area and after a year I was really struggling, so I opened up a room in the back where I'd shift some units for my dad: swings, mats, role-playing costumes. It became a real hotspot for swingers. They'd come to rent their spare rooms to other swingers through my office and buy all their gear out the back. I ended up bringing the porn gear out the front and installing a small noticeboard for the rooms-to-let ads.

'Well, business boomed and then I sold it and moved to a smarter area, suburban, nice, you know. Probably full of swingers too, but they were discrete, kept it in the family. I did a conversion cookery course, specialising in baking. Made lovely artisanal bread. It was hard work: up at four, delivering it myself. Bloody knackering, but so satisfying. Seeing all those loaves steaming in the morning chill, on their way to greet a family at the start of their day. "From warm pillow to warm loaf"– that was my strapline. But of course then the supermarkets started their home delivery and people stopped bothering about it being warm and fresh. Stuffed with bird feathers and human hair that commercial crap, but they all threw me over for it in the end. Criminal, those supermarkets. Too convenient, too cheap. They thought I couldn't compete, but I could, you know. I thought, John, I thought, I did, I thought John, what do people want that they can't get delivered by the big boys? What do people not want in their family shopping bags, for the kids to rummage through or her indoors to discover? What would they like a discrete bloke like me to drop round, under the cover of a nice warm loaf?'

He paused, as if waiting for them all to guess, but everyone except Juan, who was studying his corn dolly, had been mesmerised by the tatooed gun, which had waggled throughout as if holding them hostage to his biography, and they barely managed a collective shrug.

'Porn, of course. I started delivering porn mags and a sliced bloomer, blue movies and a pack of buns. And, well, you can probably see this coming, can't you? Yeah, the porn really took off in the suburbs and so I dismantled the bread oven to make more room for the swivelling mag racks, got in some display cases for toys. And that's the way it's been really. Every time I try and make a go of something else… So far I've set up a hairdressers, a reprographics shop, a private dental clinic, a lido, a conference centre and a theme park, but every time all they want is porn, porn, porn. So I've resigned myself to it now. I've got a chain of sex shops, all with different skews and specialisms, but the emporium is the biggest yet.'

'Well,' said Sue, once he appeared to have come to a close. 'Well, well, well…' It was unclear if she was appalled. Jørn on the other hand was fascinated.

'How refreshingly upfront you are, I have to say,' he said. 'I wish you'd open a branch round these parts.'

'It'd be closed down instantly,' said Linda. 'The Academy wouldn't stand for it. It's… it's misogynistic.'

'Oh don't come the prim wallflower with me,' said Sue. 'You'd have a jolly good browse. There'd be plenty of merchandise for us, I bet. What do you think, as a fellow woman?' She was addressing Patty, who eyed the coving thoughtfully before answering.

'I think that any hard-working woman who can afford to spend her income on vibrators and wine should only welcome such an establishment. There are many who have to go without.'

'But what about the degradation,' cried Linda, 'the objectification, the male gaze?'

'It's the female gays you should be concentrating on dear,' said Johnnies John.

'Aren't we over this "up yours" attitude towards men?' said Patty. 'Personally, I'm much more interested in what goes up mine.'

'Here here!' shouted Ida, trying to make eye contact with John, who was almost sitting in Patty's lap by now. 'What do the men think? Juan?' Nothing. 'John? Where do you stand on porn and feminism?' Her voice was strung perilously taut. Those who knew her well hoped John was careful in answering. He paused, looked at Ida, then away. He had made his decision.

'I think I stand right on the…'

PING! The sound of the oven timer cut through from the kitchen, puncturing the tension with such faultless precision that everyone, even Juan, burst out laughing, whipping up and prolonging the mirth with a 'that was just brilliant', or a 'you couldn't make that sort of thing up', while the interns brought the canapés in on the wheeled hostess trolley and passed them silver-service-style round the still chuckling diners.

'Bon appetit,' said Ida, signalling that everyone should start.

There were choruses of 'Mmmm,' and 'Delicious, Ida,' as everyone popped a warm brown splat in their mouth, some with trepidation, readying their cocktail glass should any unpleasantness need immediately sluicing away, others with game inquisitiveness.

'So, Patty,' said John suddenly, loudly, as if uncomfortable with the dip in conversation, although that was unlikely. Ida had never known him to be uncomfortable with anything yet. 'What do you think of the nationalisation of Foreign industry?'

One could feel the table brace itself. Politics already. The party must be going well, thought Ida. Patty held a piece of brown midway between plate and mouth, cocked her head to one side and spoke softly but deliberately.

'I think it is a great shame for the industries. Not because I don't support nationalisation per se, but because this Foreign government is not interested in productivity or even in economic assets. It is a matter of politics alone. These industries are being used as emotional collateral by a political party more interested in entering the history books as the party to install an independent republic and dispense with the Great Potentate. The industries will rot in their hands. Foreigners are not renowned for their maintenance programmes, and so I suspect that we have a few disasters ahead of us.' She popped the food in her mouth and chewed, absorbed by her thought.

There was no replying to that really. No one present knew enough about it. John smiled at Patty and nodded. Ida sighed loudly, as if in sympathy with the doomed industries, and took a long draft from her drink. Jørn thought of ways to introduce a new topic that would show just how unsuccessful John's conversational gambit had been.

'I could bathe in this brown stuff and ingest it through my pores,' he said.

'Yes, the saffron gives it a real majesty,' said Linda.

'Steady on,' said Sue. 'It's only a bloody canapé.'

'Oh, don't ruin it,' wailed Linda. 'I'm enjoying enjoying it.'

'And I want to eat it without having to gag on your enthusiasm.'

'I love saffron, don't you?' said someone.

'Actually,' said Ida, 'I find the aroma quite sinister. It's sexy, if you know what I mean, but it has a dark edge too, don't you think?'

'It's made from the stamen of the crocus,' said Hands.

'That would explain its sinisterism,' guffawed Sue. 'We're eating bowls of penises!'

Surprised by her animated response to his scientific comment, Hands, who felt he had risked exposure to uncomfortable amounts of attention by speaking out in the first place, dropped a canapé, which splashed onto Ida's arm, who over-reacted for comic effect, which made him jump again and knock his wine glass into her lap. He dived under the table, to hide and to wipe her lap and legs with his napkin. She played up smuttily, janing like a porn actress, which some found hilarious. John, meanwhile, at the other end of the table appeared not to notice. Ok, this was what she had asked of him, but really, he didn't have to be quite so convincing. His bland, moony expression, which was clearly him feigning detachment just to wind her up, made her furious.

But not quite as furious as when, two minutes later, John dropped his food into Patty's lap, who sat motionless, looking down at the stuff dispassionately while he fussed about on his hands and knees, dabbing away, until she simply removed her napkin to reveal her pristine silken lap beneath it.

'Well, a fancy lap that laps it up. Fancy that,' he said, getting back up to his feet.

Ida could bear it no longer. 'Er, John?'

'Hmmm?'

'Ah, I think, given your obvious expertise with the flannel, you could come help me wash up the bowls for the main course. Ok?' He muttered his assent and they disappeared into the kitchen, Ida returning some minutes later, a little pinker than when she had stepped out and asking to speak to Sue for a minute. In the kitchen. Sue went. They re-emerged, Ida asking with some vexation if anyone minded that the bisque was a little, er, lumpy?

'It's just that our soup maker seems to have broken and we don't have a sieve in the house.'

According to the dinner guests' code, all present said that yes, of course, that would be fine. They could more than cope with a lump or two.

'Oh dear,' commiserated Linda. 'What make is it? We had a Jameson for a while but it was hopeless. I always insist on a Derrida these days. Very reliable, goes on and on for years, and it has that brilliant "cream of" setting.'

'Yes,' said Sue, 'she creams anything that one. Mushrooms, beef, knickers…' Then added, 'Goodness, sorry, I don't know what's got into me tonight.'

'No, I don't either,' said Linda, looking wounded and mistrustful.

'Well mine is a Derrida too. That's what's so weird,' said Ida.

'At least you know you can get parts then,' said Jørn. 'They'll never stop manufacturing Derrida spares.' Everyone agreed.

John re-emerged from the kitchen, followed by Manfred and the two interns, wheeling a hostess trolley laden with bowls and a handsome, steaming tureen.

'Sorry about the lumps everyone,' said John chirpily. 'The knob just came off in my hand. Ida's worried you'll all think she's a terrible cook, so I should hold my hands up right now and say it was all my fault.'

Self-doubt, when expressed within an intimate relationship, is a private thing, which John had betrayed with this display of self-sacrifice and honesty. Now everyone would be thinking not about her cooking, but her vanity.

'That's very big of you John.' The steely note in her voice alerted all but Juan that the danger in the room had not yet passed. 'In fact, you've probably acted with all our interests at heart I'm sure. You're doubtless saving us from the slowing down of entropy, right?' John gave no sign that he knew what she was alluding to. 'You know, that thing about soup being dangerous for the flow of time. You told me about it after the…'

'Ah,' said Patty. 'You mean the nursery rhyme about how not chewing your food makes time stand still? Chew, chew and chew some more, until one minute turns to four…'

'Nursery rhymes?' said Ida. 'Oh, grow up.' At which everyone else burst into spontaneous conversation:

'I read your piece on Joan Jellicorse,' said Linda to Jørn; 'Hey, would you rather live in a bungalow or a tower block?' Johnnies John asked Sue, who deliberated for some time and then said 'Neither', and John presumably furnished Patty with the end of her nursery rhyme.

Ida sat quietly for a while and eyed Patty, finding fault with her smattering of freckles and her too-thin wrists. She had no idea who this woman was or what she did, but it was her flat and her dinner party and she was going to have a nice night. She turned to Hands, smiling stiffly.

'This smells nice,' he said. 'The lumps won't impair the flavour at all.'

The party was back up to volume by the time the interns had finished dishing up. The sight of great lumps of meat plopping into bowls of thinnish broth drew screeches of excitement from those diners more accustomed to silken pools of creamed and strained soups. The electricity of a group of people about to do something even just a little risqué could light a small standard lamp.

Ida gingerly spooned a chunk of flesh into her mouth and chewed, eyeballs ranging around the room as if surveying for predators that might pick her off in this vulnerable state.

'Oh Dog, it's so… what's the word. What's the word?' She had pushed the bolus of meat to one side of her mouth to ask Linda.

'Meaty?'

'No, well, I mean yes, it is meaty. But what else? It's really… oh, you know, when it's, oh… viscous? No. Shit, there are some words I always forget. I should make posters of them to put about the place. Oh, not viscous but—'

'Vicious?' said Juan thickly. Everyone turned to him, then looked quickly away, alarmed at the maliciousness he brought to the word.

'No, not vicious. That would be weird,' said Ida. 'It's like, you know, bodies and bits and innards and—'

'Visceral,' said Jørn.

'Yes! That's it. It's so visceral. I mean, it's not unpleasant, it's just so visceral.'

Linda and Sue agreed, their hands held decorously over their mouths as they chewed.

'But you enjoyed the hog roast the other day,' said Hands.

'Really?' said Linda, incredulous. 'Sliced right off the carcass?'

'It was pulled pork,' said Hands. 'Not sliced. Pulled.'

Linda winced at the image.

'Oh, it was just a bit. An experiment. It made my jaw ache, if I'm honest. But Hands was marvellous, he really was. Catching that pig all… viscerally like that.' Ida was drunk now. Drunk, dejected and repeating herself.

'Hands by name…' said Hands shyly, holding up his stubby paws and flexing his fingers.

*

By the end of the main course the diners were fully abandoning themselves to the moment, severing all ties with tomorrow. The cone of light from the overhead pendant lamp was turned almost solid with cigarette smoke, engulfing the large oval table and isolating it from the room around it. Facing inwards, everyone spoke of the world as if it were a book they'd once read, as if there had never been any reality other than this table right now. Ida cordially dismissed the interns, who had begun to startle the diners whenever they stepped forward to retrieve a fallen piece of cutlery or refill a glass. To Ida's relief, Patty used the interns' departure as cover for her own, excusing herself gracefully – she had an early start back to Edgeboston tomorrow – and thanking Ida, who told the tablecloth that it was welcome.

'I'll accompany you to the tram,' said John, shoving back his chair and pocketing his corn dolly. 'I've got a big meeting tomorrow myself. Thank you for a wonderful dinner Ida. It's been great meeting you all.'

Appalled, Ida simply sat and looked after him as he disappeared through the door. She felt her cervix shrink to the size of a pore. She wanted to cry, to scream, to kick him down the stairs then drag him back up, to jump on his back, tug his hair, pull down his trousers and humiliate him there on the onyx table. But instead, she stepped out into the landing and called 'See you later, collaborator' sarcastically to the top of his head. She could see, in the wedges of downstairs visible between steps, John helping Patty put on her coat over her long, slinky, ivory, double-satin dress, and her smiling wordlessly in response. Well, good luck to her in his disgusting bedsit, with its obnoxious cacti and eggy stench.

Ida reset her face to 'hostess' and flounced back into the dining room, plonking herself down in her seat next to patient, smiling, gentle Hands and opposite a rejuvenated Jørn.

'So,' said Jørn, 'Ida, tell us why we're all here. You said it was about your new project. What else have you got cooking for us this evening?'

'Oh… Yes, my project…' she was trying very hard to bring all of herself back into the room, and not allow her deeper recesses to follow John out of the flat. 'Yes, oil. That's why we're all here. Our new friends are all involved in oil in one way or another and, um, yes…'

'Oil?' said Sue, Linda and Jørn in unison.

'As in oil paint?' said Linda.

'I was going to say that,' said Sue.

'Well, that I don't really know,' said Ida. 'The thing with these oil types is that they generally don't know so much about art, so I haven't been able to tell whether it's the same. These oily types …' she trailed off.

'Yeah,' said Hands. 'It's not the same oil in paint as runs through pipelines. It's a question of definitions though. If by oil you mean petrochemicals produced from fossilised deposits, then paint is not made of oil; but if you mean any neutral, nonpolar chemical substance that is a viscous liquid at ambient temperatures and is both immiscible with water and lipophilic, then that's everywhere. We've been eating plenty of it tonight even.'

'How dare you!' said Ida. 'I've been slaving for hours.'

'I was referring to how you can squeeze oil from all sorts of vegetable matter,' said Hands.

'I can?'

'The most common vegetable oil used in kitchens is made from the rape plant.'

'Rape! Rape!' shouted Ida, trying to jolly herself up.

'I can tell you all about rape,' said Sue, who, as we know, had an unusual upbringing and knew all about countryside matters. 'If you suffer from hayfever, make sure you live surrounded by rape. It's insect pollinated, so doesn't waft its pollen about in the air. And what is pollen anyway but plant sperm?'

'So does that make hayfever an STD?' asked Jørn. 'Contracted from plants as they rape us?'

'Rape!' Ida was finding it hard to keep up with the swerves of the conversation.

'Exactly. But what about saffron?' said Sue. 'Can you squeeze oil from crocus cocks?'

'Oh dear, Ida, did you put something in the dinner?' asked Linda. 'Everyone is awfully smutty tonight. Sue, you're being very close to the bone.'

'Yes,' said Ida. 'Isn't it great? It must be them.' She waved her arm in the general direction of Johnnies John and Juan. 'What are you up to, you guys? Have you slipped something into our drinks?'

Jørn narrowed his eyes in a plume of cigarette smoke and took a thoughtful sip of his Castrol GTX.

'Yes,' he said slowly, 'there's a distinct whiff of sex in the air tonight. Maybe it's the influence of this oil. I know nothing about it. Tell me, gentlemen, is oil always closely associated with sex?'

Juan licked his lips, as if about to speak, but then relaxed back in his seat and yawned.

'There's loads of oil in sex,' said Johnnies John. 'There's massage oil and lubricants for starters.'

'Maybe for you,' said Jørn. 'I tend not to need such preliminaries.'

'Oil is nature. Sex is Dog given,' pronounced Juan in his thick accent, which of course caused the Darwinians in the room to bark 'No, sex is nature', which prompted the post-humanists to announce that it is a culturally informed technique of reproduction that has remained anachronistically biological for nostalgic reasons, which drew from the humanists cries of 'Sex is not just a souvenir of thought patterns embodied by temperamental meat, it is the very methodology of humane humanity.'

'And,' continued Johnnies John once the fracas had exhausted itself, 'there's a whole load of plastics in sex. That's made from oil. Do you know how to spot plastics? Seams down the length of things. Giveaway. From the moulding process.' He looked around the dining room, but all was chrome, glass, wood, wool and linen, lustrous taupes, lilacs and mahoganies enlivened by electric light – apart from a tell-tale primary blue object on the floor beneath the sideboard. 'Aha! Here you are.' He passed around the pair of pliers, their handle warm and welcoming to the grip, in contrast to the cold, hard, metal pincers. 'Plastic. See that seam? Once you start looking for it, you'll find it everywhere, especially in functional spaces. I bet there's loads of plastic in the kitchen here.'

'Fuck off, how dare you,' said Ida, before leaping from her seat and weaving out of the room.

Everyone offered scenarios they believed to be plastic-free, but Johnnies John answered each time with a list of constituent polymers and their uses. All conceivable angles of quotidian life were considered, as well as unusual situations, fantasy vignettes, nightmare scenarios and nothingness itself, which he thought could well be a fine biaxially oriented plastic film.

'But exactly which plastics are used in sex?' asked Jørn, wondering what he was missing out on.

'Well, condoms are made out of Latex, which is natural rubber, but femidoms are made out of polyurethane, which is good for those with a Latex allergy, which can be very nasty. Femidoms don't have to cling so tightly, you see. And then there's Vaseline, of course, which is petroleum jelly, so a sort of protean plastic. We shift lots of units of that… And then there's all the plastic dildos, blow-up dolls, strap-ons, butt plugs, those ball things that go up… ooh, thank you.' His stocktaking list was curtailed by the arrival of another cocktail, offered by Ida, who had returned with another jug, a good deal of it spilt down her front where she'd been tasting it straight from the pouring lip.

'Are nylon stockings a plastic? Because they've got seams,' said Linda shyly, drawing a sharp look from Sue, which was noticed by everyone and gave rise to a good-natured jeer round the table. And it was from here that the evening unravelled. The diners whooped and cawed and made half-candid admissions and hooting accusations, until the idea of good old-fashioned, unaided, organic lovemaking gave way to a pulsing petropolis of protuberances and sheathings, vibrating and shunting like an industrial behemoth guzzling oil, coughing up soot and spewing out a glossy run-off as it fucked and fucked without pause.

Come midnight, words had become confused with action. Chairs had been scraped back, the table thrust aside and the thick rug redesignated a brownfield site on which a factory of flesh was established. The industrial complex reconfigured itself at intervals to try out new lines in ecstasy with fresh anatomic combinations and updated circuits of neural stimulation, which over time generated copious volumes of liquids and auditory by-products. Until finally, once peak production had been reached and the warm, meaty smells of the kitchen had been usurped by the swelter of sweat and spittle, the factory gradually wound down, the guests pulling out one by one, making their way stealthily down the spiral staircase and staggering out into the remains of the night.

CHAPTER 31

Ida was making ready to step on to the red carpet, if not with eagerness then at least with experience. Hands contemplated its alarming course, past a throng of journalists and photographers, and considered refusing like a horse. Clinging to her arm, on the side furthest from the paparazzi, he tried to draw himself in, to become so slight that he might be mistaken for her shadow. They were halfway along when Dean Rothwell-Beer, a few steps ahead of them, tripped and fell, skirts flying, in front of the ever-hungry press. Ida braced herself for a barrage of photoflashes, but astonishingly there was not so much as a snigger.

'Now that's a national treasure,' she said wistfully as security guards picked the elder stateswoman off the floor and shielded her while she rearranged herself.

The travelator of celebrity guests into the venue was only just underway again when a crazed and filthy woman wearing nothing but a soiled and ragged pair of men's trousers flew out of nowhere, shouting something that sounded like 'Charlotte' and heading for Ida. This time the guards did not pounce so readily, but waited to assess the situation.

'I'm sorry, you seem to have mistaken me for someone else,' said Ida as good-naturedly as she could with a woman grabbing at her clothes, breathing hot alcoholic breath that stung her eyes and snarling 'I'll bring you down, I'll bury you.' Photographers greedily snapped away rolls of film before security guards lifted the demented woman off the ground and flung her back into the night. Then it was Ida, trembling from a hangover redoubled by shock, who clung onto Hands' arm, as they set off once more along the cruelly long carpet.

*

Hands had called that morning – she must have given him her number, unless he had asked John for it, which she dearly hoped so – and she was interested to note a distinct tingle in response to his voice. The morning they had spent in the haystack, she had mentally tested the idea of leaping on him, but had been checked by the puppy fat that lingered round his jaw or the shortness of his index fingers – or was it some inscrutable aroma he gave off? Or perhaps it had been that her hormones were rooting for John instead. Not having much of a history of monogamy, she found that hard to accept. Anyway, this morning the very thought of Hands was arousing. She put this mainly down to the universal lust that bubbles up from the liver after a night of drinking spirits, and tried luring him to her place for immediate gratification. He had said he was busy all day, but would be glad to see her later to advise her on the critic in residence interview at AP, which he had managed to arrange for her.

Before the phone rang, she had been thinking about John and his disappearance during dinner. She could never, ever forgive a man for going off with another woman, ever; and yet some inner governing chamber was intent on making up excuses for him. Maybe he had brought Patty after all and she was his sister. This was ridiculous. You don't look at your sister with your tongue hanging out. She would do better to forget about him.

She called him.

'What happened to you last night?' She held back her annoyance, tried to sound flirtatious, insinuating.

'What do you mean? I went home.'

'Yes, and … ?'

'And I went to bed.'

'With … ?'

'I know what you want to hear, Ida, and I'm sorry to disappoint you, but I went home alone and went to bed so I could get up and have a meeting this morning without the customary O'Dewey hangover.'

'Really? Then why were you acting so cold to me all night? And so hot with a certain other person?'

'Because you asked me to.'

And so on … His argument had been watertight. Her grievance – that he could at least have made a display of disregarding her orders – sounded pathetic, so she resorted to silent resentment and a cold 'Whatever. See you.'

Something had changed again, but she wasn't sure if it was in him, in her or in their relationship. His behaviour at the dinner party was the only empirical information to go on. It was, she decided, his problem if he was erratic and irresponsible, and she was not going to demean herself by tripping about after him trying to guess what he wanted. The safest thing to do was to destroy him. Not in reality. That would be too much effort. She would destroy him in her eyes only.

She concentrated first on his annoying argumentativeness. He was sharp and lithe enough to wrangle over anything, damn him, which he did more for the sport of it than through conviction. This made him a pedant, a splitter of hairs, a logic-chopper; he was the advocate of all devils; he liked to cut and thrust, argufy and quibble; he was cantankerous, factious, pugnacious, prickly and contrary for the hell of it; a friction builder and a barney lover; a rumpus, scrimmage, fracas stirrer; a bone picker, a crow plucker, a pugnacious, contrary duellist and a bellicose dissention sower. This argumentativeness was not even criticality, but ego-fuelled self-elevation through the rubbishing of others. A show-off and a wind-up merchant, they used to call these sorts of people. Not that she needed to be intellectually superior to a man to enter into a relationship with him – but he had to be willing to take the gloves off now and then. Everyone needs to be wrong, aimless or lazy sometimes, and this should not become a point of vulnerability, but a chance to demonstrate loving accommodation and humility. The constant friction of John's conversation had been wearing her down more than she had realised. But Hands – there was another proposition. He didn't fight her every utterance. Ok, he often didn't respond either. He was more likely to depart from her conversation at a tangent or keep his previous course, as if she hadn't spoken at all. But that was quite relaxing, actually. In fact, his keenness to share his eclectic knowledge was charming, his localised outbursts of excitement almost contagious. His shyness, or whatever it was, would be a drag, though. Still, as her girlfriends often told one another, one person cannot be everything. Maybe in his case gregariousness was the trait she had to find elsewhere. Although her aching, dried-out brain couldn't explain how an anti-social lover might be compensated for. Did this mean she should have two men on the go? One for indoors, one for out?

But going back to John. For thoroughness, she should pick over another of his faults, demolish him from another angle. She had something big lined up for this.

The problem was during sex, as he was coming to orgasm. On other men's faces, when the yoke of conscious self-control slips off, she had seen not animal abandon but pure hatred – perhaps aimed at her specifically, or at all women, or even all humanity. This malevolence was always shocking to her, and since no amount of post-coital tenderness could ever obliterate it, she would drop these men like stones. But John's face was not contorted by any such snarl as he gyrated and sawed his way to their mutual gratification. Far more disturbingly, his features remained blank, his voice silent and his eyes open but unseeing. Not that he was inattentive. In fact he was expert at delivering satisfaction, which hinges on consideration of the other. But he expressed nothing until the final rictus and shout of ecstatic arrival. Such withdrawal could only be to an abominable place, and Ida would close her eyes to shield herself from any dark light that might escape from it.

This was not something she had broached with him, though not through squeamishness. They had discussed many aspects of sex: the particularities of their erogenous zones, which in both their cases were not easy to track down; the compatibility of their most crucial curvatures; the psychology of initiating, and so on – but never this. No, his detachment was something she bore but did not mention, even to girlfriends.

She had been dwelling on this unsettling fault, which was successfully sucking dry all other positives about the man, when the telephone rang. She was annoyed to note her instantaneous disappointment that it was not John, but on hearing Hands ask in his polite monotone how she was, she was surprised to notice other sensations. And so it was that, against her more practical impulses, she asked Hands to accompany her to the biggest, glitziest event in the Academic calendar.

*

Once inside the huge characterless shed – which had been built in a hurry a few decades previously, with no allowance for finery – coats were taken and guests ushered to assigned seats at small, low drinks tables loaded up like donkeys with saddlebags of bottled spirits and chilling champagne.

'You're late' said the steward sternly to Ida. 'You need to go back out and round to the service entrance.'

'Really? Are you sure?' She was ready to burst into tears now. Was her name not on the list? 'O'Dewey plus one?'

Alarm flickered over the steward's features, he apologised and showed them to their table with excessive unction.

'Seems everyone thinks I'm someone else tonight,' said Ida as she fell onto the foiled neck of a bottle. Hands was hardly able to sit after having turned to wood in front of the cameras. 'I haven't the faintest idea who that mad woman was. Just my luck to be the random victim. I wonder what the press will make of it. Some sort of performance I hope. I must warn Sue to start spinning it. Oh Dog, will a time ever come when I'm in control of my own output? Sometimes I do wonder who is driving the vehicle that is my life…'

There were hundreds of tables dotted about the vast interior, with eight or so guests lounging at each, in low-slung, white leather armchairs and sofas. The search for Sue did not seem practical – not before a sharpener.

Ida and guest had been billeted with six pregnant wives of artists and critics who were seated at the top tables. With the gravid women's variously expanded hulls encased in pale, thin, stretchy fabric, the table took on the quality of a cliff colonised by seabirds, especially as, while they chatted, the women's eyes darted over one another's shoulders to take in the high society milling about. Ida was keen to introduce herself and see what direct or indirect connections she might unearth with these six strangers. There was always a common link to be found within just a minute of tactical questioning. Hands, on the other hand, was intent on relaying advice for the interview at AP, which was scheduled for the day after next. He started telling her about the background and history of the company, but would spend too long on some detail, and she would forget what the subject was and impatiently interrupt him with an observation. She pointed out her previous bosses and college friends who had done well, and who, among the stream of people passing their table, might be a fashion industry spy. The awards ceremony, she explained, was preceded by the announcement of the new season's lines, and spies would rush to the toilet stalls to scrawl sketches and pass them through cracks in the frosted glass windows to waiting runners, who would then fax them through to high street retailers so that the choicest items could be on the racks first thing tomorrow.

'There's the head of Narratology. I went to college with her. She's obviously connected to the fashion racket. Look at those pearlised stilettos and that alpaca shrug. Outrageous, parading it like that. I mean, you'd try and play it down a bit, right? Like Linda. She's clearly an undercover operator. No one suspects her at all. Where are those two, I wonder. You haven't spotted them, have you?'

He shook his head.

'Listen, on Friday, just don't mention what you know about us,' he said, in a last-ditch attempt to drive the most importance advice home.

'What about us?'

The huge hall suddenly boomed with music, as if someone had put a record on halfway through, and a relay of models stalked the catwalk, looking at once hunted and hunter-like. A marina of upturned faces followed them hungrily as they paced the pontoon that jutted from the stage, and the raked enclosure of black-clad photographers, like a bank of furious clouds, burst into a storm of flashes.

After a scant five minutes, the show was over as abruptly as it had begun, and Hands, eyeing a dark, wiry man approaching with the clear intent of addressing one or other of them, managed to quickly blurt out, 'Academic Petroleum. Interview. Don't mention GASMAN.'

'Hmmm?' said Ida, who had been engrossed by the fashions, thinking how absurd they were, and how glad she was to have found a way of circumnavigating the need for perpetual newness, looking instead further and further back into fashion history.

'Ida!' said the wiry man, a luxurious, glossy black beard spreading regally across his white-tie get-up. 'How are you?'

'Ah, Derek, you look marvellous. Is Suky here?'

'No. On kid duty – you know how it is.'

'No Derek, actually, no I don't. You're forgetting that I am childless, as you would say, or, as I prefer to call it, child-free.'

Hands could not know this was a running joke between them, and busied himself studying the time on his watch. Derek chuckled and asked if Ida were up for any award this year.

'Not this year. I think I'm in a transitional period. We're just tanking up, really,' she said, nodding towards Hands. 'Hands, Derek …' The men shook hands, one with interest, the other mechanically. 'How about you?'

'Yes, actually. I'm up for the punctuation gong, which is nice,' Derek said with dignified modesty. 'This is my sixth year shortlisted for one of the minor prizes, and I've won two of them. Maybe I'm inching my way towards the prestigious heights, or maybe I'm stuck in the foothills forever. But we can only keep on in order to find out.'

'Anyone who can handle semi-colons with dignity deserves a prize, if you ask me,' said Ida. 'Who was it who said they're as ugly as a tick on a dog's belly?'

'Ooh, I don't know, but if you remember, let me know. That would be a good self-deprecating quip for an acceptance speech. I mean, if I were to, you know… Long shots and all that. Erm, how about you, Hans? Any trophies you've got your eye on?'

'I hear I was considered for the methodology category, but the nomination went to someone else in the department,' said Hands without a trace of regret.

'Oh bad luck. I bet they'd just got a new publishing contract or something. Prizes always go to those who don't need them, don't they?' said Derek. 'Not that I'm saying you look like you need a prize! Goodness, me and my size elevens.'

Hands hoped that a bit of laughter on his part would be enough to signal to this complete stranger that no offence was taken. He gave out a soft burst, which would have sounded menacing to anyone who could hear it over the din of the crowd. To his companions he appeared to smirk bizarrely.

'Hey, did you heard the rumour about the big publishing award?' said Derek. Ida shook her head. 'This didn't come from me if it turns out to be completely wrong, but apparently a whole load of review copies were sent out late last night and the word is that it's incendiary. An eye-watering exposé of loads of very well-known artists and academics, apparently.'

'Really?' Ida was wide-eyed. 'Who's it by? And why? That's career suicide.'

'This is the amazing thing. I heard it's by an intern,' said Derek in the tone of voice reserved for scandal.

'No!' Ida was more disbelieving than outraged.

'Apparently so.'

'Interns are such different creature these days,' she said sadly. 'Not the lally-gagging lapdogs of our day. They really can bite the hand that feeds them. They seem to have a different conception of getting on than we did. It's sort of non-linear or something.'

'Do you have trouble with yours then?' asked Derek.

'No, they're a bunch of poppets,' she said, 'as far as they let me know.' This gave pause for thought. 'Oh Dog, it doesn't bear thinking about. If you can't trust an intern to not know what's going on, we're all in trouble.'

'Well, so long as they keep their eyes on the top of the ladder and don't try knocking us second-raters off the lower rungs,' said Derek. 'Well, better get back to my departmental cohort before they think I've defected to Philology.'

'Love to Suky,' called Ida into the crowd that had already engulfed him.

'So, that was Derek. But sorry, you were telling me something. Golly,

I should have warned you about tonight really. There's likely to be a lot of people coming over to say hello. Always on duty. Anyway, you were saying…'

Another man flopped down breathless in the vacated chair, his tie over his shoulder and his forehead damp with perspiration.

'Chip! So nice of you to drop in,' said Ida.

Chip wheeled round, a look of checked panic in his eyes. 'Ah, Ida, hello. This is turning into quite a night already isn't it?'

'Is it? You tell me. You look a bit ragged. Everything going well with Tolly?'

'Tolly? Oh, well, you know… In fact I'm sure you always knew. It's fine. Fine. I've got bigger problems right now. I'm sorry Ida, I'm going to have to dash. Trying to hide from someone. Let's go for a drink sometime soon and talk sitcoms.'

The next person to rock up, on the lookout for any unopened champagne, was Fredegund. She had swapped her white stick for a golden labrador for the night, and it was this lustrously coiffured bitch that had dragged Fredegund straight to Ida's table.

'Good booze hound. Good girl.'

'Hello Fredegund. Is that foundation you're wearing? You're looking especially matt this evening.'

'Why thank you Ida.' She sniffed the air and smiled broadly. 'Trust you, cheeky-drawers, to ride a drinks table shotgun with a bunch of pregnant women. Mind if I help you out with that magnum there? And who's your chum? What a night, eh? Have you heard about the publishing prizewinner? Incendiary, they're saying. Well, wish me luck – hopefully that'll be me bursting into flames up there. Hmmm, sorry the endorsement didn't happen, dear heart. Publishers got some artist to do it in the end. Out of my hands. Same old marketing nonsense. Anyway, listen, I'll call you in a few days, when it's all calmed back down. A bit crazy at the moment. Hopefully it's about to get worse. Must go and taunt Hastings, wherever he is. Call me.'

*

Derek was among the early recipients of minor awards, taking his place in a parade of academics still working their way up the lower-middle ranks. Ida never heard whether he had discovered who had derided the semi-colon because the crowd continued to chatter through his acceptance speech. And they talked over an unknown from the Linguistics

Department, who cried and laughed hysterically in turn at the microphone. Ida thought she seemed interestingly high key, worth keeping an eye out for. The audience did shut up, however, when a geographer in a shiny suit and swept-back hair strolled up to the microphone and cradled it like a crooner. It was widely known that he was instrumental in shaping the Academic publishing programme, since he was married to an important series editor.

'Thank you, thank you,' he said with suave assurance. 'I am honoured, of course, to accept this award. First of all, I must thank Michelle, my wonderful wife, who has given me the time and space to pursue my research. Honey, I'm truly sorry… And then there are a few other people I should mention too. I'm assuming that Tolly Adio is here. Tolly?'

A hesitant Tolly rose from his seat, his black tie aquiver beneath his damp, protruding lower lip as he cleared his throat to say 'hi' and wave a limp paw at the man onstage.

'Tolly, please, step up here a moment. I think the audience should know just how… shall we say… effectual you have been in steering my career to date.'

'Can't face a public fucking love-in. I'm off to the ladies,' said Ida, rising from her seat and leaving Hands transfixed by the body language onstage.

*

As Ida zig-zagged through the seated audience, people kept flagging her down, beckoning her over and demanding more bottles, more canapés, more mopping up of spillages. It took her a while to realise that it was her outfit causing all the confusion. It looked remarkably like the catering staff uniform, the stripes of her dress shirt melting over distance into the pale blue of their tunics, and her trousers a stylish moleskin version of their polyester. On leaving the toilets – where one guest had tipped her and another complained that she hadn't washed her hands thoroughly enough and should be sacked if she thought she was going to handle food now – she spotted the doors from which the real catering staff were emerging with large platters of canapés. Like a clay pigeon thrower, the doors would swing open and throw out a figure, who walked backwards a pace, then swivelled round to bear a laden silver platter off on its curving path through the great hall. Punters would turn their gaze towards the intermittent beacon of the kitchen light, no one hungry enough to actually stand outside in ambush, but many trying to will the waiters over.

The dinner conversation last night about culinary oil was right at the limit of Ida's memory. She remembered having a long and serious discussion about rapeseed oil, but couldn't remember if anyone had explained the link between the yellow and the black oils. Well, here was a most unusual opportunity no researcher could ignore: she effectively held a backstage pass and could nose about in a professional kitchen. And wouldn't it be a hoot to pick up a platter of canapés and take it back to their table? Or even use it as a means to gain entrance to the judge's enclosure? Had she been sober this latter adventure would never have entered her head, but right now it seemed like a splendid idea, although she hadn't gone so far as to think what she would do if she did get in there.

She watched the bona fide staff enter the kitchen. They would barely break pace to barge the door with a shoulder, and as it swung in their wake she saw them place their empty platters on a neat pile before bearing right, where she presumed the full platters must be. They avoided head-on collisions, when their entrance coincided with another's exit, by using different halves of the swing door: in, forwards on the right; out, backwards on the left.

The bright light of the kitchen shrank Ida's pupils painfully, and the hall-filling timbre of the public address system was reduced to muted inconsequence by the doors once they stopped swinging. She stood by the stack of empty platters, trying to appear purposeful.

It was hard not to think of a gallery in this bright white space. There was no let-up of hard surfaces, not a curtain, lampshade or knick-knack in sight. But here the white cube was made fussy by other means, by functional inbuilt structures of various metals, from polished chrome shelving to brushed stainless steel worktops to heavily blackened iron hobs. The floor glinted with mineral aggregate embedded in its brick-red non-slip surface, on which porters and sous chefs fretted around chefs in tall pleated hats and rubber-buttoned tunics, bent over their wipe-clean stations with intense concentration, barking out an order for more roast beef, more parsley, more caviar.

Each canapé took between one and four minutes to construct. The chefs' nimble fingers would lay out a base element – say, a tiny piece of toast or a wedge of decoratively peeled cucumber or a deftly plaited raft of seaweed – and then fly across the tops of tubs of ingredients, diving like cormorants to pick out a cube of tortilla here, a sliver of ham there, which they sculpted and installed on the edible plinths. Then finer details were added: cornices of piped tuna purée, cupolas of fluted quails' egg halves, Corinthian orders of sprigged *frisée* ... It was unclear whether each canapé was improvised or a predetermined classic. The chefs moved rhythmically, like instrumentalists caught up in the call and response of an ensemble impro, but it looked to an outsider to be happening far too quickly not to be fully rehearsed. There were not only aesthetic concerns and references to other dishes to be factored in to each decision, but also the primary function of taste and texture to consider. The musk of caviar would probably not sit so well with the sweet sourness of a crumbly cheese, and the bright green of a broad bean divested of its leathery jacket would exacerbate the dimness of a dollop of tapenade. Each canapé was the outcome of a swiftly executed, complex three-dimensional equation, and each chef a dextrous computing unit with a division of porters to superintend their raw materials. When an ingredient was running low, the porters flew to the back of kitchen, where sous chefs were simmering, steaming, boiling, zesting, flaking, paring, slicing, julienning, carving, mashing, puréeing, tossing, whipping and creaming, so that the radishes or crab paste or yellow pepper diamonds could be replenished before the old tub was empty. And when a tray was full of canapés – when the chef had finished planting a beautiful, exotic garden, featuring topographical and chromatic intricacies that could only be brought forth by the deepest knowledge of the natural world – a nod would summon a member of waiting staff, who stood for a moment in appreciation before it, then swept it up and over to the doors, the chef following it with his or her eyes – at once critical and proud – until it disappeared beyond the swinging door, through which an abstract burst of hullaballoo entered, signalling time to start on the next one.

Having witnessed the serious precision and imaginative flair that went into each platter, Ida could not bring herself to go through with her plan. She could not stand the thought of these gorgeous spreads being set upon by curators and publishers who, at most, cast a peremptory glance over the tray to identify the largest piece of roast beef. She took a step towards the nearest chef, a man about her age, with a mind to tell him how wonderful he was, they all were, how they must crave recognition and how she was willing to provide it, how all of Academia should know about their work. The man's eyes flicked towards her as he sensed her presence, their gaze meeting at an impassable border between two worlds: hers marked by pace, noise, disparity and inconsequence; his anchored and incessant, dutifully bringing forth the doomed fruits of his craft and care. Ida lowered her eyes with shame, turned and ran out of the kitchen, almost colliding with a waitress, who veered skilfully around her.

*

Back on the other side of the doors, the hall was in uproar. Where previously the crowd had more or less fulfilled the role of appreciative audience to what was happening onstage, now there was no division, no directionality. Everywhere was thronging with knots, small and large, of people doing Ida was not sure what, but doing it with more energy than she had encountered since, since... A woman flew backwards towards her from a nearby cluster, her feet clear off the ground and her mouth open wide but emitting no sound. She landed at Ida's feet with a violent exhalation, ignored the hand proffered in aid and swung terror-filled eyes about, looking for somewhere to hide.

It was a massive fight! Or rather, a series of smaller fights that erupted and reconfigured, together making up one big brawl. The huge hall was as full as it had been, but the neatly seated bodies had become messy and intertwined, taking up way more space. People were shouting at each other from a distance or up close, letting fly inexpert punches that missed their mark, then hurling themselves in for a full-contact wrestle. There was a dignified fistfight here and there, but in the main, undisciplined scraps emerged from the boiling sea of furious bodies. A hand grabbed Ida's shoulder and pulled her backwards. She screwed shut her eyes and braced herself. It was Hands. He took her by the wrist and led her towards the stage, dodging bodies as they fell left and right. Limbs lashed out at them, mouths gaped and gasped around them. Blood, grunts and fury spattered them. At the top of the stage steps Ida paused and turned to take in the mass as it trembled with indignation and pain. From this height, the thicket of flesh and noise could be seen to be made up of celebrities, friends, colleagues, acquaintances and strangers clawing the air in self-defence, or smiting, kicking and spitting with purpose, if not with coordination. Some were not directly involved, but hemmed in by spats all around them. Others had barged, fought or crawled their way to the exits, hammering at the doors to be let out. But most were spilling from one clash to the next, giving as good as they got. The amateurism of the violence belied the professional hate and envy that sustained it, and it occurred to Ida that, no matter what had sparked it, there would be no going back.

As Ida and Hands ducked across the stage, the plywood set was torn from its batons and hurled after Rothwell-Beer, who was stumbling into the wings. They followed her into the black hinterland and looked about for green exit lights to lead them onwards and outwards. Someone shouted Ida's name from behind. She wheeled round to face a battered-looking Prentice Hall, who held a book aloft and shrieked at her with more venom than she thought a human constitution could take.

'A hyped-up cream puff of a pamphlet! A pamphlet! How dare you!'

'Prentice, what's going on. You're hurt. Are you ok?'

'Don't give me your fucking fake pity, you treacherous little hussy. You're just lucky you're too irrelevant to have been on that stage tonight. Fucking climbing women. All backstabbing bitches. To make up for what you lack in your trousers.' He was gulping for breath, and spittle frothed at the corners of his mouth.

'Prentice, you're angry. You should stop talking. You'll regret it later. Come on, let's get you out of here…'

'Stop flapping your filthy female tongue at me or I'll pull it out from its roots in your dripping, bloody sack of depravity. I'll unplug it from your pathetic quivering quim, from which you are always speaking, you filthy whore…' Unused to such rhetoric and at a loss for further words, he threw the book at her head, a corner hitting her agonisingly in the temple. Luckily, before anything worse could happen, a thick-necked security guard in black puffer jacket and steel toecaps materialised from the backstage shadows, grabbed Prentice from behind and performed the mandibular angle technique, completely incapacitating him. Hands grabbed Ida's wrist again and ran, twisting through corridors until they tumbled into the puddle-pocked back alley and slammed the fire door behind them.

*

Ida was holding a napkin full of ice cubes to the side of her head. Hands had arranged his face into an expression of concern, unsure what else he could do.

'Ok, tell me from the top again, starting with what the man in the shiny suit said.'

'I really couldn't tell you. I wasn't listening, but it seemed to be very unexpected. The other one – Tolly – obviously wasn't keen on going onstage, I could see that much, but not having anything to do with the Geography Department, I didn't really know what they were talking about. The first man had been insulted by the second man and the first man wanted to confront him on it. That's as much as I got. Then the MC, like I said, managed to get them to move off the stage, but then the next person – I don't know who, a woman – got up and someone started heckling and then she began crying and then someone heckled the heckler and then someone ran on the stage and grabbed the microphone and then denounced someone else and then jumped at someone from the stage – it might have been the person they were talking about I suppose – but anyway, then everyone began shouting at everyone else.'

The agony of his vagueness far outstripped that of her head injury. They had fled to a café a few streets away from the great hall, but no one else had found their way there yet to offer a clearer picture of events. Ida cursed her bout of sentimentality in the kitchen. She had missed everything.

'Can you remember what Prentice said? He mentioned a pamphlet or something.' She winced as the waiter delivered their drinks with a loud chink.

'Yeah, a hyped-up cream puff of a pamphlet,' said Hands, raising her stiff drink to her lips, which she hadn't been expecting. The drink dribbled down her chin.

'Um, thanks, I'll manage. And all that foul misogyny! What's got into him? What's got into everyone? Oh where is everyone? I'm going back…'

But just as she was making ready to rise, other escapees in evening dress tumbled into the café clutching various parts of their anatomy, their groans and weeping echoing gauchely about the marble, mirrors and brass. A couple plonked themselves down besides Ida on the banquette. The woman began fervently leafing through a book, her cleavage juddering as she muttered to herself with barely contained terror.

'It's a bloody bonfire, I tell you,' cried the woman.

'What is?' asked Ida.

'This bloody book.'

'It's very thorough,' said the man. 'I can't think of anyone who's been missed out. Tut tut, there's going to be many a rolling head tomorrow.'

'Sorry, what is this?' asked Ida, reaching for the book, which the woman passed to her reluctantly.

'It's the most incredible dishing of dirt ever,' said the man. 'Impressive how she's gathered it all really. Beautifully written. You could learn a thing or two from this Belle LaBelle.' He directed this last comment to his companion, who slapped him round the face, rising from her chair and screaming at the top of her vocal range that now even he was against her and that was it, she was going to jump from the Fine Arts balcony. The man rushed out after her into the night, which thrilled with alarms and sirens, leaving behind the book.

'What Thinkers Really Think About,' said Ida, reading out the title. She looked to Hands for a response. He continued to count and categorise the injuries and expletives around him.

She turned the book over and read the blurb to herself.

'Oh Fredegund!' she cried.

'Where?' said Hands, looking around.

She waved the book at him.

'It's so obviously by Fredegund. The woman with the labrador from earlier.'

'But it's by Belle LaBelle.'

'Oh. You know her?'

'No. It says there.' He pointed to the cover.

'It's Fredegund, I bet you. All that earwigging and hobnobbing over the last Dog knows how many years, and she's written it as if it were the revenge text of a disgruntled intern. Genius.' She opened the book at random and read to herself. 'Woah, there are some grubby quotes in here. Strelnikov says that Tolly has the personality of a gnat, and Tolly calls Prentice's last book a load of self-centred codswallop, centred on the dullest wallop of cod he ever met. Woohoo, they'll rip each other apart tomorrow, if they didn't already tonight!' She turned to the back cover again. 'According to this, it is "the most vivid evocation of academic life to date." It is, apparently, "a cross between a genealogical romp and a car crash in slow motion." And look, it's fully indexed too. Let's see K… N… O… O… Here we are: O'Dewey. Ooh, yes, three page references! Not as much as some, but not bad. Let's see what she's got on me. Oh, a cream puff of a pamphlet – that was it. I remember saying that now. The bitch! And what else? Oh Dog, it's that episode with Sergeant Singer. Phew, he comes off the villain by the looks of it. Which is quite right. Let's just check that other one… ooh, did I say that? That's a pretty good quip. Hah, good old Fredegund. I come out of it pretty well I think. Cream puff is so anodyne compared to some of the vile things in here. Who would have thought? Tut tut… Gaw, I can't wait until tomorrow. This is going to be the best media furore ever.'

She paused in her excitement and eyed Hands as he counted the floor tiles between him and the toilets, calculating two and a half tiles per stride, which made five strides in all.

'Do you want to see if you're in it?' she asked.

'No.' Apart from the unpleasantness of it happening around him, he did not consider himself in any way involved.

'It's fabulously interesting though,' said Ida. 'All this animosity and violence. It shows just how much we believe to be at stake. You don't get this passion from the service sector, do you? Or maybe you do. Maybe cleaners and tram drivers are really critical of each other too. I'm sure there are lots of ways to clean a floor that people get passionate about.'

'Yeah.'

'But we don't really hate one another. We're just scared for our professional lives. We might think the most terrible things about others, but it's generally to make us feel better about ourselves. The weird thing is that it doesn't work if you tell people negative things about themselves directly, only if you tell someone else. It's a bit like how stars disappear when you look at them directly.'

'Yeah.' Hands started pushing back his chair, making ready to take those five strides.

'Oh you're just not bothered by any of this are you?'

'No, I mean yeah, I am. I can see it's… a thing.'

'Hands, do you realise that you never express surprise or annoyance or any emotional… I was going to say extreme, but actually I mean even mid-range emotion. Did you know that?' Hands was still half in, half out of his chair, as if stooped beneath a low bulkhead. He shrugged awkwardly. 'It's really quite important to express surprise, or even mild interest, when talking to people, otherwise they think they're telling you things you already know and then they feel boring.' She knew she was being unfair, but after all that adrenaline outlay and the subsequent incredible revelations, she really needed to express her excitement to someone who would reciprocate.

'Yeah, I know. I mean, oh! I'll try. I'll really try. I don't mean to make you feel boring. I am interested, I mean, you are interesting, really. I'm sorry, I'll try and be more surprised sounding. Oh!' His voice rose to a near hoot, and Ida couldn't help laughing.

'No, Hands,' she put down the ice pack and reached out for his hand. 'I'm sorry. I'm indulging my insecurities. You don't need to sound surprised every time I open my mouth. Although maybe a little more emoting would be good now and then. Hey, at least I mentioned this to you directly and didn't just moan to a third person.'

Hands attempted an emotion, but missed.

'Anyway,' said Ida, suddenly exhausted and keen to get on the telephone from the comfort of a huge pile of pillows. 'I'd better get off. And thanks for being my date. I think you've saved my head from a serious lump. I'm going to sleep better than some tonight.' She stood up and Hands, practically bowing as she rose, leaned across the table for an embrace and probably a full-on kiss, which Ida managed to divert into a cheek peck. Hands, in his confusion, used his tongue anyway.

CHAPTER 32

Two days on, career casualties were still being pulled from the EMMAs wreckage. Some things had been said that night that could be neither unsaid nor ignored. But no one dared add to the mess, so a peculiar politeness descended. Academics, artists, curators and critics talked only in generalities, making no mention of individuals, and the media followed libel laws to the letter, sheltering behind the conveniences of the word 'allegedly'.

The trashier rags published tables of photographs of the fallen, like victims of a massacre, drawing causal and associative links between them to pass off their tattling as scientific analysis. The more serious journals speculated that an epidemic of Imposter Syndrome was to blame, and reported high-profile cases as isolated incidents, including nothing but facts: Prentice Hall was sacked from his professorial post and Tolly Adio was expelled from pretty much everything he had been involved in. One headline caused Ida's heart to thud sickeningly. Sergeant Singer had committed suicide. No article mentioned his inclusion in Belle LaBelle's book, but a number of its passages had been dedicated to his affairs. Ida realised this would be the end of his lawsuit against her. That was a low thought. Imagine the agony that must have led him to his final action – and her first thought had been how it affected her. She was ashamed. She pondered what his death would mean if she had been in the wrong in the first place, if she had purposely skewed his words to suit her agenda. If one has done something shameful and the only other person who knows about it dies, is one released from one's shame? She wasn't sure if shame required witnesses, or if that made it mere embarrassment. Was shame an internal judgement on the self, and embarrassment social? But with neither shame nor embarrassment to contend with in respect to her original dealings with Sergeant, Ida could concentrate instead on the guilt of having felt relief that the lawsuit was over.

Sergeant's suicide changed the timbre of reporting, sparking serious editorials and interviews with ethical advisors on issues of publishing and privacy. The book, some said, was now a murder weapon, and the author a criminal. That morning Ida had phoned Fredegund, her own prime suspect, to find her fuming.

'I can't believe it. The only time I'm up for an award and the ceremony's aborted.'

'You kind of brought it on yourself though,' said Ida.

'What do you mean, twinkle-tits? I worked for two and a half years on that book. It'll be buried in an avalanche of shit by the time the next awards come round. This is not something I would have brought upon myself. It's devastating.'

'But didn't you ... ? Isn't Belle LaBelle ... ?'

'Dog! That wasn't me. That was written by a fucking intern. You don't think I'd stoop that low do you? Cheezus, puffy-muff, is that what you think of me? That I've been snooping around you all, mopping up your filth to further my own career? Ida, dear heart, I'm stricken.'

'I thought it sounded like a name you'd come up with, and you did say you were writing something explosive under a pseudonym. I guess, I, well, I'm sorry, of course you wouldn't have... But the intern thing is just scaremongering, isn't it?'

'Oh no. Teddy, that ham-faced leech at Random, told me it's for real. I saw him in De Lou's after the brawl. He'd had a skinful, the muppet, but he should know. It's one of his. And now it's all anyone can talk about. Belle La-fucking-Belle. What about my book?'

'I'm sorry, Fredegund. What was – is – your book about?'

'It's called *Dinner Quips: how to get ahead over the starter*,' she replied morosely. 'It was – is – really fucking funny. But no one's ever going to have a dinner party ever again, because no one's speaking to anyone else.'

She had a point there. Ida had rung round the morning after the ceremony and no one had picked up, even at Sue and Linda's office. She was dying to know the fallout there. A couple of their clients hadn't come off too well. Oddly, the answer machine message said the offices were closed. No reason, no reopening time, just closed. She would have called their home number, but she realised that even after all these years she didn't have it, which struck her as sad, then annoying.

She had wanted to tell them about the AP Critic-in-Residence interview too, maybe ask some advice. And now here she was, picking her cuticles in the waiting area of the Human Resources Department in the company's Academic headquarters. The conglomeration of portacabins lurked at the end of a muddy cul-de-sac far from central Academia, where only the weather was a consistent guest. The thwack of pinecones on the flat roof and the cawing of crows heightened the suspense.

Finally, a red-faced man fetched her through a flimsy door into an overheated room, where the cheap materials that had been pressed into a desk, vertical beige blinds, carpet and ceiling tiles were charged with static and body odour. The man took his seat behind the desk next to another middle-aged man, almost identical looking, with a balding grey comb-over, rectangular metal-framed glasses, a shapeless navy blue suit and a face beaten by many winds and whiskies.

'Please, take a seat. Welcome to AP,' smiled the first man. 'My name's Brewster Jenning, head of HR, and this is Orville Harden, operational development.' It was when Orville smiled that Ida discovered how to tell them apart: Brewster was the one with both his front teeth. 'We're really excited to speak to you today. We oil types rarely get to brush shoulders with celebrities, so it's a real pleasure to have you here. We've been reading about you all in the newspapers and it sounds like such a crazy life. I think we need an injection of that sort of energy around here, but perhaps without the aggro, if that's possible. Were you involved in this recent – what was it – a blowout?

'Perhaps more of a meltdown?' said Ida. Good to correct them on a technical point up front. 'Of course I'm mentioned in the book. It'd be awful not to be. But I haven't, you know, got my come-uppance like some. Not that I should, I mean, the bits about me are nothing bad. I'm not contentious. I mean, that is to say, not in that way. I do put the cat among the pigeons sometimes with some of my ideas about art. But I'm not, you know… trangressive in the wrong way.' She should stop talking and gauge what they were after before characterising herself too concretely.

Brewster turned some pages on the desk before him. She craned surreptitiously to see if she could see any other candidate's names, but he shuffled the papers quickly together and stuffed them into his desk drawer. 'So, the person we're looking for, as we told our mutual friend Hands – er, how do you know him, by the way? You're not the sort of person we usually see him out and about with, is she Orville?'

'Hot diggedy dawg, no it hoot'n toot'n sure as hanny it ain't. Wooey.'

Ida's backside lost contact with the chair at 'hot diggedy'. That was an interesting tactic he had there, expressing and passing on surprise at once.

'Ah, I, ah, we met not so long ago, through a mutual friend.' She should hold back with her ace card for now. Play it when it really counted.

‘How nice. Anyway, so, the person we’re looking for is someone to ask the really dumb questions about this place.’ Everyone in the room laughed. The word ‘dumb’ sometimes has that effect in formal situations.

‘Oh yeah, hunny pie, the really stoopid questions, like you wouldna hear from the mouths of babes, nuh-uh.’

‘Right, I see,’ Ida crossed her legs and tugged her skirt down over her knees in curt response to ‘hunny pie’.

‘You see,’ said Brewster, ‘we can all be rather set in our ways here. We’re such practical businessmen… and woman. I think we have a woman. Or maybe she left. Anyway, we’re so used to being practical and solving problems and developing new projects and expanding the business that we often overlook some of the finer, what do you call them – concepts.’

‘Yeah, uh-huh, what he said,’ said Orville, his face twitching as he spoke.

‘What sort of finer concepts?’ asked Ida, wondering if that was a good example of a dumb question.

‘Well, if we knew that we wouldn’t be here talking to you now, would we?’ said Brewster with genial sarcasm, which Ida took to mean that it had been a good dumb question.

‘So the idea is,’ said Ida, ‘that I would come in and… I mean, the person you are looking for would come in and notice things that you wouldn’t ordinarily notice, and would ask you about them?’

‘Uh-huh.’

‘And presumably it’s good if they are stupid questions, because often what seems stupid contains the kernel of innovative or unusual ideas, right?’

‘That’s about the long and the short of it,’ said Brewster, now apparently bored. Had she been too sensible just then? ‘Now, do you have anything you’d like to ask us?’

This was usually the last thing that happened in an interview, but here it was obviously a trick question. If she were to ask something practical like ‘how often would you need someone to come in,’ then that would eliminate her right away, surely.

‘How dumb is dumb?’ she ventured.

‘Aha, now, that is a very good question, isn’t it Orville?’

Was a good question the opposite of a dumb question? Would it have been dumber, in this context, to ask the sensible question after all?

‘Uh-huh, she’s hit the nail on the hot-digeddy head there, Brew ol’ buddy m’pal.’

Damn.

'We asked ourselves that question when we were thinking about recruiting, and we decided it'd really be up to you. You're probably much cleverer at gauging how dumb to be,' said Brewster, unnecessarily shuffling a stack of papers – a classic signal that a discussion has ended. But where were the questions about methodology, long-terms aims, historical comparators?

'Ok, ok, here's a dumb question for you,' said Ida, trying to prolong things, to get herself across better, or just more. 'Why use Snowdon for prospecting when you can use seismic surveying equipment?'

The two men's eyes snapped into contact with hers.

'Hunny pie, that ain't a stoopid question, that's just plain weird. You're suggesting we use a mountain to survey rocks?'

'I mean Snowdon. You know, the GASMAN,' Ida leaned forward and narrowed her eyes. The two men stared back expressionlessly.

'The underground group with the oil interests?' she prompted, but still nothing. 'No? Hmmm, I guess you're just HR. Snowdon wouldn't be within your remit. Golly, sorry, I mean, not that HR is "just" anything. It's really, really important, obviously. I just mean that it's not production. Although presumably everyone gets hired through you at the beginning. You probably interviewed for the position of gravitational diviner.'

'Actually, I'm HR,' said Brewster, 'but Orville here is from Prospecting.'

'Oh dear, I'm so sorry,' said Ida. 'As you can see I know nothing about corporate structure. But really? You've never worked with him? The guy who falls down?'

'Yeah, uh-huh, I know jus' who you hollerin' 'bout now. Garvin, he's called – plum good guy. Considering.'

'Considering?'

'Never you mind young missy. That ain't nonna yo business. We're here to hear some dumb questions and so far all I hear is probin'. You probe like a Dogdam prospector. We need to get you out in the field, that's where you should be with a nose like that.' Orville took his hat off and rubbed the back of his neck, whistling 'jeee' through the gap in his teeth. 'Wimmin,' he concluded, replacing his hat and turning to Brewster with watery eyes.

'Oh, that would suit me just fine, in fact. What I'd really like is to get on to an oil rig. And to go to Foreign. I understand that's where it all happens. I have an idea for a book, you see.'

'Miss, we're not here to work out your career for you,' said Brewster. 'We're here so that you can bring AP right up into the modern, critical age.'

'And anyway,' said Orville, 'Foreign ain't no place for lady academics. It's a wild place where even the bullhorns gotta watch their back. You sure gotta lot to learn about this business. Pfffff.'

'Oh, I know. And I am ready to ask all the dumbest questions to help me learn it.'

'Quite. Well, anyway,' said Brewster, switching to a brusquer gear. 'I think we have all we need for now. Thank you for coming Mzzzz O'Dewey. We'll let you know either way within a fortnight.'

'Pffff… women,' repeated Orville as Ida shut the door behind her.

*

'Excuse me, are you aware that Academic Petroleum are currently demanding levels of compensation that would cut into the Foreign education and health budgets, effectively blackmailing the government, and the Foreign people, into reinstating the lapsed oil concession?'

An earnest young woman with no trace of an accent was thrusting a leaflet into Ida's hand. It looked like a piece of gallery marketing, with minimal design and austere copy: 'AP's terms of Supplemental Agreement unacceptable to Foreign nationals'. The group of campaigners was too small and informative to be called a demonstration, but it was certainly drawing the attention of some men in grey uniforms. Ida thanked the woman and told her no, she wasn't aware of any of this, but certainly supported the cause. She signed her sponsorship form, or whatever it was, and told her to keep up the good work, while the uniforms slowly closed in.

*

On her way home Ida made a detour via Sue and Linda's office. With so much crumbling lately, she could really do with a dose of homely bickering and some solid professional obligation. She strode through the building's grand entrance hall, tossing a friendly greeting to the concierge, who had been working there for as long as she had been a client. He did not give out the usual jokey wink. His face turned hard and blank and he stepped out of his booth to block her way up the stairs.

'Can I help you?' he said, addressing the air above her right shoulder.

'Yeah, hi, er…' she realised she had never known his name in all these years. 'You ok? You look a bit peaky. I'm just popping up to see Sue and Linda.'

The concierge remained unaccountably distant yet obstructive, informing her that there was no one of that name here. Ida was too dumbfounded to argue, too alarmed by the sudden opposition presented by one who, to date, she had thought of fondly as inconsequential. His sudden assumption of authority caused a nauseating swivel in her reality. She glanced up the stairs, hoping to see Sue and Linda crouched round the corner of the balustrade, laughing at this rather pathetic joke. They weren't there, of course, but Ida did notice that their bronze business plaque had been removed, leaving unsightly glue marks on the wooden panelling. 'Er, I see they've taken down their plaque,' she said, pointing. 'They seem to have forgotten to tell their clients where they were moving to. I'm sure I'll hear from them today, but it's rather urgent. Do you happen to know—?'

The concierge slammed the door to his booth. Bewildered, she wandered back out into the street with the purposelessness of someone thwarted in the major plan of their day. She looked for the nearest phone box, thumbed through her little black book and dialled. No answer. She thumbed some more and dialled again.

'Hi, Hands? What are you up to?'

CHAPTER 33

Kirkpatrick was handed the goatee as she stepped to the front of the gathered GASMANs. The damp walls of the bascular housing glistened glamorously behind her and a hush descended as she composed herself in readiness to speak. She was handsome, in her early sixties and wore a heavy, dark woollen cape with a lively satin pussycat bow beneath her softening chin. There was something of the dandy about her, a figure from another era who enjoyed an opaque lifestyle. She spoke with such confidence and personability that it was impossible not to like her, and what she was saying, instantly and entirely.

'GASMANs, our time has come. As many predicted, Foreign oil interests are being left to rot. Without bought-in expertise, the installations are crumbling, the workforce has dwindled, the politicians regard their oil fields as nothing but a cipher of their pyrrhic victories. This may be close to disastrous for Academic Petroleum, who have been chased out and left empty-handed; but for the GASMAN it is the signal to move on to the next phase. We must now dedicate our attentions to Academia.

'Academia is not our natural enemy. It never has been. Some of the old guard inflect GASMAN ideology with warring rhetoric, but I think many of you will appreciate that, in practice, Academia is a great resource and an unwitting ally, and that we would do well to turn it into a witting one. Academia represents a potential oil consumer base so substantial that, if integrated, it could fund all research and exploration for decades to come. And regarding production itself, there are as yet untapped reserves throughout Academia that would postpone peak oil for we know not how long. We have started work on both user-side and production programmes, as many of you will have read in recent reports, but this evening I will be projecting forward to show you the state of things to come. And sooner than you might think.'

Kirkpatrick paused for those who needed time for information to sink in, and performed an ostentation with her cape and a pointer for those who didn't.

'Oil drilling usually happens on a vast scale, which obviously is not going to happen on campus any time soon. Whereas we're comfortable with the existence of bleak and remote offshore platforms, the landscape of the academic shires is too pastoral for most to envisage with black crude spurting up out of huge derricks. And yet there has been a nodding donkey near the Social Geography Faculty for at least 30 years, and it is by no means the only one around. It is tucked behind a hedge, the blockhead visible at its uppermost position from the narrow country road. But this has never been cause for complaint. This particular tract of land provides a transition between the dense residential spread of the halls of residence, bounded by the main east-west arterial railway line, and the Southern Zones Recreational Park. It has been settled by commuters and middle managers, who take local buses to the nearby natural beauty at weekends, but who are too busy to require it right outside their windows.'

She paused to check that her audience were following before calling up a pair of slides on the twin carousels, which beamed onto the screen a line drawing on the left, and on the right a photograph of woodlands with pale-blue mountains in the distance. 'It is through a handful of these peripheral sites that drilling has secretly been conducted in the Southern Zones over the last year. As you will see, we have been testing ways of screening the works from view with great success. The idea is that if we expand production at this site, visitors would remain unaware of the gradual shrinking of the parkland. Complex and subtle reconfigurations of footpaths and bridleways would lead them imperceptibly back on themselves, so that the longest walk would be a spiral that covers a fraction of the original acreage.' With the pointer she made a flourish towards the line drawing, which could now been seen to be an aerial diagram of just such a spiral footpath. 'The illusion is maintained by landscaping to give the impression of two different viewpoints over totally different parts of the countryside, when the viewpoints are in fact only metres apart. So this photograph is the view from this position. And this…' She changed the photograph of woodlands to one of fens with wide-open skies. '…is the view from here,' pointing to a second X on the left-hand slide, 'just ten paces on, pointing in this direction.'

The audience gave out a murmur.

'Of course, at some point the illusion will have been pushed to such an extreme that it will most likely collapse. It will only be possible to keep the reality of the landscape at bay for so long, and so it falls to us to prepare the people of Academia. They must learn to appreciate the beauty of the machined landscape; the myth of the rural idyll must be replaced by an aesthetic appreciation of form and colour. If we do not strategize this switch now, we will meet with much resistance when the time comes.'

She paused to take a sip of gin and call up another pair of slides, of what looked like mid-century abstract paintings in rich hues, bearing tiny geometric interruptions of their expressive gestures and sumptuous textures.

'The transformed region will be regularly likened, by those without this progressive appreciation, to a lunar landscape, although this would be entirely inaccurate, not only because of the diggers and dumper trucks beetling around and the tall refinery chimneys sending out their flags of smoke, but also because where the moon is famously near monochrome, the park will be aglow with colour. The copses, grass and deep chalk hills will be scraped back to form viciously scorched and scarified sweeps of craggy dykes, separating ponds died ochre, apple green, taupe, asparagus, viridian and tea. We will also have the option of these ponds of run-off being leeched through with rivulets and poolings of tangerine, aquamarine and chartreuse. The darker hues of the freshly disturbed regions could be puddled with silvery liquid, and made even more emphatically mirror-like by their reflection of the flat grey sky – although with a nudge of the perceptual apparatuses of the brain, they could become a lacework of holes with a view through to an airy beyond. The structural ridges and canals that almost control the various flows and overflows will be heartbreaking in their texture, their tortured aggregate conveying the extent of liquid forces which insist on flowing and seeping. Major causeways and minor slip roads will constitute a circulatory system around and between these pools and puddles. Vehicles, like corpuscles, will carry the spoils in slow, choreographed passages. They will be praised for their grace and nonchalance and likened to swans.'

Kirkpatrick's tone had become transportative, like a preacher's, modulating and rising to carry the listener on in raptures. Her arms were cursive in the air, her eyes more often closed than open, her notes unheeded on the chair beside her, although she still had presence of mind enough to change the slides now and then to another pair of heartbreaking landscapes. They took Ida's breath away. She would be willing to throw over the standard-issue green countryside for this gorgeous painterliness any day.

‘The occasional extra-deep gulley will suck in the sunlight and convert it into the indigo ink of a doodled line. Chalky escarpments will, here and there, persist, jolting the eye with their sudden brightness, dimmed only by slight leakages of cyans and tawnies at their edges. The orange and red trucks will look positively jolly when parked on these, and it will be a marketable highlight when a row of red dumpsters park beside a primary green pool.

‘At times a sector that has rested for a while will take on the ferrous look of a meat collation. At others, serenity will establish itself, the stagnant silt a dark scar of past action. Flooded delta plains will be marbled with the floating corpses of dead rainbows, which always mark the presence of oil. People will observe that all human emotions are represented here in the new-look National Park and how, with the removal of all foliage, it is an affecting experience, as never before.’

Kirkpatrick descended to Earth abruptly and opened her eyes. Like a hypnotist, she pointedly surveyed the audience left to right, smiling, as if to say: here we all are, back in the room, after our special time away together.

‘But all this is yet to come, unfolding over a timescale that is beyond our current funding streams. These photographs were of course taken in Foreign, where a large proportion of the land – as much as thirty per cent of the mapped territories – has already submitted to prospecting and production. In Academia, we are still speculating as to where the oil is concentrated. Our initial Snowdon surveys suggest we are not likely to enjoy the sort of oil that spouts easily but the sort that must be dragged from the ground by fracking. But it is here and we shall frack it.’ She flicked through more slides of the buildings and forested setting of Academia, as viewed from the familiar, flattering angles of the official prospectus. ‘We have found encouraging signs here, near the administration hub, where some very small dead rainbows lie about the marshy undergrowth; and here, by the psychology labs, where the leaves are dark brassica green; and behind the Dean’s block, the paths run black with promise. Oil might be lurking around the statistics blocks, or running down from the hills to the language departmental valleys, or bubbling beneath the entertainments quarter. We are only now coming to realise the magnitude of the resource beneath our feet, but we shall find it and raise it no matter how difficult, how dangerous, how objected to. The crude shall rise. Thank you very much. We will now have a short comfort break and then we will hear from my colleague on the ground, Klondike.’

Everyone clapped earnestly and Kirkpatrick glided back to her seat. Ida thought her most impressive. She loved those old-world mannerisms: the crooking of her fingers as she filled in the outlines of her ideas, the wavering of her wrists as she came to the close of a sub-clause and how her mouth appeared to sustain a smile even when she was pronouncing words with an 'o' in them.

'That was great,' she said brightly to Hands, who sat to her left, and pointedly not to John, who sat on her right. So little had she thought of John in the past few days, it caused her a genuine jolt when he had dropped down into the seat beside her.

'Hello stranger,' he had said, with a hard look not quite ruining his handsome face. 'Hands.' He sent a curt nod across her, then turned back to look her steadily in the eye. 'Been busy?'

'Very,' she replied. And so the exchange continued in terse non-sequiturs and veiled accusations, with over-sensitised Hands protecting himself from their no-nonsense body language by engaging the stranger next to him in a blow-by-blow recap of his journey there.

At first, Ida had found it difficult to ignore the sensation of sunburn that sitting next to John produced, but Kirkpatrick's intensity and those landscapes had penetrated her consciousness at an altogether different emotional frequency.

John rose from his seat, seeming to pause absent-mindedly.

'Ah, I might not see you again, before I go,' he said to Ida.

'Oh, not staying for what's he called? The next mount?'

'Klondike. Yes, but I mean I won't see you around before I go. To Foreign. Week after next.'

'That'll be nice. Have a ripping time.' She turned her back on him, the adrenaline numbing any pain she might be feeling. He shrugged and sauntered off. 'Hands, fancy something wet?' she said for something to say.

'Sure,' said Hands, 'I'll go get it. And I brought some homemade flapjacks too.' Well, John might be a salty dog, but Hands was sweetness personified.

'Lovely. Mine's a whiskey. I'll keep your seat for you.' She tried not to hope that John would come back, having realised he was unable to live without her. Oh Dog, where did she get this rubbish from? But he *might* come back to pick up an umbrella he'd forgotten, and then she could say something frank that would prompt him to be honest with himself, and with her, and to confess that he was unable to live without… No! This was not what she wanted. She just wanted him to allude to the fact that maybe he was missing her and that he was unable to...

She saw Hands approaching, his youthful pinkness looking terribly vulnerable against the craggy rock, and John beyond him, whose appearance was perfectly suited to subterranean roughness, his dark forelock glistening in the low lighting and his white smile beaming out like a coal miner's. He sat elsewhere for the next session, to Ida's relief and disappointment, which, contrary to what one might expect, are perfectly miscible.

*

When Klondike took the stand it took Ida a short while to redact the goatee from his face and identify him. Those pectorals! It was the plumber who had worked on Sue and Linda's office. His shirt seemed to be labouring to contain his torso as he delivered a report, with full aerial photographic and blueprint support, of a conversion project.

'Sounds religious,' Ida muttered to Hands, who sniffed in reply.

Klondike went on to outline how he and his colleague had been gradually, and covertly, adapting parts of Academia's plumbing and sewage system into an oil distribution network.

'Just think of all those dual-tapped basins in all those toilets and washrooms. At present we have control of around forty per cent of targeted hot taps, and we are negotiating access to at least half of the rest. Then, when we finally turn on the big stopcock, we shall be able to get the black stuff into every single building with the minimum of effort.'

There was a question from the floor about how Academics were being persuaded to go without hot water.

'Oh,' said Klondike, 'it's not in their homes, just in public and institutional toilets. We've a full folio of managers' signatures and departmental letterheaded paper, and people more or less accept any conditions they think are handed down from management. What with that, and the compensatory installation of antibacterial gel dispensers, no one has questioned the legitimacy of our business whatsoever. Biddable lot, academics.'

CHAPTER 34

Ida rolled onto her back, relieved that the task had been accomplished, from Hands' point of view anyway. She'd been less than enthusiastic about sex with him the past few times. It was tending towards sawing wood, and she couldn't tell whether this had produced her decline in interest or was a result of it. Hands, on the other hand, seemed oblivious to the significance of her dryness. What she lacked in natural juices he replaced with his own saliva, not as a sensual act but as if there were a mechanical fault to be improvised around.

Ida's sexual pride did not permit her to reject his advances. In fact, it required her to make the first move each time. When she was having sex regularly with just one person for a stretch, the frequency of the act was, to her mind, a known that remained unspoken between them. There was a certain amount of pleasure that was due, and even if she was the recipient of none of it, she felt she had to keep her end up. This was boggy ground, because every feminist knows that they owe a man nothing, that his urges are his problem; and yet Ida did not want to play into the stereotype of the woman who withholds, whether through frigidity or power games. Her macho impulse to keep up with and even to outstrip her partner would only last so long though, and after a few weeks with Hands it was really becoming a chore.

After a few respectful post-coital minutes she spoke.

'Hands. I have to stop seeing you. I'm going to Foreign. With John. It's all arranged.'

She surprised herself with her directness. She had written and rehearsed a more delicate speech, but never mind. If anyone appreciated efficiency it would be Hands.

'It's not that he and I are, you know… It's more that I won't be able to think about you so much while I'm away, and I don't think that's fair on you.' She waited for him to respond, but there was nothing. He continued lying on his back, rigid, staring at the ceiling, his lips pursed.

'Hands, say something. Even just "yeah". I'm sorry. I know it's painful, but you need to say something, otherwise I can't know that you understand.'

Hands turned away.

'Ok, we'll talk about it later.' She addressed his freckled shoulder, which from that angle looked babyishly plump, as if it were the one part of him that truly expressed how much of a boy this man was. 'Maybe we can find a way that it will all be fine.' Still no response. 'But hey, how about helping me learn the language? I thought you'd really enjoy that, being a linguist and all. Look, I made up some flashcards already.'

She fished out a pile of index cards from a drawer in the bedside cabinet and started riffling them coaxingly. She had made a first foray into the Foreign language and realised quite how foreign it was. But if she could become fluent, there would be so much new content for the taking. She didn't know of any other Academic who spoke Foreign, or indeed anyone, other than GASMANs, who had stepped foot across the border, and so she would have first dibs on whatever she might find there. And if the place is as peculiar as they say, there would be cultural quirks and social anomalies to analyse and commentate on for years to come.

At the sound of the index cards phuttering and slapping, Hands rolled over to face her, his eyes fixed on the cards. He reached out, snatched them and threw them about the room, his eyes flashing black, his mouth twisted. The cards fluttered about pathetically, making no impact worthy of his rage, forcing him to speech – a strangled, horrible sound wrenched from a part of his gut he seldom used.

'You… you… wicked, wicked cat.'

He was standing now, trembling, naked, beautiful. Ida was prone, awed.

'Oh, Hands! You made a metaphor!'

*

There are 33 characters in the Foreign alphabet, only five of which look like and sound like characters of the Academic alphabet. There are a handful of false friends, which look the same but sound different, and then there are the totally different characters, some of which look familiar but mutated, and some that are wild new fabrications. Ida took comfort from the fact that there were any letters at all. She could imagine the possibility of a language with no structural familiarity, perhaps with entire words, phrases, sentences or ideas represented by a single character. Or an alphabet made up of any old thing – dots and dashes, puffs of smoke, clicks and whistles, colours, aromas, pricks on the skin, intensities. If both Foreign and Academic were made up of sentences that were made up of words that were made up of letters, then surely the Foreign brain cannot be so dissimilar to her own.

She turned to Manfred for help, who patiently took hold of the index cards and used them to fan the little fire in her brain that was warming to this new tongue. First he tested her on words made up of letters that coincided with the Academic alphabet, then introduced a few 'false friends' to one-, two-, then three-syllable words that looked frightening but which, when read phonetically, sounded like Academic words. This built up a quite advanced but impractically esoteric vocabulary of trans-cultural phenomena that included mayonnaise, chauvinism, bar, pizza super-supreme, gymnastics, businessmen, whiskey, heavy metal rock and nylon.

Beyond this point, Manfred said, without learning the Foreign alphabet himself, he wasn't going to be able to tell if she'd got a word right or wrong, and it wasn't in his job description to learn alphabets. Ida had said just having him there was enough to discipline her into continuing, and so he sat with her as she progressed through the beginner's exercises.

She started to notice that words changed their final few letters depending on – what? She wasn't sure. She tentatively opened a book of advanced grammar, and sure enough there were chapters and chapters of tables of myriad rules governing various declensions and conjugations, lists of exceptions, and exceptions to the exceptions, and contraventions of contextual rules. What seemed like chaos – with words changing their endings apparently at will – could be completely rationalised if this blizzard of rules was learned in its entirety. As a rule, Ida liked rules; it's just that in Foreign there seemed to be a one-to-one ratio of rules to situations, which all had to be remembered. She wasn't sure if they still qualified as rules under this condition. Although the Foreign language was of pure and singular origins, in practice it didn't seem much different to the anarchic whimsy of Academic, which was a mongrel tongue fused from the many disciplines that used it.

Learning a language is like an enchanted sort of carpentry. Each word is a nail to be hammered in; but confoundingly it pops out again, so it must be hammered in again; it pops out again, and it must be hammered again, repeatedly, until it relents and stays in. Grammar is the multi-tool needed to construct corners and joints, and has many attachments and settings. Total fluency is the ability to make a beautiful smooth mahogany cabinet every time you open your mouth, and not only is it filled with the meaning you intend, but it bears just the right amount of ornamentation to suit.

One morning Ida was bricolaging a small balsa and string folly out of reflexive verbs. Manfred waited until she'd finished conjugating 'to be afraid', then blurted, 'I have a job.'

'Hmmm?' said Ida, still concentrating. 'You have a job to do what? Your bit's not the difficult bit. Like I said, I just need you to sit there to bring out the natural competitor in me. Right, to argue. I argues, you argues, he argue...'

'Sorry,' he interrupted, 'you're misunderstanding me. What I'm trying to say is that I can no longer intern for you. I have got a job – that is, a paid position in the Academy.'

'Oh Manfred that's... I hope it's a good department, with prospects.' She laid the cards aside, forgotten.

'Yes, it's in the Curating Department. I think there's plenty of room for me to grow there.'

'Ah, well, it's good that someone has benefited from the troubles. Poor old Prentice. He was a dolt, but I wouldn't wish that level of public humiliation on anyone. You know, you've grown a lot here. I've watched you bloom. I'm very proud of you. And grateful for your dedication and hard work, of course.' How adult she was being, she thought. She felt not a trace of the fury and self-pity she had been rehearsing.

'And I've learned a lot here. I'm grateful to you too.' Now they were officially of near-comparable status, he spoke with a new earnestness. Gone was his professional detachment.

'I've known this was coming for some time now. I have something for you.' Ida padded off into another room and dragged a huge cardboard box back to Manfred, who did not jump up to help as he would have just half an hour previously. 'You can open it now if you like.'

He wrestled out the staples, stripped off the packing tape and scooped out the polystyrene beans to reveal a vast crystal chandelier full of tiny rainbows and splinters of light.

'I don't know what to say,' he said. 'Thank you.'

A spangled tear fell from Ida's lashes.

CHAPTER 35

You can get all the way to Foreign from Academia by train, surprisingly enough. You need to go to Edgeboston and carry on for about two days until the flatness has almost run out. Then, when you are starting to think that the horizon is drawing you in to its ultimate conclusion, you start veering to the left. After another day of slow-moving travel, the train – a mongrel string of carriages of differing designs and liveries – will divide a number of times along the route, as other passengers peel off to the remotest regions of Academia. You, however, must stay in the ricketiest carriage until you reach the border, where it is jacked up into the air to have its wheels changed for entry into Foreign territory, where even the railway gauge is different.

Rather than undertaking this journey in one long, uncomfortable go, John suggested they stop off at Edgeboston for a few days. Since this was the closest Academic city to Foreign, albeit at some distance away still, there was quite a trans-cultural scene, which presented Ida with some opportunities to meet bi-linguists working in oil derivatives. She was thinking of it as a chance to limber up before plunging in to her research proper.

She and John had picked up where they had left off. Neither mentioned Hands or Patty, neither acknowledged their hurt or betrayal. Ida took their unspoken agreement to be that mistakes had been made, and admitted to, and that recriminations would be a waste of energy. She wasn't sure this was the healthiest way to go about a reconciliation, but if it could hold for long enough for them to have a pleasant and fruitful research trip together, that would be a good enough outcome. She enjoyed John – after Hands' diffidence, his obstreperousness stretched her – but ultimately she did not bank on him being around for long. She should stop herself from falling completely for someone who had already proved unreliable, but topple enough to enjoy a little romance. This was a fling, she told herself. No strings. No future. No nonsense. Hands was right, she had been a cat; and she must continue to be fickle in her affections and emotionally self-sufficient, occasionally torturing the man for sport, but never for sustenance.

John was being sent to Foreign by the Anthropology Department to recruit applicants to a new cross-cultural module. Ida thought this sounded rather grand, but he assured her that it was the lowest work-horse who was being sent.

'The official departmental line is that academic standards are low in Foreign, and to send a professor would be like sending Mata Hari to seduce a rigger. But really it's because the Academy, being a bunch of old women, think the whole of Foreign is about to tip into civil war. We don't have to worry though. Not being AP employees, we'll be quite safe. Foreigners love tourists.'

'Are riggers that horny? Funny, I didn't notice it in Jim.'

'I've never met the guy, but from what I hear he's too sour to be salty. Not a collaborator I'd seek out.' He shuddered.

'And don't forget that officially you're still my collaborator,' she said brightly, steering the conversation away from anything to do with Hands.

'Ah yes, your project,' he said ambiguously.

'My project? It's our project.'

'Ok, ok.' He laughed. 'Do tell me about our project.'

She told him about her thoughts so far on the meta-factional docu-tragi-comedy novel she would write about oil rigs or maybe onshore oilfields.

'And my contribution?' He seemed unenthused by the prospect of whatever it might be.

'Like I said at the beginning, you don't actually have to do much, just give me an anthropological nudge every now and then. Maybe point out some methodologies I may have overlooked, introduce me to some theories, references, that sort of thing.'

'And, like you didn't get around to saying at the beginning, what's in it for me?'

'I'm in it for you, John. All of me! For the duration of our collaboration.'

*

John's first input was to arrange an appointment with Johnnies John, who she hadn't really talked to at the dinner, but he had seemed friendly and full of content. He welcomed her warmly on the steps of his capacious porn emporium, before whisking her off on a tour of what he called his 'applied derivatives dealership'.

The building was typical of the variegated city of Edgeboston. Beyond a grandiose stone, gilt, marble and columned façade, its bulk was mainly wrought from grey concrete streaked with damp, crumbling precariously and shored up here and there with contingent bolts and braces made from whatever pieces of wood or metal had been to hand. About this, a melange of prefabricated structures were tacked-on, like the afterthoughts they were, and the entrance, sunk discordantly into the grand frontage, involved an odd triangulation of doors, black-out vinyl and a large mirror, creating a confusing kissing gate-like setup, where punters would approach their own reflections only to turn an abrupt corner, where another clutch of punters were waiting to leave through the same aperture, which was disproportionately and perversely tight, given the well-proportioned halls within. The entire building was held together by a symphony of bodge that produced an ache in the chest of those used to slick mass-production, for there was beauty in its fallible ingenuity. Inside was bright, brassy and encrusted with flashing chandeliers and plush furnishings. The look was part boudoir, part department store, part kitsch museum reconstruction.

'Plastics are well sexy,' Johnnies John was saying as they walked among the displays. 'You've got your rubber fetishwear,' he invited Ida to cop a feel of something scant and strappy, 'which isn't actually rubber, but PVC, which is a petrochemical, of course.' He strolled over to a cabinet arrayed with dozens of closely related specimens. 'And you've got your hard, thermosetting plastics in your vibrators and dildos. This discrete Prawn model is a big seller among the professional ladies, whereas couples seem to go more for this Rampant Leopard one here.' He tapped the glass, adding to the smeary fingerprints. 'As you can see, they range from the big and bendy to the pocket-sized and stiff. And just look at that range of colours and textures.'

They moved on deeper into the shop, pausing at highlights. 'Then there's all the fun fur round your handcuffs – pure nylon, that, as are your non-chafing satin love ropes. And the TPR plastic of the Dutch wives – that's latex- and cadmium-free. We're setting up a made-to-order celebrity doll service, so punters can have them made to look like, well, like you, if they want.' Ida nearly swallowed her own tongue at the monstrosity of this. 'What's really great, though, is if you haven't got the room for a full-sized blow-up doll you can have this compact version here.' He passed her an inflatable pair of breasts with a delicately wrought and self-moistening vagina planted in the cleavage. 'All the important bits there, all in a cubic foot or so. And if that's all a bit much – some blokes are intimidated by the tits, you know – then there's this cunt in a can. Tidy, eh? Looks just like a can of beer, but unscrew the top and *voilà*. And then, when you fancy a bit of back-alley action…' He turned it around and removed another lid to reveal a tightly puckered anus. Ida felt sad for all the neuroses – and worse – expressed through these redacted female forms. 'This one's made of that non-latex stuff, but you can get real flesh ones now. I sell them under the counter because it's still a bit dodgy. They're grown from pig stem cells and regulations mean we have to bring them in from Foreign, but I'm hoping the authorities will relax on that one soon.'

Johnnies John had an annoying habit of emphasising a point by clutching Ida's forearm or digging her in the ribs with his elbow, but she considered it worth tolerating for his bizarre and beautiful commentary. Exotic, multi-segmented words seem to tumble from his mouth as if his mother had sung them to him in her arms. 'I happen to know that this Motion Lotion contains propylene clycol, hydroxy-ethylcellulose, imidazolidemy urea, sodium benzoate, methyl barabene, tetrahydroxpropyl, ethylene dianure, tetrasodium EDTA, tocopheryl acetate and aloe vera. Very good for the skin, aloe,' he said, caressing Ida's cheek with the back of his fore- and middle fingers, which she stoically ignored.

'How do you know all this?'

'Because I care.'

It is generally the way, she thought, that if you care you know, but not necessarily that if you know you care, in which case you generally forget. Does this mean, then, that the way to tackle a failing memory or scant understanding is to induce more care? Can care be synthesised if it is not naturally occurring?

A couple browsing the vibrators picked up a Dick Rambone and put it back down again, with boredom rather than disdain.

'Nothing's really jumping out at me. Is it you?'

'Nah.'

It was an entirely pragmatic conversation, unembellished with lasciviousness or even with the symbolism of lust-to-come. If these were what real-live sensualists were like, then Ida thought they could do with a bit of cerebralism to think their way out of their emotional numbness. One drawback to sensualism, she realised, was that it was over-reliant on external stimuli.

They wandered up a grand central staircase to the first landing. The entrance to the next floor was flanked by two treadle machines, each with disembodied, thigh-high, patent-leather boots which worked the pedals that turned a wheel to which arabesque feathers were attached. This tickling machine was a big catalogue seller, Johnnies John explained. The off-the-street punter tended to go for the handheld non-electricals downstairs, but your mail orderer was more interested in the down-to-business sex machines (not sex toys, if you please), which ranged from the portable to the room-sized. Ida was circling these machines, incredulous, animating them in her mind and barely believing what she saw.

'So, this copulation machine has two modes. There's vibration only – that's for anal – and there's this interchangeable member for vaginal, which also moves back and forth. It's remote-controlled and runs at up to 700 beats per minute.' He obviously relished the technical side of his work, like a ferroequinologist obsessing over the serial numbers of rolling stock. He dwelt for quite some time over yet more serried ranks of dildos, drawing Ida's attention to their dimensions and materiality. Even the earliest models were impressive in their ingenuity: Renaissance-era glass shafts of a pleasing solidity were topped by rubber addendums that ranged from an abstract blob to a doll's hand with fingers outstretched like a coxcomb; there was a stainless steel one that screwed on to a shower hose, a clutch of nineteenth-century hand-cranked vibrators, which looked like rotary egg whisks that had lost their balloons, and a number of Foreign-designed utilitarian vibrators, controllable remotely by way of a lamp cord and rocker switch.

'And this seesaw is a good transition piece, bringing together dildo design, kinetic sculpture and furniture.' Two upright protuberances were placed four feet apart, awaiting the open core of the two women as they each, in turn, brought down their side of the see-saw, the cutaway in the wooden seat providing ample clearance for alternating shaftings. 'And over in the furniture department I think you'd appreciate the Rim Chair, the Voyeuristic Object, the Erotic Saddle and the various flat-pack tables with armrests, waist belts and lazy Susans.' The Voyeuristic Object was a porcelain gazunder in a Bakelite holder with small feet and a wing mirror attached for auto-voyeurism – a proclivity that Ida did not have herself, but could understand might be a thing.

'And I suppose, if you're going to be farsighted about the impact of oil, then you should take electrical goods into account too,' he said as he demonstrated the various brands of Van der Graaf cavity massagers, electromagnetic wave lengtheners and anti-masturbatory pouches, which, when touched with the bare hand, completed a circuit that sent a jolting warning up the forearm, stopping well short of the heart, but close enough to instil mortal fear in an adolescent. 'Because electricity is a by-product of oil, after all,' he added enigmatically, as he stood next to some electrical pleasuring device called Surge Gainsbourg.

Ida was struck by the paradox that electricity was used in some instances to curb an erection, and in others to stimulate one. It was interesting, too, that the sex shop did not promote indiscriminate intercourse, but encouraged the healthy conduct of individuals of all ages and persuasions, and even, in the case of over-stimulated male adolescents, promoted the deferment of sex until it could be appreciated for its finer aesthetic qualities. In the wild old unregulated days, before Edgeboston had been annexed by Academia, pumped-up bands of teenage boys had ravished everything within reach, spawning a swollen generation of unplanned brattlings and burned-out mothers, which proved a very poor basis for a settler community. The recent stabilisation of provincial society was attributed in part to the good work undertaken by a modern, self-legislating porn industry, and particularly its influence in postponing the dawn of a young man's sex life.

'Now, there's a real treat for you through that door on the left,' said Johnnies John. 'It's a cinema dedicated to antique porn. There's no dialogue. Doesn't need it. The stories never change. It's still the same plotlines today. Lots of inter-class romping between mistresses and gardeners, masters and chambermaids. The only difference is the production values. And the get-up. Of course these days the camera work is quite something – gets in real close, so you feel like you're actually there. The new 3D films are incredible. But this old stuff, well, it's all long shots and static viewpoints. The actors' techniques are pretty rubbish too – all fumbly stand-up wanking or missionary. Not at all inventive. They have choreographers on the payroll these days. Artful, it is. Anyway, I'll just go and set up a reel. The loo's down that corridor if you need it. First left, second right.'

Relieved at a rest from his talking and clutching and nudging, Ida wandered towards the loo, not really needing to go, but enjoying the autonomy. There were no signs, so she tried one door, which was locked. A door opposite seemed a little ornate for a loo, but the silver deco handle was too tempting not to try. She pushed gently and it swung open with ease – invitingly, even. She stepped into a small lobby with a stiff tufted hessian mat, on which she automatically wiped her feet, and walked, as if compelled, up the royal blue carpeted staircase.

At the top of the stairs there was a ninety-degree turn, some more steps and a landing with understated flock wallpaper on one side, a long window and viewing bench on the other. Ida was excited by the prospect of watching some equipment being demonstrated, but what she saw was completely impenetrable.

A large room was arranged around a circular, leather-upholstered banquette that faced inwards, with microphones suspended from the ceiling at the very centre. Microphones were a part of everyday life for Ida, so she accepted them readily, and the luxurious upholstery was easily read as a seat of power. The men and women in suits who intermittently occupied it were performing a ritualistic dance, she could tell that much. Every so often they would spring from the seat to crow or hiss into the microphones – the glass was very thick, like an aquarium's, but Ida could read their lips – then waggle their behinds or wheel around to make urgent gestures. They seemed to be communicating via the microphones with entities far away and passing messages on to a handful of casually dressed people hovering a few yards away, who translated this information into hand gestures and transmitted it to formally dressed men and women standing in bays lined with monitors and flashing buttons around the perimeter of the room. The eyes of the middlemen and women were trained avidly on the centre as they motioned vigorously over their shoulders; those at the periphery glanced about frenetically like hens, receiving messages, consulting readouts, talking on phones and punching keyboards.

Ida gazed on as a naturalist would, inferring scraps of logic from the flapdoodle below. Since the scene was playing without audio, there was no vocal urgency, no joy or frustration for guidance, just movement. Ida wondered if the people involved were aware of the origins and effects of the information they handled, or if they were mere conduits. But whether they knew what was going on or not, they were personally implicated, their body type, mood and sensibilities inflecting the simplest of finger whisks and thigh slaps. One woman on the nearside of the banquette, facing away from the window, moved with a singular grace and gestured with an unmatched blend of emotional pitch and professional polish. After a few minutes she turned round to leave the room, and Ida saw that it was Patty. Why that fucking thin-wristed, fairy-voiced simperer…

A loud click startled Ida. She span round to see an old bent man in overalls emerge from a wallpapered door carrying a broom and a roll of bin liners.

'Looking for the ladies?' he asked as he scuttled behind her and with short stabs swept her and a pile of dust out the door he'd just come through.

'What place is this?' Ida craned over his shoulder to see more.

'I don't ask any questions, and neither should you. Now, shoo, go on. Go down that stairwell right to the bottom then push the bar on the fire exit. It's not alarmed, so just ignore the signs.' He gave her a sharp shove with the broom, then slammed and bolted the door between them.

She clomped down the wooden staircase – impossibly, to her mind, five flights down – the door at the bottom urgent with red and green exit and do-not-exit signs. She held her breath and pushed the bar, expecting the building to explode into noise. It did not.

The city was flowing past the end of the alley. She plunged in and was soon at the entrance of the megastore, where she found Johnnies John. And Patty.

'Ah, here's where you wandered off to. All a bit much was it, the film? Yes, people get that way sometimes. Need to cool off a bit. Froth over in the heat, I say, enjoy it. Anyway, you know Patty, of course. Did she tell you she's my plastics consultant as well as my missus?' He hooked Patty round the waist, pulled her to him and bent her backwards slightly.

So, she was with *him*. Ida didn't remember them even talking to one another during the evening, let alone saying goodbye. And how come she left with John? Ida hid her confusion with a placid smile of greeting.

'Yeah, she's a real mine of information,' Johnnies John continued. 'Although I don't think they mine plastics, do they Patty?' He slapped his hand on her bottom as a means of amplifying his delight.

'No, they don't mine it,' she said, stepping forward, out of his grasp, and continuing to walk sedately. The other two fell into step, while pedestrians rushed past. 'It's usually manufactured, although sometimes it's hunted. You see, plastic is pretty indestructible and likes to get as far away from human company as possible so it can live out eternity in splendid isolation. It sticks to its own sort and is a bad mixer when it comes to other materials and life forms.' Her voice was soft and mesmeric, but oddly hard and persistent at the core, as if originating elsewhere and then channelled. 'It likes bodies of water especially, and there are massive gyres of plastics in the oceans. The seas are in fact part of a shifting chemical and economical matrix that comprises innumerable agential processes carried out by humans and more-than-humans…'

Patty had been a linguist researching semantic plasticity when, at a symposium on nominalisation, she happened to sit next to Johnnies John, who was there solely for the post-plenary drinks. They had bonded over a speaker's Freudian slip, and before long, she too had found herself in the GASMAN subterranean auditorium, where she had learned of the limitless possibilities of plastics, and the malleable and context-dependent properties of hydrocarbon chains. They reminded her so much of the conditional relations between words, phrases and sentences, with their eagerness to be seamed and warped for purpose, that she took to organic chemistry like a polypropylene duck to water, and within a year she had moved to Edgeboston, where Johnnies John swung her a job as a trader on the floor of the Plastics Exchange.

'…These might be cormorants, cod, corals, bacterial microbes… any animals, vegetables or minerals that have an agential role in the chemical and economical matrix of plastics. The sea is an archive, you might say, and by studying its composition we can piece together the various roles of these carbon workers, whose agencies break down plastics or enable it to build up or be transported.'

'So there's a lot of plastic in the sea, then?' asked Johnnies John, probably sniffing some sort of business potential – a new line in organically reared waterbeds, perhaps.

'You just need to walk along the strand line of any beach to see that the sea is blooming with plastics. There are underwater lego reefs, armadas of bottles, ghostly shoals of fruit stockings, which are scooped up and gulped down whole by fulmars and albatrosses; and the beaches are dripping in angel's tears – those microscopic beads of plastic that pose as grains of sand. There are temporal trends in plastic abundance, but it is estimated that there are tens of thousands of tonnes per one hundred square miles of ocean at the moment, which includes all the trace plastics that wash out to sea from facial scrubs, toothpastes and low-fat dairy products…'

These supermarket items provided little pegs of specificity on which Ida could hang small scraps of comprehension, but otherwise, Patty was describing a strange and beautiful fairy tale. She had a faraway look as she talked not just figuratively over the heads of her audience, but also seeming to address something taller than all of them, beyond the plastic-bag-bedecked trees and the fluttering vinyl kites of advertisers.

By now the trio were back at the front door of the porn megastore, having made a circuit of the vast block that housed it and the mysterious trading floor, and who knew whatever else may lie within. As they negotiated the mirrored entrance, their chests pressed up against one another's, Johnnies John wondered out loud if they might like to see his latest fully functioning display – a Jacuzzi dining suite with built-in commodes.

'Sounds a bit racy,' said Ida, signalling her caution loud and clear.

'Don't worry,' he said. 'Me and Patty, we have what you might call an open relationship. Don't we dear?'

'We do indeed,' said Patty smiling calmly. 'We have these bodies that can give and take so much pleasure, and we really don't see why we should be proprietorial over them. I like to consider myself just one negotiable element in a network of physical exchange.'

'But of course,' said Johnnies John taking hold of her hand, 'our hearts belong to one another. That's a different matter.'

This pronouncement had the miraculous effect of dissipating Ida's jealousy like a wind clearing smoke from a battlefield. She took comfort from the knowledge that Patty's time with John was inevitable and without consequence. She could understand the function of non-stick relationships.

'So,' pressed Johnnies John. 'Care for that Jacuzzi lunch?'

'Why not?' said Ida gamely, although Patty made her excuses. Indoors, beyond the breezes and stenches of the city, there was a distinct lavendrical aroma about her, a sweet bitterness that suited her odd otherworldiness. Ida decided, putting prejudices aside, that she liked her.

'Well Patty, I hope I will see you again before I leave. Maybe you could show me about a bit. I don't suppose I could tag along to a social or something could I?'

'By all means, Ida. I know how it is to be the new girl. Why don't you come along to the Petroleum Club next Tuesday? I'm compèring at Plastic Fantastic. I'll put you on the list.'

'Got yourself a plum invitation there.' Johnnies John raised his eyebrow. 'Stacked to the rafters with the oiligarchy, that place. You be careful now – don't know what you might pull out of that pit.' He chuckled, gave Patty a surprisingly chaste kiss on the cheek and led Ida off to discover the delights of semi-submerged luncheoning.

CHAPTER 36

From her table right in front of the stage, Ida could survey the audience that filled the club with its buzz. It was easy to tell the Academics from the Foreigners. The Foreigners had a wilder look about them, their faces fleshier, or more potatoey perhaps – not unattractive, just arranged according to different rules of taste.

But where was John? He said he'd catch her up. The cabaret was about to start. A woman stalked onstage wearing all-over fishnets in which fronds of seaweed and pearly shells were strategically ensnared.

'Good evening fantastic plastic people!'

My goodness, was that Patty? Those legs!

'Welcome to Plastic Fantastic, the club night for the petrochemically inclined. I am Patty Kim, your host for this evening, and you…' She looked about the audience, as if appealing to them all individually. 'You, I can tell, are… Plastic Fantastic!'

The audience roared with approval.

'Madam, I can see you love a polymer – that fabulous hair; and you sir, you look like you know a thing or two about resin. Nah, just kidding, you're wonderful. Isn't he wonderful, ladies and gentlemen? But what about nylon? Who doesn't love a nylon, know what I mean, sniff sniff?' She plucked some strands of her body stocking between thumb and forefinger and pulled a great tent of elasticity to her nose for a sniff. She let go and it snapped back into place. She pulled out another, and another, contorting into amazing shapes to sniff herself all over. 'But seriously people, we have a fabulous line-up this evening, and all top-notch plastic fantastics. None of your expensive imitations. You can keep your comedy gold. What do we want?' She raised her arms theatrically, summoning the swell of the audience.

'Comedy polymers!' they hollered back.

'Of course! But before we crack on with the show, I suspect some of you are wondering what happened to our very own cling film escape artiste from last week. I know a few of you were concerned because he didn't actually escape while he was here onstage. But it was fine, really, ladies and gentlemen. We cut him out backstage and, after just an eensy weensy ickle bit of mouth-to-mouth, he was absolutely fine. He's been practising all week, so hopefully we'll be seeing him again soon with his new improved act. But he's here in the audience tonight, I see, so I think he deserves a round of applause as encouragement, don't you ladies and gentlemen? Let's hear it for the Human Buttie.' A respectful smatter passed around the room.

The first act lasted a scant couple of minutes. Dressed in a few sequins with a dozen plastic hula-hoops spinning crazily around her waist, ankles, neck and wrists, Loopy Lou shuffled like a demented gyroscope from stage left to stage right, her features arranged on the disturbing side of funny. The second performer was a telepath, a grey-haired man with the manner of cold porridge, who could extract any numbers from any head. He announced that he could retrieve audience members' safety deposit box combinations. The trouble was, of course, no one was going to confirm that he was correct. To save him corpsing, Patty bounded onstage and engaged him in the retrieval of all the various numbers, codes and tallies from her own head as she led him off. She then bobbed back on to whisk the audience up before a man dressed in a loincloth swallowed a plastic pint glass whole. He was followed by Tilly, a heavy-set young woman in black lycra, who thundered onstage and laid out a series of tupperware pots of diminishing size. Starting with the largest, she folded her concertinaed limbs inside each pot and closed the lid before breathlessly bursting out and moving on to the next, smaller one. Eventually she took up as much room as a beaker of milk. 'Trapdoors,' someone near Ida whispered. Then a drummer made a virtuoso racket with a kit of washing-up bowls and storage tubs, which was followed by Plasticity, a team of shaven-headed androgens performing the most extraordinary contortions, bending their bodies into spiders teaming from a nest, a fully functioning typewriter and a representation of the second law of thermodynamics, which drifted offstage to an awed ovation.

All this was building up to the headline act of the first half, which many in the audience had come a long way for. A plastic surgeon would perform a 'racelift' on a volunteer from the audience, while together they sang a duet from the first scene of *The Barber of Seville*. With many Foreigners wishing to parse themselves into Academic society, the show of hands was dense. The selection was made by the surgeon, a buttery lyric baritone, auditioning pitches of screams until he found a countertenor he liked, who then sang from prompt cards clutched by a nervous assistant, while the surgeon cut, stuffed, moulded and bellowed.

Once the bed had been wheeled off to the last wisps of accordion accompaniment and a promise to reveal what was beneath the bandages next week, Patty skittered back on stage and announced an intermission.

Ida reverted to worrying about John. She was sure he had said he would meet her in the club, but maybe she was wrong. Had they planned to meet at the diner where they'd had lunch? Or back at the hotel? Or maybe outside the club, because Patty might not have thought to put his name on the list too. But she was sure he said 'see you in there', because she remembered wondering how he knew where it was. He was just late, she decided. And that was annoying, because if she went to the bar or the toilet she'd lose their seats; and neither could she avoid Geronimo, the anarchic troop of clowns with striped torsos and loincloths, who were terrorising the audience with irritating physical humour. They tugged her sleeves and tweaked her nose, curdling her annoyance into anger. She didn't even try to save John's chair when a woman with huge hair and a musty odour sat down in it. He could fight his own battles, if he ever had the decency to turn up.

Geronimo were the very same clowns of the St Geronimo feast-day celebrations in Foreign. They hired themselves out for the rest of the year, but with few takers, save Patty. Traditionally, the clowns were drawn from the disabled population and had licence to taunt any able-bodied person they encountered on feast-day. Not to waste a drop of precious time, they got up at midnight to devise their mummery, then descended at dawn on towns and villages in groups of ten or twelve, naked apart from loincloths, their bodies crudely painted with black-and-white rings, like hazard marks, and their hair adorned with plastic detritus: biro shafts, cable ties, electrical wiring and so on. The paint was made from cormorant shit and oil, so even their stench was a nuisance. They threw whinging children and geriatrics into rivers, intimidated the middle-aged with lewdness and forced too-small shoes on the feet of fashionable women, who were not allowed to reject them but had to mince and grimace through their day. Teenagers were jeered using words they didn't know the meaning of, the hair of groomed men was mussed, their slick suits sprayed with epaulettes of canned cream. It was traditional for the clowns, with their wheelchairs, callipers and prosthetics, to shamble about the town with impunity, to do, for once, precisely as they wished and whatever came into their heads. One year they were joined by a man suffering mild macular degeneration, who argued that disability was a matter of degrees, and that his glasses were as much a prosthetic as a false leg. The clowns tied him naked to a telegraph pole with a long-dead eel tied around his torso, and left him to stew in the hot sun.

*

The second half of the cabaret followed the form of the first, with a number of shorts building up to a major performance. Patty had changed into a mini-dress made on the principle of Venetian blinds, through which she flashed at key moments. She must have had an address book full of performers to guarantee a turnover of new acts each week, mused Ida. And indeed, between dealings on the plastics exchange floor and rehearsals of her own burlesque routines, Patty did travel the underground clubs of the world seeking plastic talent. She collected stand-ups and strippers and magicians and jugglers like academics collected references and quotations. Ida couldn't take her eyes off her all night. She was becoming infatuated with her, thinking her the paragon of cat-like independence. She recognised qualities that she herself did not possess but would like to cultivate. Patty swallowed her own stockings at the very end of the evening, which was the funniest, cleverest thing Ida had ever seen.

But before this denouement, the audience was treated to the spectacle of a young man, long-limbed and clumsy as a new-born foal, dressed head to heel in Velcro, at whom fuzzy red balls were lobbed from offstage until he was entirely covered. Then in meandered a clutch of somnambulists in long gowns chanting statistics – 'The plastics industry has an annual turnover in excess of nineteen billion and employs approximately 180,000 people. 6,218 million plastic bottles are disposed of every year. We get through 260 tonnes of plastic aggregate in toothpaste and facial scrub and bath scourer per capita per annum…' And so on, until their catatonia became infectious and the heavy lidded stagehands were barely able to cart them off.

'And now, hold on to your fight reflexes ladies and gentlemen, because here come the two most polemical women in gender studies with a special Plastic Fantastic set for you tonight. Please welcome to the stage Emmanuelle Rant and Simone de Beavoir…'

A woman of extraordinary proportions, as if there might be some shire horse in her DNA, spiralled down a pole to the side of the stage.

'Woops, sorry – forgot something,' she said with exaggerated airheadedness, and somehow spiralled back up the pole, disappearing for a split second among the lighting rig and reappearing arm in arm with a second woman, just a little less big-boned.

'Got everything now, Emmanuelle?' said the second woman. 'You don't need to go back for your self-esteem or anything?'

'Thanks Simone, but mine's not detachable. I see you serviced yours this morning. I could tell by the scratches on the formica.'

The audience cooed at the mention of the classic laminate.

Simone, the slighter but still voluptuous woman, was now sitting on Emmanuelle's lap, who in turn was perched on a high stool. Both were dressed in lilac tweed skirt suits, snug peachy cashmere jumpers, stern pulled-back dark hair and severe spectacles, and both hung a stiletto from a big toe with great expertise.

'Yes, ladies with gentle menses, as many of you picked up on, we have a formica kitchen at home, where we like to do the majority of our polemicizing,' said Simone.

'Sorry, what was that?' said Emmanuelle.

'I said we had a formica kitchen.'

'No, before that.'

'Before that I said, "Yes, ladies and gentlemen".'

'No you didn't. You slipped in some abjection or other. Something about menses.'

'Are menses abject?'

'Are menses plural?'

'Were you saying, Emmanuelle, that menses are or is abject? Are you betraying your sex?'

'No, I…'

'Will you be drumming every bleeding woman from the club and making her stand outside until she's as bloodless as a man? Will you?'

'Certainly not.'

'Sounds like you would. I heard a distinct testeness in your voice.'

There was something familiar about the quick cross talk, the identical outfits, their seated pose… Ah, it was a ventriloquism act. But it was impossible to tell which was the human, which the dummy. It seemed that the chin of both women moved slightly as the other talked, but neither mouth had the too-stiff lips with the tell-tale lines extending down from the corners. Traditionally, it would be the smaller figure, Simone, who was the dummy, but rumour had it that it was the other way round, that Simone was a live, sweating woman sitting on a giant doll's lap, manipulating its levers and cams up the front of its blouse.

'The abjection was in relation to the context not the content, my dear Simone. To invoke any bodily fluid when greeting strangers is completely puerile.'

'You mean like "saliva-ly to meet you" or "chymed, I'm sure"?'

'Yes, just like that. Totally puerile.'

'Oh, ok. Thanks for the tit.'

'Sorry?'

'I said, "thanks for the tip."'

'Not at all.'

'Really? It's not a tip?'

'Huh?'

'You seem to be giving me etiquette tips and then refuting them.'

'No, what I was saying was, don't mention it.'

'Why not? Are they not supposed to know it's not a real tip?'

'Who, the audience?'

'Yes, that mass of indifference we see before us.'

The audience had fallen silent some time back, and did not rise to the provocation.

'I don't think they need tips on courtesy from me,' said Emmanuelle.

'I could give them a pointer or two though.'

'Oh yes?'

'Yes. Like, laugh every now and again to make the people onstage feel comfortable. It's just good manners you know.'

'I think we have to earn that first, Simone. I think we're boring them.'

'Speak for yourself. At least I was slipping a bit of spice into things, wasn't I ladies and genital men?'

'You're doing it again.'

'What?'

'Being puerile.'

'I beg your hard-on?'

'Listen, we should get on with the act. We're not being paid to sit up here bickering about crudities.'

'One of us isn't being paid at all.'

'No, but we split what we do get fifty-fifty. In recognition of the fact that neither of us could do it without the other.'

'Speak for yourself.'

'Will you stop saying that.'

'What?'

'Speak for yourself.'

'Sorry. That was insensitive.'

'Thank you. Now, we really must get this polemic rolling…'

'Go on then.'

'I'm trying…'

'Good.'

'Listen…'

'I'm all ears.'

'Right then, here we go…'

'I'm buckling up.'

'Shut up!'

'Really? You want me to shut up?'

'Yes.'

'…'

'Just for a little bit.'

'…'

'I mean until I get the provocation out. Then I want you to talk.'

'…'

'You won't be able to help yourself once we get going.'

'…'

'Ok, I'll just start without you.'

'That's what you said last night.'

'Ah, I didn't think you'd be able to resist that one.'

'Of course not. You handed it me on a platter.'

'Know you too well.'

'Or so you think.'

'Oh I know you like the back of my ... Look, let's stop this. There are things to debate.'

'Will we have a mass debate? In public?'

'I'm ignoring that.'

'No you're not.'

'Ok, ladies and gentlemen, this evening's issue, the hot potato that's on everyone's lips…'

'That's stupid.'

'What is?'

'A hot potato on everyone's lips. It would burn.'

'Unless you've got lips of polybutylene terephthalate.'

The audience rustled very slightly.

'Anyway, what we're really here to discourse on this evening is…'

'What is your position on the nationalisation of Foreign oil and plastics industries?' shouted a man from the very back of the club. The audience stirred and muttered.

'Well that must be the dullest heckle I ever heard,' said Simone.

'Don't be rude,' said Emmanuelle. 'Every audience is different. Not everyone likes entertainment. This gentleman obviously likes a good, long, dull discussion. Thank you sir for the question. We'll be only too glad to debate it. Care to start Simone? Foreign nationalisation? What's your thoughts?'

'I think it's …'

'Uh-oh,' said Emmanuelle, 'I can see from the wild signalling in the wings that our time is up. And we were just getting going. Shall we at least … ? No, that really is it from us tonight. Well, thank you ladies and gentlemen. It's been really great. You've been great. We've been two. And remember – one of us is made entirely of plastic, but we don't like to brag …'

The pair spiralled back up the pole to a smattering of claps and Patty sprang onstage, working for a full minute to bring the clapping up to tempo and volume through legwork alone.

'Now, it's time to strike up the music, maestro. And please, ladies and gentlemen, put your hands together for the one, the only – they broke the mould when they made her – Ri-i-i-igid Bridget!'

A woman embedded in expanded foam was wheeled onstage by a chorus of individually shrink-wrapped naked men. The room hung on the disarming waver in her voice as she sang 'The Ballad of Rigid Bridget', the men crinkling in time and doo-wopping through perforations in their plastic wrapping. It wasn't until the song's crescendo, when Rigid Bridget fought her way out of her rugged, brittle yellow casing as a metaphor for something no one quite followed, that Ida recognised Sue.

Ida barely heard the final act with its chorus of six men dressed as toothbrushes and a pneumatic soprano dressed as a denture. So upside-down had her world been turned, her senses ceased to draw any sense from it. The musty smell of the large-haired woman, the braying teeth on stage, the flat warm tang of the end of her pint and the hot sweat of the crowd collapsed into the memory of Sue's wide-open mouth delivering a high C-sharp, driving Ida, staggering, to the toilets.

*

'It's just an extension of my role at the exchange,' said Patty, now in her off-stage clothes. 'Same thing, at base. Gauging what's required and finding the resources to fulfil it. It's all production and performance, behind the scenes and masquerade. And a little bit of firefighting. Like with the ventriloquist.'

'Yes, they were quite something. Which was the doll?'

'Nobody knows. But did you hear that heckle? He was an industrial plant. There's lots of them around at the moment, with the situation being what it is in Foreign. He was hoping to stir up a bit of anti-nationalist rancour. Had to cut it right off. The girls were furious. But they would have been more furious if he'd got any further than he did. Could've got ugly. I felt terrible pulling them off like that, but really, it was for the best. It's terrible, these AP operatives trying to stir up trouble.'

'AP? Really? Why?'

'With the Nationalisation Bill fully ratified it's clear that diplomacy's failed, so they're whipping up dissent now, probably trying to precipitate a coup.'

'Crikey, it's all too complicated for me,' said Ida. 'Never had the memory for politics – people swapping allegiances and policies all the time. But hey, what about Rigid Bridget?'

'Ah yes, Sue. I met her at yours that night, didn't I? It was so funny her turning up here. Not the sort of person I'd usually expect to come knocking.'

'Let's give her a surprise. Could you send a message backstage that an anonymous fan would like to buy her a drink?'

Patty signalled to one of the staff and ten minutes later Sue appeared, her shy grin freezing at the sight of Ida.

'Well, that was… phenomenal,' said Ida, beaming dubiously.

'You two probably have a lot to catch up on,' said Patty, springing from her seat. 'Excuse me, I must go make sure the other performers haven't overshot their riders.'

Ida glared at Sue, breaking into a sweet smile as Patty turned to ask, 'Same time next week?' Sue nodded eagerly and Patty disappeared backstage.

'What the fuck … ?' growled Ida. Sue shrugged, looking embarrassed. 'What's going on Sue? The office, the agency? I've been trying to find you for days. It's all going on back there and you've just dropped it all for… for… well, I don't even know what you call it, but it's bloody irresponsible, actually, that's what I'd call it.' Ida was panting.

'D'you know what?' Sue was eerily calm. 'I am so fed up with you all.

All of you and your little vanities and big egos and your careers and your petty squabbles and big ideas that never go anywhere but into a book. I am through with all your climbing and one-upmanship and paranoia. I am leaving you all to stew in your own academic juices because I have found cock and now I am finding myself. I can finally see a future that I like the look of.'

'Cock? Cock!' Ida shrieked. Heads turned towards them. She dropped her voice. 'But what about Linda? And the agency? You love all that business. And I really could have done with your help – your paid help, may I add – during that debacle with the intern's diaries. I'm assuming you heard about that?'

'Yes. And bloody well done Belle LaBelle, is what I say. It's just what the Academy needed. A jolly good drubbing from the inside.'

'Sue, this is bizarre.' In reality people didn't change so completely, so abruptly. 'What on earth happened to you? Actually, what did happen? You look fabulous, by the way.'

'Oh thanks. That'll be the adrenalin. Even just standing on a public stage raises the heart rate, and the average cabaret slot is equivalent to a significant workout at 70 per cent capacity, rising to 85 per cent if it involves speech. I feel great.'

'And what about Linda. Does she know where you are? Does she know about the cock epiphany? Whose cock was it, anyway?'

'You introduced us, actually. Johnnies John. And Jørn. And the little guy. Couldn't get round to the weirdo though. You two were too busy climbing inside one another. That was one hell of a dinner party. I don't know why I skirted the penis for so many years. If you squint until your eyes are just out of focus, they're actually quite cute little chappies. But yes, it was time to let Linda go, to let her become the person she needs to be without me terrorising her into being what I want her to be. She doesn't know where I am, by the way, and soon she'll think I'm dead. Please don't tell her otherwise. Go along to the memorial service and play the role of the grieving client, if you don't mind. We all owe her that much.'

'Crikey Sue, would Linda really prefer you dead than cock-happy? Let me talk to her when I get home. There's no need to plant your dentistry in a van and push it over a cliff, or whatever you've been planning.'

'I guess… put it that way… Yes, thank you, if you speak to her – gently – when you get back, that probably would be a better way of dealing with it.'

'Good. That's more like it. And actually, while we're being sensible, even if you have run off with the circus, can you give me one last piece of advice? For old time's sake?'

'Shoot.'

'This big new project I'm working on, it's a meta-factional docu-tragi-comic novel about the anthropology of oil and plastic derivatives in sexuality and art. It's still a bit convoluted yet, because I'm in the phase where everything seems relevant. But it'll focus itself. You know how these things go.'

'Sounds promising,' said Sue, finding her agent's instinct involuntarily unfurling. 'I look forward to having a cameo in it – but please do change the name. Anyway, what's the problem?'

'I'm just wondering how funny it should be. Do you think Academia is ready for humour yet?'

'The thing is, Ida, Academia is one big comedy. Go for laughs and people will see reality reflected back to them.'

'Sue, you have become infinitely wise. I'll go get us a couple of drinks to celebrate the new semen-stuffed you. What do you want?'

'Surprise me.'

By the time Ida returned Sue had gone. She knew this would be the last time she would see her old friend – had she been a friend? She wished her luck.

CHAPTER 37

Ida let herself into the hotel room.

'Where've you been? I've been waiting here all night. I thought we were going to a club,' said John, as he stuffed some papers into a card wallet.

The thrill of the evening and the high-pitched humming in her ears deserted her instantly. Was he really angry? She couldn't tell.

'Really? We said we'd meet here? Golly, I'm so, so sorry. I honestly thought we'd arranged to meet there.'

'Well, how could I know where "there" was?'

'I was wondering that at the time, but you seemed to know where I meant.'

'Nope. I've been waiting all evening for a telepathic transmission, but you must have sent it to someone else. I hope they had a good night. I hope you did.'

'Oh crikey, I'm really sorry. A total misunderstanding. My fault...'

'Oh, don't worry about it. I had some important paperwork to finish – must fax it off in the morning.'

They sat on the edge of the bed. He undressed himself first, then her, while she gave him an account of the cabaret, of Sue and not so much of Patty.

'It was pretty inspiring seeing Sue. She's changing everything about her life. It got me thinking about this project. We should really make it as big as we can. As daring as possible. I think we can do something really, really important.'

John smiled at her, got up to make one last note in his notebook, and pulled back the counterpane.

'You're pissed. It's late. Let's go to bed. We've an early start.'

*

The train station that served Foreign sat on a small parcel of Foreign territory within Academia. Its fairy-tale castle of a façade, with columns, spires and stucco icing, were built by forced Foreign labour during the period of great expansion to express the scale and timbre of Foreign ambitions. Ida was waiting for John in the area behind, where rows of tawdry prefab sheds housed depressed cashiers and paranoid guards, and where porters roamed the platforms and waiting areas, dealing with confused or angry passengers.

Ida was making her way incrementally to platform three, stopping for as long as possible every ten yards or so to wait for John before being chivvied along by someone bearing one of the many uniforms and insignia of Foreign authority. When they left the hotel, John had gone to make some calls and fax his paperwork. He would meet her at the station directly. It was now ten minutes until departure. She should drag their suitcases to the door of their carriage so they could hop on at the last minute. But what if he couldn't figure out which platform? That wasn't likely, he was a bright chap, but you never know. People develop strange blind spots when they're travelling. Unless they know the route well, that is; but John had admitted this was his first trip to Foreign. They had both been so excited. He can't have bailed out. He wouldn't do that to her. Not on purpose. He must be hurt or sick. He must have… what? Been run over by a tram? Struck down with cholera? Hardly realistic. Maybe he had said to meet her at the hotel again. No, she was positive he had said the train station. She remembered not asking where precisely in the station because she didn't want to come across as a panicky traveller. He was probably just stuck on public transport somewhere, sweating and cursing and worrying about her. She should wait nearer the entrance. It would be the nice thing to do. Then again, he wasn't one to appreciate nice. He would probably prefer a display of independence. And what if she was waiting there and he ran in last minute and they were miles from the platform? Then they'd miss it, whereas if she was already by the train with the luggage, he could sprint through and catch it. That's probably why he gave her his valise, for just this situation.

She stood beside the green and chrome carriage, craning to look at the sleeping quarters inside. They looked small but clean, and hilariously old-fashioned, decked with doilies and chintz. A formidable woman with a chest like a sofa and a face like a fist shooed her on to the train. She clambered half aboard, intending to leave one foot on the platform until John arrived. The woman snarled something at her in Foreign, rushed at her, almost knocking her over, and slammed the door. Horror surged. Where was he? He had precisely one minute to show up. Maybe he had jumped on a carriage further up at the last minute. She dragged her suitcase along the corridor, peering through the windows into the next carriage, but other passengers were blocking the sightline. She found their compartment and tried the windows. They were the sort that did not open. She craned her neck to look towards the station. A figure passed along the platform wearing John's colours. It was trotting sedately, flashing in and out of view among the people waving off their loved ones. It approached her carriage – it *was* John, his trot not quite matching the gathering speed of the train. 'John! Oh no!' cried Ida. He held up a sign. 'I'll meet you there.' 'Fuck!' she mouthed. 'Fuck! Fuck!' She pointed at his valise. He shrugged and smiled and waved. She sank into her seat. Panic turned to desolation. How many days travelling on her own now? John could catch up, there were plenty of other trains, but this was the bit she really needed him for.

*

Three days later, following a number of short but intense relationships with fellow travellers, Ida had learned a lot: how to barter ruthlessly with the generations of women who boarded the trains at every station to hawk berries, chicken and fungi from their gardens; she had grasped, via pidgin Academic, the criminal unfairness of the Foreign taxation system, and she had discovered, to her hot embarrassment, that 'egg' and 'testicle' were synonymous in the Foreign language. This did not bode well for gender politics in the region, if men were laying claim to eggs too.

An old woman, whose name had withered, dropped off and been replaced by 'Granny' decades ago, boarded at some Dog-forsaken halt which seemed to serve nothing but a shed. She immediately pulled the blinds down, locked the door and rolled into the lower bunk, while her son, who also had not taken a name – but in his case probably through sloth – stood guard in the corridor for the rest of the journey. The old woman was quick to tell Ida, in Foreign, that she had 28 grandchildren, and was scandalised to discover that Ida had not a single offspring. 'By me there is no hasbund,' Ida added, just to see what happened. But all that happened was that the old woman rolled over in disgust and went to sleep. The son, meanwhile, growled fiercely at Ida for disturbing his mother's rest whenever she emerged to use the lavatory; and so Ida retreated to the bunk and crossed her legs, as the train lolloped across the fringes of Foreign, of which she saw not a chink of the landscape. She finally pupated fully bored, what felt like weeks later, at her final destination – the commercial and cultural capital of Foreign.

Travel, while broadening, as some claim, is also narrowing, since it quickly becomes evident that humans around the world have encountered the same problems and come up with similar solutions. Architectural structures may have different styling, but the principle of a roof and walls holds; and infrastucture such as transport hubs, bins and bars are always identifiable. Never has anyone from abroad accidentally put a spent banana skin in a baby carriage or tried to catch a train from a chemist's.

Ida worked on the principle that any moving concentration of people was likely to lead to a transport node of some sort, and so after dragging her huge suitcase and John's valise first to a sports ground and then a political rally, she eventually found the underground system and stood gazing at what she hoped was a map of its interchanges and destinations.

'Thank Dog I learned the alphabet, at least,' she thought, as she enunciated each place name on the underground map until she found one that sounded like what John had made her learn parrot fashion in case they were separated. She successfully negotiated the multi-coloured tangle of lines, the tiled tunnels and huge, heaving platforms, emerging some distance away, at the correct station, to take up her map and walk to the hotel.

Despite various GASMANs' promises that the capital was dual language, it was not. It was a distinctly un-Academic town. Signage formed a cloak of impenetrability across the city. Ida stood before a street sign, repeatedly voicing it slowly and phonetically, speeding up until she achieved what sounded like words. It wasn't even possible to use visual cues to swiftly extract the sort of thing a sign was alluding to. Street names and adverts, burger joint logos and police insignia were graphically indistinguishable, all apparently made by a novice designer with a knock-off Pantone palette. If a man in a uniform approached bearing paperwork, there was no way of telling whether he was going to give you a money-off voucher for a foot-long sandwich or demand to see your ID.

After a few false starts and reorientations, Ida found the hotel and told the man at reception she had a 'reservoir', which he refused to understand. She grappled with her dictionary and found the right word, but still the man seemed to have no idea why she might be there with a suitcase telling him about reservations. Ida wondered if the word had a few meanings, as it does in Academic. Maybe she was telling him she wasn't sure if she wanted to stay there, or maybe she appeared to be demanding to know where the protected wildlife was. There were no other guests to help her out, so she reached for her wallet to retrieve the phone number on Patty's business card. She would triangulate by telephone with a bilinguist. The man brightened enormously at the sight of her wallet, licked his lips and held out one hand while reaching with his other for the keys hanging on the wall behind him. So it was cash he wanted. She had heard about this, but never quite believed it. She handed him what seemed to be enough to secure his good humour, and he loaded her up with thin, crispy grey towels from a cupboard at his feet and showed her to a grim little room. Not wishing to hang about in a cell that was taller than it was broad, and which had alarming gouges in its paintwork, Ida dumped her luggage and left the hotel to explore.

Foreign is the sort of place where man greets man by grasping forearms, but they do not smile; they dress uniformly in faded blue or grey-beige and are slack faced with pale blue eyes, hard like marbles. It's also the sort of place where the women walk around on short pointy stilts and wear clothes so fitted that you can see the sinews working as they walk; their faces are an immaculate mask of paint so realistic that it takes time to realise it is trompe l'oeil, and their hair is styled so carefully that every strand is individually placed to create a pattern so intricate that neither maths nor nature could replicate it. As Ida had suspected, the gender-politically interested could write volumes here. And everywhere there were children, unaccompanied by adults, roving in packs or idling singly. They were dirty and badly dressed, hungry-looking and up to something.

The buildings in the capital were enormous and bullying. Older buildings in the city centre were bedecked with brightly coloured domes, columns and turrets, and were scarred at their corners, above doorways and under the eaves. Modern ones, which made up the bulk of the urban sprawl, were little more than vast cream-coloured boxes with slight decorative detailing to mark the entrance or announce the purpose or name of a building. It was clear from this marked architectural difference between the centre and the suburbs that a major paradigm shift had occurred at some point, but it seemed that this had not been a revolution powerful enough to warrant total eradication of the old guard. Perhaps the remains of the old buildings reminded citizens how bad things had once been, making them grateful for the new regime. The problem was, though, that the old architecture was so much more lovely.

Ida was starting to understand the nature of the language, if not the language itself, now that she had seen the people that spoke it at close quarters. The severity of the men matched the hard clusters of consonants that stopped up her mouth awkwardly; and the stream of women all following the same narrow band of fashion was, she thought, like the many long, multi-segmented words built from rearrangements of a handful of phonemes. The grammar she related to the authoritarian architecture and social governance. She was starting to sense how the tables and tables of rules and exceptions of rules extended to public and civic life, with the result that she was as unsure about walking into a building as she was about conjugating verbs or employing cases.

Installed at a table in what she took to be one of the classier joints, she consulted the menu. The language guides only ever taught the words for foodstuffs an Academic liked to eat – soup, sandwiches, canapés – none of which were to be seen here. The waitress approached on impatient, clacking stilts to take her order. Ida closed her eyes and made a stab with a forefinger.

'Yes?'

'Oh, hillo. Geeve my please, I wood like, erm… lights?'

That was a word she recognised. Should be fairly safe.

'Lights. That comes with bread, potatoes or rice.'

'Yes… thanks you.'

'Ok. Lights with bread, potatoes and rice. Any beverages?'

'Wart?'

'What can I get you to wash it down with?'

'Wart?'

'Drink! What do you want to drink?'

'Ah, drink! Warter police.'

'Water. Sparkling or still?'

'Police?'

'No, no police here today thank you,' said the waitress, smiling dryly.

'Sawry?'

'Would you like sparkling water?'

'…?'

'Fizzy water? With gas?'

'Gaz?'

'Phssst.'

'Ah, no, withart phssst. From the, ah, how yah say?'

'From the other side of the world? Very superior non-carbonated water.'

'Er, yes ... ?'

And so, after a lunch of multiple carbs, lights, which are really lungs, and a bottle of water that buoyed the local economy for a week, Ida emerged financially lighter, queasier and a tiny bit wiser. She had picked up some new words and she had learned that unless you know how to draw a line around a purchase they will just keep adding to it. She had been tempted to buy a pair of Foreign stilettos to surprise John when he turned up, but she'd had to abort the adventure when the sales assistant tried to load her up with leather-care creams, cloths, brushes, storage bags, a spare pair of identical shoes and an accompanying pair of flats for sprinting for buses in. The man had screamed what she assumed were obscenities as she fled the shop.

She was confused by the Foreign disposition. It was difficult to gauge whether these terse people enjoyed an argument or not. They seemed to be quick to anger, but then they were liable to make things difficult in the first place, so presumably they liked being annoyed. And yet they were unexpectedly sentimental. The streets were frequently blocked by a slow procession headed by a jeep mounded up with men holding aloft a photograph of another man. Actually there seemed to be two men that these people were equally fond of. One was young, handsome and suited, the other older, with a sad, long face and grey pyjamas. There was camaraderie among the men on any one jeep, but since she never saw the two groups meet she could not tell if they were likely to feel the same about one another. She assumed it was to do with the political situation – the stand-off between the prime minister and the potentate, was it? – but for her the startling thing was that these were men loyal to a cause and proud of it. Each group's cohesive passion was so far from the abrasive singling out she was treated to that she found the contrast, frankly, insulting.

After just two days she longed for the blanket indifference of Academics in public space, and ached for an ally to support her in her daily skirmishes. Travelling is always a bit of a battle, made up of a string of one-to-one combats. The traveller really wants something that the vendor has: cab rides, food and drink, a sight to see. And the vendor really wants what the traveller has: money. A traveller is always presumed to have money, because travel is a luxury commodity, so quite what happens when that traveller doesn't have any money for whatever reason is anyone's guess. Ida was still awash with Anthropology Department funding, and welcomed the restaurant episode as the subject for a feature on the socio-economics of relational consumption. But after a week of this continual squeezing by the Foreigners, which she became increasingly aware of but powerless to stop, she felt utterly embattled.

One particularly bruising episode presented itself when she tried to visit a swimming pool. In Foreign, all prospective swimmers must present a certificate of foot health and prove that they live within the locale of the pool. Ida had managed to convey her needs to the hotel receptionist who, at a price, gave her a letter of temporary residence and called a local doctor to make an appointment. Two days later she was sitting in the doctor's waiting room. Someone called out a Foreign approximation of her name, which in the local language meant 'tyre manufacturer of some note', and she entered a dark and fusty room, where a middle-aged man with a veiny nose motioned for her to sit down.

'So you want to go swimming,' he said after a few difficult minutes.

'Yahs, ploice, I love to sweem. I need to sweem.'

'And your feet are perfectly healthy, I take it?'

'Mine feet?' Ida bent over in her chair and started to unlace her shoes and peel off her socks.

'No, no.' She froze at the doctor's sternness. 'I don't need to see your damn feet. Just tell me, give me your word. You look healthy enough to me. Glossy hair's a good sign of foot health.'

'Hair?' Ida looked back limply.

The doctor sighed, took a form from the filing cabinet, signed it and handed it to Ida.

'Here, take this to reception.'

'Reception? I go now?'

'Go to reception.'

'I go.'

She handed the form to the ancient receptionist, who stamped it, printed off a small chit, which she also stamped and wrote something on, then pointed over to a small window where an ancient man was waiting. The chit was taken, numbers were punched into a till and a ting produced another slip of paper and a demand for more money than Ida would care to admit to having handed over.

You might think that this was a local scam, that the swimming pool was owned by a relative of the doctor and that the two had cooked it up between them. But no, these sort of procedures are part of life in Foreign. No moment of negotiation is without a multi-step mercantile process, for it is part of the Foreign psyche. It is also democratic, because it keeps money moving constantly among the people. Everyone at some point in the day will have something that someone else wants. This might be an actual thing, like a necklace, or it might be an action with an outcome, like making a cup of coffee; or it might be the withholding of a thing or an action, like not smashing your car windscreen with a brick. And so it is impossible in Foreign society for there to be a massive divide between the haves and have-nots, because everyone, even a child, has a little something, or an absence of something, they can sell.

*

There is something usefully reckless that kicks in during one's middle years. Perhaps it is the vestiges of youthful arrogance not yet cramped by decrepitude, or maybe a level of wisdom that takes the edge off juvenile idiocy without eradicating it altogether. Whatever the mechanism, a week into her stay in Foreign Ida was starting to like being on her own among strangers. Fuck John. She was going to visit that swimming pool and have a swim, Dogdammit.

With the mid-afternoon light chasing small, choppy waves about its surface, the vivid rectangle of chlorinated water was inviting. The old, ornate architecture had been unsympathetically renovated, the original shiny blue and green tiles replaced with matt beige ones to give it a contemporary feel, which unfortunately erred towards the corporate. The multi-coloured bunting looked a little self-conscious against the sobriety of the vaulted ceiling, but with the red ropes strung with plastic buoys, the large clocks with only swift sweeping second hands, the elegant diving boards and numbered starting blocks, the place was cheery nonetheless. The yelps of mock fear and hollers of delight of those bathing for leisure and the rhythmic splashes and gasps of the power-swimmers fused into a soundscape magnified and made radiant by the tiling.

Ida stood at the edge, wondering which lane to join. She had borrowed a swimsuit – a meagre scrap of stretchy silver-grey – from John's copious wardrobe of activewear. He said it belonged to his sister, but she knew it was an ex-girlfriend's. Which was absolutely fine. Everyone has exes at their age. It fitted her nicely and she thought it made her look like she knew what she was doing, even though she was just copying what others appeared to be doing. She had thought about John as she stepped into the swimming costume, wondering if he really was on his way. She told herself that actually she was glad he missed the train, otherwise he would have done all the talking for her, because his Foreign was better. As it was, her Foreign was coming along nicely, although her apologies, which were frequent, were a little ornate. When she had followed a woman from the changing room, thinking there might be a shower she had to use before entering the pool, she had almost bundled into a toilet cubicle with her. The woman had slammed the door before Ida was even halfway through begging a thousand forgivenesses from her and her livestock.

When it came to picking a lane, Ida aimed to make a sensible and independent decision. The fast lane was a busy motorway of bodies of variable dimensions and curvatures in shiny lycra sheaths. Up and down, up and down they went, some with the regularity of a machine or the grace of a marlin, others flailing and splashing inefficiently, their heads lurching upwards for air before ploughing on mightily. They shuttled and bumped, caught up and overtook; some stopping in the shallow end, pretending to adjust their goggles while they panted, others clocking up the laps without pause, turning underwater like sleek mammals at either end. Ida would clearly cause problems if she joined the fast lane, but the slow lane was clogged with people bobbing about with little or no forward impetus. Some were enjoying the play of the water on their bodies in a large, sociable bath; others were trying to swim but not quite grasping the technique. Brightly coloured objects littered the surface: hoops and balls, odd butterfly shapes and fat noodles on hand for beginners to help with floatation while they figured out propulsion. Ida was prepared to downgrade to this lane if necessary, but it would be a shame to start at the bottom. In the middle lane there were a few slowies, a terrible splasher who brought his left arm down like an axe, the water shouting back in response, and two others, in caps and goggles, who had the deportment of strong but not flashy swimmers. Ida lowered herself down the steps backwards and waded with her arms out horizontally above the water towards this motley bunch. She bobbed under the lane ropes, checked that no one else was making ready for the off, then ducked underwater, sprang off the wall and surged towards the deep end.

Three minutes, five mouthfuls of chlorinated minestrone, a slight entanglement with the ropes and a good deal of gasping later, Ida was back at the shallow end. Two full lengths of breaststroke. She was amazed to find she could swim. She tried another lap to check it wasn't beginner's luck, but no, she could definitely swim. Her stroke lacked the precision and regularity of the trained, but within her flailing there was definitely the armature of technique. She tried a length of crawl, which was rather more blurred and frenetic, but she could breathe first one side, then the other, remaining facedown in the water in between. She must have learned when she was young. She tried but failed to recall the pressure of inflatable armbands on her biceps, the sting of chlorine going up her nose and hitting her brain, drawing from it a short-lived but intense ache, and the reverb that trailed every cry, shout and whistle blow.

Two women in the slow lane leaned with elbows propped on the side like it was a bar, watching the women emerging from the changing room pull the lycra further down over their buttocks before crossing the tiled expanse and lowering themselves backwards into the pool.

'Lovely, isn't it?' one of the women said to Ida, who was taking a short breather. 'Can't beat a swim, I always say Sheila, don't I? Makes everything seem better. It's how I gave up smoking. Now I indulge the death wish by lying face down in water whilst really out of breath. Cheaper than sucking on ciggies.'

Ida smiled apologetically, said something that sounded to the women like, 'I don't know nuts, for which I offer apologies more than you can imagine', then plunged downwards once more and sprang forth like, she felt, a missile from a launcher.

Four more lengths and another rest. The two women were still there, chatting, nudging and pointing. They hadn't swum a stroke yet. They were obviously keen to entrap swimmers in conversation as they rested, but had realised Ida was not up to much chat. If only she had spoken better Foreign. She could have discovered that these two women were senior counsels on the mergers and acquisitions commission, taking a break from the assessment of yet another hostile take-over in the oil extraction sector. And she might have realised that at any moment of any day the pool housed a pantheon of upstream and downstream workers and representatives. The dark-skinned, doughy young man in the tie-died knee-length shorts, for instance, was starting out in microseismic monitoring; the pot-bellied man floating morosely on his back had been stuck for decades in the middle rungs of an investment management company that specialised in the energy sector and, unbeknownst to him, the younger, peroxided, mean-mouthed woman in an aggressively skimpy bikini was quite high-up in the rival investment management company that had just sold a pension scheme, involving a large proportion of oil and gas shares, to the Academy. The serene breaststroker, who was not going to let her beautiful face get wet for anything, was thinking intently about a vertical integration issue she had been paid to resolve as advisor to a deep-water project manager, and the wiry man with the strawberry blonde tinsel on his shoulders and a nose like a keel fin, who had dived over her spectacularly, drawing the chastising whistle of the lifeguard, was helping his brother turn round a struggling rig fleet coordination outfit. Elsewhere in the changing rooms, the café, the first aid room and the pool manager's office there were shippers, drillers, upstream and downstream service providers, geophysical surveyors, reservoir testers, well sinkers, hole enlargers, waste managers, subsea landing string organisers, risk managers, insurers, accountants, advertisers and brand redevelopers, financial analysts, brokers, industry forecasters, importers and exporters, as well as commissioners, ombudsmen and legislators on all of these branches and sub-branches of an industry as thronged with people with ambitions, frustrations and families to feed as the pool was brimming with water. But without clothing, language or context by which to assess them, all Ida could see were people with better or worse strokes than hers.

A statuesque old man sliced through the water in front of her with the agility of a manatee, stopping to say sorry in case she had been making ready to set off herself. She pardoned him, taking in the sight of his unusual body. He was wrinkly top to toe, front and back, apart from the smooth, purple dome of his swimming cap. Usually the wrinkles of the aged are concentrated on the face, the neck and the back of the hands, and relax into more generalised sagging across the larger expanses of thighs, back and stomach. This man, however, was tightly wrinkled all over, including his uncannily intact six pack. And was it her imagination, or was that butterfly stroke intended to impress her?

After a little more bobbing and splashing, she padded off to the changing room and tackled the difficult process of drying and dressing, getting everything out in the wrong order, having to drip back and forth between locker and cubicle for this and that, and pouring talcum powder inside items of clothing to ease them on over damp skin. An elderly woman watched from the mirror with amusement while styling her impeccable, complex hair.

Ida emerged from the changing rooms feeling energised, but stopped in her tracks when she clocked a vision of a man leaning against the railings and watching a pair of boys poke a dying pigeon with a stick. The dome of his head was as smooth as a rubber swimming cap, and below it a strong body strained at its clothing. His eyes shone with health above a wry half smile bearing a bib of kempt stubble. Looks after himself, thought Ida, which can go either way. But whichever way it went for him – self-obsession or healthy centeredness – it was of little consequence to her, because he was obviously waiting for a woman who was taking her time getting changed.

'Hey,' he said, shifting his weight to both feet, righting himself and smiling directly at her. Blimey, *she* had been the woman taking her time. And was that Academic he just spoke?

'Hey,' she responded.

'What's a broad like you doing in a joint like this? Fancy splitting a herring some time?'

'I'm sorry, do I know you?'

'Yeah, sure, I was in the pool just now. We met at the shallow end.' Good Dog! It was the wrinkly old man from the pool. You could see the similarity in the eyes. Although, of course, it wasn't a similarity – they were the same eyes. But how had he got so young so quickly? He looked about ninety in the pool, but on dry land he was thirty-five at a push.

'Was that… do you…'

'Prune up all over if I stay in the water too long? Yeah.'

She wondered how she was going to erase the vision of him as a nonagenarian, which is what she would have to do if they were to going to get it on, which is what seemed to be going on here.

'Anyway, if you wanna go split that herring later, or even just bump gums, here's my number.' He handed her a card. 'Ask for Spengler.'

'Nice to meet you Mr Spengler. I'd like that. The herring I mean. Maybe you could show me round some places too. I tend to get a bit lost and my Foreign is, well, not great, so it's nice to meet someone who speaks Academic.'

'I learned from the flicks,' he said with modesty. 'But sure, I can be your tour guide. What sorta thing turns your crank?'

'Oh my crank is turned by a lot of things. Don't suppose you know anything about oil?'

Spengler slapped his thigh, threw back his head and guffawed, showing off his splendid teeth.

'Do I know anything about oil? Lady you are eyeballing the oiliest cat either side of the Munros.'

CHAPTER 38

'Hey, press the flesh and grab a flop,' said Spengler, holding out his right hand and indicating with his other the threadbare swivel chair on the other side of the table. Ida was unsure which hand to obey, but since shaking the right would have involved clambering over the desk, she grabbed the flop instead.

'And get with the agenda Brenda, kapeesh? I'm gonna need that report,' he hollered after his assistant. 'Totally corn-fed, that Brenda, and a bit leaky, but gets the jellyroll going, if you dig. Poached her from the AP top cat. Heh, she sure knows which side her chop suey's buttered on. Now, you ready for some gum bumping?'

'Golly, I don't know. Um, yes?'

The office was dim and beige, with dull linoleum tiles and a nicotine-stained ceiling. The ashtray on the desk between them bristled with stubs. An empty airfield with a lonely control tower was visible over Spengler's shoulder, through the grimy Venetian blinds. His feet were lodged on the desk next to the telephone and a streamer of blue smoke rose from his left hand. Ida sat up stiffly, a notepad on her lap.

'Fresh out of Cuban candles, I'm afraid, but care for a coffin nail?' Ida declined the pack of ancient, dried-out cigarettes of dubious branding. 'You want to dip your bill? Here, have one on the city.' He poured a glass of water from a jug and handed it to her, all without taking his feet off the desk. 'So, you're here to pad your skull, huh?'

'Er, possibly. But thanks for meeting with me Mr Spengler. Um, really, I was just curious to know, well, what is it that you actually do?'

'I'm a flow guy.'

'Oh. Flow…?'

'Yeah. I was head honcho of AP's multi-phase flow research project, which is not as cubistic as it sounds. Anything that went through pipelines was my business. Kept me busy as a one-legged tap dancer. A lot of the time it isn't all liquid flow or all gas flow, it's a combination. Multiphase, they call it.'

'Fascinating. Can you tell me more about it?'

'Sure. The hardware I was tangling with made things flow and made them flow for longer, but it had to be nix on the heat. And without insulation, kapish? We wanted to let the pipes go colder than morgue meat without copping a slurry. That'd be like sending ice cream down a line. And I was the go-to in their offshore engineering outfit too. I got sent round PDQ to sort things out. A lot of the foul-ups never got into the fishwrappers though.'

'Fishwrappers?'

'Tucson blankets. Scream sheets.'

'Oh… yes, of course. How awful.'

'Yeah, maybe it sounds real fly being Johnnie-on-the-spot, but if you want turkey-talk, so long as we got the stuff flowing again they didn't care about dopes like me. It was just "get yourself on a sky train tomorrow and we don't know when you're coming back." They'd pour water on a drowning man, those big barracudas.'

This guy could talk. He seemed to be responding to her questions well.

'What sort of things went wrong?'

'Well, your vanilla spill would be down to corrosion. You see, when you've got oil and gas, you've got cloud juice too; and along with that comes CO_2. These buddy up and rust, so AP's supposed to put inhibitors in the line and keep their lamps on the prowl. But they don't of course – most of them minnows were born tired, and the big fish, why they're a bunch of bottom dealers and nickel-nursers. So the upshot is I had to clean up a whole heap of foul-ups. There was one time they spanked all the cabbage for inhibitors in the first month and they knew they were riding for a fall. There was a spill and that got into the fishwrappers, and then there were a couple more that didn't, and this was when the bringdown started for me.' Ida made a sympathetic noise – she had known the agony of being overlooked by the press, which was almost as painful as being looked at too much. 'I got wise to all the no-goodniks, the bum raps, the slab traffic, the numbers racket. I should've tipped the hole card, raised some sand, but…'

He stared at his hands. They were big, their knuckles surprisingly hairy, like tropical fruits. He seemed to slump further into melancholy and swivel his eyes to somewhere beyond Ida, perhaps at a rig far away, through a curtain of lapsed time. Ida could all too easily picture him as an old man in a day room, looking out on to a rainy driveway that only ever bore cars full of visitors for other residents.

'You ever hear of intelligent pigging?' he said suddenly, brightening.

'No, but I like the sound of it.'

'Well, a pig is another way of clearing the lines – gives me the large charge, real righteous. The easiest way is to put a soccer ball in the pipe – snug as a dog in a bun – and send it down to sweep out the sky juice. That's pigging. There's all sorts of pigs, all used for cleaning.'

'Ironic,' said Ida, thinking of the greasy pig she'd eaten in the countryside.

'We had a clever pig, the cat's pyjamas. It was a magnetic flux wall thickness detector. Real on-the-beam stuff. Got these brushes and callipers and mechanical gams for moving and measuring and detecting cracks. And its own juice pack and fusebox. They send it through the fancier lines every three years. Eats up a lot of chimes. And cabbage.'

'Hey, could you use a pig to transport people do you think?' asked Ida.

'Never heard of it, but that doesn't mean…' Spengler tailed off with the modesty of a scientist not willing to pronounce on a discipline not his own.

'Maybe you could tell me a bit more about drilling. I've done a bit of reading, so I know you don't just blow a hole in the ground and scoop it out. I read something about rednecks drilling their names in the rock.'

'Measurement while drilling, they call that. Writing their monikers… I've never eyeballed it, but it's modernistic alright. Lots of bozos think the oil is in a big hole, but it's not – it's in the rock, which is like a sponge, and the oil kinda seeps out.' He took his feet off the desk and shuffled the chair over to a flipchart. He drew a blob and shaded it in, presumably representing the oil-saturated rock. 'And sometimes it's in places where you can't drill straight down.' He added another blob above the first one, this time unshaded. 'Once AP wanted to build a fake island in the middle of one of the hoppingest tub lanes in the world, put palm trees on it and jetties and all that baloney, and then drill rigs, so they could suck out the oil like a clown with a straw in a jar of nosepaint.' Bold squiggles and dashes transformed the blob into just such an island, with a dotted line representing the drinking straw-cum-pipeline down to the oil. 'They paid a whole lot of rhino to the council and talked up a heap of applesauce too. That raised the public's gauge, I can tell you. But then some cat came up with directional drilling. They send the drill bit down and circulate mud…' He started drawing a confusing insert that did not appear to honour the scale of the rest of the drawing.

'Mud? Pigs again?'

'Not that sort. This is far-out mud, made out of... Let me put it this way: you can have an oil-based mud or you can have a water-based mud. The oil-based muds are A-1 bentonite slurry.' He abandoned the smaller detail of the diagram and readdressed the problem of extracting the shaded black stuff from the lower blob. He drew another blob, filled in with dots, way off to the left, labelled it 'harbour' and started extruding a dotted line downwards from here. 'So, you're sending down the drilling mud to the drill bit, and you're drilling a hole with this wig-flipping bit and then it's all coming back up. Well, someone who was smart in the top storey thought of using the mud to pulse a signal to an angulated drill bit. So, after a certain amount of drilling vertically, there's what we call a kick-off, starting in at an angle, you dig my lick?' The dotted line took a turn to the right, making for the oily blob. 'You can plant the drill bit by pulse-mud telemetry and tool it hydraulically like an eighty-eight. They're actually jiving with the bit as they drill. And this is how, once you've gone down into the bed a-ways, you can drill pretty much as horizontal as a hooker. A step-out well, we call it.' The dotted line found its mark and the shaded, oily blob was sucked dry.

'And this means you can keep sucking the oil up from anywhere then? Is there a lot of it about?'

'When I was a greenhorn redneck, there was this guy called Hobart Blip who thought the oil was going to run drier than a cork leg any moment. But we're still going. There'll be blackouts soon though, 'cause AP decided not to run some gas contracts, and the Foreigners are going to have the rest of you over a barrel.'

'Gas?'

'Yeah, on the QT, gas is the real hitch. Oil seems to be flowing for now, but they'll all pitch a bitch when we can't turn the Edisons on anymore. In the meantime, though, we just gotta be more and more smart with the tech. The latest big sound is hice.'

'Hice?' In Ida's mouth it sounded like a frightfully posh person saying 'house'. 'What's hice?'

'Hice is seabed hydrates. Looks like ice, got the chassis of ice, but buddied up with methane. It forms under high pressure, where methane's beating it from the bottom. Get this: there's more hice than all the gas we've ever used up 'til now. The problem is digging it. I mean digging as in *dig*, not...'

'Ah yes, I... dig...?'

'See, for every cubic metre of hydrate you land yourself a hundred and thirty cubic metres of gas. Real wig-frying stuff. Rub is, when you try and dig it, it comes apart like a two-bit suitcase. I've seen it in the arms of an ROV and it just boils away like rubes on a barbecue stool. Pretty hincty stuff.'

It was at this point that Ida's chair, which she'd been swivelling gently back and forth throughout, chose to drop a couple of inches, making her shriek and almost pee herself. 'Oh my Dog, oh my Dog, I've broken your chair. I'm so sorry.'

'Don't vip another vop,' said Spengler, laughing as he dismounted his own chair and switched the two, so that Ida towered above him, and his feet, once back up on the desk, were almost level with his head.

'And then another time,' he continued, 'one of these hydrates formed a plug real close to a main sub-sea line offshore. They were tying in a new development, and had cheapskated like a hobo riding the blinds. They'd only put one valve in, and that leaked. This solid plug formed, cranking up a 1200psi pressure differential.' He paused for effect.

'Sounds awfully dangerous,' Ida guessed.

'You can sing two choruses of that. Would've been like throwing lead out of a heater if it'd blown. There'd've been a lot of cancelled Christmases. A lot of schmucks carried by the handles. Of course nobody wanted to shut down the line 'cause it was worth a lot of cabbage, and AP bosses are so mean they won't even spend a weekend. So we had to try and fix it while it was still operating. Three months we had the heebie-jeebies on that one.'

'And the mud? Can you go back to the mud and the oil?' She worried that hice might be going off topic.

'Sure. Mud's like a high-strung frill, but weight it and you won't get a blowout. But if you hit a high-pressure gas pocket you're gonna get a full-on Red Adair situation. When they're drilling they eyeball the pressure, making sure the drill bit's higher than what they're drilling through, so if there's a kick it won't blowout. Problem is, if you've weighted it with lead shot – like in your bentonite slurry – and there's too much pressure when you find a whole heap, you're gonna louse up the caper by squirting it full of gypsum.'

'Does a blowout happen often?'

'Straight from the cookhouse? Too often. The Gulf of Foreignness copped a blowout and some. The mud drivers was all in a heap and the hardware that should have nixed the blowout didn't. Either up jumped the devil or AP really loused up.'

'Which do you think it was?'

'Sounds off the cob, but this is such a shady business. It's underground and real messed-up. And the other hush-hush thing is the greed and arrogance. I knew there was a load of four flushing going on and risks being took, 'cause of all the friends in the bank, and this is what got my head in a sling. That last big one in the Gulf of Foreignness flew it through to Endsville for me. I remember one weekend we were going to run this funnel down we'd designed to square the beef, and on the Sunday they said it had been a bum steer. But turns out they hadn't done a thing we told them to. It was all just publicity hooey whistling through the graveyard. I got a letter saying I had to go sing in court, but I said no soap, told them they were talking on a dead phone, I wasn't going to stand by them, because I didn't believe in jack they were doing. They were shooting a line about the rate of the leak, working a snow job on the scream sheets, because what was actually happening would send you to sauce a little on the much side. It put eleven men in the bone orchard, you know… the more gen I scooped on the dice the more bent out of shape I got. Yep, the chill was on for me. AP wasn't ever going to eat crow, so I just had to cut the scene.'

'But if you've washed your hands of the whole business, what do you do now?'

Spengler swung his feet off the desk and leaned forward, picked up a pen and started jabbing its retractable nib in and out, in and out as he spoke.

'Well I got to noodling it out, and I figured – and I ain't grandstanding here – but I figured I still got a lot of draw in this game.' Clickety click. Clickety click. 'What's more, and this ain't no onion ballad now, but I kinda dig flow, you dig?' Clickety click. Clickety click. 'So, no, I ain't washing my lunch hooks of it just yet.' Clickety click. 'I've set my peepers on going into teaching, and if you could help me with that, I'd be much beamy.' Clickety.

He put down the pen.

'Teaching?' Ida was starting to understand why he'd asked her there, and was a little miffed.

'Yeah. You're in with the mortarboards. A frill with a big fusebox and vocab to match. I want you to tap me a face-off with a top dog, then I'm one bird's gonna pull his freight round these parts.'

'But why teaching? You've no experience.'

'An' what, doll, is the best way to get it? I ain't putting on the dog, but I got vision.' The feet went back up on the desk in a gesture of expansiveness as he leaned back, hands behind his head, elbows out like a wing-nut. 'With AP escorted off the premises, Foreign's gonna have to overhaul its own fuseboxes, get the cats hep to real A1 tech gen. Right now, with this nationalisation bust-up, things are going down the pan. It's a real shit show in a diaper dumpster. But 'stead of humping round the miseries, I'm gonna set up my own college. First, though, this goon from Saskatoon gotta learn how to dole out his own learnin'.'

'Well, I do know of someone who teaches part-time in the Physics Department. Maybe when I get back… But I can't promise anything. He's rather snotty about the Foreigners that work for AP. Reckons you're all dumb rednecks. Maybe if I introduce you as the former, what was it? Head of Flow? Then he can find the Foreign bit out for himself.'

'If I can get to his shell-like, the jive'll do the rest. Any dude, even the sourpusses in this business, can't resist a jaw 'bout bubblin' crude. Like they say: oil gets everything moving.'

There was a knock at the door followed by Brenda's nut-brown head with an expectant look on its face.

'Sorry Spengler, Kirkpatrick's going to be ten minutes late…'

The head disappeared.

'Why, that broad'd take the clothes off a fish...'

'Kirkpatrick?' said Ida excitedly. 'Handsome woman with a cape? I think I might have met her. Well, I've been in the same room as her.'

'Oh yes, there's only one Kirkpatrick. She's on the mattress route that one and she's going all the way. Sometimes I wish I was still AP's go-to guy, then she'd be taking off the step-ins and giving out the box gravy for a leg-up from me. Anyhow, about our deal… You hot to trot?'

'I don't know. What would be in it for me?'

'I still got oil contacts AP don't even know exist. I can get you on a rig quicker than you can say jackrabbit. And if that don't turn you on, sister, you ain't got no switches.'

'And Kirkpatrick. Can you introduce me to her?'

'Kirkpatrick? Sure. You two'd break out like the measles, I bet. And I'd like to come and watch.'

He got up from his chair and opened the door. She gathered her coat and bag, but when he didn't do likewise she asked, 'Er, aren't we going to look at some civilians tapping the pipelines? I thought…'

'Sorry doll, Kirkpatrick and me've got some air to fill. Go play with the traffic and I'll send her your way later.'

CHAPTER 39

Ida usually performed her bedtime routine with precision and vacancy, having honed each constituent action – cleaning the teeth, brushing the hair, passing the water – and the dance-like transitions between them to such automated reiterability that she often couldn't recall executing them at all. On the whole, she felt this was more of a good than a bad thing, for it cut down on energy expenditure in the ever-depleting mental sector. But, considering it from another angle, perhaps this mindlessness was not to be encouraged: shouldn't every moment of every day be experienced with every fibre of her being?

Since it had been a wearing day, in which an alien world had revealed itself a little more, she decided to luxuriate in her preparations for bed. The familiarity was a comfort. Then, once she was swaddled in her gingham silk pyjamas and the stiff hotel bedclothes, she would send up a rocket of pleasure from the launch pad of physical desire into the firmament of her imagination. But first her immediate bodily needs, usually consigned to the corridors of dull necessity, must be given license to parade with pride in the civic space of conscious thought, to let down their hair and kick up their heels, consume class-b drugs at a non-threatening, recreational intensity, and experiment with free love and mutual culpability. So invigorated would they be by their new freedoms and visibility that they would change the way they dressed, swapping their customary worsted for flamboyant cotton prints; they would take more time over their hair, dying it and trimming and bobbing it into daring asymmetrical styles; their speech would become infused with wild imaginings and—

This wasn't quite the sort of fantasy Ida had had in mind. Her thoughts had run loose too soon. She reined them in and began again.

It was key to her nocturnal fantasies that she selected as their object someone she has already met. They should be credible – not a stratospheric public figure or a stranger she has glimpsed, nor an implausible griffin cobbled from real people's best bits. This evening Spengler was the obvious choice. She would particularly enjoy puppeteering his machismo in the comfort and controllability of her own imagination. Importantly, she could easily evoke his voice and mannerisms – she just had to think of the black-and-whites she'd wept through on those days when an old movie is the only safe place to be. She rehearsed a few sentences: 'Kiss me. Kiss me as if it were the last time'; 'I'm scared of walking out of this room and never feeling the rest of my life the way I feel when I'm with you.' Sweet nothings are a meaningless cliché in the abstract, but when voiced in a real situation they can be magnificent.

So, she thought, let's get this scenario underway. It's mid-afternoon and Ida and Spengler are in his office. No, too anodyne – not enough at stake. What if they were in the Art Department seminar room between sessions? Plenty of risk there, but it was too familiar. They need to be somewhere with the prohibitive frisson of the academy, but fewer everyday associations. Perhaps they're in a hospital. That is a structured and disciplined place. But it also attracts suffering and pity, which isn't sexy. Ah, maybe it's a public arts centre on a performance day: everyone is serious and focused, their roles fixed and their movements more predictable. Yes, that's it. The yet-to-couple are in a windowless dressing room in the backstage complex. These places are far more seedy than people imagine, which is just the ticket. Carpet- and ceiling-tiled with sock-rich air, it is an extravagantly degraded setting. The door has just clunked shut as the producer leaves to check on ticket sales. No, we need to get them out of the room for longer than that. The producer has gone to make three hundred copies of the script for the chorus. Yes, it's a very lavish production, a Busby Berkeley showdown with girls a go-go. Goodness, no, of course there isn't a huge chorus of fabulous women. There must be only slight competition, easily vanquished. A huge chorus of plain women then? Or a small chorus of only mildly attractive women? Not knowing Spengler's standards in that department, maybe for safety's sake it should be an all-male cast.

Ok, so it's a musical with a large male chorus, which is set… where? On a submarine? It'd have to be a submarine in the past though, because these days such a setting wouldn't preclude female crewmembers. There'd likely be a foxy yeoman ruining everything. Bitch. But a vintage submarine – where would you get one of those? And how would you get it through the stage door? No, no, it would have to be set within a rectilinear architecture easily represented onstage.

Hmmm, which squarish buildings contain only men? Ah, a prison!

Yes, it's a musical set in a prison. Lots of men doing chin-ups on bed frames. But wouldn't it be dominated by arias in solitary and duets set next to an open toilet? Depressing. If the male lead is a method actor he'd be too dejected for any fun. But hang on, he's not a method actor, or any sort of thespian. He's an engineer. Ida was forgetting. So, how about setting it somewhere he'd be at home, and more likely to be a happy, thoughtful lover? How about in an engine factory, but one where there's only male workers because, because… Well, maybe not always male-only – that would be a bit unrealistic. Maybe the women have all been given the day off for mammograms. It's a very caring company.

So, a factory it is. An engine factory. And Spengler. We've got Spengler in an engine factory. But where exactly? Never having been near a factory, Ida was at a loss to visualise this. Let's find the CEO's office, then. She could take a few liberties with that, performing an exegesis on academic offices she has known, throwing in a few imagined details – this is a fantasy after all. In which case, why not invent the factory production lines from scratch too? All that noise and heat could be so exciting. Hang on though, we've lost the thread now. Is this actually a factory or is it a musical set in one? Did we decide that? It should probably be a theatrical representation of a factory, because she's more likely to find herself in a theatre than a factory. It's way more realistic. Ok, so we can just sketch the factory equipment in – we don't have to actually build the white-hot foundry, the milling, turning and riveting machines and the heavy chains and hooks loaded up with half-built engines swinging down the lines like flanks of flayed meat. But there is theatrical equipment too, which we would have to build: the set pulleys and flats, the lighting rig and trapdoors. Lucky he's an engineer really.

But wait a minute, is he an engineer? If this is a musical, then he is an actor after all, an actor playing an engineer in a factory. Which is a shame, because actors can be so self-absorbed. Maybe he's an am-drammer, an engineer who likes to act in his spare time, and is playing a factory worker in a musical. Hmmm, an amateur though. Amateurism is only attractive if you already love someone and find it touching. It wouldn't be sexy if he kept fluffing his lines or was totally wooden. And it would draw too much attention to the construction of the fiction within the fantasy, which would be distracting. Ok, we could have an actor playing the engineer, a great actor who looks exactly like Spengler, and the liaison happens within the matrix of the play, with the character of the engineer rather than the actor playing him. So does that mean that

Ida is playing herself or someone else? Or is someone else playing Ida?

Ah, hang on a minute, she's got it: he's a theatre technician. An engineer transposed into the theatre context. Yes, that could work.

So, it's mid-afternoon and Ida and the theatre technician are in a second-floor room within the backstage complex. There are no windows, the door is… Oh, someone forgot to lock the door. The members of the cast all pile in with balloons, party poppers, cheap sweets, triangular sandwiches on trays and crisps in clogs (from a previous production). It is the director's birthday. Damn. How come everyone else knew? Nobody tells her anything around here.

Ida reset the fantasy, emptied the room and started again. But this time proceedings were interrupted within seconds by a fire drill. She tried again. And again. But each time there was a fresh disruption: a bout of cramp in Spengler's calf muscle, an infestation of furniture beetles, the arrival of a pratfall of clowns. The interruptions became more and more frequent until the fantasy was a juddering, jammed cycle of unusable brevity, an untenable stutter that eventually halted altogether. Ida just didn't have the will to redirect the situation from the top. It obviously wasn't working out with Spengler.

She supposed she could break her first rule, and cast an imaginary lead. She could get up right now and do some research, referencing an image from here, a description from there. Except she'd forgotten she wasn't in her own bed. She was thousands of miles from her library. She could put the project on ice until she got home, or she could go out into Foreign and find herself a real grease monkey in a real factory, then try again another evening. A good slathering of reality should lubricate things a bit, easing the way for the oily shovelling hands of a man with a dungaree strap drooping over his gleaming bicep above his fine forearms… and… and… his greasy hair flopping over his forehead like a come-hitherly question mark and… and… a paunch… no, a haunch like a panther's; an oil-black panther lounging along a branch, its front paw dangling like a python, a hissing, mesmerising python… and… and… and off she drifted into a deep, lubricated sleep.

*

The next morning Ida woke with Spengler's words caught in a neural loop: 'Oil gets everything moving… oil gets everything moving…' She sat up in bed, propped on an escarpment of pillows, and savoured the vestigial sensation of smooth mechanical shunting and rotating, which trailed her sleep like vapour.

Experiential physics, she mused, is dominated by the drag of gravity and friction. And art too, if you think about it, constantly presents obstacles and induces resistance. It takes the long way round an idea, expending untold energy on trifles, and does its best to stem easy, free-flowing meaning. This inefficiency is called criticality, and it fuels the Academy. How interesting, then, that an engineer would aspire to the opposite, to unobstructed movement. Could she learn something from this? Could it be that some thoughts or actions should be lubricated, not inhibited? But don't artists also employ lubriciousness as a hindrance? Ambiguous images, objects and actions offer no purchase to fixed meaning. A slippery idea, it is hoped, provokes fluidity of thought. It dislodges entrenched opinions and raises consciousnesses that have become stiff from lack of exercise. And presumably, when a consciousness is raised, it doesn't turn into another obstruction, but lifts out of the way entirely, permitting freer passage. And it can also provide a higher vantage point from which to spot further problems. But isn't this the umpire's chair again, the re-establishment of hierarchies? Isn't this what we're trying to avoid?

Such abstract embranglements were exasperating to Ida, but luckily a tangible research option presented itself instead. Spengler had sent a message to the hotel, which the receptionist sold to her for the price of a good, hot dinner. She was to meet Kirkpatrick at a metro station in an outer district and accompany her on a studio visit. A studio visit? This was surprising on a number of counts. Firstly, Ida had assumed that Kirkpatrick, being a GASMAN, would not be into art; and secondly she didn't realise there were any Foreign artists. If there were, they had no profile in Academia. This could be fantastic, she thought. She could be the first to write about a whole new art scene.

Nothing is ever black and white; neither is it made up of shades of grey. There are often hues where you wouldn't expect them, and so the fact that there are artists working in Foreign shouldn't be so surprising. The cultural landscape of Academia may be skewed towards art, critical theory and soup, but this did not preclude people also having sex, experimenting with chewing gum, doing yoga and performing other mindless deeds. Similarly, in Foreign the body was dominant, but did not displace all intellectual activity. Art was made, exhibited and appreciated, although admittedly it was not so popular as to warrant televising; and granted, little of it had the conceptual dimension of Academic art.

‘I don’t know anything about art,’ said Kirkpatrick as they walked through a grimy area of the city. The sky was even flatter and more dour than usual, and low- and high-rise blocks were set about a huge expanse of wasteland as if they’d grown from the mindless scattering of seeds. ‘I’m here in my corporate capacity today.’

Ida eyed her side-on. She was handsome out of doors too. She seemed a little larger than most people, not in a corpulent way, but as if she were made out of larger cells and occupied a greater space in the minds of others. Some people do that: their shine extends them.

‘Corporate? I didn’t think GASMAN was a corporation.’

Kirkpatrick stopped short at this and looked at her strangely. She wondered if she had make a terrible gaff.

‘I know a GASMAN,’ said Ida quickly. ‘He took me to a meeting once. Twice. I saw you speak. You were excellent.’

‘Ah, yes, of course, you have known a couple of Bergs, am I right?’

Ida blushed. Was this the archaic use of ‘known’?

‘Yes, they’re members, but I don’t think you know them, or have known them. So anyway, you were saying about your corporate capacity?’

‘Yes, with AP. I’m their strategy consultant.’

‘You can do that and be a GASMAN?’

‘Naturally.’

Ida fell silent, not understanding at all the dynamics of this world, but it was not her habit to confess ignorance immediately. There were usually some clues to be gleaned if you let things roll on for a while. Perhaps not in this instance though. She felt that Kirkpatrick would not stand for vague responses. She plumped for changing the subject instead.

‘What’s the collective called we’re going to see? You did say, but…’

‘Deadly Clever Bestiary. Not so memorable, is it? Sounds terrible in translation, but it’s really beautiful in Foreign. We’re sponsoring their current project, so I’ve been roped in to make an appearance. By we, I mean AP, hence the corporate capacity. Of course the artists are keeping it hush-hush about this sponsorship deal, given the current political climate. If anyone asks, we’re private patrons, ok?’

‘Right. Deadly Clever Bestiary. Yes, that is awful. So you speak Foreign?’

‘Brought up bilingual,’ said Kirkpatrick as she pressed the doorbell of a concrete bunker of a building. ‘My father was a pioneering prospector.

Got oil in my veins. Well, half of them. There's gin in the other half.'

With the impatience of the high-powered, she was about to press again when the metal door scraped open to reveal an imp of a man in racing-green dungarees, with a tiny beard just below his bottom lip and of such a particular shape that it must be for something special, like resting a panpipe.

'Kirkpatrick, welcome.' He grabbed Kirkpatrick by the shoulders, standing on tiptoe to kiss her on one cheek, then the other, then the first again. He looked at Ida, still smiling kindly. 'Hillo?' he said in effortful Academic.

Kirkpatrick introduced Ida, with plenty of explanation in Foreign that Ida couldn't follow. The man, who we shall call Spider, for we are working in translation, nodded and looked at Ida and nodded some more. He seemed to be weighing things up, said something quite long and serious sounding, and then, with a 'plees, plees,' to Ida, bade them follow him along a dark corridor which smelt of damp sand.

'I've just told him who you are, although I'm not too sure myself. I said you were a novelist. I hope that's accurate enough for now. Anyway, he said you are more than welcome – of course he would, we're bankrolling them – and that you must sit for them too.'

'Sit? As in … ?'

They emerged from the corridor into an old hall with a large wooden floor, a stage with parted red velvet curtains at the far end and tall windows down the two sidewalls, their long blackout blinds half raised. Dusty beams of weak daylight fell on dozens and dozens of figures. Men, women and children stood, lay, sat and splayed about the stage and assembly floor; some huddled in groups, others in a world of their own; some were nude, some dressed in contemporary fashions, others in archaic garb.

Ida wandered respectfully around the forest, taking the opportunity when her host was out of view to tap them. She had thought they were made of wood, or maybe painted brass, but the sound was too dead and hollow. All human history was here: Roman and Greek gods, major and minor, plus Graces, Furies and Classical philosophers; Thors, Odins and Freyjas; Christs, his apostles and Marys, with and without baby; Buddhas and devas; Shivas, Ganeshas, Durgas and Vishnus; green men and Pucks; emperors, kings, aristocrats, generals and politicians; celebrity waxworks and idealised shop mannequins …

'It ees beautifully,' said Ida shyly in Foreign.

'It's terrifying, is what it is,' said Kirkpatrick in Academic.

Spider looked quizzically from one woman to the other. 'Nice?'

'Nice,' agreed Ida in Foreign. 'How you… How…?' She switched back to Academic. 'Would you mind asking him how they're made. What is this material?' She tentatively tapped the toe of Aristotle.

Kirkpatrick quizzed Spider and relayed back to Ida: 'It's a polyethylene-based polymorph apparently, malleable at relatively low temperatures. I asked him if it's bad for the skin but he assures me it's not, but anyway, we'll have plenty of petroleum jelly to protect us.'

'Protect us?' said Ida with some alarm. 'What do we need protecting from?'

'The plastic I suppose. I don't quite understand. I'm not a downstream kind of girl. Give me a barrel of crude any day.'

So these were casts of real people. This would explain Thor's weak chin and Aphrodite's Adam's apple – but what about Venus De Milo's stumps?

'So when they say "sit for us" they mean…' began Ida.

'Yes,' said Kirkpatrick. 'They mean sit, stand or lie for us. You choose. But make your choice wisely, because this stuff lasts forever. Who will it be?'

Ida had long craved legacy, but in the event she was reticent to commit. Her psychology would be laid bare by her choice of character, which was presumably the point of the artwork, but if she didn't want to reveal her own aspirations, what other criteria were there? Admiration for another, she supposed. But real historical figures should be avoided. You never know if some dreadful future revelation might render them scandalous or ridiculous. Mythical figures, on the other hand, are more or less fixed in the collective imagination, and their allegorical qualities universal. They were the safer choice. But before she could make a firm decision, she felt she should know more about the conceptual angle of the piece.

'Oh, I don't think you have to worry about that,' said Kirkpatrick.

'On the contrary, it's really important. I need to know the context within which I'm being represented. There may be some meta-framing that impacts on my decision. Even the title would make a difference. What if the installation were called *Look at These Sad Bastards' Opinions of Themselves*?'

'Ok, I see your point. I'll ask them, but I wouldn't hold out for too much complexity.' Kirkpatrick translated for Spider and two other members of the collective, a young man and an even younger woman, also in green dungarees. They looked to Ida, then to one another, then jostled between themselves to elect someone to explain.

'The title is *Untitled*, in brackets *People*,' relayed Kirkpatrick. And that's the conceptual framework.'

'Erm,' said Ida, 'the concept being ... ?'

'People, I suppose.'

'Is that a concept?'

'I don't see why it wouldn't be. Not being much into art myself, I'm not well-placed to expand on it.'

'But maybe you should ask them about the figures' pan-historical transliteration of ideological positions and intellectual paradigms. And ask them if they're referring to Kierkegaard's assertion that the deepest form of despair is to choose to be other than oneself.'

'Sure, I'll ask them,' said Kirkpatrick sweetly. She switched to Foreign and told the artists that Ida had said, great, thanks, that's all really clear. Ida took from their general smiles and nods that, although they may not be as sharp as Academic artists, the ideas she had referred to struck a chord with them.

'Ok,' said Ida, 'you can tell them that I wish to appear as Laocöon.'

'Who?'

'Laocöon. He was an ancient Greek – not a god, I wouldn't be so presumptuous – but a priest, I think. He tried to warn the Trojans against accepting the wooden horse, which for some reason, I never really understood why, really annoyed Athena, who was the goddess of wisdom, and she sent two serpents to kill him. So, in short, he suffered a divine death because he intuited more than wisdom herself knew.'

'Ok, well, I'll relay that on to the Bestiary. They'll need to do a little research, find some serpents and so on.'

'And you? Who will you sit as?'

'I'm going to be Red Adair.'

'Oh. Nice. Was she—'

'*He* was a pioneering oil fire and blow-out fighter. He put out the devil's cigarette lighter, which you might not recall, but it burned up billions of barrels of crude.'

'Sounds fantastic. But that does raise a rather important question, doesn't it? About cultural relativism. I mean, you hadn't heard of Laocöon and I didn't know who Red Adair was. Can you ask them how they plan to deal with that? Will there be information panels, wall texts, a handout or anything?'

Kirkpatrick passed on the query. The young woman's face blotched pink, her bottle lip trembled. Spider put his arm around her and addressed Ida directly.

'Plees. Plees stop.' Then he spoke passionately in Foreign to Kirkpatrick.

'Enough of the Academic criticism, I think,' said Kirkpatrick. 'They're not trained to take it in the same way. Quick – say something nice.'

'Golly, I'm so sorry,' said Ida. 'I had no idea. I mean, I wasn't thinking. Um… Something nice? Well, um… I have to say that there are a lot of them, aren't there? They must have worked very hard. And they all look so real!'

Kirkpatrick translated. The young woman burst into tears and ran out.

'What? What did I say?' said Ida, horrified.

'Oh, don't worry. They're always over-emotional. You should have seen them when we first commissioned them. I dread to think what will happen when the sculptures are destroyed.'

'Is that likely to happen?'

'Absolutely. They can't keep renting this place once AP sponsorship is retracted, and this new nationalist government are not going to tolerate such a pan-cultural production as this. They'll take chainsaws to the sculptures the moment they get wind of them. The new cultural vision for Foreign is exclusively Foreign, I'm afraid.'

'That's terrible. It's so oppressive. Is there anything we can do? Although Academia probably won't be so open to Foreign art either, but that's just because it's not very good. It's nothing ideological. Hey, I tell you what though, I could write a framing essay to introduce the piece to the Academic media in a way they'd understand. I could zhoosh it up with a bit of conceptual rigour. Want to ask them if they want me to do that?'

'I don't think I'll mention it just yet,' said Kirkpatrick as she examined a naked man on all fours, his beard trailing the floor beneath him and his stricken face turned to one side, as if someone had just called out to him. 'They haven't quite joined the dots up yet between their art and what's going on around them. I don't think they've even noticed that their sponsors have been expelled from the country. It's my job to break it to them that the contract's now void, but I'm waiting until they've made me into Red Adair. I haven't come all this way for nothing. It would make a fantastic centrepiece for the garden at home. I could plant red-hot pokers all around it.'

'Funny they're not politically aware.' Ida was absent-mindedly fingering a dimple in Lilith's buttock. 'It's a bit of a prerequisite for being an artist back home. I guess here it's political enough being an artist in the first place, right?'

'Most likely,' said Kirkpatrick as they were ushered out of the hall.

*

Ida and Kirkpatrick stood naked in a warm workshop while the entire corpus of Deadly Clever Bestiary introduced themselves and shook hands one by one. They all seemed very nice, if a little too mild for artists. Except for someone whose name translated as Wolf. Even though Kirkpatrick neglected to translate anything he said, Ida could sense the toxicity leeching through his comments. Still, she thought, every collective needs one of those.

'My, what strange nipples,' said a plain woman whose name meant Cassowary, as she measured the sitters with a carefully warmed tailor's tape measure. 'Very neat.' Kirkpatrick turned to have a look, but was reprimanded for moving.

After an hour and a half of intense measuring – the distance between the nostrils, the diameter of each nostril, the thickness of the nostril wall, the distance between the naval and the mons, the curvature of the mons, the increment of swell of the inner left thigh, the inner right thigh, and so on and on and on – Spider announced that they could get dressed. Then they all sat around with tea and biscuits, the artists pointing out the eminent sitters among the forest of kings and goddesses.

'The Great Potentate's cousin Alexandra, that's her, there, with the partridge in her mouth, yes, she had the most terrible wind during the casting. And the newsreader – that's the chap with the wreath next to Aesculapias – he got edgy if he couldn't use the telephone every ten minutes. And this sprite here, she is actually a famous industrialist who is rumoured to have killed all her brothers and sisters to inherit the family parrot. She is so suspicious of everyone she wouldn't accept a drink from us, even though being cast makes you very thirsty. And just to give you the heads up, we also insert a catheter. Full-body casting is an intimate process. I look forward to your next sitting.'

CHAPTER 40

'Got time for a coffee?' asked Ida as she and Kirkpatrick reclaimed the pavement after a cramped and fractious bus ride back to the city centre.

'I'm meeting someone actually. Perhaps another time.' Kirkpatrick tilted her discretely expensive watch, then checked her reflection in a shop window, empty save for a rotating podium flaunting a single tub of foot-care product.

'Another time, yes, I'd like that,' said Ida. She was wondering what she was going to do for the next few days, before their casting session. She could tone up in the pool in preparation, but she was keen to see more of the city too, and not just random suburbs and business districts, which was all she had managed to find so far. 'Could you perhaps show me round some of your favourite places?'

'Certainly. You can come with me to the horseracing the day after tomorrow if you like. Do you like a flutter?'

'I haven't the faintest idea.'

'I'll pick you up from your hotel at eleven. And wear something fabulous.' Kirkpatrick turned on her heel and marched off.

Ida wandered idly in the same direction, being careful to let Kirkpatrick get far enough ahead for it not to look like she was following her. She wasn't following her – not exactly. It was just that she would be more likely to find something of interest if she went in the general direction of someone interesting. It would be churlish not to take a lead when it was presented.

She could still make out the sage green of Kirkpatrick's hat, its striped feather bobbing urbanely. The feather bore left, mounted some steps and disappeared through a doorway. She tried to bear right – it would be too embarrassing to be seen again so soon – but every time she stepped towards the kerb to cross the road another jeep loaded up with men holding their pictures of men roared past, shouting and jabbing guns in the air. In a final attempt not to bump into Kirkpatrick as she came back out of the doorway, or to pass close to a window she might be sitting next to, Ida pushed her way once more to the kerb, this time at an official crossing, but a great mass of bodies was surging across the road from the other side. People were running and elbowing, swinging their bags to clear a path. Women's ankles buckled above their stilettos and men's necks bulged over their shirt collars, making not so much an uproar as a low murmur of determination. People were not trampling one another, but herding together, flowing around the street furniture and forging towards a common goal. Ida was carried along, alarmed, but not scared. It was interesting to be part of something at last, instead of feeling debarred from the workings of Foreign society.

The swell reached the doorway that Kirkpatrick had entered. It was a café and the clientèle were at the window, looking with confusion at the scene before them. Ida felt proud to be part of the spectacle. She waved at Kirkpatrick as she was bustled past, but Kirkpatrick had turned away to speak to… Was that John? She recognised the forearms reaching out with a coffee cup in each hand, and the rolled-up cuffs of a pink and green shirt that she'd spent half an hour ridiculing once. It was definitely John.

She scrambled and shrieked and clawed her way back, but the current was too strong. The undertow pulled her down. The eddies flung her off to the right. A tributary from a side street engulfed her and channelled her into a district that took on a derelict aspect – perhaps a market, trade having puttered out for the day. She was drawn deeper into the maze of ironwork, soiled tarpaulin, crumbling brickwork and corrugated iron. As far as she could tell, she was in the middle of the horde – she could not see its edges, but could sense the repercussions of whatever was happening where it met with the buildings and the street. She heard smashing and cracking noises, and even the occasional small explosion, which would produce an abstract, undirected excitement at the centre. Those around her ululated softly, their voices never raised, no word uttered.

Frantically trying to commit to memory every corner turned in this seemingly endless landscape of unadorned utility, Ida felt panic rising in her throat.

'Let me off!' she cried, as if she were five again on a too-fast Waltzer. 'I want to get off!'

Swimming hard up-tide towards the rear of the fray, she was finally released as wrack on the pavement beneath a lamp post that guttered and went out, leaving her marooned in the gloaming. The crowd receded into the distance, carrying its unsettling mutedness with it.

For over an hour she tried to retrace her steps back to the café where she'd seen John. The comparative friendliness of backlit shop signs and grudging customer service desks were nowhere to be seen in this seamy, business end of commerce. Such double-acts as health and safety, weights and measures, standards and hygiene did not tour here. Trucks, vans, lock-ups and holding bins denuded of graphic niceties stood rusting and listing. Trails of cabbage leaves, dripped pig's blood and deep scores made in the compacted debris by corners of crates, filled with shoes or lampshades or tins of fish, attested to the rude journeys made from lorry park and canal-side to splintery holding sheds and rusty cages, to battered stalls knocked up out of ply and flaky painted scaffold. This was the backstage of Foreign trade and Ida, never having seen the equivalent back home, could only imagine it was symptomatic of this thoroughly unpleasant society. These were people whose food was dragged to them along the floor, but who then made a ludicrous display of foot hygiene in swimming pools. Her tiredness and confusion was collapsing into contempt.

Dotted around the quarter, and providing the landmarks by which she tried to orientate herself, were innumerable churches, all in varying degrees of disrepair. She was reminded of Johnnies John's porn emporium by one chapel, which seemed to have borrowed a door with mirrored portholes and broken neon from an old nightclub. The broken stained glass of a neighbouring, or perhaps rival, church hung precariously in its lead, the vestry of another was nothing but a scarp of flints. Ida tried to recall what she had read in guidebooks about Foreign history and culture, guessing these ruins to be evidence of a popular decline of organised religion, much like what had happened in Academia the previous century. It was only when she encountered an ornate basilica with its vaulted wooden roof alight that she began to understand. These were churches not in disrepair, but wilfully and very recently damaged. This must be what the edge of the surging mass of people had been busy with, and which she had perceived through transmission at its centre. She was lost in the aftermath of a religious looting.

She hugged the shadows as she moved through the streets, fancying she could hear scrabbling and groans inside churches and down alleyways between warehouses, and swearing she saw figures flitting through her peripheral vision. She hurried, turning left and right arbitrarily now. The district could only be so big. She had to emerge at some point.

Just as she was deliberating the wisdom of ducking into a bin enclosure to relieve the painful pressure of a shit brought on by fear, a fleet of shiny brown vans careened out of the dimness behind her, passing so close that her hair whipped across her face, blazing copper in their headlights. Running blindly after these faintly familiar heralds of a respectable civilisation, she turned a corner she wouldn't have thought of turning otherwise – so dreadful did the street smell – and hurtled along a stinking rivulet, losing the trucks, but catching sight around a bend of a commercial district decked in the gauche signage she never thought she'd be so happy to see.

Reorienting herself by way of a subway map, she eventually found the café where she'd seen Kirkpatrick and John, her heart hammering out her hopes as she approached the window. Of course no one drinks coffee for three hours, but she looked, nonetheless, for a bobbing feather or a gleaming forelock. The café had been turned over to some evening activity – an open-mic poetry evening perhaps. A young woman stood intoning darkly while a morose audience listened mostly in silence, emitting a collective sound of dissent now and then.

'Tough crowd,' thought Ida.

She traipsed back to the hotel, at last relaxed enough to analyse her circumstances and how she might have got into them. Did John know she had been with Kirkpatrick? Probably not at first, but after a conversation, surely Kirkpatrick would have mentioned her. Not that Kirkpatrick knew Ida and John were whatever it was they were. But why was John meeting Kirkpatrick at all when he should be rushing to her to make sure she was all right? Why hadn't he phoned? Why wasn't he waiting on the stairs? Outside her door? In her hotel bed?

CHAPTER 41

To drown out the unhelpful brew of bio-chemicals that a sleepless night secretes in the head, nerves and joints, Ida ingested several small, dark, sweet coffees, which gave her instant cystitis. Determined not to let a nagging urethra deter her, she launched herself into the city nonetheless, and started looking for John.

This was a ridiculous idea, she thought, after having ducked into half a dozen cafés. She would place an order, use the lavatory and quit, leaving a trail of uneaten eggs to chart her lack of progress: two scrambled, a poached, a fried and a couple of benedicts. What had she expected? To find him sitting waiting for her in a strange café in a strange land? She should have stayed at the hotel. But maybe he'd lost their itinerary and couldn't remember where they were staying. Although she was forgetting – he remembered everything. Oh, this was useless. She was losing the ability to recognise how her own common sense might map on to somebody else's. She needed to describe the situation aloud to someone and then gauge from their reaction how overdramatic, or not, she was being.

*

'I'm sorry, he left this morning, and I'm leaving this afternoon, if it isn't too late,' said Brenda.

'What do you mean too late?' said Ida, the tremble in Brenda's voice proving infectious.

'Haven't you heard, on the radio? The imperial forces have been captured. The government were tipped off and have tanks all over the city.'

Ida looked out her hotel window and saw just a carrier bag waving insolently at her from a tree.

'I don't understand Foreign,' said Ida. 'I have no idea what's going on. What *is* going on?'

'The fucking coup is backfiring. I'm ex-AP. They're going to suspect me immediately. I should have gone last week. But no, I stuck around for Spengler. Seems he was sticking around for someone else. Now he's upped and gone. Walking arsehole.'

'Look, let's meet. I'm sure if there are two of us we'll be less alone.' Ida flinched at her own literalness. 'We can figure out together what to do, I mean. I can't even speak Foreign. I really need your help.' She heard Brenda's attention snap to an abrupt sound in the background. 'Stay where you are. I'm coming to find you.' Ida pictured her standing in Spengler's office, the phone still in her hand, as a group of partisans in double denim, hanging off a tank and holding aloft a picture of a man, drove through the walls, not even noticing her slight frame as the caterpillar tracks mushed her up in their tread and trundled forth, trailing a length of shiny, curly, black cable behind them.

Ida turned on the television set in the hotel room while she collected herself. The first channel was broadcasting a report on cotton prices in Academic with Foreign subtitles. The only other channel was off-air, its ominous high-pitched tone filling the hotel room like the canned scream of a nation. Ida threw all her belongings into her suitcase, except her notebooks and dictaphone, which she strapped to her torso along with her Foreign currency. She tucked her pens down her socks. John's valise stood by the wardrobe, so far unopened. There might be something she could use in it – a penknife or a compass. She pulled it onto the bed, released the fasteners and lifted the lid. It was full of packs of babies' nappies and Academic telephone directories.

*

Spengler's office was locked up as though it never expected to reopen. Through the venetian blinds round the back Ida saw a fly-blown lunch on the desk: sandwiches dismantled and stripped of their filling, an apple with a single bite taken out, its flesh turned brown, and a packet of corn snacks shaped like, what was that… feet? Ida rattled the door and called 'Brenda' through the letterbox in case she had resorted to hiding in a cupboard. But Brenda had, at last, got with the agenda and fled.

Ida was still round the back of the building, hiding her suitcase in the shrubbery, planning to come back for it once she'd found John, when a tank rolled up. Seeing the place deserted, it chucked a bit of ammunition by way of a calling card, and drove off, looking faintly ridiculous as it trundled up and down curbs. Cowering in a hydrangea, Ida couldn't see whether the man on their banner was the young debonair one or the older chap in grey pyjamas. But as she had no idea which man meant what, and which of them would be on her side, it didn't really matter. Images without context – how inert they are, she thought.

Her plan was now reformulating itself into forgetting John and getting to the train station as quickly and surreptitiously as possible. She unstrapped her notebooks and extracted the pens for ease of movement, sighing at the symbolism of the moment. The dictaphone had slipped down her trouser leg at some point and was probably lying in the road somewhere. She'd be back, she vowed. A coup couldn't keep a good researcher down. She set off, her suitcase grasped to her chest, aping the behaviour of Foreigners she saw in the street, who dashed forth and hither in bursts of movement between cover proffered by doorways, bins, vans. Cars and jeeps continued to pass in clouds of dust. Banners bearing splendid paintings of the younger man were hung from high-up windows. A barred wagon carrying a band of dejected-looking soldiers in red coats with gold buttons and blue sashes pulled up outside a square building with a stern emblem above its door. The soldiers were hustled in by men in khaki. Moments later gunshots rang from within the building, and Ida, face-down under a car, missed the sight of dozens of red-coated infantry men teaming into the street and scattering through the city, knocking on doors and raising men and boys from their kitchen tables and arming them with rakes, gateposts, cricket bats.

Ida came to, how much later she wasn't sure, still under the car. She had nodded off from fear, like she had always felt the impulse to before public speaking. Sleep had seemed the most alluring place to hide, offering a respite from decision-making and consequences – but unfortunately not a respite that lasted. That was the preserve of death alone. Awake again, she was still in the same tight spot, with the same lack of understanding of what to do for the best. The best. An absurd idea. How could anyone ever know what that would be? She rolled on to her back and contemplated the undercarriage of the car. She may as well have been looking at the surface of another planet or the inside of her own pancreas. In the timid daylight that cowered under there with her, she could make out nothing she knew the name of. Not so much as a screw. All these miraculous panels, ducts and vessel-like components required tools that only a specialist knew how to ask for. She imagined Suky driving around in the car. The thought was extremely sinister from this angle. Suky sitting above all this unknowability, and... Actually, Suky hurtling around at dozens of miles per hour above all this unknowability. The blind trust involved was terrifying. Whose expertise was Suky unthinkingly relying on? When they are not personally implicated in the outcome of an action, humans are hardly renowned for their dependability, selflessness and attention to detail. Bureaucracy, legislation and customer service were, she realised, supposed to synthesise care, but they could only ever produce a brittle sort of impersonal attention. Understanding, mastery and love – all these had been traded for warrantees and compensation. It was in this sliver of space beneath the car that the expanse of human despair made itself visible to Ida.

She crawled out and resumed her zigzagging course towards the train station. She was incredibly thirsty but could find no shop open. Shutters were pulled down in every street, their neons off and A-boards stowed. The entire city had mobilised. Cars, vans and bicycles, sprouting men holding pictures of a man, spurted and lurched through the streets, throwing up dust that settled in a dulling layer on everything.

Citizens were converging in the square in front of the parliament building, the most imposing of all latter-day Foreign architecture. They jumped from their vehicles, abandoning them to a growing barricade. An orchestra established itself, as men bashing on xylophones and snare drums and blowing through horns gravitated towards the scene. At first, no voices joined in to give form to the verses, until women, dressed in tight mini-dresses and high heels, started gathering in sociable knots, waving their manicured hands in the air and singing loudly in beautiful harmonies. One woman grabbed Ida by the wrist and flung her hand up in the air, forcing her to sway along. It was not an aggressive gesture, but Ida did not want to find out what would happen if she did not comply. She swayed and attempted to sing along, stumbling out occasional Foreign words she recognised, a beat behind everyone else. The woman soon found someone else more enthusiastic to buddy up with, and Ida backed cautiously away from the intensifying crowd, making in the direction of a sign that she knew for sure was pointing out the train station.

The last thing she saw, before turning into the station approach road, was a conclave to the side of the vast civic square trying to restore a fallen statue, using ropes and posts to lever it upright and back onto its plinth. If Deadly Clever Bestiary had been commissioned to make that statue, she thought, you could have a coup and a counter-coup every few minutes. The realisation that the gravity of bronze and stone as sculptural material was both actual and metaphorical occurred to her suddenly, with a loud and painful clonk.

CHAPTER 42

Topped by a crashing headache, Ida's entire body was sore and her urethra screamed with urgency. The last thing she could remember was having some sort of interesting insight, something to do with … no, she couldn't recall anything but the sensation of having the thought. And then blackout. Had she been drinking? She ran her tongue over her teeth. She couldn't taste any beer fur or tannin. She called 'Manfred' weakly; then, recalling the recent past, 'John?'; then, with creeping clarity of thought, 'Kirkpatrick?'

A man pulled her up by her arm. A blanket smelling of stale sweat and cheese fell to the puddled floor. He led her into a stark room with a desk and two chairs. She sat in the chair, wondering whose drab clothing she was wearing, and itching to check if her underwear was her own, which she resisted for fear of giving out mixed messages. She tapped her foot to distract her from her need to pee, which agitated the man, so she continued, putting more of a swing into it. Another man in uniform entered, whispered something to his colleague and left. The clock ticked as if thoroughly bored of its job. The first man produced a form from the desk drawer, chewed the end of his pen and deliberated the ceiling tiles, as if about to embark on a delightful composition, then wrote a few lines with such vitriol and downward pressure that the tips of his fingers turned from pink to pale yellow. He slapped the sheet in front of Ida, obviously for signing. She stared at him. He jutted his jaw. She motioned towards the sheet with open hand, palm upwards, and shrugged. He withdrew a gun from the desk drawer and slowly docked it in his holster. She signed as best she could using the Foreign alphabet, which Manfred had helped her learn all those weeks, months, centuries ago.

The man left and returned five hours later, by which time Ida had almost desiccated from anxiety and the airlessness of the room. Cystitis had forced her to pull the drawer out and use it as a shallow, non-flushing lavatory. Since mere droplets were issued each time, she had days before it would be full. The man sat sourly before her, oblivious to the little lake of fire by his right elbow, turned on a tape recorder and spoke in slow, flat Foreign into its built-in microphone.

'Officer Cartridge, interrogation room four, Sunday the fourteenth of November, twenty-one hundred hours. Suspect present.' He leaned back and she felt his eyeballs slithering over her chest and arms, then homing in on her face and rolling to a momentary rest at her own eyeballs, before moving on in their tour of her body. She shivered. 'Looting is a federal offence that is punishable by banishment to a labour camp. Treason, I need not remind you, attracts the ultimate punishment. You,' at this point he pored over the paper she had signed earlier, 'Ira Doughy, have been arrested on suspicion of both offences and are pending trial. You have elected to be represented by the state and have passed over your rights to a phone call.'

'I no understand,' she wailed. 'What happens?'

'This is your statement, which you have signed of your own free will, did you not?' He pointed at her signature and pointed at her. 'You?'

'My name is Ida O'Dewey,' she said calmly, in perfectly acceptable Foreign.

'And you verify that you attest to the evidence given in the statement here and here?' He pointed to paragraphs on the sheet, then levelled his gaze at Ida, whose vision was becoming dim at the periphery. Her need to pee was mounting. She jiggled her leg, but that aggravated her headache.

'I know nothing. I am not well. In my head.'

'Very droll, Ms…' he had to glance at the paper again, pronouncing her name as if it were a rotten vegetable in his mouth, 'Ms Doughy. You'll find that any claims of diminished responsibility do not work here in Foreign. There is no point insisting on a doctor's examination.'

'A doctor – yes, yes please. I want for doctor.'

'We can call a doctor if you insist, but you will either be pronounced insane and sent to a secure unit or you will be pronounced sane and sent to a secure unit. The choice is yours. Do you withdraw your request for a doctor?'

'For doctor? Yes. Please.'

'Good, I hereby submit to the recording that the suspect has withdrawn her request for a doctor and thereby admits to soundness of mind.' Cartridge leant forward, pressed pause, then slumped back into his chair, letting out a foul-smelling belch. He pressed play again and read from the sheet. 'Looting, damage to state property and employees, carrying disguises with intent to smuggle criminals across the border, resisting arrest, assaulting a police officer… Need I go on?'

'Sorry, no understands.'

'Maybe you understand pictures.'

He withdrew some photographs from a file and shoved them across the desk at her. She bent her head painfully to look at the top one. The photograph was of a charabanc of clowns.

'Oh… It's a joke. Oh very funny. Was this all John's idea? It's a very elaborate set-up. He could've just put a crank call through to my hotel room or something. But still, I appreciate the effort.' Her laughter had a crazy edge that ricocheted about the room and turned abruptly to hiccups when Cartridge's giant craggy hand slammed the desk and, horrifyingly, a droplet of urine escaped into whosever underwear she might be wearing. He reached over and brought another photograph to the top of the pile, pointed at a small figure in the background and said 'You.'

Despite her private humiliation and desire to sit still lest more moisture should go on the move, Ida peered closer. It *was* her in the background, facing the other way, towards a large imperious square in the background. She remembered the protesters' struggle with the statue, and the insight into materiality and power flashed through her mind once more. This time though, she thought it too obvious a subject for an essay. The photograph had been taken from a window, the second floor perhaps, and caught a party of curly wigged clowns carrying televisions and stereo systems back to their charabanc. She leafed through and saw that in another picture the goods were restored behind shop windows, a clown's arm raised, stone in hand, ready to liberate them. Another, taken with a zoom lens, caught three clowns face-on. These could not be painted faces, but masks, for each clown bore identical features: an average nose beneath its red plastic addendum, quite large eyes slightly far apart, and neither overly full nor overly thin lips. They all wore dark dungarees. Cartridge leaned over with a fat felt-tip pen and coloured a clowns' wigs in orange.

'You. They're all you.' He took pleasure in his artwork, cocking his head to one side to appreciate it properly.

Ida gasped and grabbed a photograph for a closer look, but its graininess broke down under scrutiny. She drew it back to arm's length and squinted.

'Oh my good Dog! How…? Deadly Clever Bestiary! Kirkpatrick?… John?'

Connections, coincidences, accidents and irrelevances whirled around in a sandstorm of horror. She thought she might throw up in her own lap. Which way was up? These masks, the studio visit, when was that? A day ago? A week ago? If she were a man she'd be able to tell by the growth of her facial hair.

'It's a set-up. Deadly Clever Bestiary. Kirkpatrick. John. It's them,' she pleaded, unable to access any Foreign words now.

The phone rang. Cartridge snatched up the telephone receiver, listened, rumbled something sinister into it, hung up and turned back to Ida with intense hostility.

'Filthy AP shit-stirrers. I should lock you up and throw away the prison.'

He looked at his big, fat, black watch, clinging to his wrist like a leech, sighed more halitosis into the room and reached for his keys, which dangled in a swollen machismic bunch between his testicles and his gun. His mind was more on what was in the lunch tin in his locker than how to best achieve justice. If it wasn't interesting his wife would get an earful when he got home. He'd shake her awake and then give her an earful. He did so hate shift work. It plays havoc with routines.

Seeing him reach for his gun, Ida shouted in panic.

'This is madness! I want to speak to the Academic consulate immediately. Get me the consulate, get me Kirkpatrick. No, not her. Get me Spengler… Patty… Mum… get me someone, anyone. Get me them now!' She resorted to screaming to draw someone else into this exchange. She was getting nowhere with this man and she really needed the loo.

Cartridge's hand diverted from his keys, reaching instead for a button on the underside of his desk. A white-coated woman appeared, apparently without even having to open the door, with a syringe held out like a lance and aimed at Ida's jugular. The man sighed – lunch was going to have to wait.

CHAPTER 43

Ratta-ta-chah, ratta-ta-cha, ratta-ta-cha. Ida woke to a swaying percussion that she instantly recognised as a train. Mmmm, cosy. She rolled over and went back to sleep, dreaming of forearms like snakes winding round her, loving her, lauding her, raising her up. Ratta-ta-chah, ratta-ta-cha, ratta-ta-cha.

CHAPTER 44

Rosa Kress can't believe she just nodded off. Last night is catching up with her. She hopes no one noticed her jolting awake. Trust her to sit next to a boffy showy-offy question-asker like Gwynne, she thinks. Everyone is turning round to look, and she only has make-up on one eye, thanks to that whatever-his-name-was last night / this morning. If she twists round more, maybe no one will notice that only one lid is mauve. She hopes Gwynne doesn't spin it out, asking the same thing in four different ways. She doesn't know how people can pipe up, just like that. All those faces looking, judging.

'Hi, John, I just wanted to ask: when you say we are dissociated from,' Gwynne checks her notes, 'the matrices of power, you make it sound like it's our fault. Are you saying that we should be more aware? I mean, are we to blame for this, er, dissociation. Are the matrices of power… I don't know how to put it… I mean, do you think we can re-associate ourselves or… How can we know what these, um, matrices are? I mean, in your book, is it all the protagonist's own fault?'

Rosa doesn't know what Gwynne is getting at. It all seems very abstract to her. She wishes someone would give an example. She hopes the lecturer will now. He really is a dish. John. She must remember that. She's forgotten her notebook and writes it on her hand instead. She wonders if he is giving tutorials afterwards. She might try and sign up. Except she only has one eye made up. Shit.

'Yes, and no,' John is saying.

Rosa thinks he is being overly gentle. Come on John, there's no need for the softly-softly with Gwynne. She's a fucking barbarian in crits.

'But tell me – sorry, what's your name?'

'Gwynne.'

'Ok, Gwynne. In fact, if you could all tell me your names when you ask questions that would be friendly. You all know mine, after all.' He laughs a plastic little laugh.

That's fair enough, thinks Rosa. Or is it creepy?

'But tell me, Gwynne, could you say right now precisely which forces compelled you to think whatever thought it was that made you want to ask that question?'

There is a ripple of amusement as Gwynne shakes her head. Maybe she'll think twice about putting her hand up in the future if she sees there could be comeback. Ha ha, thinks Rosa.

'No, of course you can't,' says John. 'It would be ridiculous to operate at that level of self-analysis all the time. Instead, we use a sort of shorthand for what we think or hope or assume is going on. You might say curiosity made you ask it, for instance, but what is curiosity? It's not something a primary school teacher hands to you in your first lesson. Neither is it a singular chemical impulse that comes from your hippocampus. It's all sorts of things, real, symbolic and imaginary, which coalesce into a sort of power, which appears to originate in you, your parents, society, history, culture – all mulched down into a word that you attach to yourself, knowing that it's not exactly that, but that it gets the general idea across. You see, we all feel dissociated from power not because we are alienated by it, but because we produce it collectively in complicated ways and pass it on in abstract forms. We can't describe it to ourselves, let alone name it for anyone else's benefit, because it's going to look different from where they're standing.

'In *The Lost Imposter* the protagonist can sense power as Other, but she can never actually point to it. This is because a finger that points cannot be included in what is being pointed at. And anyway, when we point, it's only ever from our own individual position, unless someone else can actually physically get inside our skin and look along our arm and through our own eyes.'

Gwynne smiles and nods slowly, impressed. She pretends to make some more notes, hoping he won't ask her anything else. Rosa is impressed too. She has heard about *The Lost Imposter*, or more specifically about its author's sensational acceptance speech at the EMMAs, and she is definitely going to read it now. She hopes it has his photograph on the back cover.

'Now, there was another question down here.' A forest of hands sprouts throughout the auditorium. Rosa wonders what criteria he uses to pick people out. Speed of hand? Length of arm? Alertness of features? 'You, in the cerise. Yes. And don't forget to say your name.'

'Yeah, hi, my name's Jojo. Um, this is more of an observation than a question really.' Jojo laughs lightly, self-deprecatingly. 'I like how, even though you're an anthropologist, you write as a person we can identify with and you don't just write about someone else, like in a case study or something. I really like how it reads as a novel, and we get to see things from the inside. Warts and all. Actually, maybe I do have a question after all. Is this a real person or did you just imagine her?'

'Yes, she is a real person, although I took the ethical decision not to reveal her identity in the book. As for writing it from the first-person perspective, well that was more of an accident that turned out to be really useful. You see, when psychologists publish case studies they sometimes protect their subjects' identities by referring to them by their first initial, and in this case that would have been an 'I', which became really confusing. So I thought, what if I actually wrote it in the first person? From the position of "I"? This way I could screen the subject's identity while achieving a sense of intimacy that the academic study usually can't for danger of overstepping certain lines. As for how I selected the subject, well, that was easy: she actually approached me and asked to collaborate. So a lot of serendipity really.'

Rosa is only an undergraduate student, and she isn't confident in her own judgement by any means, but she's not sure that ethics is just to do with naming someone or not.

'How about a guy this time? Yes, you in the, what is that, a Rothwell-Beer T-shirt? Old school! Cool!'

Rosa recognises the next questioner by the sound of his throat clearance. Oh crikey, she thinks, John's going to cop it now. Hetro always asks the most difficult question, not because he knows a lot, but because he has a supernatural ability to find weak spots. It's horrible to watch. The lecturers start faltering, turning purple, grasping for longer and longer words to hide behind. Why would you want that from your education experience? Rosa supposes he just gets a kick out of humiliating others. An interesting fuck, no doubt.

'Yes, hi, I'm Hetro.'

John smiles.

'I was just wondering… and this is a follow-on from Jojo's question in a way… but, ok, I get how you can write "I" when you're not that person when it's a novel, and you can say "I thought this" or "I thought that", because it's all made up; but what I don't get is how in an anthropological study you can sort of get inside the person's head like that. You mentioned ethics just now, but what are the ethics of putting thoughts inside someone else's head?'

Not one of his thorniest questions, thought Rosa, unsure if an easy ride was quite what she had wanted for John after all. She enjoyed seeing others dealing with their emotions. It was a rare excitement in Academia.

'Good question, Hetro. Very good. Yes, what you're asking there is about the documentary imperative, the author-subject relation, radical subjectivity, empathy – all those tricky things that the anthropologist has always had to deal with. And actually, this is one of the progressive aspects of *The Lost Imposter*. I got so close to my subject I started to over-identify, as they say. I lost all objectivity and so thought the only way to deal with this is to completely run with that, to live alongside her, within her, to become her… I can't really go into my methodology, because that's where the creative copyright kicks in, but yes, you have indeed spotted the uniqueness of the project.'

'Does she like it?' asked Hetro. 'Your book, I mean?'

'This isn't the sort of book you can publish without a subject's approval, even if they are incognito. So I can say categorically that "I", as we have to call her, loves it. Says she couldn't have written it better herself.'

At this point the course leader, who had invited John to give the lecture, steps in.

'Yeah, John, I have one last question, if you don't mind. Then we'll have to wrap things up. I was just wondering about your response to responses to your book. A number of commentators have criticised you, and specifically the bit in your acceptance speech where you talked about your project in the light of the furore at the previous year's awards ceremony. Were you already working on *The Lost Imposter* when the Imposter Syndrome epidemic broke? And how do you counter those who say you have been opportunist, or even, dare I say, exploitative?'

John puffs out his cheeks and exhales slowly while pacing the stage, like a panther, Rosa thinks, in his black jeans and polo neck.

'Well, that certainly is a final question, thanks Gray.' John's laugh has a bitter edge. 'Yes, it is problematic to say it was good timing, in that the crisis gave my book a very public context. Without that, it would have been picked up by an obscure imprint and categorised under quackery, no doubt. But as it was, the condition was suddenly and widely acknowledged. It was prioritised for medical research in fact. What the situation was crying out for was a narrative context for what would otherwise be perceived as a rash of singularities. My book provided a view onto a system that didn't excuse, but went some way to explaining, these instances of slander, blackmail and, in one sad case, suicide. It has helped psychologists, systems analysts, geographers, economists, cultural legislators, academic managers and so on to rebuild, reform and re… recruit. It may be immodest of me, but rather than accusing me of being opportunist, I think the Academy should acknowledge I was there to help pick up the pieces.'

'And your subject? This "I". Is she doing well? Did she succeed in her project?' Gray is disappointed that John's position is so well-rehearsed. He has to wind the session up now and wants to pull focus from John himself in whatever small way possible.

'Oh she's very happy, yes. She found what she was looking for in the end. The last time I saw her she was in the thick of it. I'm sure we'll be reading all about it soon.'

Gray announces that a sign-up sheet is on the noticeboard and people should grab a tutorial slot if they want one, at which a dozen or so people fling themselves towards the lecture hall doors. He is starting to tell John about another book he has read on interdisciplinary collaborations while John packs away his slides. Rosa approaches shyly, having arranged her hair over the unmade-up eye.

'Hi, sorry, John, I wanted to ask you something, but I don't like asking in these big lecture theatres, but anyway, I was wondering…'

CHAPTER 45

Ida woke to the familiar smell of brine, oil and mensch sweat, and the alarm clamouring for attention. She rose, dressed in the freezing, ozone-drenched cabin and went straight on shift. The dawn scrum over meagre breakfast rations was too rude an awakening. She preferred to savour what little sleep had managed to linger as sweet fog in her recesses. Her legs were heavy and reticent, and her still-tender vision strobed in the stark strip lighting as she made her way along the corridor to the latrine.

After relieving herself and gulping down some rusty water from the tap, she pushed on out of the quarters house, towards the helideck, to conduct final prep and checks for the guard changeover that afternoon. One of the roustabout's duties was to clear the communal corridors and exterior platforms of litter. Three days previously she'd had to clear away a used tampon, which, since there were no women guards on duty that week, must have been brought on-rig in its already bloodied state by one of the male guards and kept in a fridge for a week before warming it back up to body temperature. That such forethought went into the prank made it all the more dreadful. But while Ida would much rather have found an unused one, since they were the most precious contraband on the rig, she could draw some comfort from the familiar sensation of the warm, soft bullet in her hand. And the spirit of pranks was not altogether lost on her either. She had dim memories of some students erecting a cast of a house on top of the great dome of a departmental building overnight. She used to think it both sad and brilliant that they had expended so much effort on such a pointless act. What she now realised, from her position within the jostling social strata of a prison camp, was that these efforts weren't at all pointless, but a vital means of maintaining hierarchies. To inconvenience the other is a definitive assertion of power.

This morning, however, there was little more than the occasional foil from a cigarette packet and a sticking plaster that had slipped off greasy skin and stuck fast to the linoleum. Until the helideck level. There on the metal gridded walkway, just outside the external door, where the wind blustered, full of spray, and the oppressive waves a hundred metres or so down roared and slapped and gurgled just about forever, lay a dead pollack. It was the length of Ida's thigh, plump and silver-gold, like a lesser-known soft metal. The fins, top and bottom, were folded back, as if in resignation. The other prisoners often talked about fishing. They described spinning for pollacks from piers using jelly worms as teenagers. Even the tiddlers, they said, had been hard-fighting, and so she could imagine the struggle of landing a daddy like this one.

She hid the fish behind a bulkhead while she checked the heliport risers, standpipes and spray systems – vital in case of dimensioning fire – and then tucked it down inside her burlap trousers. She stopped off at the communications room to empty the bins – a job she'd made up for herself but that had as yet gone unquestioned – grabbing from it a good few feet of discarded seismic readout and stuffing that down her trousers too. Then she headed to the galley to hand the pollack over to someone who could prepare it out of sight of the guards.

*

The fish lay on the formica table, like a smoking gun. Two guards stood glowering at the assembled prisoners. The one called Fuji was a notoriously brutish banksman with a soft, delicate, almost angelic face and no regard for the prisoners' lives. He found their being swept over the sides of the rig a minor annoyance that interrupted his train of thought, which was usually about the fighting dogs he bred back on the beach to clean up with in the waterfront bars. The other guard, Eiger, was more compassionate, although this was hard to tell from his potato of a face. He could empathise with his wards, for he too would much rather be back on dry land, working creatively with his hands. His propensity to breed small but hungry humans in multiple had forced him to take this dangerous but well-paid work.

Fuji, being from a coastal family, could tell that the fish had not been stored in a freezer. Its eyes had the just-faded light of a very recent catch. No other guard had claimed the fish, and so the question remained, which of the inmates had fished it and how?

'Maybe it was dropped by a seabird,' suggested someone, although a murmur of 'bloody big bird' and the noted lack of claw marks more or less put paid to that. Nothing useful was offered up as alternative explanation, and since whoever had hidden the fish in the oven was obviously not going to own up, Fuji settled on symbolic random punishment.

Forcing half a dozen prisoners to scrub the rig with a toothbrush in high winds without a harness sounded fair to him. Eiger talked him out of this, saying it would be punishment enough for the guards to be seen enjoying sashimi while the prisoners forced down half rations of seaweed soup.

Ida listened to their discussion, memorising it word for word so that she could write it down on the thin strip of soggy, fishy paper still stashed at her crotch. Her new project was progressing well. Her understanding of oil had grown exponentially since she had been forced to become part of the workforce that pumped it up from the ocean bed. She had been covered in it head to toe for five years now. It was tinting her skin and fusing with her corpuscles. She had even developed one of those itinerant aches she'd heard about somewhere – she forgot where. And that was another thing. Her long-term memory – always a bit ropey after, what, she couldn't quite recall – was now unravelling as quickly as she could fill it with new information and thoughts. Perhaps her grasp of the Foreign language, which she had necessarily picked up quick-smart, had come at a price. The brain as a roll-on, roll-off system. Or maybe her past was dissolving into the vast grey expanse of sky and sea that spread outwards from the rig to infinity.

Two years or so ago she had given up trying to escape or even hoping for a regime change to bring about the release of political prisoners, which she guessed she must be, given that she had committed no crime. She had ceased to worry about those at home who must be worrying about her, and she had even stopped wondering what had happened to her. She was only thinking ahead now, of the completion of her book. It would be a sensation. She would have no trouble finding a publisher when she was released in another few years. But the problem was how to smuggle off the rig what by then would be a mattress full of carefully numbered paper shreds? Perhaps she would have to start memorising the text, or sending it ashore in stolen bottles, or seducing a guard. She wondered how feasible this latter option would be. She hadn't seen her own reflection for years. Did she look as unattractive as she felt? For now, though, she must tuck this difficult thought away. To avoid confiscation of her day's food or sleep, she must report to the banksman for slinging operations so that the drilling would continue unabated.

ACKNOWLEDGEMENTS

This book was written with the generous support of the Patrick and Joan Leigh Fermor Arts Fund. A research trip to the Sex Museum, Prague, and Akademgorodok, Siberia, was part-funded by the Joanna Drew Travel Bursary. Other aspects of research and development were facilitated by Kent County Council; Whitechapel Art Gallery, London; Eastside Projects, Birmingham; Project Arts Centre, Dublin, and Cranfield University.

For support of various kinds, including space, time, technology, advice and knowledge, I would like to thank Nicky Sim, Caro Howell, Tessa Giblin, Catherine Herbert, Nicole Mollett, Sir John O'Reilly, Professor Feargal Brennan and Paul Fairhurst – and the Grinkevich family in Novosibirsk and London, for their hospitality and help.

I am also grateful to Matt Rogers, Nicholas Stewart, Milly Thompson, Sean Ashton and Melanie Manchot, whose input and encouragement helped me to press on through earlier drafts.

First published by Eros Press, 2016

ISBN 978-0-9934268-8-9

Design by Sami Jalili

Eros Press
9 Noel Rd.
London
N1 8HQ

erospress.co.uk